D0843859

Bilingual Language Development and Disorders in Spanish-English Speakers

edited by

Brian A. Goldstein, Ph.D.
Temple University
Philadelphia, Pennsylvania

Baltimore • London • Sydney

Paul H. Brookes Publishing Co.
Post Office Box 10624
Baltimore, Maryland 21285-0624

www.brookespublishing.com

"Paul H. Brookes Publishing Co." is a registered trademark of
Paul H. Brookes Publishing Co., Inc.

Typeset by Barton Matheson Willse & Worthington,
Baltimore, Maryland.
Manufactured in the United States of America by
Victor Graphics, Baltimore, Maryland.

The individuals described in this book are composites or fictional accounts based on the authors' actual experiences. Individuals' names have been changed and identifying details have been altered to protect confidentiality.

Library of Congress Cataloging-in-Publication Data

Bilingual language development and disorders in Spanish-English speakers /
edited by Brian A. Goldstein.
    p.   cm.
  Includes index.
  ISBN 1-55766-687-3 (pbk.)
  1. Bilingualism in children.   2. Language acquisition.   3. Language disorders in children.   4. Spanish language—Acquisition.   5. English language—Acquisition.   I. Goldstein, Brian.

P115.2.B555   2004
420′.4261′0973—dc22

                      2004016584

British Library Cataloguing in Publication data are available from the British Library.

Contents

About the Editor

Brian A. Goldstein, Ph.D., Associate Professor, Department of Communication Sciences, Temple University, 110 Weiss Hall, 13th and Cecil B. Moore Boulevard, Philadelphia, Pennsylvania 19122

Dr. Goldstein received his bachelor's degree in linguistics from Brandeis University in Waltham, Massachusetts, and his master's and doctorate degrees in speech-language pathology from Temple University. He teaches in the areas of clinical management, phonetics and phonology, and language and culture. In addition to teaching, Dr. Goldstein has done clinical work at the Massachusetts General Hospital in Boston and the Rainbow Community Head Start in Philadelphia, working closely with Latino children and their parents.

An American Speech-Language-Hearing Association (ASHA) fellow, Dr. Goldstein has published many works on communication development and disorders in Latino children, with a focus on phonological development and disorders in monolingual Spanish and Spanish-English bilingual children. He is the author of *Cultural and Linguistic Diversity Resource Guide for Speech-Language Pathologists* (Singular Publishing Group, 2000). He has served as editorial consultant for numerous journals and is currently the editor of *Language, Speech, and Hearing Services in the Schools,* published by ASHA. He has been a member of numerous state and national committees, including the Multicultural Issues Board, the Publications Board, and the ASHA Council of Editors.

About the Contributors

Raquel T. Anderson, Ph.D., Associate Professor, Department of Speech and Hearing Sciences, Indiana University, Bloomington, Indiana 47405

Dr. Anderson conducts research in the area of grammatical development and skills in monolingual and bilingual children. She is particularly interested in patterns of Spanish language loss in children with language impairment. She teaches in the areas of atypical language development, speech and language diagnostics, diversity and clinical practice, and bilingualism in children.

Lisa M. Bedore, Ph.D., Assistant Professor, Department of Communication Sciences and Disorders, The University of Texas at Austin, Austin, Texas 78712

Dr. Bedore's research interests are in the areas of language development and language disorders in Spanish-speaking and Spanish-English bilingual children. Her most recent work has focused on the description of specific language impairment in Spanish-speaking children.

Ann Derr, M.A., Speech-Language Pathologist, St. Paul Schools, St. Paul, Minnesota 55116

Ms. Derr is a bilingual (Spanish-English) speech-language pathologist who has worked on the St. Paul School Birth to Five Assessment Team for 20 years. She is co-chair of the Minnesota Speech-Language Hearing Association's Multicultural Affairs committee and has been involved in mission work in Guatemala involving individuals with cleft palates.

Vera Gutiérrez-Clellen, Ph.D., Professor, Department of Communicative Disorders, College of Health and Human Services, San Diego State University, San Diego, California 92182

In addition to her work in the department of Communication Disorders, Dr. Gutiérrez-Clellen is Director of the Bilingual Speech-Language Pathology Certificate, School of Speech-Language-Hearing Sciences at San Diego State University and Co-Principal Investigator of a contract funded by the National Institute on Deafness and Other Communication Disorders to develop and validate a language test for Hispanic children speaking nonstandard English. Her research focuses on the nature of language disorders in bilingual children as well as its effects on the acquisition of literacy during the preschool and school years.

Carol Scheffner Hammer, Ph.D., Associate Professor, Communication Sciences and Disorders, The Pennsylvania State University, University Park, Pennsylvania 16802

Dr. Hammer's research interests include language and literacy development in African American and Hispanic populations, parental beliefs about language and literacy development, and the relationship between environmental factors and language and literacy development. She conducts longitudinal research in collaboration with Adele W. Miccio on the language and literacy development of bilingual children attending Head Start.

Donna Jackson-Maldonado, Ph.D., Professor, Department of Languages and Literature (Facultad de Lenguas y Letras), Universidad Autónoma de Querétaro, Querétaro, Mexico

Dr. Jackson-Maldonado is a researcher and professor who has worked extensively in the areas of normal development and language disorders in Spanish-speaking monolingual and bilingual populations. She also has worked for the Mexican government's special education and communication disorders program, doing in-service training, writing books and manuals, and developing language assessment instruments. She was co-developer, with Elizabeth Bates and Donna J. Thal, of the MacArthur Inventarios del Desarrollo de Habilidades Comunicativas, a translation and adaptation of the MacArthur-Bates Communicative Development Inventories (both available from Paul H. Brookes Publishing Co.).

Ellen Stubbe Kester, Ph.D., Research Associate and Lecturer, The University of Texas at Austin, Austin, Texas, 78712

Dr. Kester conducts research in the area of bilingual language acquisition and the assessment of bilingual language skills. Specific research interests include the development and representation of lexical/semantic language skills in bilingual children and psychometric issues related to the language assessment of bilinguals. Dr. Kester teaches courses in normal speech and language development and measurement and evaluation in speech-language pathology.

Kathryn Kohnert, Ph.D., Assistant Professor, Department of Speech-Language-Hearing Sciences, University of Minnesota, Minneapolis, Minnesota 55455

Dr. Kohnert's research investigates the relationship between first and second languages in developing bilinguals and between language and basic cognitive processes in diverse learners with and without language impairments. She has a strong interest in early identification of language disorders as well as the under- and overidentification of communication disorders.

Adele W. Miccio, Ph.D., Associate Professor, Communication Sciences and Disorders and Applied Linguistics, The Pennsylvania State University, University Park, Pennsylvania 16802

Dr. Miccio teaches courses in clinical phonetics and phonology. Her research interests include typical and atypical phonological acquisition in at-risk populations, the relationship between phonological development and later literacy abilities, and treatment efficacy.

Janet L. Patterson, Ph.D., Associate Professor, Department of Speech and Hearing Sciences, University of New Mexico, Albuquerque, New Mexico 87131

Dr. Patterson has extensive teaching and clinical experience in child language assessment. She has published research on lexical development among Spanish-English bilingual toddlers, and her current research focuses on parent and teacher perceptions of language and communication characteristics of bilingual preschool children.

Barbara Zurer Pearson, Ph.D., Research Associate, Department of Communication Disorders, University of Massachusetts, Amherst, Massachusetts 01003

Dr. Pearson has conducted research on first and second language learning with a special emphasis on young bilinguals. With the University of Miami Bilingualism Study Group, she collaborated on the book *Language and Literacy in Bilingual Children* (Oller et al., 2002, Multilingual Matters). At the University of Massachusetts she is Project Manager for the interdisciplinary team that developed a dialect-sensitive assessment test, *Diagnostic Evaluation of Language Variation (DELV)*, published in 2003 by The Psychological Corporation.

Elizabeth D. Peña, Ph.D., Associate Professor, Department of Communication Sciences and Disorders, The University of Texas at Austin, Austin, Texas 78712

Dr. Peña teaches coursework in the area of child language and measurement, with an emphasis on bilingualism. Her research focuses on semantic development in bilingual children and on dynamic assessment.

Nan Bernstein Ratner, Ed.D., Professor and Chairman, Department of Hearing and Speech Sciences, University of Maryland at College Park, College Park, Maryland 20742

Dr. Ratner is the editor of six volumes and the author of more than 35 articles and 20 chapters addressing language acquisition and fluency in children. Her current research focuses on the origins of stuttering in young children, the interactions between fluency and language development in children with and without language impairment. For a number of years, she served as division coordinator of ASHA's Special Interest Division on fluency and fluency disorders.

María Adelaida Restrepo, Ph.D., Associate Professor, Department of Speech and Hearing Sciences, Arizona State University, Tempe, Arizona, 85287

Dr. Restrepo is a bilingual speech-language pathologist. Her research deals with differentiating language differences from language disorders and clinical and theoretical issues relating to bilingual and Spanish-speaking children with specific language impairment, such as characteristics, assessment, and language maintenance and loss.

Barbara L. Rodriguez, Ph.D., Assistant Professor, Department of Speech and Hearing Sciences, University of New Mexico, Albuquerque, New Mexico 87131

Dr. Rodgriguez's research interests include bilingual language development, literacy development in Spanish-speaking children, and Hispanic parents' beliefs and practices. Specifically, her research focuses on the processes of second language acquisition, the language socialization practices of Mexican American families, and the cultural variability of parental beliefs.

Acknowledgments

This project began when Elaine Niefeld, Publisher (then Editorial Director) at Paul H. Brookes Publishing Co., contacted me. She felt the time was right to consider a book on language development and disorders in bilingual Spanish-English learners. She shepherded this project from its inception through its publication. I thank her for her patience, calm demeanor, support, and guidance. I also thank Assistant Editor Amy Perkins, Production Manager Lisa Rapisarda, and Senior Book Production Editor Leslie Eckard at Brookes for their support and hard work on behalf of the book and its authors. I would also like to thank Liz Peña for her providing suggestions on themes and organization of the book and Kathryn Kohnert for reviewing Chapter 11.

I thank all of the chapter authors for being willing to participate in this project. The success of this book hinges on the fact that these scholars are doing outstanding research in all areas of language development and disorders in Spanish-English bilingual children. Research of this type usually cannot take place without external funding support. Thus, we are indebted to agencies that have generously funded much of the research reported here.

On behalf of all of the authors, I would like to thank all of the children and their families, centers, and schools who gave us the opportunity and permission to do research. Their generosity and understanding of the research process has led to more appropriate speech and language services for bilingual children.

I also acknowledge the pioneers of research related to bilingual speech and language development and disorders. The authors of this book and our peers are predominantly the second generation in the field, so to speak, and we owe a debt of gratitude to those who blazed the trail before us.

Finally, words cannot express my gratitude to my wife Linda and my two children, Lauren and Jenna, for giving me their tireless love and support, and for understanding my incessant need, in the words of Lauren, "to hog the computer."

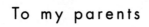
To my parents

Setting the Stage

CHAPTER 1

Bilingual Language Development and Disorders

Introduction and Overview

BRIAN A. GOLDSTEIN

The years since the 1970s have seen a marked increase in the number of individuals in the United States who speak a language other than or in addition to English (U.S. Bureau of the Census, 2000). According to the most recent census, approximately 47 million such individuals in the United States, almost 18% of the total U.S. population, fall in this category (U.S. Bureau of the Census, 2000). Of those 47 million individuals, almost half (45%) report that they speak English "less than very well." Almost 60% of this group (28.2 million) report Spanish as the language they use other than or in addition to English. Globally, Spanish is spoken as a first language by somewhere between 322 and 358 million speakers; that number rises to approximately 417 million if second language speakers are included (Grimes, 2003). The relatively large number of individuals in the United States who speak a language other than or in addition to English include numerous children who are English language learners (ELLs) (historically termed limited– and non–English proficient, LEP/NEP). Estimates indicate that as of 2001, there were approximately 4.6 million ELLs in the U.S. schools, a 105% increase since 1990 (Kindler, 2001). Of those children identified as ELL, 79% (3.6 million) speak Spanish. These figures actually may underestimate the number of ELLs, in general, and Spanish-speaking children, in particular. The U.S. Bureau of the Census (2000) estimated that approximately 6.8 million 5- to 17-year-old Spanish speak-

The writing of this chapter was funded in part by the National Institute on Deafness and Other Communication Disorders contract #N01-DC-8-2100.

ers live in the United States. This relatively large number of ELLs in the United States has caused institutions (e.g., the school system) and professionals (e.g., teachers, speech-language pathologists, psychologists) to attempt to plan for these individuals' academic, linguistic, and societal needs.

According to Ruiz (1988), the United States has had three main orientations to language planning. The first, rooted in the 1950s, is Language-as-Problem. Bilingualism was seen as a problem of modernization; that is, how to deal with issues such as code selection, standardization, literacy, orthography, language stratification, and so forth. In the 1950s, language issues were linked to the so-called "disadvantaged," similar to other social issues such as poverty, low socioeconomic status, and lack of social mobility. Bilingualism, then, was perceived as a problem to be overcome and viewed mostly as a deficit. That is, speaking two languages was not seen as a skill that increased cognitive ability and metalinguistic flexibility (e.g., Palij & Homel, 1987), but rather, limited them. Thus, one language had to be eradicated. The assumption was that non–English-speaking children had "handicaps to overcome" (Ruiz, 1988, p. 7). To improve these "handicaps," many "experts" advocated making a transition to and acknowledging the dominance of English rather than allowing bilingualism (i.e., supporting both languages).

Even though Ruiz first noted this phenomenon in the 1950s, bilingualism itself has existed in North America since before the arrival of Europeans (Ferguson & Heath, 1981; Taylor, 1981). In fact, Taylor noted that many bilingual speakers of two American Indian languages often were trilingual after adopting a *lingua franca* as a third code. Even after the arrival of Europeans, bilingualism was not a rare occurrence. In the 1500s, it was not uncommon for individuals to speak Spanish and a Native American language (Craddock, 1981). In 1787, Franklin College (later to become Franklin and Marshall College) was founded as the first bilingual college in the United States (Feinberg, 2002). In 1879 in New York, 1,376 people were enrolled in bilingual classes; that number increased to 36,000 by 1905 (Molesky, 1988). During the first half of the 20th century, many public and private bilingual programs were ended; this trend accelerated when the United States became less hospitable to immigrants and immigration itself slowed. At the beginning of World War II, there was a renewed interest in language education, particularly from teachers. For example, the first teachers of English as a Foreign Language enrolled at the University of Michigan in 1940 (Feinberg, 2002).

Between World War II and the 1960s, not everyone viewed bilingualism as a problem. Increasingly during this period, language was being recognized as a civil right. In the 1960s, the Language-as-Right movement was manifested as government forms, ballots, instructional pamphlets, judicial proceedings, and civil service exams were printed in languages other than English. In addition, individuals could not be discriminated against for using languages other than English, and they were allowed to use their language(s) of choice in daily activities. Historically, in the United States, neither language diversity nor non-English language maintenance is encouraged. There is, however, current support on some fronts for a Language-as-Resource perspective. This attitude advocates the conservation of language abilities of non–English speakers and an increase in language requirements at universities (if for no other reason than the need for linguistic diversity for business purposes). There is, however, a contradiction because most individuals support foreign-language instruction in schools but ask non-native English speakers to lose their first language.

Although non–English speakers in the United States may become monolingual English speakers or remain monolingual in their first language, most children and adults gain some facility with English (Segalowitz, 1997) and fall between these ends of that continuum. The fact remains that large numbers of bilinguals live in the United States with varying degrees of skill in each language.

The rapid growth of young ELLs has greatly challenged our present support system for assessing and treating ELLs with communication disorders. The *23rd Annual Report to Congress on the Implementation of IDEA* indicated that "a significant number of LEP students also have a concomitant disability; those students are at even greater risk for negative educational outcomes" (U.S. Department of Education, 2001, pp. II-38). The same report also noted that Latinos with speech and language impairments composed 12.7% of students ages 6–21. If the prevalence rate of 12.7% for speech and language impairments is applied to the 6.8 million Spanish-speaking children between the ages of 5 and 17, then some 870,000 Spanish-speaking children exhibit communication impairments in their native language.

Despite the relative size of the bilingual population in the United States, especially Spanish-English bilingual children, there is a dearth of research focusing on language development and disorders in these children. However, the way in which institutions and professionals understand language development and disorders in Spanish-English bilingual children (the focus of this book) will determine these children's success in the larger society. A book like this, solely devoted to language development and disorders in Spanish-English bilingual children, is possible only now because of the critical mass of scholars doing programmatic research in all domains of bilingual language development and disorders.

FOCUS AND THEMES OF THE BOOK

A growing number of sources on Spanish language development have become available in recent years. The sources that are available, however, 1) tend to focus almost exclusively on monolingual speakers of Spanish, 2) have not integrated "best practices" for assessment, and 3) have not attempted to synthesize current thinking on intervention to an approach that might cut across language areas. The purpose of this book is to present current research findings on language development and disorders in Spanish-English bilingual children and link those findings to the assessment and treatment of Spanish-English bilingual children with communication disorders. To that end, the goals of this book are to

- Present developmental data on speech and language development and disorders in bilingual (Spanish-English) children. Most chapters also contain data on monolingual Spanish speakers (and some comparison data on monolingual English speakers as well) given that the preponderance of data exist for monolingual speakers

- Present assessment "best practices" within each speech and language domain

- Present a comprehensive chapter on intervention that integrates research findings across all areas of speech and language

The way in which more than one language is acquired has been the subject of much debate in the literature on bilingualism. Individuals in diverse fields such as linguistics, sociology, psychology, education, speech-language pathology, and anthropology, to name a few, have attempted to account for the acquisition and development of bilingualism across a variety of dimensions. Because of this lack of agreement, then, it is important to delineate what this book is and what it is not. The book *does* attempt to provide state-of-the-art information on bilingual speech and language development (and some information on speech and language disorders) for Spanish-English bilingual children being reared in the United States. In addition, the authors attempt to apply that research to best clinical practices for assessment and intervention. The book *does not* attempt to include everything known about bilingualism because that type of information is available from many sources (e.g., Baker, 2001; Romaine, 1995). Thus, the authors did not include topics such as bilingual education, language planning, and language attitudes that did not relate to the overall goals of this book. Again, the focus is on current research on Spanish-English bilingual speech and language development and disorders, specifically relating to clinical assessment and intervention.

The book focuses mainly on bilingual children ages 4–7, simply because most of the data collected thus far are from children in this age range. A number of chapters, however, do provide information on younger children (e.g., Chapter 4 on lexical development and Chapter 7 on early morphosyntactic development) and older children (e.g., Chapter 3 on language processing and Chapter 10 on narratives) than those in the 4- to 7-year-old range.

The most consistent theme of the book is that the processes of first and second language acquisition are interrelated but may be expressed in different ways by bilingual children as compared with monolingual children in either language. In many ways the research presented supports the view of many researchers that bilinguals are not two monolinguals in one (e.g., Grosjean, 1989). The findings outlined in this book support research indicating that practitioners and researchers should take a holistic view of bilingualism; in other words, they maintain that a bilingual individual is an integrated whole who cannot be easily separated by his or her component languages. What exists in the bilingual is a "complete linguistic entity" with a "unique and specific linguistic configuration" (Grosjean, 1989, p. 6). The adoption of this view, Grosjean argued (and which is supported by the research reviewed here), will lead to the study of the bilingual individual as a whole, the examination of both of the bilingual's languages, the investigation of how bilinguals organize and use both languages, and the determination of how individuals become bilingual and maintain (or lose) their skills in each language.

The research presented in this book also supports the notion that acquiring more than one language is a life-long, complex task with great individual variation and a developmental trajectory that is not uniform; skills ebb and flow over time. As Kohnert notes in Chapter 3, bilingual language acquisition is a process that involves multiple interactions between the first and second language and the developing child based on social, cognitive, and linguistic forces. That is, families may use each language differently for different purposes, with different people, for different tasks as dictated by the community (e.g., home, school, peers) (Wong, 1988). Thus, in order to understand the developing communication skills in bilinguals, both researchers and speech-language pathologists (SLPs) alike need to

- Examine aspects of each speech and language under various conditions with different interlocutors and then examine direction and rate of speech and language change

- Examine variations in performance and error types

- Understand the circumstances for acquisition, including the nature and rate of input and output

- Obtain a detailed language history noting input and output

In addition, given that the research outlined in this book indicates that bilingual children are both similar to and different from monolingual children of either language, SLPs need to examine what is common to both languages and unique to each language. Most important, the data support the view that notions such as *proficiency* and *dominance* are moving targets altered by differences in tasks, topics, and demands.

CHAPTER ORGANIZATION

The volume contains 13 chapters divided into five sections. With the exception of this first chapter, Chapters 2–12 each provide

- Specific developmental data on speech or language acquisition in monolingual Spanish speakers (detailed data on monolingual English-speaking children are generally excluded because they are already widely available)

- Developmental data on speech or language acquisition in bilingual (Spanish-English) speakers

- Research findings related to speech or language disorders in bilingual speakers (when possible)

- Appropriate assessment information within each language area. That is, each author provides information on least-biased assessment for that specific speech or language domain

- Information on best practices for intervention for that specific speech or language domain

Finally, Chapter 13 provides a comprehensive focus on intervention across all language domains. A brief overview of the content of Chapters 2–13 follows.

The first section of the book, *Setting the Stage*, provides the context for the remaining chapters. This first chapter presents the themes, organization, and focus of the volume. After this introduction and overview, Hammer, Miccio, and Rodriguez focus on the mechanisms in which child socialization affects bilingual language acquisition. They argue that historical definitions of language emphasizing language form do not account for the tremendous variety noted in the language of bilingual speakers. They indicate, as did Grosjean (1989) and Wong (1988), for example, that bilingual language development is predicated as much on interaction with the environment as it is on acquiring the rules of the language. This interaction with the environment, the chapter authors note, depends on a number of critical factors, including amount of input, opportunity for output, interlocutors, support of the community, parental beliefs about language acquisition, attitudes toward bilingualism, parents' perception of their role in the educational system, and general child-rearing practices. They conclude that the relationship between child socialization and bilingual language development is complex and is mitigated by a number of factors but that it is clear that bilingual language development must be seen through the lens of the family and its relationship to language acquisition.

The second section, *Lexical and Semantic Aspects*, focuses on the relationship between vocabulary and meaning. In Chapter 3, which discusses language processing in early sequential bilinguals, Kohnert brings together research from cognitive science, psycholinguistics, and speech-language pathology to put lexical processing in bilingual learners into context. Kohnert states that as opposed to monolingual children, bilingual children may have different linguistic experiences in each of their languages, often at different times in their development. Bilingual children, in contrast to bilingual adults, have different levels of cognitive development through which these linguistic experiences are processed. The complexity of bilingual language processing, she argues, comes from the interaction or collision of these cognitive, linguistic, and social forces. Taking an information processing perspective, Kohnert outlines bilingual language development as an interaction between general cognitive processing mechanisms and individual experiences, which results in a constant interaction between the child's two languages and changes over time. She presents longitudinal data indicating that over time, bilinguals showed significant increases in lexical production and comprehension accuracy, along with increases in fluency. Moreover, in the participants that she studied, overall gains in processing tasks over time were greater in English than in Spanish. Noteworthy is that gains in receptive language came earlier than gains in expressive language, leading Kohnert to question the notion of language dominance testing in bilingual children. Finally, her results reflected the variability often witnessed for bilingual speakers. One year after their initial testing, bilingual children showed some increases, some decreases, and some stability in performance that indicate between- and within-child variability. Her results suggest that practitioners should examine each of the bilingual's languages over time and under varying processing demands.

In Chapter 4, on bilingual lexical development, Patterson and Pearson focus on the fact that vocabulary acquisition is a multidimensional skill that involves social, cognitive, and linguistic factors. They also note that lexical learning involves phonological, morphological, syntactic, and semantic domains of language. Similar to the other authors in this text, Patterson and Pearson emphasize how pragmatics (e.g., in what situation and with whom the item was learned) and the heterogeneity of bilingual children inform vocabulary development. This heterogeneity is based on the circumstances in which bilingual children acquire, process, and use words, including the age at which the children acquire words in each language, the amount of input in each language, and the contexts of input for each language (e.g., home, school, community). Size of the lexicon is related to contexts and amount of exposure in each language, although there may be a threshold (as age increases) at which the link between amount of exposure and lexical development is not as strong. This finding again emphasizes the point that bilingual language development changes over time depending on the situation. Studies of lexical development also aid in determining the level of interaction between the bilinguals' languages. Patterson and Pearson report that vocabulary learning does not always transfer from one language to the other. Results from studies examining lexical development in bilingual speakers indicate that vocabulary size should be examined in both languages by determining how bilingual children learn and use words in both languages and by assessing how bilingual children link form and meaning.

In Chapter 5, Peña and Kester focus on theory, assessment, and intervention related to semantic development. The authors suggest that differences in salience for specific features in each of the two languages will result in different trajectories for development of those features. For example, high frequency words or categories of words in one language may be lower frequency in the other language. This difference in frequency may be one factor that results in an individual's acquiring words or categories of words differently in each of his or her two languages. In addition, different points in the acquisition process likely will result in different patterns of semantic development. Finally, as has been noted for other domains of bilingual language development, semantic development also may be influenced by when and how each of the languages was acquired. Taken together, these differences may determine how bilinguals store and link the lexical item and the concept it represents. The strategy that bilinguals use to make this connection may change over time depending on how and when each language is acquired and the individual's relative proficiency in each language. As was noted for other areas of language acquisition, semantic development also is mediated through one's culture (e.g., bilingual children might name *hamburgers* in English as a food they would eat at a birthday party but list *arroz* [rice] in Spanish). Finally, in a series of studies, Peña and her colleagues have found that bilingual children perform differently in each of their languages and that they perform differently than predominantly monolingual children of either language. These findings suggest that semantic skills are not distributed evenly across the two languages and that it is important to consider not only what skills bilinguals have in each language but also how the two languages influence each other.

The third section of the volume, *From Grammar to Discourse*, begins with Chapter 6, in which Jackson-Maldonado examines the relationship between vocabulary and verb morphology. The chapter author describes this topic by noting similarities and differences in verb morphology by monolingual and bilingual children. She clearly shows that the acquisition of the verbal system by both groups of children is gradual depending on the type of verb being acquired. As authors in other chapters also indicate, different morphological markers may be acquired differently depending on input and on cognitive and pragmatic factors. In studies of emergent bilingual children (i.e., those children who use only Spanish at home but who may be exposed minimally to English), Jackson-Maldonado shows that mean length of utterance and vocabulary level often determine how and when a morphological form appears. This determination also results from the specific verb form being acquired. Jackson-Maldonado argues that practitioners then should elicit specific verb types (e.g., change of state, activity) with specific morphological markers (e.g., present tense, past tense, present progressive) and avoid assessing only a limited number of verb types and morphological markers.

In Chapter 7, Morphosyntactic Development, Bedore examines morphosyntactic acquisition from a slightly different aspect than Jackson-Maldonado. Bedore focuses mainly on the question of whether bilingual morphological acquisition is different than monolingual morphological acquisition. She begins by noting that the morphosyntactic systems in Spanish and English are different. Spanish, unlike English, is regarded as a morphologically rich language with many morphological markers. English, unlike Spanish, however, has relatively fixed word order. Differences such as these may help to determine similarity of morphosyntactic development in bilingual and monolingual children. Another factor affecting morphosyntactic development, especially for speakers acquiring Spanish, is dialect. Bedore notes that in some dialects of Spanish, segments such as /s/ that act as morphophonemic markers often are deleted as part of the dialect. Thus, practitioners will need to be careful in determining which language changes are the result of dialect and which are the result of true error. Considering these and other factors, Bedore notes that morphosyntactic developmental milestones for bilingual children are similar to monolingual children, if the bilingual children are provided the means and opportunity to hear and use both languages. She cautions, however, that the rate and order of morphosyntactic development are unknown at this time given the limited scope of the studies in this area.

As noted previously, bilingual language development constitutes an interaction between the individual's two languages and the environment (broadly comprising caregivers, level of input, and community, to name a few). In Chapter 8, Anderson further explores the relationship between those variables as they extend to first language loss in Spanish-speaking children and implications for clinical practice. Anderson strongly makes the case that when two languages come in contact, skills in each language will be affected. She describes a pattern of language shift that takes place in communities in which only one language is prominent. As speakers of the minority language increase their contact with speakers of the majority language, the majority language is often adopted as the primary means of communication. The subsequent generation experiences a decrease in the use of the native (i.e., minority) language with a potential loss of receptive and expressive skills in the language. By the third generation, speakers often can communicate only in the majority language. The gradual diminution of language skill in the native language across generations is gradual, although the term *language loss* is usually reserved for a more rapid decline in native language skills. From a clinical perspective, it may be difficult to distinguish bilingual children undergoing loss from children with language disorders because many features of both conditions are similar (e.g., lexical loss, deletion of morphological markers, decreased use of complex clauses). As Anderson notes, verb morphology appears to be especially vulnerable to language loss. Thus, disentangling the nuances of early verb development (as discussed by Jackson-Maldonado), morphosyntactic development (as discussed by Bedore), language loss (as discussed by Anderson), and grammatical impairment (as discussed by Restrepo and Gutiérrez-Clellen) has proven to be a challenge to researchers and practitioners alike. To extricate some of these features, Anderson recommends examining each child's use of language over time in relation to the community norms in which the child lives. Attempting to locate normative data related to language loss, she argues, will not yield productive differential diagnoses. Instead "normative" data will come from measuring how the two languages are used depending on the situation in relation to the linguistic norms of the community.

In Chapter 9, Restrepo and Gutiérrez-Clellen continue the discussion of bilingual children who have difficulty with language acquisition in both languages. From the outset, the authors note that Spanish-English bilingual children with grammatical impairments will not necessarily exhibit the same difficulties in each language. Different grammatical characteristics of each language result in different developmental timetables and thus would dictate different features of the impairment in each language. Of note, the authors indicate that features of specific language impairment (SLI) often noted for English-speaking children (e.g., errors in inflectional morphology on past-tense markers) are relatively uncommon in Spanish-speaking children. Spanish-speaking children with SLI are more likely to have more difficulty with features such as articles and clitic pronouns. Thus, in attempting to differentiate bilingual children with SLI from those with language loss, for example, Restrepo and Gutiérrez-Clellen recommend measuring grammatical forms that are reported to be difficult in each of the bilingual's languages. In addition, as Bedore also noted in Chapter 7, dialect features of bilingual speakers, particularly in Spanish (e.g., omission of inflectional morphology markers), need to be considered. Finally, the authors recommend a specific criterion to diagnose grammatical impairments in bilingual children.

In Chapter 10, Narrative Development and Disorders in Bilingual Children, Gutiérrez-Clellen indicates that monolingual Spanish-speaking children develop episodic (i.e., story grammar) structure like that of other children who are monolingual in other languages. She also notes that it is important to measure other aspects of narrative development such as causal, referential, spatial, and temporal cohesion and complex syntax. She finds that these features may be exhibited differently depending on the language being acquired, based in part on the typological differences between the two languages. For example, Gutiérrez-Clellen reports that Spanish-speaking children use more relative clauses in narratives than do English-speaking children but that English-speaking children use more detail in their descriptions of motion events than do Spanish speakers. She also notes that evidence of transfer may be found in the narratives of bilingual children. For example, when producing narratives in English, Spanish-

English bilingual children might delete obligatory subjects as is permissible in Spanish. Conversely, when producing narratives in Spanish, bilingual children might over-use pronouns to reintroduce referents. Amount of transfer, she cautions, may be a function of relative exposure to each of the languages. Gutiérrez-Clellen cites research indicating that high exposure to both languages decreases the frequency of transfer from one language to the other. Spanish-English bilingual children undergoing loss of their first language (usually Spanish), however, are at greater risk for transfer effects in their narratives. Gutiérrez-Clellen also reports on the narrative skills of bilingual children with language disorders. The narratives of this group of children, she notes, are characterized by a lack of cohesion throughout their narratives, omission of referents for pronouns, and limited episodic information. These difficulties do appear to be similar to deficits exhibited in the narratives of monolingual children with language disorders. Thus, Gutiérrez-Clellen recommends obtaining narratives in both languages in different contexts and using a dynamic assessment approach to disentangle the effects of language-specific characteristics from true deficits.

The fourth section, *Speech Characteristics*, focuses on the phonological and fluency components of bilingual development and disorders. Goldstein focuses, in Chapter 11, on phonological development and disorders in bilingual children. He concentrates on the issue of whether the phonological system in bilinguals is represented as one system that separates into two over time or whether the phonological system is separate from the earliest point of development. Sources of evidence for how the phonological system is represented in bilinguals include cross-linguistic effects (i.e., transfer), accuracy on sounds common to both languages and unique to each language, and bilingual phonological development. The evidence indicates that bilingual children exhibit relatively little transfer between languages and are more accurate on sounds shared between the two languages than on sounds unique to each language. It also indicates that bilingual phonological development is similar, although not identical, to monolingual development in either language. These results suggest that bilingual children seem to represent the languages separately, although interaction between languages occurs. Just as Peña and Kester suggest for determining semantic deficits in bilingual children, identifying phonological disorders in bilingual children necessitates examining the bilingual's phonological skills in each constituent language and then determining how the two languages interact with one another.

In Chapter 12, Bernstein Ratner focuses on the fluency of bilingual children. Bernstein Ratner notes that different cultures view fluency and stuttering differently, especially specific features that might be used to diagnose stuttering. One cultural view about stuttering is that it may be caused or exacerbated by speaking more than one language. That is, some hold a belief that bilingualism itself is a risk factor for stuttering. Bernstein Ratner notes that there is little empirical support for this viewpoint. Thus, even for bilingual children who stutter, removing one of the two languages from the environment will not ameliorate the fluency disorder. The author also notes that if a bilingual child stutters, dysfluencies will occur in both languages. As Bernstein Ratner reports, no cases of stuttering in only one language have been reported. Stuttering severity, however, may be different across the two languages because of the structural differences between the two languages being acquired and the person's relative proficiency in each language. Code-switching, a common characteristic of bilinguals, is often misinterpreted as stuttering. According to Bernstein Ratner, there is some indication that the frequency of stuttering is higher during instances of code-switching, possibly because of processing demands placed on the individual during moments if increased linguistic complexity (i.e., lexical access necessary to code-switch). This finding supports the results noted by Kohnert (Chapter 3) that language processing is key to understanding bilingual language development. Bernstein Ratner cautions that for bilingual individuals, especially for bilingual children experiencing language loss, it is important to distinguish stuttering from difficulties in language formulation. One way to make that determination is to collect samples of fluency in both languages, remembering that stuttering will be exhibited in both languages while language formulation difficulties may be evident in only one language.

The data presented in Chapters 2–12 provide some clear suggestions for assessing communication disorders in Spanish-English bilingual children. SLPs must complete a language history for the family, including language input and output by time and interlocutor. In addition, SLPs should collect information from these children using both formal and informal means and take into account the dialect that the children use and to which they are exposed. That information, however, must be compared with a database of bilingual children acquiring their languages under the same circumstances. It is simply not appropriate to compare the English or Spanish language skills of bilingual children to the skills of monolingual children.

The data presented in this book also have implications for intervention related to communication disorders in bilingual children, specifically related to the language of intervention. The research findings presented here indicate that the languages of intervention for Spanish-English bilingual children likely need to be both Spanish and English. Most certainly, during the course of treatment, intervention will need to take place in both languages given the linguistic differences between English and Spanish. So the relevant question in terms of language of intervention does not seem to be "In what language should I treat?" but rather, "When do I treat in English and when do I treat in Spanish?"

Moreover, SLPs should be guided not only by language of intervention but also by the short-term goals of intervention. A number of authors have suggested that SLPs make treatment decisions by determining what goals are similar for both languages (e.g., increasing categorization skills) and what goals are unique to each language (e.g., use of the subjunctive in Spanish). Thus, language of intervention is determined by the goal itself. (These issues are detailed in Chapter 13.) There is a caveat, however. Even for goals that seem to be common across the two languages, SLPs cannot assume, predict, or expect that the same or similar skill in one language will transfer to the other language. Finally, as motivated by the research on speech and language development and disorders in bilingual children, intervention choices might hinge on how the child acquired the two languages and how these two languages are used in his or her environment.

A NOTE ON TERMINOLOGY

Individuals included in studies attempting to account for bilingual language development are defined and described in a myriad of ways (see, e.g., Baker, 2001; de Houwer, 1990; Hakuta, 1986; Romaine 1995; Valdés & Figueroa, 1994, for detailed discussions of this issue). The classic categorization bifurcates bilingual development into two categories: simultaneous and sequential acquisition. Defining these terms, however, has proven to be elusive. For example, McLaughlin (1978) argued that the label *simultaneous* should apply to children acquiring more than one language before age 3. Padilla and Lindholm (1984) indicated that *simultaneous* should apply only to children exposed to more than one language from birth. These definitions imply, of course, that children acquiring a second language after age 3 (McLaughlin's definition) or soon after birth (Padilla and Lindholm's definition) would be labeled as *sequential* bilinguals. In an attempt to define these categories with more specificity, Swain (1972) and Meisel (1990) referred to children who acquire more than one language from birth as "bilingualism as a first language" and "bilingual first language acquisition" (BFLA), respectively.

Although these terms (i.e., simultaneous, sequential, BFLA) are the ones most frequently used to describe bilinguals, Wei (2000) listed some 35 other terms that also have been used to describe bilinguals. Perhaps, describing types of bilinguals using these labels is much ado about nothing. Romaine (1995) argued convincingly, however, that the matter of the "label" of bilingualism is not a trivial one because the label is used, in part, to define the language characteristics of the particular group of individuals who participated in the given research study. These characteristics (e.g., language history, amount of input and output over time, community support for bilinguals) are necessary to detail, she argued, in order to make valid comparisons with monolingual speakers and to control for the variety of conditions under which bilinguals acquire their languages. Thus, for example, Romaine (1995) posited six types of childhood bilingual acquisition, depending on characteristics such as parents' languages, language(s) of the community, and parents' strategy for language input. Valdés and Figueroa (1994) proposed classifying bilinguals based on six foci: 1) age of acquisition, 2) functional ability, 3) relationship between the languages, 4) context of acquisition, 5) stages in the lives of bilinguals, and 6) circumstances leading to bilingualism. Unfortunately, exact definitions and inclusionary and exclusionary criteria for these categories have proved to be elusive (Romaine, 1995).

Why is it so difficult to define childhood bilingual acquisition? It is possible that we are unable to define it because these labels are a construct that we have imposed for convenience. For example, if simultaneous bilinguals are only children who acquire two languages from birth, then everyone else is sequential—quite a heterogeneous group. Given that the categories typically associated with bilinguals (i.e., simultaneous, sequential, BFLA) may be limiting because they do not detail the conditions under which bilingual children acquire their languages, how can we account for the heterogeneity in the bilingual children that we are studying, while at the same time impose some type of common vocabulary? In this volume, the authors categorize children in one of two general categories, simultaneous and sequential, to describe the way in which they acquire their languages. More important, although the authors of the individual chapters define these terms somewhat differently, they adhere to Spolsky's (1989) notion that it is important to indicate who uses what language and under what conditions. Thus, the authors provide detail on the language and community characteristics of the participants in their studies. Some readers (understandably) will take issue with the authors' decision to proceed in this manner. The authors believed, however, that instead of trying to impose a strict definition of these terms, they would maintain the slight variations in definitions across chapters, in part to reflect the situation in the literature and to let each author describe, in detail, the individuals participating in their studies.

REFERENCES

Baker, C. (2001). *Foundations of bilingual education and bilingualism* (3rd ed.). Clevedon, UK: Multilingual Matters.

Craddock, J. (1981). New World Spanish. In C. Ferguson & S.B. Heath (Eds.), *Language in the U.S.A.* (pp. 196–211). Cambridge, UK: Cambridge University Press.

de Houwer, A. (1990). *The acquisition of two languages from birth: A case study.* Oxford, UK: Oxford University Press.

Feinberg, R.C. (2002). *Bilingual education: A reference handbook.* Santa Barbara, CA: ABC Clio.

Ferguson, C., & Heath, S.B. (1981). Languages before English: Introduction. In C. Ferguson & S.B. Heath (Eds.), *Language in the U.S.A.* (pp. 109–115). Cambridge, UK: Cambridge University Press.

Grimes, B. (2003). *Ethnologue: Languages of the world* (web version). Retrieved September 16, 2003, from http://www.ethnologue.com/web.asp

Grosjean, F. (1989). Neurolinguists, beware! The bilingual is not two monolinguals in one person. *Brain and Language, 36,* 3–15.

Hakuta, K. (1986). *Mirror of language: The debate on bilingualism.* New York: Basic Books.

Kindler, A. (2001). *Survey of the states' LEP students 2000–2001 summary report.* Washington, DC: National Clearinghouse for English Language Acquisition.

McLaughlin, B. (1978). *Second-language acquisition in childhood.* Mahwah, NJ: Lawrence Earlbaum Associates.

Meisel, J. (1990). Grammatical development in the simultaneous acquisition of two first languages. In J. Meisel (Ed.), *Two first languages—early grammatical development in bilingual children* (pp. 5–22). Dordrecht, The Netherlands: Foris.

Molesky, J. (1988). Understanding the American linguistic mosaic: A historical overview of language maintenance and language shift. In S.L. McKay & S.C. Wong (Eds.), *Language diversity: Problem or resource? A social and educational perspective on language minorities in the United States* (pp. 27–68). Boston: Heinle & Heinle Publishers.

Padilla, A., & Lindholm, K. (1984). Child bilingualism: The same old issues revisited. In J. Martinez, & R. Mendoza (Eds.), *Chicano psychology* (pp. 369–408). Orlando, FL: Academic Press.

Palij, M., & Homel, P. (1987). The relationship of bilingualism to cognitive development: Historical, methodological and theoretical considerations. In P. Homel, M. Palij, & D. Aaronson (Eds.), *Childhood bilingualism: Aspects of linguistic, cognitive, and social development* (pp. 131–148). Mahwah, NJ: Lawrence Erlbaum Associates.

Romaine, S. (1995). *Bilingualism* (2nd ed.). Oxford: Blackwell Publishers.

Ruiz, R. (1988). Orientations in language planning. In S.L. McKay & S.C. Wong (Eds.), *Language diversity: Problem or resource? A social and educational perspective on language minorities in the United States* (pp. 3–25). Boston: Heinle & Heinle Publishers.

Segalowitz, N. (1997). Individual differences in second language acquisition. In A. de Groot & J. Kroll (Eds.), *Tutorials in bilingualism: Psycholinguistic perspectives* (pp. 85–112). Mahwah, NJ: Lawrence Erlbaum Associates.

Spolsky, B. (1989). *Conditions for second language learning.* Oxford, UK: Oxford University Press.

Swain, M. (1972). *Bilingualism as a first language.* Unpublished doctoral dissertation, University of California, Irvine.

Taylor, A. (1981). Indian lingua francas. In C. Ferguson & S.B. Heath (Eds.), *Language in the U.S.A.* (pp. 175–195). Cambridge, UK: Cambridge University Press.

U.S. Bureau of the Census. (2000). *Languages spoken at home.* Retrieved September 25, 2003, from http://www.census.gov

U.S. Department of Education. (2001). *23rd annual report to Congress on the implementation of IDEA.* Washington, DC: Author.

Valdés, G., & Figueroa, R. (1994). *Bilingualism and testing: A special case of bias.* Norwood, NJ: Ablex.

Wei, L. (2000). Dimensions of bilingualism. In L. Wei (Ed.), *The bilingualism reader* (pp. 3–25). London: Routledge.

Wong, S.C. (1988). Educational rights of language minorities. In S.L. McKay & S.C. Wong (Eds.), *Language diversity: Problem or resource? A social and educational perspective on language minorities in the United States* (pp. 367–386). Boston: Heinle & Heinle Publishers.

CHAPTER 2

Bilingual Language Acquisition and the Child Socialization Process

CAROL SCHEFFNER HAMMER,
ADELE W. MICCIO, AND BARBARA L. RODRIGUEZ

A number of factors influence children's language acquisition. Many of these factors, particularly those that refer to children's socialization practices, are often discussed informally or anecdotally in studies of children's early language development. Traditional linguistic definitions of language, however, do not explain the language varieties that bilingual communities create (Zentella, 2002). Languages are not merely sets of rules but are flexible systems of communication that are intertwined with a speaker's identity and the communicative context (Zentella, 2002). As stated so well by Schwartz more than 20 years ago, "Language is a part of culture so essential to the specification of human nature that it both pervades the rest of culture and is most readily taken as its controlling metonymic analogy" (1981, p. 7). That is, in order to understand bilingual children's language acquisition, one must also understand the social-cultural context in which development takes place. Social and cultural factors that influence children's language acquisition include parental language input, the community in which the children are raised, parents' beliefs about language development, child-rearing practices, and environmental factors.

Relatively few investigations have been conducted on language acquisition and social-cultural factors affecting language acquisition of Spanish-

The work on which this chapter is based was funded in part by Grant #1R01HD39496-02 as part of the Biliteracy Research Network (funded by the National Institute of Child Health and Human Development and the Institute of Education Sciences) and a grant from the American Speech-Language-Hearing Association.

English bilingual populations living in the United States. Information from the studies that have been performed can be augmented with the findings from investigations on the language acquisition of bilingual children living outside of the United States and investigations on environmental factors that influence children's language acquisition. This chapter addresses the research in these areas and supplements this information with findings from a longitudinal investigation of Spanish-English bilingual Head Start children (Hammer & Miccio, 2000) and a study of Mexican American mothers and their children with language disorders (Rodriguez & Olswang, 2002).

THE CONTINUUM OF LANGUAGE INPUT

Before discussing parental and community influences on children's language development, it is important to acknowledge the different types of input to which bilingual children may be exposed.

Types of Input

In general, scholars agree that the pattern of exposure to two languages, as opposed to the language of the parents or the dominant community, is the critical variable for understanding children's language acquisition (Bhatia & Ritchie, 1999). The terms *simultaneous* and *sequential* language acquisition have been widely used since the 1980s to refer to the different conditions under which bilingualism develops. More or less equal exposure to both languages from birth is referred to as simultaneous language acquisition; whereas, the term sequential language acquisition indicates that the child is exposed to one language in infancy and the second language sometime later, for example, when entering preschool at age 3. No agreed-on cutoff point has been established to distinguish between the simultaneous and sequential acquisition of two languages (McLaughlin, 1984; Meisel, 1994). In fact, de Houwer (1995) argued that designating age 3 as the time at which the child begins to acquire the second language was too late. She preferred the terms *Bilingual First Language Acquisition* (BFLA) in reference to the child exposed to two languages from birth and *Bilingual Second Language Acquisition* (BSLA) to refer to second language exposure, which she believed to begin at least 1 month after birth but before the age of 2. Alternatively, Bhatia and Ritchie (1999) proposed that simultaneous learners were those who were exposed to two languages prior to the one-word stage of language development. These authors also acknowledge that these distinctions are all in need of empirical support.

The role of different types of inputs in bilingual children needs to be examined systematically. In order to do so, researchers need to begin with the simpler differences (e.g., simultaneous versus sequential acquisition), and as more data inform the differences, researchers can then determine other qualitative differences in the acquisition of two languages. It is generally acknowledged, for example, that most children in the United States, even those from monolingual Spanish-speaking homes, are exposed to English in the greater community and through television and other media. These activities, however, do not require children to follow directions, answer questions, and interact with peers and family in two languages. Learners of two first languages, such as Spanish and English, have continuous exposure to two languages and live in homes in which they are expected to follow directions, answer questions, and interact with peers, family, and the community in both Spanish and English. Sequential learners, however, are children raised in Spanish-speaking homes in which they are not expected to follow directions, speak, or interact with their community using English until they attend school at age 3 years. The sequential learners are exposed to English through the television, trips to the grocery store, and other excursions into the English-speaking community. They are not, however, placed in situations in which communicating in English is required, expected, or encouraged until they attend school (Hammer, Miccio & Wagstaff, 2003).

Overall, input can be described as a continuum with one end characterized by the total separation of the two languages and the other by the total mixture of the two languages; to tease out the important differences between simultaneous and sequential acquisition, researchers need to describe children's patterns of acquisition and also the pattern of the input and the context in which it takes place.

The Influence of Language Input on Children's Development

The role of input is more complicated in the bilingual child than in the monolingual child. Monolingual children receive relatively uniform and homogeneous input from speakers in the family and in the community. Bilingual children, on the other hand, have divided input. A commonly held belief is that parents who are raising their children bilingually should keep the two languages separate, a strategy referred to as "domain allocation." Common versions of this strategy include one-parent/one-language, in which one parent speaks one language and the other parent another; one-place/one-language, in which one language is used in a certain place such as the living room and another language, elsewhere; a language/time approach in which one language is used during specific times of the day and the second language during other times; and a topic-related approach in which a particular language is associated with particular topics (Bhatia & Ritchie, 1999). The underlying assumption is that if caregivers keep the two systems separate, then the task of separating the two languages will be easier for the child. This approach has several limitations. First, these unnatural strategies to maintain a balance between languages lead to a pattern of input that is different from that provided by a more natural environment. Second, it cannot be assumed that input in the two languages will be balanced. If, for example, the mother spends most of the day with the child and the father only sees the child on occasion, then the influence of the two languages will differ. Third, the presence of other speakers in the home such as a grandmother or caregiver will alter the pattern of the input. Consequently, an unnatural input condition may create a socially unnatural environment for language use that can lead to bilingual children's failure to acquire pragmatic competence. Kessler noted, "Bilingualism requires the continued use of both languages in communicative naturalistic settings" (1984, p. 35).

In addition, researchers have documented that the total separation of two languages in the input is extremely difficult, if not impossible. Goodz (1989), for example, found that language mixing is more common than not; even parents who thought they were using only one language with their children used utterances containing elements from two languages. Others have documented that the natural language mixing that occurs in bilingual homes does not have a negative effect on children's language acquisition. Garcia (1983) found that Spanish- and English-speaking preschoolers who received Spanish-English mixed input from their mothers experienced no difficulty keeping the two systems separate themselves.

Regardless of the degree of separation of the two languages, the quantity of exposure to each language that a bilingual child receives is smaller than that of the monolingual child, because exposure to one language must alternate in some way with exposure to the second language. Consequently, the bilingual child is not simply two monolingual children in one (Grosjean, 1982). Depending on the degree of exposure to a particular language and how the exposure was provided, bilingual children may be viewed as existing on different points on a continuum, and, as a result, these children will show varied acquisition characteristics (Bhatia & Ritchie, 1999).

The language acquisition of a bilingual child who is not exposed to both languages from birth or who does not receive relatively equal exposure to two languages may follow a different trajectory from that of a child who receives continuous exposure to two languages from birth. In some cases, one language will likely dominate due to the differentiated exposure over time. Spanish- and English-speaking bilingual children, for example, may be English-dominant and subsequently, are fluent in English but have weak knowledge of their native language (Portes & Rumbaut, 2001). Spanish-dominant children, alternatively, are fluent in Spanish and less fluent in English. These situations result in a delay in the development of one or both languages compared with the development found in monolingual individuals. In some cases the non-dominant system is eventually lost and English fluency is obtained; in others cases, children lose their native language but do not become fluent in English, making them limited bilinguals (Portes & Rumbaut, 2001). Alternately, a child's fluency in one language or another may be subject to temporary progression and regression when there is a change in his or her language environment. A child may, for example, travel to Puerto Rico and speak only Spanish for several months. This child may eventually lose the ability to retrieve English easily. On return to the U.S. mainland, however, English may be retrieved in a relatively short length of time and Spanish may then undergo a subsequent plateau or loss. Because the linguistic environment of the bilingual child is likely to change, it is not unusual that input from one language may be interrupted for a relatively long period of time; as a consequence, some loss or attrition is likely (Kessler, 1984; Schlyter, 1993). Hansen-Strain (1990) concluded that both age and the degree of competence in two languages before a change in input occurs play a role in a child's ability to continue to use two languages. These complexities of language input and use distinguish bilingual language acquisition from monolingual language acquisition.

Several factors appear to support children's bilingual language acquisition, as determined by Portes and Rumbaut (2001), who studied the development of immigrant children during their junior high and high school years. Portes and Rumbaut (2001) found that having two native-born parents or parents who only speak a non-English language in the home supported children's ability to become fully bilingual. The length of time the children lived in the United States also affected their language development. "With other factors controlled, U.S. residence leads to a net decline in the probability of bilingualism of about 1% per additional year in the country" (Portes & Rumbaut, 2001, p. 140). Parental socioeconomic status (SES) affected children's language abilities as well, with children of parents with higher socioeconomic status more likely to become bilingual. It appears that the added resources of parents of higher status assisted them in counteracting the effects of living in the United States over time.

Another factor that predicted bilingualism was gender. Girls were 6% more likely than boys of similar backgrounds to become bilingual. The final factor was being of Latino origin. Children whose native language was Spanish were more likely to preserve their first language than children from other immigrant groups. Latino children had a 51% greater probability of maintaining their native language than children from other cultural groups (Portes & Rumbaut, 2001). As discussed in the next section, the community in which families live also affects children's language usage and development.

Role of the Community

In societies in which bilingualism is natural and supported by government educational policies, children receive input from two languages on a regular basis and become bilingual (Bhatia & Ritchie, 1999). In societies in which the language of a minority group is distinct from that of the majority community, and consequently not viewed as valuable (and in fact, is often stigmatized), communities and families must adopt alternative strategies if they wish to ensure that the family language is not lost. The latter is the experience of Latino children living in the United States, who attend public educational systems that promote acquisition of the English language and, in many cases, provide no or limited support for the children's home language. Programs for at-risk preschoolers and families including Head Start and Even Start have policies that support English language acquisition, but do not stress the maintenance of children's first language. At the elementary and secondary school level, the states of California, Arizona, and Massachusetts have passed legislation that severely reduces or eliminates bilingual education for children whose first language is not English (Massachusetts Department of Education, 2003; National Association of Bilingual Educators, 2001). These policies have great implications for Latino children's development. First, children who come to school speaking Spanish require 2–3 years to develop the ability to communicate in English at an interpersonal level. The same children need 5–7 years before they achieve a level of proficiency in English that will allow them to learn academically (Cummins, 1981). If they receive academic instruction in English without having sufficient opportunities and time to learn English, they may fall behind academically simply because they do not have the necessary language foundation to acquire the material.

Second, children exposed to such policies quickly learn that English is the preferred language and that there is limited value in using and maintaining Spanish (Portes & Rumbaut, 2001). Despite parental support for their native language, children often prefer English. In a study of the immigration process of adolescents from primarily Asian and Latin countries, Portes and Rumbaut (2001) found that preference for English increased over time and was nearly universal. During junior high, 72% of the children in the sample preferred English to their native language and the percentage increased to 88% by the time the children graduated from high school. Mexican American children differed from this during their junior high years, with the majority preferring Spanish to English; however, by the end of high school, 75% preferred English.

As a result, children's opportunities to become bilingual are limited, which is unfortunate as bilingualism has numerous benefits. On the one hand, maintenance of the Spanish language enables identification with members of the community that share the same histories and assists one in making sense of situations encountered in the U.S. mainland. Speaking and understanding English, on the other hand, smoothes individuals' integration into the larger community and school (Zentella, 2002). This situation results in children being able to accommodate their linguistic abilities to the diversity around them. Those who are in regular contact with both monolingual Spanish and English speakers learn to switch rapidly from one to the other. In addition, bilingualism has many documented cognitive benefits including heightened sensitivity to semantic relationships, better phonological awareness abilities (Bialystok, 1986, 1988, 1992, 1997), greater awareness of linguistic rules and structures, enhanced creativity, and better academic outcomes (Hakuta & Diaz, 1985).

Therefore, attitudes of the family, the school, and the society at large are important and will affect a child's language usage. A child may not feel as though he or she has the opportunity to use both languages in all situations. One language may be seen as more appropriate in a given situation, particularly with respect to the people involved in the conversation, the topic, the location, and so forth. Because of the value placed on one language versus another, a child may choose to speak the language that he or she feels is better suited to the task, activity, or location, even when the child knows a conversation partner shares a common first language. Consequently, the question of exposure and usage is very complex.

PARENTAL BELIEFS

In recent years, two trends—increased interest in cross-cultural approaches to child development and a particular interest in the family—have come together to produce a literature specifically concerned with parental beliefs. Several scholars have argued that parental beliefs influence the goals parents have for their children, and these goals affect which behaviors are emphasized in the contexts of child development (Garcia Coll et al., 1996; Hoffman, 1988; LeVine, 1988). Parents' beliefs underlie their practices, which are consequently viewed as contributing to children's developmental outcomes. Thus, parents' beliefs about their children's learning guide parents' actions with their children (Neuman, Hagedorn, Celano, & Daly, 1995). They also characterize the parent–child relationship from a cultural perspective (Sigel & McGillicuddy-De Lisi, 1984) and mediate child outcomes (Rubin, Mills, & Rose-Krasnor, 1989).

Murphey (1992) proposed a general model of the role of parents' beliefs in affecting child outcomes. Parental beliefs are both global and specific. Global beliefs are broad views about the child such as those regarding the child's developmental process. Specific beliefs are parents' views about particular tasks and skills such as those related to a child's verbal assertiveness or ability to engage in complex play. Global and specific beliefs vary across cultures (Cashmore & Goodnow, 1986; Okagaki & Sternberg, 1993; Quirk et al., 1986) and evolve over time, reflecting patterns of coping with and adapting to the surrounding environment. Parents' global beliefs about language development, bilingualism, and their perceived roles in the educational system may have a considerable effect on their linguistic behavior toward their children and characterize the nature of children's language learning environments.

Beliefs About Language Development

Relatively little research has been conducted on parents' beliefs about language development and their role in supporting their children's acquisition of language, and even fewer have been conducted on the beliefs of mothers from diverse backgrounds. One study by Super and Harkness (1986) illustrated the influence of maternal beliefs on language development. They noted the relationship between maternal views about how children acquire speech and the amount of language input, topics of conversation, and frequency of verbal interactions provided by the mothers. Mothers who believed that young children learned to talk primarily from other children rather than from themselves were less likely to encourage language development and more likely to use commands, for example. Maternal language behavior also reflected cultural goals and values (e.g., training for obedience and responsibility versus individual verbal expression).

Limited information exists on Latina mothers' beliefs about language development. Mendez Perez (2000) studied Spanish-speaking Mexican

American mothers who had young children with language disabilities. Results of the investigation revealed that the mothers' age, and not acquisition of expected milestones, was used to gauge children's language development (Mendez Perez, 2000). These mothers did not expect their children to speak until the age of 3, and, therefore, they were not particularly concerned about their children's communication difficulties. The mothers did not associate limited verbal skills, reliance on nonverbal gestures, or poor retention skills with disabilities, and they believed their children would eventually catch up.

The mothers verbalized the importance of facilitating their children's language development, however. They saw themselves as active participants in their children's language learning and described what they did to facilitate language growth, including listening to their children, interacting with them, labeling objects and ideas, and creating opportunities for interactions with others. Mexican American mothers may be more likely to view "mothering" rather than "teaching" as their primary responsibility, thus focusing more on the nature and content of communication rather than on the rate of acquisition (Garcia, Mendez Perez, & Ortiz, 2000). Although this research yields valuable information, additional investigations are greatly needed in this area to better understand the role of culture in bilingual children's language development.

Attitudes Toward Bilingualism

In addition to understanding parents' views about language development, parents' attitudes about language usage and bilingualism need to be understood because parents' attitudes may influence the linguistic choices parents make during interactions with their children (de Houwer, 1998) and children's language choice. For example, a parent's negative attitude to early simultaneous bilingualism may result in a conscious decision to limit exposure to one language in order to emphasize the other. Zierer (1977) believed that exposure to a second language during the first few years of language development would hinder a child's acquisition and maintenance of his or her primary language and, therefore, prohibited second language input.

Conversely, a positive attitude toward early bilingualism may result in a parent's decision to use two languages in the home. Saunders (1988) reported that because he and his wife both had positive attitudes toward bilingualism and the specific languages involved (English and German), this contributed to their decision to raise their children in a bilingual language-learning environment. Parental attitudes relate to the language practices in

the home, which Fishman (1991) argued is the most critical factor in pre-
dicting whether a language will be maintained over generations.

Attitudes about bilingualism appear to be related to ethnic identity.
Schecter and colleagues (1996) reported findings from a recent analysis of
Latino parents' attitudes regarding bilingualism and their personal decisions about home language use. In-depth interviews were conducted with
Latino families in which parents chose to maintain the use of Spanish in the
home. The most frequent rationale cited for maintaining the use of Spanish in the home concerned the instrumental benefits of speaking more than
one language. Parents argued that knowledge of Spanish would serve their
children well academically, help their children to adapt to geographic relo-
cation, and give their children an edge in a competitive job market. Parents
also perceived knowledge of Spanish as an important part of their children's
sense of Latino identity and emphasized their commitment to the minority language as an act of affirmation of group identity. Similarly, Hurtado
and Gurin (1987) provided evidence that ethnic identity fosters positive
views of bilingualism among individuals of Mexican descent.

Despite these findings, relatively little is known about the attitudes
about language usage and bilingualism of various Latino groups living on
the United States mainland. Hammer and Miccio (2002) investigated the
attitudes of Puerto Rican mothers living in Pennsylvania whose bilingual
preschoolers attended Head Start. In this preliminary study, 34 mothers
completed a survey that elicited their attitudes about Spanish, English, and
bilingualism; 14 mothers had children who learned Spanish and English
sequentially and 20 had children who learned the two languages simultaneously. Nearly all mothers reported that they valued both languages. All
mothers believed that it was important for parents to understand and speak
Spanish well and for children to understand Spanish well; to be bilingual;
and to understand, speak, read, and write well in English. A large majority
of mothers felt that it was important for parents to speak English well and
for children to speak, read, and write well in Spanish.

When the two groups were asked more specific questions about their
attitudes toward Spanish (Hakuta, 1994), differences were observed between the two groups' answers. Nearly 80% of the mothers of sequential
learners as compared with 55% of the mothers of simultaneous learners
felt that an individual who was bilingual had more opportunities to express
his or her feelings. Approximately 80% of the mothers of the sequential
learners agreed that speaking Spanish fostered positive feelings about one-
self as compared with 60% of the mothers of the simultaneous learners.
Although a larger number of mothers in both groups believed that a per-

son "should" use Spanish daily as opposed to "needing" to communicate in Spanish daily, differences were observed between the two groups. Nearly all mothers of sequential learners felt that a person should use Spanish on a daily basis as compared with 75% of the mothers of simultaneous learners. Only 42% and 35% of the mothers of the sequential and simultaneous learners, respectively, reported needing to use Spanish to communicate on a daily basis. The groups were more similar with respect to their attitudes as to whether it was acceptable for a person to be raised speaking Spanish and then forget it. More than two thirds of the participants in the two groups indicated that this was not acceptable. As of 2004, it was unknown how these beliefs related to parents' language usage and their children's language development. This issue will be addressed at the conclusion of the 5-year investigation of bilingual Head Start children's language and literacy development.

Parents' Perceived Roles in the Educational System

Parents' perceptions of their roles in the educational system are important factors that affect the relationships that are developed between individual families and professionals. Researchers have found that parents' knowledge of school-related activities was an important factor in their level of involvement. Delgado-Gaitan reported that among Mexican American parents, social isolation from other families and their lack of English language proficiency "created a knowledge gap" (1990, p. 141), which influenced their involvement patterns. Mexican American parents often believe that the role of the home and school should not interfere with each other (Chavkin & Gonzalez, 1995). Many Mexican American families believe that they are being helpful by maintaining a respectful distance from the educational system (Peña, 2000) and maintain traditional educational beliefs.

Mothers' educational beliefs were the focus of an investigation of Mexican American and Anglo-American mothers (Rodriguez & Olswang, 2002). Sixty mothers (30 Mexican American and 30 Anglo-American) of children with language impairments completed the *Parental Modernity Scale* (Schaefer & Edgerton, 1985), designed to probe parents' educational beliefs. Results indicated the educational beliefs of Mexican American mothers were more strongly traditional and authoritarian than those of Anglo-American mothers. These beliefs included the notions that the school is primarily responsible for educating children, that parents should not question the teacher's teaching methods, and that obedience is an important concept to teach children.

When working with Latino families, it is important to keep in mind that the mother's education level and the family's socioeconomic status are particularly relevant to understanding how mothers define their role with respect to their children's education. Research has demonstrated that educated mothers tend to view their participation as "part of their job" more than do less-educated mothers, with mothers with at least a high school education playing a greater role in their children's education (Moreno & Lopez, 1999). In addition, working-class parents have been shown to believe that their role was to prepare children for school by teaching them manners and rudimentary skills and to be supportive but not to intervene in their children's program (Lareau, 1989). Similarly, Puerto Rican parents tend to relinquish control over their children's education and discipline to the school while retaining parental control over the children's home activities (Casanova, 1987). Goldenberg (1987), however, found that when Latino parents with low income perceive themselves as being influential in helping their children learn to read, they have a direct impact on their children's outcomes.

In conclusion, Latino families are interested in their children's education, but they often believe that they should not interfere in the educational process. In addition, parents may lack the confidence to attend school functions or to approach their children's teachers because of lack of familiarity with the U.S. educational system and/or because they do not feel comfortable communicating in English (Delgado-Gaitan, 2001). As a result, professionals may view families as uninterested and uninvolved in their children's education. Delgado-Gaitan (2001) demonstrated how successful relationships could be fostered between school personnel and Latino communities. These alliances can help eliminate cultural misunderstandings between families and professionals. Professionals need additional knowledge about Latino cultures in order to maximize their interactions with Latino families.

ASPECTS OF CULTURE

Before discussing specific cultural parenting behaviors, it is essential to address what culture is and to discuss the interrelationships between culture, communication, and parenting. No universally accepted definition of culture exists; however, there are three aspects of culture on which anthropologists agree (Hall, 1976): 1) culture is learned; 2) its facets are interrelated; and 3) culture is shared and serves to define the boundaries of each cultural group. Two additional aspects of culture that relate to children's development also appear to have researchers' consensus. First, cultural values and beliefs are reflected in the child-rearing practices of a cultural group whose main goal is to teach its youngest members how to become competent members of that community (Ochs & Schieffelin, 1984; Ogbu, 1988; Rogoff, 1981; Schwartz, 1981). Second, language is inextricably linked to culture, a concept that is expressed by Schieffelin and Ochs, who stated, "From our perspective, language and culture as bodies of knowledge, structure of understanding, conceptions of the work, collective representations, are both extrinsic to and far more extensive than any individual could know or learn" (1983, p. 116).

When these notions are applied to parenting, it can be concluded that the interactive and language behaviors of mothers when engaged with their children, as well as the behaviors of other members of the culture, are influenced by and reflect the values and beliefs of that culture (Ochs & Schieffelin, 1984; Peters & Boggs, 1986). "How caregivers and children speak and act toward one another is linked to cultural patterns that extend and have consequences beyond specific interactions observed" (Ochs & Schieffelin, 1984, p. 284).

Language development researchers have noted three universal features of culture and language development. First, all children who are typically developing acquire language at about the same age in all cultures (Crago, 1992). Second, caregivers in all cultures use language, show affection, and guide their children's learning, and children help structure their own learning by participating in activities and choosing with whom they interact (Crago, 1992; Rogoff, 1990). Third, variations in the individual behaviors of members of a given culture are found within all cultures (LeVine, 1984; Rogoff, 1990; Schieffelin & Ochs, 1983; van Kleeck, 1994).

All members of a given culture do not universally agree on the goals and values of the culture (Rogoff, 1990; Sameroff & Fiese, 1990), and families will have varied successes when trying to meet the more global goals of their culture, "because of differences in their genes, their family's position in the community, their material resources, and the chance circumstances in life" (Rogoff, 1990, p. 118). In other words, familial and individual preferences for various child-rearing practices of a given culture result in variations within a cultural group (Sameroff & Fiese, 1990). Keeping these aspects of culture in mind, the following section addresses the cultural practices of Latino families. Because limited information is available about the child-rearing practices of Latino families and even less information exists about the practices of particular Latino cultures, most of this information pertains to Latino families generally, and the reader should keep in mind that differences do exist between and within the various Latino cultures.

Collective Orientation of Latino Cultures

A collective orientation is the guiding framework for Latinos (Vega, Hough, & Romero, 1983). Emphasis is placed on community and, more important, the family (Zuniga, 2004). Families, including extended family members, support their members by offering emotional and monetary support and by sharing resources. Additional support may come from godparent systems and close friends. Latino households tend to be large, with close to one third of families living in the United States consisting of five or more people (Therrien & Ramirez, 2001). Often more than one generation lives in a home and/or family members may live within the same neighborhood and may have daily contact with one another. This results in families being close-knit. Actions and decisions must consider the family and not just the individual.

Marriage and Child-Rearing Practices

Marriage serves an important function in Latino families, and divorce is viewed unfavorably. As a result, the divorce rate for Latino couples is lower than that of non-Hispanic whites and African American families (Kreider & Fields, 2002). In more traditional families, the husband is considered the provider and the wife is responsible for raising the children. Because having children is the primary purpose for marriage in this culture, the parent–child relationships are considered more important than the relationships between husbands and wives (Zuniga, 2004).

Because children are viewed as important, parents try to provide their children with nurturing environments. Positive interactions between parent and child are desired and expressions of negative emotions including anger and aggression are seen as unacceptable. As a result, parental behaviors may seem permissive or indulgent to individuals from the mainstream culture. Emphasis may not be placed on individual achievement and early attainment of developmental milestones. It is thought that these attitudes may be related to the value placed on interdependence that exists among family members. Independence and individualization are not important goals for children (Zuniga, 2004), whereas interdependence and closeness within the family are valued.

Traditional Latino parenting practices emphasize "adherence to convention, respect for authority, and identity with the family" (Zuniga, 2004, p. 198). Children should be well educated, which means that they have been taught skills for engaging in human relationships and interacting with others in a respectful manner (Zuniga, 2004).

Communication Styles

Consistent with the emphasis on human relationships, interactions are to be harmonious and should focus on the individual. Importance, therefore, is placed on participating in "positive personal interactions that convey empathy for others, harmony in interpersonal relations, and [de-emphasized] negative behaviors in circumstances of conflict" (Roseberry-McKibbin, 2002, p. 83). As a result, conversations are typically initiated on a personal note, and questioning and conflict are avoided. Close personal distances are maintained and embraces and physical contact between individuals are common.

Because children are to be respectful of their parents and elders, children are not expected to take part in adult conversations, to interrupt adults, or to express their preferences or opinions. Children may refrain from maintaining direct eye contact with parents in order to demonstrate respect. Teaching interactions between parents and children are not stressed, and as a result, parents do not ask children factual questions in which parents know the answers already or ask children to make predictions or talk about what they are doing. Instead, importance is place on respect and politeness (Roseberry-McKibbin, 2002).

The reader is reminded that the information shared about Latino cultural practices applies to more-traditional families. Differences exist between families based on parental education and social class, region of the country, generational status, and acculturation stage (Zuniga, 2004). Families who have lived in the United States for a period of time may be bicultural or may have integrated practices of the mainstream culture into their behaviors.

ENVIRONMENTAL FACTORS
AFFECTING CHILDREN'S DEVELOPMENT

A number of environmental factors may affect a family and the environment in which a child is raised. These factors include immigration and acculturation, parental education, parental economic resources, income/socioeconomic status, and parental psychological status.

Immigration and Acculturation

Many Latino families are recent immigrants to the United States. Since 1960, 52% of all immigrants arriving in the United States come from Latin America and the Caribbean, with 28% arriving from Mexico (Portes & Rumbaut, 2001). According to Portes and Rumbaut, immigrants differ greatly based on "1) their individual features, including their age, education, occupational skills, wealth and knowledge of English; 2) the social environment that receives them, including the policies of the host government, the attitudes of the native populations, and the presence and size of a co-ethnic community; and 3) their family structure" (2001, p. 46). Immigrant groups that are similar to the mainstream society of the United States in terms of physical characteristics, social class, and language receive a more favorable reception; therefore, Latino families, who typically do not have these similarities, are likely to face greater obstacles in gaining access to opportunities and integrating into society.

Moving into an ethnic community assists families in coping with the adaptation process. Immigrants often experience culture shock, acculturative stress, and cultural fatigue because they must learn new habits, values, and communication processes and potentially, a new language (Zuniga, 2004). Residence in a community of people of similar ethnic backgrounds provides immigrants with access to social capital, "giving them a better chance to put to use whatever skills they brought from their home country and sometimes providing additional entrepreneurial training" (Portes & Rumbaut, 2001, p. 64). In addition, ethnic communities support parental authority and help preserve marriages by enforcing norms against divorce. Children from two-parent families have better outcomes because the presence of two parents doubles the resources available to children (Portes & Rumbaut, 2001).

Over time, immigrants assimilate into the mainstream culture to varying degrees, a process that may be affected by several factors. These include the history of the first generation, such as reasons for leaving their native country, the pace of acculturation of the parents and children, cultural and economic barriers that impede adaptation to the new culture, and family and community resources that assist in confronting the barriers (Portes & Rumbaut, 2001).

As immigrants assimilate in the mainstream society and learn the cultural norms and values of the predominant culture, immigrants' acculturate or incorporate mainstream behaviors in their patterns of behavior (Randall-David, 1989). The acculturation process can follow different trajectories and may differ between parents and children, resulting in three types of acculturation. As defined by Portes and Rumbaut (2001), dissonant acculturation occurs when children learn English and American values and beliefs and lose their culture at a different and faster rate than do their parents. As a result of this process, roles of parents and children are reversed because children are able to communicate in English and understand the behaviors of the mainstream culture, whereas their parents are not. This, in turn, may lead to the undermining of parental authority, as children no longer look to their parents for support when confronting mainstream society.

Consonant acculturation takes place when parents and children learn English and the new culture at approximately the same time. "This situation is most common when immigrant parents possess enough human capital to accompany the cultural evolution of their children and monitor it" (Portes & Rumbaut, 2001, p. 55), which in turn assists parents in maintaining their authority and ability to guide their children's behaviors and development. Selective acculturation occurs when both parents and children are learning the new language and customs of the mainstream culture while they are embedded in a large ethnic community. This tends to slow the cultural shift and supports the retention of the families' native language and norms. Selective acculturation typically results in a lack of conflict between generations, and full bilingualism of the children.

Not all Latino families are new arrivals to the United States—an important concept to consider—and Puerto Rican families are citizens of the United States; however, these families also cope with issues of maintaining their native culture and language while going to school and working and living in communities throughout the United States.

Parental Education

The relationship between parental education and children's development has been studied extensively. Research consistently demonstrates that higher maternal education fosters better outcomes for children. In general, children of parents with higher levels of education have higher academic achievement, perform better on cognitive measures (Auerbach, Lerner, Barasch, & Palti, 1992), and have better language outcomes than children of parents with lower educational levels (Beitchman, Hood, & Inglis, 1992; Hart & Risley, 1995; Hoff-Ginsberg, 1991; Schacter, 1979; Tomblin, Hardy, & Hein, 1991; Tomblin et al., 1997). Research on maternal education and children's outcomes in Latino families is limited; however, no evidence currently exists that suggests that positive relationships between maternal education and children's outcomes would not be found in Latino families.

Parental Economic Resources

The availability of economic resources helps support children's development, and, conversely, lack of such resources places children at risk. Poverty represents a constellation of environmental conditions such as lack of employment, stress on the parental system that may cause families to break apart, crowded and unsafe housing, and lack of access to quality healthcare and educational systems (Bradley, 1995; Hanson & Lynch, 2004). Parents typically experience significant stress that is caused by living conditions, lack of financial resources (i.e., not having sufficient funds to pay bills and not knowing how much money will be available in the future), parenting responsibilities, and extended family (McLloyd & Wilson, 1991).

Living in poverty negatively affects children's cognitive, language and academic outcomes (cf., McLanahan, 1997; McLloyd, 1998; Smith, Brooks-Gunn, & Klebanov, 1997). Persistent poverty has even greater effects on children's IQ scores, verbal ability, and achievement scores. The timing of when children live in poverty does not appear to make a difference on children's outcomes; in other words, poverty has negative effects at any time in a child's development (Smith et al., 1997).

Hispanic families are categorized at all economic levels; however, a larger percentage of families live below the poverty level in comparison with the general population. In 2001, the poverty rate for the U.S. population was 10% as compared with 21% of all Hispanic families (Proctor & Dalaker, 2002). Hispanic children are at even greater risk for poverty, with 29% living in poverty as opposed to 16% of all children living in the United States (Federal Interagency Forum on Child and Family Statistics, 2002).

Three factors have been associated with higher income levels and economic status of immigrant parents: Having a post–high school education, having a knowledge of English, and being male (Portes & Rumbaut, 2001). Differences, however, have been found in the economic successes of different groups. Regardless of the length of time they have been in the United States, Mexicans and Nicaraguans, as a group, earn less money than other recent immigrant groups after education, knowledge of English, and occupation are controlled for.

> In other words, no matter how long these immigrants have lived and worked in the United States, their net earnings remain flat. This is not the case for

Cubans and Vietnamese, for whom each additional year of experience in the country yields a small but significant gain. (Portes & Rumbaut, 2001, p. 84)

Parental Psychological Status

In addition to educational level and economic resources, parents' psychological well-being needs to be considered. Research has consistently shown that parental depression is related to less-than-optimal parenting and child outcomes. Specifically, maternal depression has been associated with lower quality of mother–child interactions (cf., Cohn, Campbell, Matias, & Hopkins, 1990; Cox, Puckering, Pound, & Mills, 1987; Leadbeater, Bishop, & Raver, 1996), more negative maternal views of offspring (Fergusson, Hons, Horwood, Gretton & Shannon, 1989), and lower cognitive abilities in infancy (Field, Estroff, Yando, del Valle, Malphurs, & Hart, 1996). Chronic maternal depression also has been associated with lower cognitive-linguistic functioning and school readiness at age 3 (NICHD Early Child Care Research Network, 1999).

Parents living in poverty are more likely to experience psychological distress than parents with higher incomes because of the economic pressure they face and the negative life events they experience. Not only can depression affect cognitive, language, and academic outcomes of poor children but also it can affect children's emotional status (McLloyd & Wilson, 1991). McLloyd and Wilson provided the following explanation for this relationship:

> Our interpretation is that when a mother is in poor mental health—a state that increases as her economic situation worsens—she is less satisfied with the parenting role and less likely to behave positively and supportively toward her child. This behavior, in turn, appears to contribute to feelings of depression and anxiety in the child. (1991, p. 127)

Limited research has been conducted depression in Latino mothers. Hammer and Miccio (2000) investigated the emotional well-being of the mothers of the bilingual children attending Head Start whom they followed from ages 3 to 6 years. Home visits were conducted with the mothers twice a year, during which time the Center for Epidemiological Studies Depression Scale (Radloff, 1977) was administered. Preliminary results from the first three home visits conducted with the mothers over the first 2 years of the study revealed that the percentage of mothers who showed depressive symptoms at a given time ranged between 40% and 60%. Many mothers received scores in the depressed range at all three time points, indicating that many Latina mothers may show signs of chronic psychological distress.

The effects of depression, however, can be buffered through social support, as has been shown in Hispanic populations (Guarnaccia, Angel, & Worobey, 1991; LaRoche, Turner, & Kalick, 1995; Leadbeater & Linares, 1992). In addition to moderating the effects of depression, increased social support has been found to decrease the occurrence of illness and stress (De La Rosa, 1988; Sandler, Miller, Short, & Wolchik, 1989; Weinraub & Wolf, 1987). Studies have also shown that parents with higher levels of social support have characteristics associated with optimal parenting; they tend to view their children more positively, are less overwhelmed by parenthood, and are more satisfied with their role as parent (Crnic & Greenberg, 1987; Crnic, Greenberg, Robinson, & Ragozin, 1984). In addition, parental access to larger and higher quality networks is associated with more positive child outcomes (Melson, Ladd, & Hsu, 1993). Thus, it appears that both poverty and lower parental educational levels directly affect children's outcomes, with maternal depression and social support networks affecting children's development as well.

IMPLICATIONS FOR ASSESSMENT

The information presented in the preceding sections has significant implications for professionals who work with Latino families when there is concern about a bilingual child with possible language impairment. The first priority is to establish a rapport with the family and to develop an understanding of the family's culture, beliefs and practices, and views about the child. Because of the cultural emphasis on a collective orientation and positive interpersonal relationships, families are likely to place high value on a professional's personal qualities, such as how approachable they are and how much interest they show in the family (Roseberry-McKibbin, 2002). Several steps must be taken in order to establish a positive rapport with the family (Hammer, 1998). If the professional is unfamiliar with the family's culture, it is important to obtain background information about child-rearing practices, communication styles, medical practices, and views of disabilities. Due to the fact that most information in books and articles about cultural practices is either written about Latino families in general or about Mexican families, it may be beneficial to talk with elders or community members from the family's specific culture in order to gain more insight. Discussions with professionals who have been successful working with families from a particular culture may also serve as a valuable source of knowledge.

Once background information has been gathered on the family's culture, the professional is ready to meet and interview the family. When talking with the family, it is important to involve the entire family and to talk to both the mother and father, recalling that in traditional families the father is likely to be the decision maker (Roseberry-McKibbin, 2002). Visits with the family should begin on a personal note, prior to getting to the official purpose. Titles should be used unless the parents ask to be called by their first names. Once the professional begins interviewing the family, he or she explains the purpose of the interview and the assessment and conducts a semi-structured interview (Hammer, 2002).

Semi-structured interviews differ from more traditional interviews in two ways. Unlike structured interviews in which the professional asks a standard set of questions, generally in a particular order, semi-structured interviews are modeled after a conversation (Taylor & Bogdan, 1984). The interviewer does not direct the conversation but allows the family members the opportunity to share information that is important to them (Rubin & Rubin, 1995). In addition, a semi-structured interview is not designed to simply obtain information from the family; it is also designed to acquire insights about the family's views, culture, and perceptions about their child. In order to do this, the professional develops guide questions that cover topics he or she anticipates discussing with the family. Questions may tap information about the child's medical history and language abilities and the family's concerns. These questions are then used to guide the interview. Questions are asked one at a time, with follow-up questions occurring to explore a topic thoroughly. Succeeding questions then follow logically from the information the family members have provided until all topics are discussed. For more information about conducting semi-structured interviews, the reader may refer to Rubin and Rubin (1995), Hammer (1998), Patton (2002), and Westby (1990).

Conducting the interview and all meetings in the language that the family is most comfortable using is imperative. If Spanish is the home language, the professional works with a trained interpreter if he or she does not know Spanish. If at all possible, asking the family to invite another family member or friend to serve as the interpreter should be avoided, as families may feel uncomfortable sharing personal information with a relative or friend present (Roseberry-McKibbin, 2002). If the family tells the professional that the meetings may be conducted in English, it is important to monitor the family's comprehension of what is said because some families may think that the professional expects them to communicate in

English or does not value Spanish. As a result, the family may say that they are comfortable communicating in English when they are not. The professional should not assume that a family is literate in Spanish, because some families may not have completed their education in their native country (Zuniga, 2004). In addition, we have found that many mothers of Head Start children who have been educated in English in the United States are more comfortable talking in Spanish but have not been taught how to read or write in Spanish.

When interviewing a family, it is important to determine the family's goals for their child, their approach to raising their child, and the child's communication partners and the contexts in which interactions occur (Hammer, 1998; van Kleeck, 1994). Assessments are most successful when the professional is open to the family's cultural style and tailors the intervention to the family's beliefs and practices (Hammer, 1998; Hammer & Weiss, 2000). Cultures that value a collective style and a cooperative mode may have different goals and approaches to guiding their children's development than the mainstream culture (Zuniga, 2004). Professionals need to be aware of these potential differences and demonstrate respect for families' parenting style and goals.

It is also important to determine if the family has recently immigrated to the United States and to assess the family's adaptation processes to determine any problems that may be present. Such problems could cloud the family's ability to focus on the needs of the identified infant or child (Perez Foster, 2001). This understanding will most likely develop over time as the professional works with the family.

Regardless of whether the family has recently immigrated to the United States, it is important to be attuned to the parents' psychological state. Immigration and the process of assimilation and accommodation, poverty, and limited knowledge of English can serve as stressors (McLoyd & Wilson, 1991). When concerns exist, referrals for mental health services may be called for or it may be appropriate to connect family members with counseling services available through their local church as religious networks are often important to Latino families (Zuniga, 2004).

Following the interview with the family, the child's language is assessed. It is imperative that the professional determine what languages the child uses and in which contexts he or she uses the languages. Recall that Hispanic children may be fully bilingual, English-dominant with knowledge of Spanish, Spanish-dominant with knowledge of English, or limited-bilingual without a completely developed system in either language. In addition, some children may be monolingual Spanish or monolingual

English speakers, although most children who speak English are exposed to Spanish at home through communication with grandparents or other family members. Thus, bilingual children's language experiences are different from those of monolingual children learning English. In most cases, children's language abilities are assessed in both languages in order to develop an understanding of the children's complete language system.

When assessing a child's Spanish language abilities, considerations must be made about the communicative partner who evaluates the child. A child may respond differently to a bilingual speaker who is not from his or her community than to a bilingual speaker from the same community. In addition, in a school setting, where English is valued, a child may speak in English even when the conversational partner is from the home community and speaks Spanish to him or her (Miccio, Hammer, & Toribio, 2002). According to de Houwer (1995), a bilingual child has more options than a monolingual child and must, from a very early age, make contextually sensitive choices. A child's choices for language preferences are determined by his or her perceptions of the situation and the topic in addition to the language of the conversation partner (Torres-Guzman, 1998). Therefore, it is important to obtain language usage information from the child's parents and school personnel to determine how representative the child's performance is during the language assessment.

The many factors discussed in this chapter show that the social-cultural processes that surround a bilingual, Latino child's language development are extremely complex. Differences in language exposure and input as well as cultural and environmental factors make every bilingual child unique. This situation presents exciting challenges to professionals who work with bilingual children and families. Care must be taken to establish a rapport with the family so that a true understanding can be obtained of the parents' practices, beliefs, and goals, and their approaches to interacting with their child. Through the development of a positive working relationship, services can be maximized to foster a child's bilingual language development.

REFERENCES

Auerbach, J., Lerner, Y., Barasch, M., & Palti, H. (1992). Maternal and environmental characteristics as predictors of child behavior problems and cognitive competence. *American Journal of Orthopsychiatry, 62*, 409–420.

Beitchman, J.H., Hood, J., & Inglis, A. (1992). Familial transmission of speech and language impairment. *Canadian Journal of Psychiatry—Revue Canadienne de Psychiatrie, 37*, 151–156.

Bhatia, T.K., & Ritchie, W.C. (1999). The bilingual child: Some issues and perspectives. In W.C. Ritchie & T. Bhatia (Eds.), *Handbook of child language acquisition* (pp. 569–646). San Diego: Academic Press.

Bialystok, E. (1986). Factors in the growth of linguistic awareness. *Child Development, 57*(1), 498–510.

Bialystok, E. (1988). Levels of bilingualism and levels of linguistic awareness. *Developmental Psychology, 2*(4), 560–567.

Bialystok, E. (1992). Attentional control in children's metalinguistic performance and measures of field independence. *Developmental Psychology, 28,* 654–664.

Bialystok, E. (1997). Effects of bilingualism and biliteracy on children's emerging concepts of print. *Developmental Psychology, 33,* 429–440.

Bradley, R.H. (1995). Environment and parenting. In M. Bornstein (Ed.), *Handbook of parenting.* Mahwah, NJ: Lawrence Erlbaum Associates.

Casanova, U. (1987). Ethnic and cultural differences. In V. Richardson-Koehler (Ed.), *Educator's handbook* (pp. 379–393). New York: Longman.

Cashmore, J.A., & Goodnow, J.J. (1986). Influences on Australian parents' values. *Journal of Cross-Cultural Psychology, 17,* 441–454.

Chavkin, N., & Gonzalez, D.L. (1995). *Forging partnerships between Mexican American parents and the schools.* Washington, DC: Office of Educational Research and Improvement. (ERIC Document Reproduction Service No. ED388 489)

Cohn, J., Campbell, S., Matias, R., & Hopkins, J. (1990). Face-to-face interactions of postpartum depressed and nondepressed mother-infant pairs at two months. *Developmental Psychology, 26,* 15–23.

Cox, A., Puckering, C., Pound, A., & Mills, M. (1987). The impact of maternal depression in young children. *Journal of Child Psychology and Psychiatry, 28,* 917–928.

Crago, M. (1992). Ethnography and language socialization: A cross-cultural perspective. *Topics in Language Disorders, 12*(3), 28–39.

Crnic, K., & Greenberg, M. (1987). Maternal stress, social support, and coping. Influences on early mother–child relationship. In C.F.Z. Boukydis (Ed.), *Research on support for parents and infants in the postnatal period* (pp. 25–60). New York: Ablex Publishing.

Crnic, K.A., Greenberg, M.T., Robinson, N.M., & Ragozin, A. (1984). Maternal stress and social support: Effects on the mother–infant relationship from birth to eighteen months. *American Journal of Orthopsychiatry, 54,* 224–235.

Cummins, J. (1981). The role of primary language development in promoting educational success for language minority students. In California State Department of Education, *Schooling and language minority students: A theoretical framework.* Los Angeles: Evaluation, Dissemination, and Assessment Center.

de Houwer, A. (1995). Bilingual language acquisition. In P. Fletcher & B. MacWhinney (Eds.), *Handbook of child language* (pp. 219–250). Oxford: Basil Blackwell Ltd.

de Houwer, A. (1998). Environmental factors in early bilingual development: The role of parental beliefs and attitudes. In G. Extra & L. Verhoeven (Eds.), *Bilingualism and migration* (pp. 75–95). Berlin: Mouton de Gruyter.

De la Rosa, M. (1988). Natural support systems of Puerto Ricans: A key dimension for well-being. *Health and Social Work, 13,* 181–190.

Delgado-Gaitan, C. (1990). *Literacy for empowerment: The role of parents in children's education.* New York: The Falmer Press.

Delgado-Gaitan, C. (2001). *The power of community: Mobilizing for family and schooling.* Lanham, MD: Rowman & Littlefield Publishers, Inc.

Federal Interagency Forum on Child and Family Statistics. (2002). *America's children: Key national indicators of well-being 2002.* Washington, DC: U.S. Government Printing Office.

Fergusson, D., Hons, B., Horwood, B., Gretton, D., & Shannon, F. (1989). Family life events, maternal depression, and maternal and teachers' descriptions of child behavior. In T. Miller (Ed.), *Stressful life events* (pp. 619–623). Madison, CT: International Universities Press.

Field, T., Estroff, D., Yando, R., del Valle, C., Malphurs, J., & Hart, S. (1996). Depressed mothers' perceptions of infant vulnerability are related to later development. *Child Psychiatry and Human Development, 27,* 43–53.

Fishman, J.A. (1991). *Reversing language shift: Theoretical and empirical foundations of assistance to threatened languages.* Philadelphia: Multilingual Matters.

Garcia, B., Mendez Perez, A., & Ortiz, A.A. (2000). Mexican American mothers' beliefs about disabilities: Implications for early childhood intervention. *Remedial & Special Education, 21,* 90–102.

Garcia, E. (1983). *Early childhood bilingualism.* Albuquerque, NM: University of New Mexico Press.

Garcia Coll, C., Lamberty, G., Jenkins, R., McAdoo, H.P., Crnic, K., Wasik, B.H., & Vazquez Garcia, H. (1996). An integrative model for the study of developmental competencies in minority children. *Child Development, 67,* 1891–1914.

Goldenberg, C.N. (1987). Low-income Hispanic parents: Contributions to their first-grade children's word-recognition skills. *Anthropology & Education Quarterly, 18,* 149–179.

Goodz, N. (1989). Parental language mixing in bilingual families. *Infant Mental Health Journal, 10,* 25–44.

Grosjean, F. (1982). *Life with two languages.* Cambridge, MA: Harvard University Press.

Guarnaccia, P., Angel, R., & Worobey, J. (1991). The impact of marital status and employment status on depressive affect for Hispanic Americans. *Journal of Community Psychology, 19,* 136–149.

Hakuta, K. (1994). Distinguishing among proficiency, choice, and attitudes in questions about language for bilinguals. In G. Lamberty, & C. Garcia Coll (Eds.), *Puerto Rican women and children: Issues in health, growth and development* (pp. 191–209). New York: Plenum Press.

Hakuta, K., & Diaz, R. (1985). The relationship between degree of bilingualism and cognitive ability. In K. Nelson (Ed.), *Children's language* (Vol. 5, pp. 319–344). Mahwah, NJ: Lawrence Erlbaum Associates.

Hall, E.T. (1976). *Beyond culture.* New York: Anchor Books.

Hammer, C.S. (1998). Toward a 'thick description' of families: Using ethnography to overcome the obstacles to providing family-centered services. *American Journal of Speech-Language Pathology, 9,* 1–22.

Hammer, C.S. (2002). African American mothers' views of their infants' language development and language-learning environment. *American Journal of Speech-Language Pathology, 9,* 126–140.

Hammer, C.S., & Miccio, A.W. (2000). *Bilingual preschoolers: Precursors to literacy.* Grant application funded by the National Institute of Child Health and Human Development, National Institutes of Health (1 R01 HD39496).

Hammer, C.S., & Miccio, A.W. (2002). *Puerto Rican mothers' attitudes about language usage and bilingualism.* Unpublished manuscript.

Hammer, C.S., Miccio, A.W., & Wagstaff, D. (2003). Home literacy experiences and their relationship to bilingual preschoolers' developing English literacy abilities: An initial investigation. *Language, Speech, and Hearing Services in Schools, 34,* 20–30.

Hammer, C., & Weiss, A.L. (2000). African American mothers' views of their infants' language development and language-learning environment. *American Journal of Speech-Language Pathology, 9,* 126–140.

Hansen-Strain, L. (1990). Attrition of Japanese by English-speaking children, an interim report. *Language Sciences, 12,* 367–377.

Hanson, M.J., & Lynch, E.W. (2004). Families in poverty: Cumulative risk and resilience. In M.J. Hanson & E.W. Lynch, *Understanding families: Approaches to diversity, disability, and risk* (pp. 89–122). Baltimore: Paul H. Brookes Publishing Co.

Hart, B., & Risley, T.R. (1995). *Meaningful differences in the everyday experiences of young American children.* Baltimore: Paul H. Brookes Publishing Co.

Hoff-Ginsberg, E. (1991). Mother–child conversation in different social classes and communicative settings. *Child Development, 62,* 782–796.

Hoffman, L.W. (1988). Cross-cultural differences in child rearing goals. In R.A. LeVine, P.M. Miller, & M.M. West (Eds.), *Parental behavior in diverse societies* (pp. 99–122). In W. Damon (Series Ed.), *New directions for child development* (No. 44, Summer). San Francisco: Jossey-Bass.

Hurtado, A., & Gurin, P. (1987). Ethnic identity and bilingualism attitudes. *Hispanic Journal of Behavioral Sciences, 9,* 1–18.

Kessler, C. (1984). Language acquisition in bilingual children. In N. Miller (Ed.), *Bilingualism and language disability: Assessment and remediation* (pp. 26–54). London: Croom Helm.

Kreider, R., & Fields, J. (2002). *Number, times, and duration of marriages and divorces: 1996* (U.S. Census Bureau Report: 70-80). Washington, DC: U.S. Bureau of the Census.

Lareau, A. (1989). *Home advantage: Social class and parental intervention in elementary education.* New York: The Falmer Press.

LaRoche, M., Turner, C., & Kalick, S.M. (1995). Latina mothers and their toddlers' behavioral difficulties. *Hispanic Journal of Behavioral Sciences, 17,* 375–384.

Leadbeater, B.J., & Bishop, S.J. (1994). Predictors of problems in preschool children of inner-city Afro-American and Puerto Rican adolescent mothers. *Child Development, 65,* 638–648.

Leadbeater, B.J., Bishop, S.J. & Raver, C.C. (1996). Quality of mother toddler interactions, maternal depressive symptoms and behaviour problems in preschoolers of adolescent mothers. *Development Psychology, 32,* 2, 280–288.

Leadbeater, B.J., & Linares, O. (1992). Depressive symptoms in black and Puerto Rican adolescent mothers in the first 3 years postpartum. *Development and Psychopathy, 4,* 451–468.

LeVine, R. (1984). Properties of culture: An ethnographic view. In R. Shweder & R. LeVine (Eds.), *Culture theory: Essays on mind, self and emotion* (pp. 67–87). New York: Cambridge University Press.

LeVine, R.A. (1988, Summer). Human parental care: Universal goals, cultural strategies, individual behavior. In W. Damon (Series Ed.) & R.A. LeVine, P.M. Miller, & M.M. West (Vol. Eds.), *New directions for child development: Parental behavior in diverse societies* (No. 44, pp. 3–11). San Francisco: Jossey-Bass.

Massachusetts Department of Education (2003). English Education in public schools. Retrieved February 11, 2003, from www.doe.mass.edu/lawsregs/03news/Q2_wrkdft.pdf

McLanahan, S.S. (1997). Parent absence or poverty: Which matters more? In G. Duncan & J. Brooks-Gunn (Eds.), *Consequences of growing up poor* (pp. 35–48). New York: Russell Sage Foundation.

McLaughlin, B. (1984). Early bilingualism: Methodological and theoretical issues. In M. Paradis & Y. Lebrun (Eds.), *Early bilingualism and child development* (pp. 19–45). Lisse, The Netherlands: Swets & Zeitlinger.

McLoyd, V.C. (1998). Socioeconomic disadvantage and child development. *American Psychologist, 53,* 185–204.

McLoyd, V.C., & Wilson, L. (1991). The strain of living poor: Parenting, social support, and child mental health. In A. Huston (Ed.), *Children in poverty: Child development and public policy* (pp. 105–135). Cambridge, UK: Cambridge University Press.

Meisel, J. (1994). Code-switching in young bilingual children: The acquisition of grammatical constraints. *Studies in Second Language Acquisition, 16,* 413–439.

Melson, G.F., Ladd, G.W., & Hsu, H. (1993). Maternal support networks, maternal cognitions, and young children's social and cognitive development. *Child Development, 64,* 1401–1417.

Mendez Perez, A. (2000). Mexican-American mothers' perceptions and beliefs about language acquisition in infants and toddlers with disabilities. *Bilingual Research Journal, 24,* 277–294.

Miccio, A.W., Hammer, C.S., & Toribio, A.J. (2002). Linguistics and speech-language pathology: Combining research efforts toward improved interventions for bilingual children. In J.E. Alatis, H.E. Hamilton, & A-H. Tan (Eds.), *Georgetown University Round Table on Languages and Linguistics 2000: Linguistics, language, and the professions* (pp. 234–250). Washington, DC: Georgetown University Press.

Moreno, R.P., & Lopez, J.A. (1999). Latina mothers' involvement in their children's schooling: The role of maternal education and acculturation. *JSRI Working Paper Series, 44,* 1–18.

Murphey, D.A. (1992). Constructing the child: Relations between parents' beliefs and child outcomes. *Developmental Review, 12,* 199–232.

National Association of Bilingual Educators. (2001). Bilingual education in the states. Retrieved February 17, 2003, from http://www.nabe.org/policy_bilingualedinstates.asp

Neuman, S.B., Hagedorn, T., Celano, D., & Daly, P. (1995). Toward a collaborative approach to parent involvement in early education: A study of teenage mothers in an African-American community. *American Educational Research Journal, 32,* 801–827.

NICHD Early Child Care Research Network. (1999). Chronicity of maternal depressive symptoms, maternal sensitivity, and child functioning at 36 months. *Developmental Psychology, 35,* 1297–1310.

Ochs, E., & Schieffelin, B. (1984). Language acquisition and socialization: Three developmental stories and their implications. In R. Shweder & R. Levine (Eds.), *Culture theory: Essays on mind, self, and emotion* (pp. 276–320). New York: Cambridge University Press.

Ogbu, J. (1988). Cultural diversity and human development. In D.T. Slaughter (Ed.), Black children and poverty: A developmental perspective (pp. 11–28). San Francisco: Jossey-Bass.

Okagaki, L., & Sternberg, R.J. (1993). Parental beliefs and children's school performance. *Child Development, 64,* 36–56.

Patton, M. (2002). *Qualitative evaluation and research methods.* Thousand Oaks, CA: Sage.

Peña, D.C. (2000). Parent involvement: Influencing factors and implications. *The Journal of Educational Research, 94,* 42–54.

Perez Foster, R.M. (2001). When immigration is trauma: Guidelines for the individual and family clinician. *American Journal of Orthopsychiatry, 71,* 153–170.

Peters, A.M., & Boggs, S.T. (1986). Interactional routines as cultural influences up on language acquisition. In B. Schieffelin & E. Ochs (Eds.), *Language socialization across cultures* (pp. 80–96). New York: Cambridge University Press.

Portes, A., & Rumbaut, R. (2001). *Legacies: The story of the immigrant second generation.* Berkeley, CA: University of California Press.

Proctor, B., & Dalaker, J. (2002). *Poverty in the United States: 2001, Current Population Reports,* P60-219. Washington, DC: U.S. Government Printing Office.

Quirk, M., Ciottone, R., Minami, H., Wapner, S., Yamamoto, T., Ishii, S., Lucca-Irizarry, N., & Pacheco, A. (1986). Values mothers hold for handicapped and nonhandicapped preschool children in Japan, Puerto Rico, and the United States mainland. *International Journal of Psychology, 21,* 463–485.

Radloff, L.S. (1977). The CES-D scale: A self-report depression scale for research in the general population. *Applied Psychological Measurement, 1,* 385–401.

Randall-David, E. (1989). *Strategies for working with culturally diverse communities and clients.* Washington, DC: Association for Care of Children's Health.

Rodriguez, B., & Olswang, L.B. (2002). *Mexican-American and Anglo-American mothers' beliefs about child rearing, education, and language impairment.* Unpublished manuscript.

Rogoff, B. (1981). Adults as peers as agents of socialization: A Highland Guatemalan profile. *Ethos, 9,* 18–36.

Rogoff, B. (1990). *Apprenticeship in thinking: Cognitive development in social context.* New York: Oxford University Press.

Roseberry-McKibbin, C. (2002). *Multicultural students with special language needs* (2nd ed). Oceanside, CA: Academic Communication Associates.

Rubin, H., & Rubin, I. (1995). *Qualitative interviewing: The art of hearing data.* Thousand Oaks, CA: Sage.

Rubin, K.H., Mills, R.S.L., & Rose-Krasnor, L. (1989). Maternal beliefs and children's competence. In B. Schneider, G. Attili, J. Nadel, & R. Weissberg (Eds.), *Social competence in developmental perspective* (pp. 313–331). Dordrecht, The Netherlands: Kluwer.

Sameroff, A., & Fiese, B. (1990). Transactional regulation and early intervention. In S. Meisels & J. Shonkoff (Eds.), *Handbook of early childhood education* (pp. 119–149). New York: Cambridge University Press.

Sandler, I., Miller, P., Short, J., & Wolchik, S. (1989). Social support as a protective factor for children in stress. In D. Belle (Ed.), *Children's social networks and social supports* (pp. 277–307). New York: John Wiley & Sons.

Saunders, G. (1988). *Bilingual children: From birth to teens.* Clevedon, UK: Multilingual Matters.

Schacter, F., with Marquis, R., Shore, E., Bundy, C., & McNair, J. (1979). *Everyday mother talk to toddlers.* New York: Academic Press.

Schaefer, E.S., & Edgerton, M. (1985). Parent and child correlates of parental modernity. In I.E. Sigel (Ed.), *Parental belief systems: Psychological consequences for children* (pp. 287–318). Mahwah, NJ: Lawrence Erlbaum Associates.

Schecter, S.R., Sharken-Taboada, D., & Bayley, R. (1996). Bilingual by choice: Latino parents' rationales and strategies for raising children with two languages. *The Bilingual Research Journal, 20,* 261–281.

Schieffelin, B., & Ochs, A. (1983). A cultural perspective on the transition from prelinguistic to linguistic communication. In R.M. Golinkoff (Ed.), *The transition from prelinguistic to linguistic communication* (pp. 115–131). Mahwah, NJ: Lawrence Erlbaum Associates.

Schlyter, S. (1993). The weaker language in bilingual Swedish-French children. In K. Hyltenstam & A. Viberg (Eds.), *Progression and Regression in language: Sociocultural, neuropsychological and linguistic perspectives* (pp. 289–308). Cambridge, MA: Cambridge University Press.

Schwartz, T. (1981). The acquisition of culture. *Ethos, 9,* 4–17.

Sigel, I.E., & McGillicuddy-De Lisi, A. (1984). Parents as teachers of their children: A distancing behavior model. In A. Pellegrini & T. Yawkey (Eds.), *The development of oral and written language in social contexts* (pp. 71–92). Norwood, NJ: Ablex Publishing.

Smith, J.R., Brooks-Gunn, J., & Klebanov, P.K. (1997). Consequences of living in poverty for young children's cognitive and verbal ability and early school achievement. In G. Duncan & J. Brooks-Gunn (Eds.), *Consequences of growing up poor* (pp. 132–189). New York: Russell Sage Foundation.

Super, C.M., & Harkness, S. (1986). The developmental niche: A conceptualization at the interface of child and culture. *International Journal of Behavioral Development, 9,* 545–569.

Taylor, S.J., & Bogdan, R. (1984). *Introduction to qualitative research methods.* New York: John Wiley & Sons.

Therrien, M., & Ramirez, R. (2001). *The Hispanic population in the United States* (U.S. Census Bureau Report P20–535). Washington, DC: U.S. Bureau of the Census.

Tomblin, J.B., Hardy, J.C., & Hein, H.A. (1991). Predicting poor-communication status in preschool children using risk factors present at birth. *Journal of Speech and Hearing Research, 34,* 1096–1105.

Tomblin, J.B., Records, N.L., Buckwalter, P., Zhang, X., Smith, E., & O'Brien, M. (1997). Prevalence of specific language impairment in kindergarten children. *Journal of Speech, Language, and Hearing Research, 40,* 1245–1260.

Torres-Guzman, M.E. (1998). Language, culture, and literacy in Puerto Rican communities. In B. Perez (Ed.), *Sociocultural contexts of language and literacy* (pp. 99–122). Mahwah, NJ: Lawrence Erlbaum Associates.

van Kleeck, A. (1994). Potential cultural bias in training parents as conversational partners with their children who have delays in language development. *American Journal of Speech-Language Pathology, 3,* 67–78.

Vega, W., Hough, R., & Romero, A. (1983). Family life patterns of Mexican Americans. In G. Powell, J. Yamamoto, A. Romero, & A. Morales (Eds.), *The psychosocial development of minority group children* (pp. 194–215). New York: Brunner/Mazel.

Weinraub, M., & Wolf, B. (1987). Stressful life events, social supports, and parent-child interactions: Similarities and differences in single-parent and two-parent families. In C.F.Z. Boukydis (Ed.), *Research on support for parents and infants in the postnatal period* (pp. 114–135). Westport, CT: Ablex Publishing.

Westby, C. (1990). Ethnographic interviewing: Asking the right questions to the right people in the right ways. *Journal of Childhood Communication Disorders, 13,* 101–111.

Zentella, A.C. (2002). Latina languages and identities. In M. Suarez-Orozco & M.A. Paez (Eds.), *Latinos: Remaking America* (pp. 321–338). Berkeley: University of California Press.

Zierer, E. (1977). Experiences in the bilingual education of a child of preschool age. *International Review of Applied Linguistics in Language Teaching, 15,* 143–148.

Zuniga, M. (1988). Chicano self-concept: A proactive stance. In C. Jacobs & D. Bowles (Eds.), *Ethnicity and race: Critical concepts in social work* (pp. 71–83). Silver Spring, MD: National Association of Social Workers.

Zuniga, M. (2004). Families with Latino roots. In E.W. Lynch & M.J. Hanson (Eds.), *Developing cross-cultural competence* (3rd ed., pp. 179–198). Baltimore: Paul H. Brookes Publishing Co.

Lexical and Semantic Aspects

CHAPTER 3

Processing Skills in Early Sequential Bilinguals

KATHRYN KOHNERT

E arly sequential bilinguals are children who learn a single first language (L1) from birth and begin the systematic learning of a second language (L2) during childhood (generally considered between 2 and 12 years of age). Traditionally, the abilities of early sequential bilinguals have been described within competence- or knowledge-based theoretical frameworks. Researchers and others were primarily interested in linguistic knowledge in L2, as measured through the use of standardized tests or language sampling. From this perspective, a child's proficiency in L2 was viewed as attaining the grammatical rules governing the language, as well as learning the core vocabulary. Much less attention was given to L1 and to the processing of linguistic information in either language. Current thinking about early sequential bilingual development, however, has broadened to address both L1 and L2. Moreover, cognitive and skill-based information processing theories can be used to frame our thinking about language proficiency in developing bilinguals. Recent empirical findings in the fields of cognitive science, psycholinguistics, and child language impairment provide a context for considering the processing of information in early sequential bilinguals. Insights from these diverse literatures can be used to inform our clinical practice with school-age children learning an L2.

The purpose of this chapter is to review the literature on language processing in school-age children who speak Spanish as L1 and English as L2, with specific attention given to clinical implications. The first section

The writing of this chapter was supported by research grants from the National Institute of Deafness and Other Communication Disorders (R03 DC05542-01) and the University of Minnesota (Grant-in-Aid of Research, Artistry and Scholarship).

presents an overview of main issues, including general stages of language development, a broad theory of interactive processing, and a model to frame our thinking about language proficiency. The second and third sections present specific characteristics of sequential Spanish-English bilingual school-age children and their performance on experimental measures of lexical processing. The fourth section looks at processing skills in monolingual children with and without developmental language impairment (LI). The final sections describe implications of processing perspectives for clinical language assessment and intervention with school-age children learning an L2.

LANGUAGE LEARNING: WAVES AND STAGES

Children who learn a single language from birth proceed through at least two general "waves" or stages of development. The first wave of language development is characterized by the acquisition of consistent form-function mappings or "rules"—essentially, linguistic knowledge or competence. Here, among other things, children learn to differentiate between the vowels of their language, to comprehend and produce core lexical referents for items and actions, and to use grammatical forms to indicate tense, aspect, number and gender (e.g., Bates & Goodman, 1997; Berko Gleason, 1997). Knowledge-dependent measures of language typically profile the forms present in the child's linguistic system, such as the grammatical structures familiar to the child or the number of words in his productive vocabulary. This first stage of linguistic form learning is well under way in typically developing monolingual children by the time they enter kindergarten (at age 4 or 5). For example, the typically developing 5-year-old child who learns English from birth has amassed a vocabulary of several thousand words, and adheres consistently to the phonological, morphological, and syntactic constraints of his or her language.

A 5-year-old is not as skilled in processing linguistic information as a 15-year-old, however. Real-time language use requires more than just knowing the correct forms. Efficient language use requires the ability to recall, access, and deploy known linguistic information with extraordinary temporal and perceptual precision. Consider that conversational speech among adult native speakers of any language takes place at a rate of approximately 125–225 words per minute (e.g., Foss & Hakes, 1978). While working at this speed, speakers construct the meanings they want to convey, select words from tens of thousands of alternatives, sequence these words according to language-specific rules, and assign grammatical inflections as needed. These meaningful linguistic strings are then produced fluently through the coordinated effort of more than 100 muscles while following the appropriate rules of social interaction.

In order to comprehend the spoken message, listeners must first perceive the signal, then retrieve the speaker's intended meaning from a stream of sounds that are exceedingly fast (i.e., an average of 5–8 syllables and 25–30 phonetic segments per second) with overlapping borders between meaningful units (Fowler, 1980; Fromkin & Bernstein Ratner, 1998; Liberman, 1970; Yeni-Komshian, 1998). Given the exquisite temporal precision required during natural language processing, temporal disruptions as brief as 50 milliseconds could have cascading effects, impeding language processing even in individuals who "know" all the rules of the language (Milberg, Blumstein, Katz, Gershberg, & Brown, 1995). Moreover, in order to process linguistic information in real-time, conversational participants need to do so automatically, resisting interference from either internal or external distractions. Given these constraints, it is clear that typical language development involves much more than the acquisition of linguistic forms or knowledge.

The second general wave of language acquisition, then, is characterized by a refinement of performance skill resulting in increased speed and efficiency in processing known linguistic information. The temporal calibration of linguistic knowledge required to be a competent language user continues to develop through adolescence (e.g., Kail, 1991). Gains in the ability to process information efficiently are accompanied by continuing growth in the areas of lexical-semantics, pragmatics, and metalinguistic skills. In contrast to knowledge-dependent measures of language, processing-dependent measures are concerned with the efficiency with which individuals can gain access to, recall, or manipulate basic linguistic units in real time. For example, most would expect greater speed and fluency of language use by the 15-year-old than the 5-year-old. This greater facility with language for older children relative to younger children is most evident under increasing processing demands (e.g., background sounds that either degrade the signal or compete for a child's attention).

The two general waves of development described here are characterized by accelerations in different aspects of language. The first wave of development is characterized by the accumulation of linguistic forms, such as sounds and words, and rules for how these forms can be combined in the language. This accumulation of linguistic knowledge is critically dependent on language-specific experiences. The second wave of language development is characterized by gains in the efficiency with which this known information is used. The efficiency in using these known forms is dependent on cognitive development and the integrity of the language processing system.

Although these two developmental waves are generally consecutive in single-language learners (with some obvious overlap), this is not necessarily the case for the sequential bilingual child. The child who learns a single language from birth and then begins to learn a second language at age 5, for example, has different experiences in each language as well as different levels of cognitive (and social) development through which these language experiences are processed. Here, it is likely that these knowledge and processing waves in L1 and L2 do not appear in a simple sequential manner, but converge or collide to produce complex outcomes. Preliminary research that uses knowledge-based measures of language indicates that the impact of an L2 on the home language (L1) may result in "language loss" (in which the L1 skills stagnate and then regress with relative disuse) or "semilingualism" (in which the child fails to fully develop either language system) (e.g., Schiff-Myers, 1992; Wong-Fillmore, 1991). In some situations, however, L1 skills may continue to develop.

In the following section, a framework for considering the interactions between cognitive processes and language experiences in sequential bilinguals is presented.

LANGUAGE PROCESSING IN AN INTERACTIVE THEORETICAL FRAMEWORK

An interactive information processing theory considers basic cognitive mechanisms (e.g., perception, memory, attention, emotion) to be integral to efficient language learning (Bates & MacWhinney, 1987; MacWhinney, 1997; Segalowitz, 1997). The general underlying idea is that cognition and language are linked at some very basic level and that, in fact, specific linguistic functions are acquired and maintained through the application of more general cognitive processes. These general cognitive processes underlie the speed and efficiency with which language is learned and used. The theoretical models included in this interactive framework assume bidirectional ("top down" and "bottom up") exchanges among different information types, both within the language domain (e.g., phonology interacting with semantics); across cognitive-linguistic domains (e.g., language interacting with basic levels of attention); and, in the case of bilinguals, across languages (L1 affecting L2 and vice versa). Interactive frameworks are generally consistent with both functionalist theories and the highly parallel, distributed processing models instantiated in neural computational networks, known as connectionism (e.g., Bialystok, 2001; Elman et al., 1996). (Refer to Gillam, Hoffman, Marler, & Wynn-Dancy, 2002, and Snyder, Dabasinskas, & O'Connor, 2002, for a review of top-down and bottom-up approaches and other terms used in the psycholinguistic processing literature.)

Working within a general cognitive-linguistic interactive processing framework, we can view early sequential bilingualism (i.e., the learning of a single language from birth and an L2 prior to adolescence) as a product of individual experience interacting with general cognitive processing mechanisms. Bilingualism is thus considered to be a dynamic system in which there is constant interplay between the languages (both positive and negative transfer as well as some competition for resources). Bilingualism is viewed as a matter of degree, with relative levels of L1 and L2 potentially shifting across the lifespan as a function of both social and cognitive influences (e.g., Hernandez, Bates, & Avila, 1994; Liu, Bates, & Li, 1992). This highly interactive perspective emphasizes change and plasticity over time, in direct contrast to static typologies of bilingualism (e.g., competence-based models that invoke strict notions of critical periods for L2 acquisition). This view is consistent with the holistic view of bilingualism, which emphasizes not only the co-existence of two (or more) languages in the bilingual but also their potential interactions within a single representational system (Grosjean, 1982). An interactive processing framework is also consistent with a limited processing capacity theory of language breakdown in children with developmental language impairment (see Leonard, 1998, and Ellis Weismer & Evans, 2002, for reviews).

Within a general interactive processing theory, we can systematically explore potential shifts in relative L1–L2 skills with respect to both cognitive-linguistic processing and language experience across development. From this perspective, we can also broaden our definition of language proficiency. This is important because measures of language proficiency are a cornerstone of clinical and educational assessments with early sequential bilinguals.

Language Proficiency

The term *proficiency*, like language itself, refers to a complex, multifaceted, global construct (e.g., Bialystok, 2001). At a minimum, proficiency in any single language involves the acquisition of knowledge (consistent form–function mappings) as well as the efficient use of this known information (in terms of the processing speed required during real-time communicative exchanges). Each of these knowledge and processing dimensions of the proficiency equation can be further broken down by linguistic levels (e.g., phonological, lexical, syntactic, pragmatic) and by channels or modes of communication (e.g., comprehension, production). As previously noted, skill or proficiency at the processing level involves both efficient access of known forms as well as control of the system in the face of competition from linguistic or nonlinguistic sources. Measures of bilingual skill are designed to index selected aspects of this overall language proficiency equation (e.g., lexical or syntactic skills in comprehension or production, at either the knowledge or processing end of a continuum). Although we cannot fully separate linguistic knowledge from processing in the assessment process, we can develop measures that selectively emphasize one aspect over the other.

Language proficiency in bilinguals is most often understood in terms of relative cross-linguistic proficiency. When skill level is comparable across the two languages, it is called "balanced bilingualism." In contrast, when one language is stronger than the other (as is most often the case) this language is considered "dominant." Competence-based models of language proficiency are primarily concerned with the acquisition of static, abstract representations, quantified with respect to the linguistic knowledge presumed present in native, monolingual speakers of a language. In contrast, interactive processing-based models of proficiency consider the efficiency with which known information is used in each language, control and interaction of the dual-language system (as when code-switching or language mixing), and the integrity of the language processing system. The standard for comparison, in this case, is performance by others who share similar experience and levels of cognitive development (most often indexed by chronological age). From this perspective, an important part of the proficiency equation is the speed, efficiency, and effort with which known linguistic information is used relative to the constraints and demands of real-time communication.

We can consider bilingual language proficiency as the linguistic output (in L1 *and* L2 across linguistic levels and modalities) that results from language-specific experiences interacting with the individual's general cognitive processing system. Input in each language is processed by cognitive processing mechanisms that communicate with each other, thus allowing for bi-directional L1–L2 transfer effects. The product of these complex cognitive–linguistic interactions (i.e., language output) is what is actually measured during language testing. The language output level is, in the broadest sense, the totality of language knowledge (in terms of consistent forms and rules in each language) and performance/processing skill (the ability to efficiently use or manipulate linguistic information).

In a series of studies, my colleagues and I began to explore one specific part of this overall proficiency equation. Specifically, we looked at lexical processing in Spanish-English bilinguals across development and experience. In the following section, important characteristics of participants in these studies are described.

SAMPLE CHARACTERISTICS

In a world in which more than half the population speaks at least two languages, children learning an L2 represent the fastest growing subset of bilinguals (e.g., Bialystok, 2001; Goldstein, 2000; Grosjean, 1982). In the United States, children learning an L2 (primarily English) are from homes in which Spanish, Hmong, Korean, Tagalog, Urdu, or one of a hundred different languages are spoken. The majority of these children are typical language learners and, with time and appropriate experience, will become proficient users of the L2. Consistent with the overall prevalence rates of language impairment in monolingual children, however, we can reasonably anticipate that a subset of children learning an L2 will have a primary language impairment for which timely identification and intervention is needed to ameliorate negative long-term effects. Identification of language impairment in a child is made relative to children of the same age who have had similar language-learning experiences. In order to identify primary language impairments in school-age children in the process of learning an L2, the boundaries of typical language performance with respect to experience and development must be understood clearly. Systematic research exploring the acquisition and maintenance of basic skills in both languages of typically developing early sequential bilinguals at all linguistic levels is needed. Without this baseline information, professionals can neither adequately assess children's progress nor identify a breakdown in the language acquisition process when it occurs.

In the following section, results from a series of studies investigating lexical processing skills in school-age sequential bilinguals are presented (Kohnert, 2002; Kohnert & Bates, 2002; Kohnert, Bates, & Hernandez, 1999). In these studies, my colleagues and I attempted to limit the amount of variation among participants on those factors believed to influence sequential language development. These factors included age, differences in the context of input, typological distance between the two languages (e.g., children learning Spanish and English may differ from children learning Cantonese and English), level of L1 development, and social and cultural status of the L1 and L2 (see Bialystok, 2001, for discussion). We attempted to control for variation among participants on these factors in order to allow for comparisons between age groups that would reveal any discernible patterns of language development against the overall background of variability that is a hallmark of early sequential bilingualism.

In each of two cross-sectional studies, 100 individuals participated, 20 at each of the following age levels: 5–7 years, 8–10 years, 11–13 years, 14–16 years, and 18–22 years (Kohnert & Bates, 2002; Kohnert et al., 1999). A third study was conducted to follow up on a subset of participants from the lexical production study (Kohnert, 2002). All participants were from Spanish-speaking families and learned Spanish as L1. Caregivers of the children reported Spanish to be their primary or sole language. All participants reportedly began the systematic learning of English as their L2 between 4 and 6 years of age. Systematic English learning was defined as consistent exposure to English through the educational system. No study participants had attended dual immersion educational programs, which seek to maintain or increase skills in L1 (Spanish) along with systematic instruction in L2 (English). Rather, participants in the lexical processing studies described in the following section were all in educational programs in the United States designed to further their English-speaking skills, with little attention given to the improvement of their Spanish-speaking skills. This emphasis on instruction in English for students in a language minority is consistent with that reported elsewhere (Krashen, 1999; Macias, 1997; National Center for Education Statistics, 1997). Although Spanish was the primary language used at home for all participants, exposure to English prior to beginning formal education had occurred via television, older siblings, and community professionals. Important for study purposes, however, was the fact that this exposure was relatively constant within and across the five age groups studied.

Both child and young adult participants lived in large cities in southern California, were from working-class socioeconomic backgrounds (parent education at most 12 years; at least one parent was employed full-time), and were of Mexican American descent. In summary, for participants included in the studies described in the following section, no significant differences in the timing or context of L1 and L2 learning were identified, and all participants were from similar cultural and socioeconomic backgrounds. All children passed hearing screenings and were considered to be typical language learners by their parents and/or teachers.

LEXICAL PROCESSING IN TYPICAL SCHOOL-AGE L2 LEARNERS

This section reports on three studies designed to investigate lexical processing in early sequential Spanish-English bilinguals. The primary objective of these studies was to investigate changes in basic-level lexical skills in L1 and L2. Potential change in each language was investigated as a function of participants' age and corresponding years of L2 experience, response modality (receptive versus expressive), and varied cognitive-linguistic processing demands (in single-language versus mixed-language conditions). As described in the previous section, all participants (5–22 years of age) were typical sequential bilinguals, with Spanish their L1 and English their L2. A primary goal of the research was to shed light on the process of typical L1–L2 learning by school-age children as it interacts with the continued development of basic-level cognitive skills and increasing experience in the L2.

Research Design and Stimuli

The stimuli and response variables used in both the receptive and expressive experiments emphasized lexical-semantic processing. To ensure that our results would reflect processing dynamics rather than only the extent of participants' word knowledge, we used items that are typically present within the vocabulary of monolingual English- and Spanish-speaking children of preschool age. We did this for two reasons. First, measures of the breadth of word knowledge are dependent on experience. This experience varies considerably as a function of cultural and linguistic background (see Kohnert et al., 1999, for review). Despite the attention given to participant selection, as reviewed in the previous section, differences in language experience are always a factor. At present, no valid measures have been taken of lexical knowledge in both the L1 and L2 of early sequential Spanish-English bilinguals.

A second reason for our relative emphasis on lexical processing over vocabulary knowledge, per se, comes from the monolingual literatures on language development and language disorders in school-age children. Research with English-speaking children indicates that skill in the efficient use (in terms of response speed) of linguistic information continues to develop through adolescence (e.g., Kail, 1991; Wulfeck, 1993). In addition, although school-age children with language impairments may "catch up" to age peers in their knowledge of specific linguistic features, they continue to lag behind in their ability to efficiently deploy these acquired representations (a point taken up further in the following section, Comparison to Monolinguals). Thus, a number of sources combine to support a relative emphasis on lexical processing over vocabulary knowledge in profiling skills in both the first and second languages of early sequential bilinguals.

In the timed production task, participants named pictures of these familiar items as quickly as possible in each of three conditions. The first two were considered low demand in that the participants were to name items in Spanish only and then in English only. The third, considered a cognitively demanding, mixed-language processing condition, entailed the participants alternating between Spanish and English on every third picture. In the receptive task, children saw a picture of a common object at the same time that they heard the name of an item. Children pushed the green "happy face" button if the word they heard correctly named the picture. If the spoken word and pictured object were a mismatch, children were to push the red "sad face" button as quickly as possible. Again, stimuli were presented in blocks of Spanish, blocks of English, and mixed-alternating language conditions. Pictures were randomized across conditions and participants saw each picture only one time. All studies were administered using a computer interface. Response speed and accuracy were the dependent variables measured.

Results and Implications

For present purposes, at least three findings from these studies advance our theoretical and practical understanding of children learning an L2. First, both L1 and L2 experienced positive developmental effects. In terms of the 5–22 years age range studied here, we observed significant increases in lexical production and comprehension accuracy accompanied by increases in fluency (i.e., faster speed for accurate responses) in both Spanish (L1) and English (L2) the older the participants were. These results are consistent with the monolingual literature that documents continued gains in processing skills through adolescence (Kail, 1991; Wulfeck, 1993). The positive impact across age was most evident in the condition that required the greatest control of processing skills at the cognitive-linguistic interface. Recall that in the production task, children were asked to name pictures in either a single language or in a mixed-language condition. After a 1-year interval between testing on the picture-naming task, participants showed the greatest improvement in performance in the mixed-language processing condition while using English (Kohnert, 2002). Improvement here reflects increases in cognitive control of the dual-language system across de-

Table 3.1.   Language dominance by response variable on lexical processing tasks

Age group	Mean years of systematic English (L2)	Comprehension: Accuracy	Comprehension: Response time	Production: Accuracy	Production: Response time
5–7 years	1.5	=	=	Spanish	*
8–10 years	4.3	=	=	Spanish	English
11–13 years	6.8	English	English	=	=
14–16 years	10.3	English	English	English	English
College age	14.0	English	English	English	English

Source: Kohnert & Bates, 2002.

Note: Statistically significant (*p* < .05) difference between Spanish and English on a given response variable is indicated by the name of the language in which performance was better (faster or more accurate). Comparable responses across Spanish and English, within a given age group and response variable, are indicated by =. The asterisk (*) indicates faster mean group response time (RT) in Spanish, which approached but did not reach statistical significance.

velopment, as well as gains in L2 (English). Documenting differences in the efficiency with which the language system is controlled has important implications for developing standards of performance for L2 learners in that we would expect more efficient resource allocation over time in children with intact language-learning systems.

A second important finding from these studies relates to relative cross-linguistic proficiency and shifting language dominance. Despite increased lexical processing efficiency in both L1 and L2 across the age range studied, overall gains were greater in English (L2) than in Spanish (L1). Over time, the L2 (English, in this case) emerged as the stronger language, as measured by processing-dependent picture naming and picture identification tasks, with skill acquisition spanning years. This shift to L2 "dominance" (i.e., relative language skill) came earlier in the receptive mode (evident after an average of 6.8 years of systematic English) than in production (evident only after approximately 10 years of systematic English). Table 3.1 shows performance within and across age groups for each lexical processing experimental task. Youngest participants, 5- to 7-year-olds with an average of 1.5 years of systematic English experience, were dominant in Spanish on the production task but showed no difference between their two languages on the basic-level receptive processing task. The next group of participants, 8- to 10-year-olds who had an average of 4.3 years of English, was split in their performance on the production task (faster in English naming but more accurate in Spanish). On the receptive task, their cross-linguistic performance was relatively balanced. By 11–13 years of age and an average of 6.8 years of English experience in school, participants were clearly stronger in English for the receptive task and performed equally well in Spanish and English on the production measure. Adolescents, 14- to 16-year-olds with an average of 10.3 years of systematic L2 experience, were now dominant in English on both receptive and expressive measures. This pattern of English dominance at the processing level held for adult participants as well.

This split in lexical processing skills across modalities challenges a clear notion of language dominance (in which one language is considered uniformly stronger than the other) at critical stages in developing bilinguals, calling into question the practical implications of traditional language proficiency assessments often recommended in educational settings. Furthermore, these modality-specific L1–L2 asymmetries can change across the course of development, with shifts in dominance taking place in one modality (comprehension) before they take place in another (production). These patterns are consistent with interactive skill-learning models of first and second language acquisition, which predict gradual change based on learning, varying across different components of the task. They are harder to reconcile with discontinuous models in which language dominance is a unitary phenomenon hooked to a finite critical period. (Refer to Kohnert & Bates, 2002, for discussion of differences found in cognitive resource control between receptive and expressive tasks as well.)

A third finding of interest from the lexical processing studies relates to variability. Given that variability within and across groups is considered a hallmark of bilingualism, it was important to look closely at changes in individual in addition to group performance over time. A subset of children included in the original cross-sectional picture-naming study was tested on the same picture-naming task a second time, approximately 1 year later (Kohnert, 2002). All participants experienced positive change in the 1-year interval from time 1 to time 2 testing on at least one response variable (response speed, accuracy, or cognitive control) in Spanish and/or English. No child demonstrated gains on all dependent variables, however. These typically developing sequential bilingual children experienced some gains, some losses, and some stability in lexical performance across time. Of importance is the finding that this variability was present not only in absolute terms but also in individual performance relative to that of language peers. Thus, in addition to the significant variability that exists between children learning two languages, we see that there is also considerable variability *within* each child. The overall trajectory, however, was upward, with gains in speed, accuracy, or control of the lexical systems across development and language experience.

Findings indicate that by looking at multiple aspects of language performance (e.g., response time and accuracy in low and high cognitively demanding conditions at different points in time in both L1 and L2), we gain a much more complex and potentially richer picture of developing sequential bilingualism. These findings also provide empirical validation for the clinical recommendation to look at multiple aspects of both languages, under varying conditions, when conducting language assessments with school-age children developing two languages sequentially (Goldstein, 2000; Roseberry-McKibbin, 1995). Results here suggest that we should document patterns of relative performance over time and under different processing demands, however, looking both at the direction and rate of change to quantify and qualify the integrity of the cognitive-linguistic processing system in a sequential language learner.

An interactive cognitive-linguistic processing theory assumes continuity within and across linguistic levels. Given that the theory predicts continuity across linguistic levels (e.g., strong associations between lexical and grammatical skills), results from the current studies on lexical processing provide a foundation for the generation of more specific hypotheses at other linguistic levels. Within the context of an interactive processing framework, results from these three studies clearly indicate that the learning of L2 by children is not simply an additive process. Rather, L2 learning is a process that involves multiple interactions between the first language, the second language, and the developing child. Descriptive profiles of this dynamic process are needed for constructing more specific usage-based theories of L2 learning by children to guide clinical practice. Research on L2 learners with and without language impairment from a processing perspective is still in its infancy. Recent advances in the monolingual processing literature, however, provide an important foundation. In the following section, a review of the literature on language processing in monolingual children with and without developmental language impairment is presented.

COMPARISON WITH MONOLINGUAL SPEAKERS: PROCESSING IN LANGUAGE IMPAIRMENT

Epidemiological studies conducted since the late 1990s indicate that approximately 7% of white monolingual English-speaking U.S. school-age children have a developmental language impairment (LI, also referred to in the literature as specific language impairment, or SLI) that cannot be attributed to a sensory, neurological, or cognitive disorder (Tomblin et al.,

1997). Within the language domain, the most salient features of LI change across development. For example, toddlers at risk for LI have low vocabulary; during the later preschool years, a hallmark of LI is morphological deficits; and during the school years, LI may manifest as poor discourse and academic skills. Despite the changing face of LI as a function of the developing child and shifting environmental demands, the underlying deficit in language processing remains (Ellis Weismer, & Evans, 2002; Leonard, 1998). Before turning our attention to language processing skills in children with LI, it is important to note that differences between monolingual children with LI and their language-intact peers also extend into the *nonlinguistic* processing domain (see Leonard, 1998; Miller, Kail, Leonard, & Tomblin, 2001; Windsor & Hwang, 1999). Although a discussion of nonlinguistic processing in children is beyond the scope of this chapter, future research that investigates the nonlinguistic processing skills along with language processing in bilingual children with and without impairment has the potential to advance our understanding of the nature of LI as well as to add to our clinical assessment and treatment methods (Kohnert & Windsor, in press).

Evidence suggests that language-based processing measures are more sensitive to language impairment in school-age children than are standardized measures of LI (Bishop, North, & Donlan, 1996; Dollaghan & Campbell, 1998; Ellis Weismer et al., 2000). This increased diagnostic sensitivity for processing-dependent measures at school age may relate to the way in which the waves of language development interact with LI. As previously discussed, typically developing children go through general waves of language development, which are characterized by accelerations in either linguistic knowledge (the first general wave) or language processing efficiency (the second wave). Similarly, the most salient characteristics of LI change across age and development. For example, although preschoolers with LI lag behind peers in their production of verb morphology in English, by school age these same children have caught up in their linguistic knowledge in this area but continue to lag in performance efficiency. Thus, processing-dependent measures may be better suited to capture the differences between school-age children with and without LI.

Processing-dependent measures profile children's speed, efficiency, or capacity to manipulate linguistic units. The linguistic units included in these tasks are intended to be equally familiar to all children (e.g., high-frequency vocabulary words, grammatical structures known by school-age children with and without LI) or equally unfamiliar to children (e.g., nonsense words that do not exist in the language). The idea is to "level the playing field" and minimize the role that prior language experience may have on performance (Campbell, Dollaghan, Needleman, & Janosky, 1997). In this way, experimental processing-dependent measures attempt to measure the integrity of the underlying language-learning system.

Timed measures of language processing have revealed consistent differences at the group level between children with LI and their peers without language impairments. For example, when asked to provide the names of familiar pictures or to judge whether a string of phonemes was a real or made-up word, children with LI were slower than their age peers without LI—even after controlling for differences in response accuracy (Edwards & Lahey, 1996; Lahey & Edwards, 1996). Montgomery and Leonard (1998) looked at the real-time grammatical processing skills of school-age children with LI. Children listened for a target word (e.g., cookies) embedded in a sentence context, then pressed a button as quickly as possible to indicate target word detection. In half of the sentences, a morphological inflection was absent from an obligatory context that immediately preceded the target word (e.g., "Every day he races home and eat cookies"). Children with LI showed no difference in their response times to target words which followed verbs missing low-substance obligatory inflections (e.g., -s, -ed) relative to their response times following correctly inflected verbs. This pattern of response differed from that of age peers, indicating that English-speaking children with LI are less sensitive to low-substance linguistic information during real-time sentence processing.

A number of experimental studies using phonological and verbal working memory tasks have shown significant diagnostic promise for identifying children with LI. Of particular interest are studies done in which performance on a phonological working memory task (non-word repetition) was used to successfully differentiate children with intact and impaired language skills who were from culturally diverse backgrounds (Campbell et al., 1997; Dollaghan & Campbell, 1998; Ellis Weismer et al., 2000). In these studies, performance on standardized, discrete-point measures of language knowledge did not differentiate culturally diverse (primarily African American) school-age children with and without LI. When children were asked to repeat made-up words (developed to adhere to the phonological constraints of English), however, researchers could successfully differentiate between impaired language learners and language learners who exhibited normal variation relative to their cultural background.

Another experimental verbal working memory task is the competing language processing test (CLPT) developed by Gaulin and Campbell (1994). Here, children were asked to respond on-line to the veracity of simple statements (e.g., "Pumpkins are purple"), while increasing demands were placed on their ability to recall linguistic information (e.g., repeat the last word from an increasing number of simple statements). Ellis Weismer, Evans, and Hesketh (1999) found that monolingual English-speaking children with LI performed more poorly on the word recall portion of the CLPT and demonstrated distinct patterns of word recall errors relative to their same-age peers who were typically developing. Moreover, the CLPT has been shown to be a less-biased assessment measure with some culturally diverse populations. Campbell and colleagues (1997) found that children from diverse groups who were typically developing and English speaking performed as well as peers from the mainstream population on the CLPT, despite significant differences between these two groups on a standardized measure of language. Here again, performance differentiated culturally diverse children with and without LI with greater accuracy than did performance on knowledge-based standardized language tests. The success of processing-dependent measures in distinguishing culturally diverse children with LI from their peers without LI has led researchers to consider these tools as non-biased assessment measures for both culturally and linguistically diverse populations (Campbell et al., 1997; Dollaghan & Campbell, 1998; Ellis Weismer & Evans, 2002). Language assessment measures that can be sensitive to differences and disorders in a richly diverse population are an exciting prospect. In the following section, clinical assessment issues and findings relevant to comparisons between bilingual and monolingual children on experience- and processing-dependent measures are considered.

IMPLICATIONS FOR ASSESSMENT AND INTERVENTION

Language Assessment with School-Age Children

When we compare typical L2 learners and monolingual children with LI on traditional knowledge-based measures of language (including language samples and vocabulary tests), there appears to be considerable overlap between the two groups (Hakansson & Nettelbladt 1996; Paradis & Crago, 2000; Schiff-Meyers, 1992). From an interactive information-processing perspective, the documented poorer performance on traditional language measures by both children with LI and typical sequential bilinguals relative to their language-intact monolingual peers is explained in very different ways. Specifically, children with LI perform more poorly on knowledge-dependent tasks because something is wrong with their language-learning system—a deficit internal to the child. In contrast, children who are in the process of learning an L2 have intact language learning systems (i.e., cognitive processing mechanisms) but may perform poorly on language tasks relative to monolingual age peers because of differences external to the child. Different language-specific experiences often mean that school-age L2 learners have had fewer opportunities to learn or use the language being tested. Moreover, linguistic knowledge may be distributed across the two languages of developing sequential bilinguals in ways that are not readily comparable to children who speak a single language (Kohnert, 2000).

Applying Processing Principles to Language Assessment

In the clinical assessment of language in school-age children, processing-based measures are an important complement to more traditional knowledge-based measures. Traditional competence-based assessment measures attempt to describe what is currently known in a given language. Processing-based measures are aimed at assessing the integrity of the system used in the service of language and documenting changes in performance across differing task demands. Ellis Weismer and Evans described assessment from a processing perspective in this way:

> Variability would be expected as a function of factors such as familiarity of information to be processed, linguistic complexity of the forms, and degree of communicative/social pressure within the situation. As cognitive resources are stressed, trade-offs in accuracy and/or timing would be anticipated across linguistic domains within an utterance or across larger units of discourse (such as conversational turns). Both accuracy levels and latency of responses are important to consider within this type of assessment approach, as difficulties may become especially apparent with respect to the efficiency with which the child is able to access and utilize linguistic knowledge. (2002, p. 25)

This perspective is consistent with both general interactive processing theories of early sequential bilingualism as well as a limited processing capacity account of developmental language impairment. It guides us to look at changes in language performance in both L1 and L2 across differing task demands.

Within each language, we can vary processing demands in a number of ways. For example, if we change the rate of input while holding the level of linguistic complexity constant, does the child's performance change? Are there more errors in carrying out a three-step instruction if the input rate is relatively fast? Does performance improve if we slow the rate of input or increase pause time before certain target structures? Alternatively, if we increase the linguistic complexity but maintain a reduced speed of input, is performance maintained? We can also vary processing demands by manipulating the degree of competing internal or external stimuli. Does performance change in the presence of background noise? If the child is asked to wait a few seconds before responding to simple linguistic information, does performance get better or worse? With bilinguals, we may want to alter cross-linguistic constraints as well to determine their effects on performance. For instance, does performance improve in a bilingual context when code switching is allowed? Does performance on fluent access tasks improve if mixed-language input is encouraged (e.g., "Name as many animals as you can in either Spanish or English")? Limited training tasks to determine the facility with which a child learns novel stimuli can also be very informative. From an interactive processing perspective, we can also ask what effect introducing top-down strategies has on lower level (bottom-up) processing efficiency. An example of this is using explicit instruction to help a child attend to the phonological overlap in cross-linguistic cognates (*trompeta*/trumpet), and testing to determine if these strategies are applied to nontrained Spanish-English cognates. Published processing-dependent measures include the rapid color- and shape-naming subtests included in the English and Spanish versions of the Clinical Evaluation of Language Fundamentals (Semel, Wiig, & Secord, 1995, 1997) and the nonword repetition subtest of the Comprehensive Test of Phonological Processes (Wagner, Torgesen, & Rashotte, 1999; Spanish version is in development).

Across modalities and basic linguistic levels in L1 and L2, interactive processing-based approaches instruct us to look for variations in performance, such as patterns of errors and response trade-offs, as a function of top-down and bottom-up manipulations. As Ellis Weismer and Evans noted, "The pattern of breakdown that occurs when we stress the system gives us valuable information about the extent to which the knowledge is robust or automatic and provides insights into factors that influence language processing for a particular child" (2002, p. 25). For children learning an L2 who have difficulties with language or learning, a primary goal of the assessment process is to determine the differential contribution of reduced linguistic knowledge and processing skills to the overall deficit. Processing-dependent assessment measures are an important complement to more traditional descriptive measures.

Reducing Bias in Assessment: Future Directions

Processing-dependent measures of language are an attractive resource for individuals working with bilingual children for another reason. Processing-dependent measures attempt to reduce the role of cultural and language-specific experience needed for optimal performance and assess the integrity of the language-learning system. If this is possible, it provides clinicians with a foothold for separating differences from disorders in children who are in the process of learning an L2. In the literature reviewed previously on monolingual children with LI, we saw that two verbal working memory measures, nonword repetition and CLPT, were found to be sensitive to LI in children from culturally diverse populations. Despite the cultural diversity of children included in the previous studies, all participants were monolingual speakers of English. It is important to know if the less-biased nature of processing-dependent tasks, relative to knowledge-dependent measures, holds for children learning English as their L2 as well.

Little research is available investigating sequential bilingual performance on language-processing tasks. Thorn and Gathercole (1999), however, used a nonword repetition task to compare L2 learners with their monolingual peers. As is conventional in these tasks, nonsense words were created to adhere to the phonological rules of the test languages (French and English in this case). Monolingual children performed significantly better than did the typical L2 learners. This advantage for monolingual children over L2 learners on nonword repetition indicates that performance on even very basic-level language processing tasks is dependent, to some extent, on language experience. In a study in progress, my colleagues and I are using a nonword repetition task in English to compare performance between monolingual English-speaking children with and without LI and typically developing Spanish-English bilinguals (Kohnert & Windsor, in press). Preliminary results indicate that, when using a strict scoring system that fails to account for phonological differences between Spanish and English, the task does not differentiate between typical L2 learners and monolingual children with developmental LI. Although these studies are preliminary, they serve to remind us that although we can emphasize the role of processing over experience in our assessment measures, we cannot completely separate language processing from language knowledge and experience. Additional studies investigating processing skills in developing bilinguals are needed to further our understanding of appropriate language assessment procedures. Pending the realization of these studies, we can critically apply principles and techniques of interactive processing approaches to clinical assessments with bilinguals. In so doing, we must be always mindful of the potential interactions between experience and performance, within and across languages.

Intervention: Promoting Gains in Processing Skills

Clinical implications for intervention from an interactive processing perspective indicate that our ultimate goals must be to increase the child's speed, accuracy, and efficiency in processing language during real-time communicative interactions. For the bilingual child, this implies that a goal should be to increase performance in both languages. This does not necessarily require that direct intervention be implemented in L1 and L2, although this may be optimal in some cases (see Gutiérrez-Clellen, 1999). Rather, a holistic, interactive information processing perspective requires that we plan for generalization of treated gains across languages. This goal is reasonable in that the focus of intervention is on improving the efficiency with which linguistic information, in any language, is learned and used.

Immediate intervention goals and procedures are determined based on an analysis of the child's performance in the varying assessment contexts. Based on the individual child's patterns of errors, trade-offs, and responses to specific training manipulations within and across languages, service providers select the most appropriate combination of intervention procedures. In order to make gains in the speed, accuracy and/or efficiency of information processing, it may be necessary to target several areas. Possible candidates include 1) increasing verbal working memory skills, 2) facilitating gains in perceptual and attentional skills related to language input, 3) promoting increased automaticity of language output, and 4) developing strategies to improve overall communicative functioning.

In intervention, a number of different specific techniques may be combined to promote gains in any one of these areas. In the area of verbal working memory, for example, the rate of input for the child who has a slower processing system may be reduced. We can also help children to be more automatic in retrieving core linguistic information through guided repetition, gradually increasing the processing demands by imposing time constraints and/or extraneous stimuli. Montgomery explained "much directed practice at processing/interpreting various language forms (e.g., words, syntactic structures) that have been troublesome may promote more-readily accessible language knowledge and more automatic language processing procedures" (2002a, p. 80). Explicit teaching techniques can be used to train top-down verbal working memory strategies, such as prediction, chunking, and verbal rehearsal. For bilingual children, an additional interactive processing strategy to facilitate greater depth of processing and cross-linguistic transfer is to help the children transfer information from one language to the other (through parallel home and school programs, translation activities, and mentored peer interactions on structured tasks). From a processing perspective we would attend to the cognitive, perceptual, and social demands in which our tasks are embedded, creating a hierarchy of processing demands through the combined use of bottom-up and top-down procedures. (See Ellis Weismer, 2000, and Montgomery, 2002b, for additional discussion of implications for assessment and intervention from a processing perspective.)

Clearly, effective language use, in both monolingual and bilingual children, requires the successful integration of language-specific knowledge and broader information processing systems. This information is seen as complementary in assessment and intervention. This chapter emphasizes the processing side of the proficiency equation in school-age children who are learning two languages sequentially. A critical need exists for studies that investigate applications of information processing frameworks to bilingual children with language impairment. In the absence of direct evidence, we cautiously generalize from the combined literatures on monolingual developmental language impairment, and typical sequential language learning.

REFERENCES

Bates, E., & Goodman, J. (1997). On the inseparability of grammar and the lexicon: Evidence from acquisition, aphasia and real-time processing. *Language and Cognitive Processes, 12*, 507–584.

Bates, E., & MacWhinney, B. (1987). Competition, variation, and language learning. In B. MacWhinney (Ed.), *Mechanisms of language acquisition* (pp. 157–193). Mahwah, NJ: Lawrence Erlbaum Associates.

Berko Gleason, J. (Ed.). (1997). *The development of language* (4th ed). Boston: Allyn & Bacon.

Bialystok, E. (2001). *Bilingualism in development: Language, literacy, & cognition.* Cambridge, UK: Cambridge University Press.

Bishop, D.V.M., North, T., & Donlan, C. (1996). Nonword repetition as a behavioral marker for inherited language impairment: Evidence from a twin study. *Journal of Psychology and Psychiatry, 37*, 391–403.

Campbell, T., Dollaghan, C., Needleman, H., & Janosky, J. (1997). Reducing bias in language assessment: Processing-dependent measures. *Journal of Speech, Language, and Hearing Research, 40*, 519–525.

Dollaghan, C., & Campbell, C. (1998). Nonword repetition and child language impairment. *Journal of Speech, Language, and Hearing Research, 41*, 1136–1146.

Edwards, J., & Lahey, M. (1996). Auditory lexical decisions of children with specific language impairment. *Journal of Speech and Hearing Research, 39*, 1263–1273.

Ellis Weismer, S. (2000). Intervention for children with developmental language delay. In D.V.M Bishop & L.B. Leonard (Eds.), *Speech and language impairments in children: Causes, characteristics, intervention and out-come* (pp. 157–176). East Sussex, UK: Psychology Press.

Ellis Weismer, S., & Evans, J. (2002). The role of processing limitations in early identification of specific language impairment. *Topics in Language Disorders, 22*(3), 15–29.

Ellis Weismer, S., Evans, J., & Hesketh, L. (1999). An examination of verbal working memory capacity in children with specific language impairment. *Journal of Speech, Language, and Hearing Research, 42*, 1249–1260.

Ellis Weismer, S., Tomblin, J., Zhang, X., Buckwalter, P., Gaura Chynoweth, J., & Jones, M. (2000). Nonword repetition performance in school-age children with and without language impairment. *Journal of Speech, Language, and Hearing Research, 43*, 865–878.

Elman, J., Bates, E., Johnson, M., Karmiloff-Smith, A., Parisi, D., & Plunkett, K. (1996). *Rethinking innateness: A connectionist perspective on development.* Cambridge, MA: MIT Press.

Foss, D.J., & Hakes, D.T. (1978). *Psycholinguistics: An introduction to the psychology of language.* Englewood Cliffs, NJ: Prentice-Hall.

Fowler, C. (1980). Coarticulations and theories of extrinsic timing. *Journal of Phonetics, 8*, 113–133.

Fromkin, V.A., & Bernstein Ratner, N. (1998). Speech production. In J. Berko Gleason & N. Bernstein Ratner (Eds.), *Psycholinguistics* (2nd ed., pp. 309–346). Orlando, FL: Harcourt Brace.

Gaulin, C., & Campbell, T. (1994). Procedure for assessing verbal working memory in normal school-age children: Some preliminary data. *Perceptual and Motor Skills, 79*, 55–64.

Gillam, R., Hoffman, L., Marler, J., & Wynn-Dancy, M.L. (2002). Sensitivity to increased task demands: Contributions from data-driven and conceptually driven information processing deficits. *Topics in Language Disorders, 22*(3), 30–48.

Goldstein, B. (2000). *Cultural and linguistic diversity resource guide for speech-language pathologists.* San Diego, CA: Singular/Thomson Learning.

Grosjean, F. (1982). *Life with two languages: An introduction to bilingualism.* Cambridge, MA: Harvard University Press.

Gutiérrez-Clellen, V. (1999). Language choice in intervention with bilingual children. *American Journal of Speech-Language Pathology, 8*, 291–302.

Hakansson, G., & Nettelbladt, U. (1996). Similarities between SLI and L2 children: Evidence from the acquisition of Swedish word order. In C.E. Johnson & J.H.V. Gilbert (Eds.), *Children's language* (Vol. 9, pp. 135–151). Mahwah, NJ: Lawrence Erlbaum Associates.

Hernandez, A., Bates, E., & Avila, L. (1994). Sentence interpretation in Spanish–English bilinguals: What does it mean to be in-between? *Applied Psycholinguistics, 15*, 417–466.

Kail, R. (1991). Processing time declines exponentially during adolescence. *Developmental Psychology, 27*, 259–266.

Kohnert, K. (2000, November). *Distributed skills: A snapshot of the developing bilingual lexicon.* Paper presented at the annual convention of the American Speech-Language-Hearing Association, Washington, DC.

Kohnert, K. (2002). Picture naming in early sequential bilinguals: A 1-year follow-up. *Journal of Speech, Language, and Hearing Research, 45,* 759–771.

Kohnert, K., & Bates, E. (2002). Balancing bilinguals II: Lexical comprehension and cognitive processing in children learning Spanish and English. *Journal of Speech, Language, and Hearing Research, 45,* 347–359.

Kohnert, K., Bates, E., & Hernandez, A.E. (1999). Balancing bilinguals: Lexical-semantic production and cognitive processing in children learning Spanish and English. *Journal of Speech, Language, and Hearing Research, 42,* 1400–1413.

Kohnert, K., & Windsor, J. (in press). In search of common ground—Part II: Non-linguistic performance by linguistically diverse learners. *Journal of Speech, Language, and Hearing Research.*

Krashen, S. (1999). *Condemned without a trial: Bogus arguments against bilingual education.* Portsmouth, NH: Heinemann.

Lahey, M., & Edwards, J. (1996). Why do children with specific language impairment name pictures more slowly than their peers? *Journal of Speech and Hearing Research, 30,* 1081–1097.

Leonard, L.B. (1998). *Children with specific language impairment.* Cambridge, MA: MIT Press.

Liberman, A.M. (1970). The grammars of speech and language. *Cognitive Psychology, 1,* 301–323.

Liu, H., Bates, E., & Li, P. (1992). Sentence interpretation in bilingual speakers of English and Chinese. *Applied Psycholinguistics, 13,* 451–484.

MacWhinney, B. (1997). Second language acquisition and the competition model. In A.M.B. de Groot & J.K. Kroll (Eds.), *Tutorials in bilingualism: Psycholinguistic perspectives* (pp. 113–144). Mahwah, NJ: Lawrence Erlbaum Associates.

Macias, R. (1997). CA LEP enrollment slows but continues to rise. *Linguistic Minority Research Institute, 7*(1), 1–2.

Milberg, W., Blumstein, S.E., Katz, D., Gershberg, F., & Brown, T. (1995). Semantic facilitation in aphasia: Effects of time and expectance. *Journal of Cognitive Neuroscience, 7*(1), 33–50.

Miller, C., Kail, R., Leonard, L., & Tomblin, B. (2001). Speed of processing in children with specific language impairment. *Journal of Speech, Language, and Hearing Research, 44,* 416–433.

Montgomery, J.W. (2002a). Information processing and language comprehension in children with specific language impairment. *Topics in Language Disorders, 22*(3), 62–84.

Montgomery, J.W. (Ed.). (2002b). Information processing: Implications for assessment and intervention [Special issue]. *Topics in Language Disorders, 22*(3) vi.

Montgomery, J.W., & Leonard, L. (1998). Real-time inflectional processing by children with specific language impairment: Effects of phonetic substance. *Journal of Speech, Language, and Hearing Research, 41,* 1412–1431.

National Center for Education Statistics. (1997). *1993–1994 schools and staffing survey: A profile of policies and practices for limited English proficient students.* Washington DC: U.S. Department of Education, Office of Educational Research and Improvement.

Paradis, J., & Crago, M. (2000). Tense and temporality: A comparison between children learning a second language and children with SLI. *Journal of Speech, Language, and Hearing Research, 43,* 834–847.

Roseberry-McKibbin, C. (1995). Distinguishing language difference from language disorder in linguistically and culturally diverse students. *Multicultural Education, 4,* 12–16.

Schiff-Myers, N. (1992). Considering arrested language development and language loss in the assessment of second language learners. *Language, Speech, and Hearing Services in Schools, 23,* 28–33.

Segalowitz, N. (1997). Individual differences in second language acquisition. In A.M.B. de Groot & J.F. Kroll (Eds.), *Tutorials in bilingualism: Psycholinguistic perspectives* (pp. 85–112). Mahwah, NJ: Lawrence Erlbaum Associates.

Semel, E., Wiig, E., & Secord, W. (1995). *Clinical Evaluation of Language Fundamentals* (CELF, 3rd ed.). San Antonio, TX: Psychological Corporation.

Semel, E., Wiig, E., & Secord, W. (1997). *Clinical evaluation of language fundamentals (CELF, Spanish edition).* San Antonio, TX: Psychological Corporation.

Snyder, L.E., Dabasinskas, C., & O'Connor, E. (2002). An information processing perspective on language impairment in children: Looking at both sides of the coin. *Topics in Language Disorders, 22*(3), 1–14.

Thorn, A., & Gathercole, S. (1999). Language-specific knowledge and short-term memory in bilingual and non-bilingual children. *The Quarterly Journal of Experimental Psychology, 52*(A), 303–324.

Tomblin, J.B., Records, N.L., Buckwalter, P., Zhang, X., Smith, E., & O'Brien, M. (1997). Prevalence of specific language impairment in kindergarten children. *Journal of Speech, Language, and Hearing Research, 40,* 1245–1260.

Wagner, R., Torgesen, J., & Rashotte, C. (1999). *Comprehensive Test of Phonological Processing* (CTOPP). Austin, TX: PRO-ED.

Windsor, J. (2002). Contrasting general and process-specific slowing in language impairment. *Topics in Language Disorders, 22*(3), 49–61.

Windsor, J., & Hwang, M. (1999). Testing the generalized slowing hypothesis in specific language impairment. *Journal of Speech, Language, and Hearing Research, 42,* 1205–1218.

Wong-Fillmore, L. (1991). Second-language learning in children: A model of language learning in social context. In E. Bialystok (Ed.), *Language processing in bilingual children* (pp. 49–69). London: Cambridge University Press.

Wulfeck, B. (1993). A reaction time study of grammaticality judgments in children. *Journal of Speech and Hearing Research, 36,* 1208–1215.

Yeni-Komshian, G. (1998). Speech perception. In J. Berko Gleason & N. Bernstein Ratner (Eds.), *Psycholinguistics* (2nd ed, pp. 107–156). Orlando, FL: Harcourt Brace.

CHAPTER 4

Bilingual Lexical Development
Influences, Contexts, and Processes

JANET L. PATTERSON AND BARBARA ZURER PEARSON

exical development is a key area in child language acquisition, assessment, and intervention. A comprehensive approach to bilingual lexical
development requires consideration of the special aspects of bilingual
acquisition and an understanding of the general processes of lexical acquisition that apply to monolinguals as well as bilinguals. The focus of this
chapter is the developmental processes of lexical acquisition among bilingual children; in other words, what is involved when bilingual children
learn new words?

Learning vocabulary is a visible and important part of language acquisition from a child's first words through high school and beyond. Lexical
development is a multifaceted process that involves social, cognitive, and
linguistic realms. Children do not learn new words in a vacuum; lexical acquisition occurs in the context of social interaction and cognitive development. Furthermore, lexical acquisition is linguistically complex. Phonological, morphological, syntactic, and semantic information intersect in lexical
development. Learning a word not only involves linking the phonological
and/or orthographic form of a word and its meaning but also involves
knowing how a word can combine with other morphemes and the syntactic roles a word can fulfill in sentences (Clark, 1993). Pragmatic aspects of
lexical acquisition also are important; children learn the contexts in which
words are most effectively used as part of developing and selecting appropriate registers and styles.

Although families and teachers usually do not use terms such as
phonology, *semantics*, *morphology*, and *syntax* to describe different aspects of
lexical acquisition, the concepts behind those terms are implied in every-

day talk about children's language. Parents and teachers often discuss a child's pronunciation of words, and they often differentiate this from discussions of whether the child understands the meaning of the word or is "misusing" it in a charming and/or misguided way. Parents and teachers also notice a child's use of over-regularized forms such as "foots," and teachers often require children to use a word in a sentence as part of vocabulary learning assignments. In clinical contexts, parents and teachers may focus on a child's vocabulary when describing concerns about possible language-learning problems (e.g., "She has a limited vocabulary," "He does not know very many words," "She has trouble putting ideas into words").

Among bilingual children, lexical form–meaning relationships are even more complex than they are among monolinguals. How are word forms in two languages related to each other and to meaning(s)? Does knowing a word in one language make a difference when learning an equivalent word in the other language? These aspects of bilingual lexical acquisition, in addition to the general processes and influences on lexical acquisition shared by monolingual and bilingual children, must be taken into consideration in well-grounded approaches to assessment and intervention.

In this chapter, we summarize the heterogeneous circumstances of bilingual lexical acquisition, especially as they relate to variations in the amount, timing, and contexts of children's experiences with each language. We then focus on two major components in lexical acquisition: 1) the amount of language input and the contexts in which children experience input in each language and 2) children's lexical acquisition strategies at various stages of development (i.e., what children "do" with the input). Implications for designing assessment and intervention strategies that are consistent with the complex, interactive nature of lexical acquisition are discussed at the end of the chapter.

HETEROGENEITY AMONG BILINGUAL CHILDREN

Lexical development in each language and relationships among lexical items in the two languages vary widely depending on the circumstances in which the languages are learned, the patterns of input a child experiences in the two languages, and the child's level of proficiency at the time of exposure. In considering lexical development and language input, the timing of the child's initial exposure to each language, overall proportion of input in each language, and contexts of input are important variables. These aspects of language input occur within the larger family, community, and social contexts, as described by Hammer, Miccio, and Rodriguez in Chapter 2.

A child who grows up in a home in which two languages are spoken has very different experiences with language input compared with a child from a monolingual home who is first expected to understand and use a second language when entering school or preschool. In this chapter, we use the term *simultaneous bilingualism* to characterize children who have significant input in two languages before they are 3 years old, and *sequential bilingualism* to refer to children whose major exposure to a second language occurs after the age of 3, after considerable learning of the first language has taken place. The young simultaneous bilingual children who participated in the studies of lexical development reviewed in this chapter experienced input in both Spanish and English on a regular basis well before they were 2 years old, and many were exposed to both languages since birth. Although reasons certainly exist to make more fine-grained distinctions in timing of children's initial exposure to and acquisition of two languages, the major distinction between simultaneous and sequential bilingual children serves our purposes in this chapter (see Chapter 2 for a more detailed discussion and critiques of these terms).

In addition to the timing of initial exposure to the two languages, the proportion of exposure to each language is another important input variable. For example, among simultaneous bilingual toddlers, some children experience more input in Spanish than in English (e.g., input is composed of 75% Spanish and 25% English), whereas others may have the opposite pattern, and some children may have relatively equal experience with input in the two languages. Similarly, among sequential learners, amount of exposure to the second language may vary depending on the educational programs in which the child is enrolled. English immersion programs, for example, use almost 100% English from the first days of kindergarten, whereas dual language programs generally target a 50/50 balance between languages. Input from home and school exert different influences on the child's developing lexicon, as well (Oller & Eilers, 2002).

Contexts of exposure to each language are another set of input considerations. Considerable attention has been paid to the distribution of languages across speakers in the homes of simultaneous bilingual children (de Houwer, 1995; Patterson, 1999). For example, in some homes, each parent may speak primarily one language with the child (e.g., the mother speaks English and the father speaks Spanish). In other homes, one or both parents (and one or more siblings) may speak both languages with a child. Contrary to the common belief that separate input in the two languages is necessary to prevent "confusion" of the two languages on a child's part, no evidence supports this viewpoint, and reasons can be given to regard this advice with some caution, as Hammer and colleagues point out in Chapter 2. Particular patterns of lexical acquisition may be related to a child's experiences with others who use one or both languages when interacting with him or her, however.

Situational contexts are also of importance. Home and school experiences are major considerations among school-age children. Many different patterns of use of the two languages may be exhibited within home and school environments, from both languages in all contexts to division of languages by activity. For example, older children in some bilingual homes may interact among themselves primarily in English when playing and arguing, whereas their parents may interact with them primarily in Spanish during household routines and family meals, and homework assignments may be discussed between parents and children primarily in English. It is not uncommon, however, for all individuals in a household to use both languages within the same context. For example, a dinner-table conversation may move between Spanish and English while family members are taking turns speaking, or code-switching may occur within speaking turns. In schools with bilingual programs, some subjects may be taught in English and other subjects may be taught in Spanish, and both languages may be used together in games on the playground.

Another way in which bilinguals vary is in their proficiency in each of the two languages. Among Spanish-English bilinguals, one child may be more proficient in Spanish than in English, another child may have roughly similar degrees of proficiency in the two languages, and a third may be more proficient in English than in Spanish. Among adult sequential second language (L2) learners, Kroll (1993) found that the degree of proficiency in L2 is an important variable in whether the learners appear to process the second language through the first language or whether they access their second lexicon more directly; a similar distinction is likely to be found in both simultaneous and sequential bilingual children. Furthermore, an individual's relative proficiency in the two languages is likely to change over time; for example, in Chapter 3, Kohnert provides evidence of a shift from greater proficiency in Spanish to greater proficiency in English across the school-age years among a group of sequential bilinguals in the United States. Another aspect of change in proficiency over time is the loss of L1 proficiency among some children (see Chapter 8), sometimes called *subtractive bilingualism* (Lambert, 1977).

LEXICAL DEVELOPMENT AND LANGUAGE INPUT

Amount of Language Input and Vocabulary Size

One way to look at the relationships between input and children's lexical development is to ask whether more input results in children having larger vocabularies. In order to answer this question, some measure or sample that estimates a child's total vocabulary or that ranks the child's total vocabulary compared with peers is used. Among monolingual English-speaking children, total vocabulary size is positively related to the amount of language input provided by parents (Hart & Risley, 1995).

Bilingual children's vocabulary sizes can be examined in several ways. Studies that have measured vocabulary size in Spanish-English bilingual toddlers and preschool children have found that when bilingual children's vocabulary in both languages is taken into account, their total vocabulary size is comparable with the total vocabulary size of monolingual children, both for receptive and expressive vocabulary (Pearson, 1998; Pearson, Fernández, & Oller, 1993). Among bilingual children, total vocabulary is distributed across two languages, whereas among monolingual children, total vocabulary is restricted to one language. Two common measures of bilingual children's overall vocabulary are Total Vocabulary (TV; Language A + Language B) and Total Conceptual Vocabulary (TCV; Language A + Language B minus translation equivalents [TEs] in Language B) (Pearson, 1998; Pearson et al., 1993). Translation equivalents are words that mean the same thing in the two languages but are counted only once. For example, consider a child who knows the words *oso* (bear) and *agua* (water) in Spanish (Language A) and *bear* and *juice* in English (Language B). The total number of words (TV) is four, but because *bear* and *oso* are TEs, the child's TCV would be three: *bear, agua,* and *juice.*

In addition to these composite measures of vocabulary in two languages, one can also look at vocabulary size in each language separately for bilingual children, depending on the kinds of information one needs about the individual's capacities and experience and the goals one has for this information. A single-language measure of a child's second language, for example, could give a sense of how much exposure the child has had to that language and could help guide an educational plan for the child. If one is measuring vocabulary as part of an assessment to determine if the child is making age-appropriate progress in language development, however, then it will be important to take vocabulary learned in both languages contexts into account.

Studies of the relationship of amount of input and vocabulary size among bilingual children have focused on whether the relative amount of input in each language systematically relates to relative size of vocabulary in each language. Studies of simultaneous Spanish-English bilingual toddlers (Marchman & Martínez-Sussman, 2002; Pearson, Fernández, Lewedeg, & Oller, 1997) have demonstrated substantial correlations between children's vocabulary size and amount of exposure within each language. Similarly, among bilingual elementary school children, those with more overall exposure to Spanish (taking both home and school environments into account) performed better than bilingual children with less overall exposure to Spanish on a wide range of Spanish language measures, including vocabulary tests (Oller & Eilers, 2002). The same finding held for amount of exposure to English, through second grade. By fifth grade (i.e., by the time children are approximately age 10), however, no significant differences were found on measures of performance in English when bilingual children who had been in an almost exclusively English-speaking school environment were compared with bilingual children who had been in dual-language school programs in which they heard English for only half of the school day. These results indicate that amount of input may be an important determinant of vocabulary and other language skills within each language, up until a threshold in the amount of input is reached. In summary, it appears that amount of input in each language is related to language development (including vocabulary), but only until a critical mass is reached, at which point the association between input and development becomes much weaker.

Although children's development and use of each language is systematically related to the amount of input in that language, Spanish-English bilingual children in the United States use more English than would be predicted based on the amount of time they are spoken to in each language. Among a sample of New Mexican bilingual toddlers with approximately equal amounts of input overall in English and Spanish (as a group, the children were spoken to an average of 54% of the time in English and 46% of the time in Spanish), the children's average expressive vocabulary based on a parent report checklist was almost twice as large for English words (98) as for Spanish words (50) (Patterson, 2002). Marchman and Martínez-Sussman (2002) reported a similar pattern in their findings for a group of bilingual toddlers in Texas. Their group of toddlers were also exposed to each language to similar degrees overall (an average of 45% exposure to English and 55% exposure to Spanish), but the toddlers were reported to use an average of 220 words in English and an average of 150 words in Spanish on more extensive parent report checklists. Furthermore, in separate laboratory sessions using Spanish and English, the same group of children also named more items in English than they did in Spanish. Proportionally greater use of English than expected based on the amount of input experienced in each language has been reported among Spanish-English bilingual toddlers (Pearson et al., 1997) and elementary school children (who were simultaneous bilinguals and sequential learners) in Miami, Florida (Oller & Eilers, 2002). These findings of disproportionately high use of English are most likely due to a combination of circumstances; as Hammer and colleagues note in Chapter 2, even young children raised in primarily Spanish home environments in the United States have some exposure to English through the media and the wider community. Estimates of language input in young children have not focused on this type of language exposure. In addition, the higher-than-expected proportion of English use may be a reflection of cultural and language shifts and attitudes toward the two languages.

Another factor affecting the relationship between input and lexical learning is the type of word being learned. Evidence suggests that the close correlation between input and vocabulary learning holds for content words in a language (i.e., nouns, verbs, and adjectives), but not for function words (i.e., articles, prepositions, bound morphemes) (Dale, Dionne, Eley, & Plomin, 2000). Yet for function words, such as gender-based articles in Spanish, work by Gathercole (2002) showed short-term effects of exposure on those elements, but a lessening of the effect when vocabulary was measured over a longer term. It should be noted, however, that Dale and colleagues focused only on preschoolers, whereas Gathercole studied children through grade 5.

For many domains, learning in one language enhances similar learning in other languages. According to Cummins's (1984) notion of the interdependence of languages, the level of attainment in a second language reflects the individual's level of attainment in the first. He proposed that knowledge in one language facilitates learning in the other. Support for this hypothesis came from numbers of Canadian studies of French-English speakers (Lambert & Tucker, 1972; Swain & Wesche, 1975). Even among those studies, however, vocabulary knowledge did not always appear to transfer from one language to the other (Harley, Hart, & Lapkin, 1986), so the concept of interdependence or facilitation across languages may hold for some domains of language but not for all.

Cobo-Lewis, Eilers, Pearson, and Umbel (2002) tested for interdependence in several domains of literacy and oral language development in school-age children learning English and Spanish. These researchers performed a factor analysis on scores from 18 standardized tests (9 in English and 9 in Spanish) taken by 952 children ranging from 5 to 11 years old. Results indicated that the literacy scores in English and Spanish did indeed load on a single factor, indicating a high degree of interdependence and thus suggesting some facilitation across languages for learning literacy skills. By contrast, the oral language tests, particularly single-word receptive and expressive vocabulary tests, showed the opposite pattern (i.e., independence). The results indicated that there were separate language factors for English and Spanish, suggesting that time spent learning English vocabulary does not facilitate learning Spanish vocabulary. Importantly, though, significant negative values were not observed, so a subtractive model for those children was not supported either. The learning of English vocabulary did not appear to have a significant relationship, either positive or negative, to learning Spanish vocabulary, and vice versa. Pearson (2002) reached a similar conclusion through a correlational analysis of narrative, syntactic, and lexical measures derived from a story retelling in both languages by the same children. Considerable evidence, then, argues against interdependence of vocabulary learning across languages.

Contexts of Language Input

In addition to the amount of input in a language, the particular situations in which children hear and use the language are important. Among studies of bilingual children, a major focus has been the child's experiences of different speakers' use of each language. The one-parent/one-language strategy has been advocated in the past, founded on the belief that children would do best if they had experience with each language in a separate context. Research with children whose parents speak both languages shows that the children develop age-appropriate language milestones and language-specific grammatical structures (García, 1983; Patterson, 1998). In addition, exposure to parental code-switching is an important context for learning to participate in bilingual communities in which code-switching is the norm, as is true for many bilinguals throughout the world (Romaine, 1995). Little research exists investigating the effects on children's lexical development related to experience with input in one language per parent versus input that includes parental code-switching. Some researchers speculate that children whose parent(s) use more than one language when interacting with them will have a higher proportion of TEs or words with equivalent meanings across the two languages (Pearson, Fernández, & Oller, 1995).

The types of activities in which children experience language input are another important contextual variable in studies of vocabulary development among monolingual children. Joint book reading is one type of special context for word learning. Participation in adult–child joint book-reading activities is linked with higher scores on a variety of language measures, including vocabulary scores (Bus, van IJzendoorn, & Pellegrini, 1995; Scarborough & Dobrich, 1994). Among bilingual toddlers, similar patterns were found within, but not across languages; joint book reading related to children's vocabulary size in each language, even when the child's overall proportion of input in each language was taken into account (Patterson, 2002). These relationships were language-specific; vocabulary size in Spanish was related to frequency of joint book reading in Spanish and not frequency of book reading in English, and vocabulary size in English was related to joint book reading in English, but not in Spanish. Thus, it appears that although some aspects of input may result in transference to the other language, vocabulary size is related to input in the same language and for young children, joint book reading has a language-specific positive relationship with vocabulary development.

DEVELOPMENTAL CONTEXTS AND STRATEGIES IN LEXICAL ACQUISITION

Phases of Lexical Development

Lexical development does not occur in isolation; it is embedded in the context of a child's social, cognitive, and linguistic development. Although there is certainly overlap and continuity in many aspects of lexical development among toddlers, preschool children, and school-age children, children's development and the contexts in which they encounter and learn new words continually change and shift.

Lexical development is a central focus of the early stages of language acquisition. Toddlers' understanding of words and the first words they say are highlights of early language development. Very young children develop an understanding and use of words largely in the context of social interactions (Nelson, 1985). As they participate in social interactions, children learn word meanings in the context of understanding the focus and intentions of others (Akhtar & Tomasello, 2000), and in the context of learning how to make their own intentions known (Bloom, 2000). An essential ingredient for word learning, then, is children's ability to participate in joint reference within social interactions. Another ingredient is children's conceptual development. Children's understanding of words moves from "prereferential" (strictly context-bound usages of words associated with general event representations), to the understanding that words can be used to refer to different instances of conceptual categories (e.g., objects, actions, attributes) in multiple contexts (Nelson, 1985).

In the preschool years, children's lexical development reflects continuing conceptual development along with an understanding of the use of words to refer. Children add new words and refine their understandings of words in a variety of conceptual categories, such as kinship and color terms (see Chapter 5). In addition, development of grammatical morphological abilities expands children's ability to formulate bi- and multimorphemic words (e.g., *dog* → *dogs, play* → *played, player, tie* → *untie*), a process that continues into the school-age years.

In the school-age years, vocabulary learning is a key aspect of school performance. Reading comprehension is correlated with vocabulary size and the majority of new words are learned from reading texts, with the meanings of new words inferred from multiple exposures in varied written contexts (Stahl, 1999; Sternberg, 1987). This type of vocabulary learning occurs across the curriculum, in expository texts from science to history as well as in fiction. In addition to providing opportunities for contextually based learning of many words, some texts provide definitions of selected terms. This requires that children understand metalinguistic, text-based definitions and explanations of new vocabulary (Norris & Hoffman, 1993). These researchers provided an example of a text in which the terms *atmosphere, troposphere, stratosphere,* and *ozone layer* are all defined in relationship to one another within two paragraphs. During the school years, children's ability to perform many tasks requiring a focus on relationships among words increases; this is seen in activities such as providing antonyms and synonyms and including superordinate category information in word definitions, such as *A bear is a mammal* (Owens, 2001).

Lexical Acquisition Processes, Cues, and Strategies

Theories of word learning are not specific as to the number of languages being learned, and for the most part can apply to learning in two languages as well as in one. Because the link between a word and its referent is arbitrary, knowledge of one word does not specifically prepare the learner for knowledge of another word. Words are learned one by one. For each word learned, a word-learning "event" specific to that word must occur.

The strategies children use to translate input into vocabulary have been subjects of research and debate (see Golinkoff et al., 2000, for a collection of writings from diverse viewpoints). Clearly, learning words involves some form of associative learning—a pairing of sounds and meanings. But how do children settle on the meanings they associate with forms?

Although children are subject to making underextensions and over extensions of word meanings compared with those of adults, children overall are quite accurate in making form–meaning links that are similar to those of adults. Why is this? Why does a child infer that the word *cat* refers to the whole cat and not its ears, fur, or tail? Why, in fact, does the child settle on the animal at all, rather than the floor it is walking across?

As discussed previously, social-pragmatic views of acquisition situate lexical acquisition in communicative contexts. Children focus on words others use that relate to children's intentions (Bloom, 2000), and children also infer meanings of words based on what they interpret to be the adult's focus of attention (Ahktar & Tomasello, 2000). Within these interactive contexts, children's linking of forms and meanings involves multiple skills and draws on cues to meaning.

The first requirement in learning a new word is to make a phonological representation of it, that is, to represent the string of sounds in one's mind so the word can be recalled. Hoff (2003) tested monolingual and bilingual 23-month-olds on their ability to repeat nonsense words accurately in an experimental setting. The bilingual toddlers' performance was similar to the monolinguals' performance on nonsense words. (The monolingual toddlers were better than the bilingual toddlers at repeating real words, however, presumably as a function of their larger English-only vocabularies at that point.) In terms of phonological representation of novel words, though, no significant difference was found between the performance of monolingual and bilingual toddlers. Other studies of early phonological development (Navarro, Pearson, Cobo-Lewis, & Oller, 1995; Pearson, Navarro, & Gathercole, 1995) also revealed basic equivalence of phonological skill between bilinguals and monolinguals, even when bilinguals' skill in only one language was taken into account. These findings indicate that bilingual children bring the same tools as monolinguals to that part of the task.

Representing the sounds of words is only one part of learning a new word. Researchers studying early monolingual lexical acquisition have proposed several strategies that children may use to guide their hypotheses about what a new word means. With some adjustments, these strategies may be helpful to bilinguals. For novel nouns, the most prominent strategies include the *mutual exclusivity bias* (Markman & Wachtel, 1988), the *basic-level word bias* (Clark, 1993), and a *whole object* or *shape bias* (Landau, Smith, & Jones, 1988; Macnamara, 1982). The mutual exclusivity strategy, also referred to as the *principle of contrast* (Clark, 1993), limits the potential meaning of a novel word by excluding any objects in the context for which the child already has another name (and for bilinguals one would need to add "another name in that language"). The basic-level bias suggests that words like *dog* or *bird* are accessible conceptually to very young children and, therefore, are more likely to be encoded lexically. The whole object bias directs the child to the most general meaning possible given the situation. So, hearing "gobble" in the presence of a rabbit, the child will opt first for the whole animal (and not some part of the rabbit). However, even 18-month-olds will learn the word as a proper name if there is not an article before "gobble" (Macnamara, 1982). Although the child's first hypothesis about a novel word's meaning will be a whole object of the shape depicted, this bias can be overridden when another quality is made more salient, such as the object's function (Gathercole & Whitfield, 2001).

The problem is different for verbs, for which, unlike nouns, speaking a word while simultaneously indicating the referent (as by pointing) will generally be insufficient. Also, strategies that apply to learning the names of things (e.g., whole object biases) are not useful for learning verb meanings. Verbs are often used before or after something occurs (e.g., "He will come," "It fell") and the meanings of common verbs often are not visible ("She likes"). Even when meanings are visible, as for verbs labeling actions ("He is kicking"), when parents are interacting with children they are less likely to use a verb concurrently with the action. Rather, they are more likely to refer to impending actions ("Put it up there"). Furthermore, impending action references may be a particularly important context for learning action terms. In a series of studies of novel verb learning, 2-year-olds learned new verbs more in an impending action context than in situations in which the verb was used as the action was taking place (Tomasello, 1995).

Children may use grammatical information such as subjects and objects as cues to decide among possible meanings of verbs, a process called *syntactic bootstrapping* (Gleitman, 1990). Shown a scene of a dog chasing a cat, for example, the phrase "The dog is chasing . . ." directs the child's attention to what the dog—the noun in subject position—is doing. If the sentence is "The dog is chasing the cat," the child must focus on the dog's action—whatever it is—as it relates to the cat; that is, the dog cannot just be running; its running somehow must be directed at the cat. Fisher (1996) and Naigles (1990) showed that children can make judgments like these for concrete verbs when they are as young as 2 years old. As with adults, hearing the verb in several sentence frames appears to help children narrow the range of possible meanings. Several cross-linguistic studies of verb learning have been conducted (e.g., Choi & Gopnik, 1995), but such studies of bilinguals have not been done.

Some research indicates that initial word learning involves what has been called *fast-mapping* (i.e., the child acknowledges that a certain phonetic shape is a word and associates it with some very general information as to its meaning). In an experiment by Carey (1978) known as the "chromium" experiment, for example, most of the children realized that "chromium" was a color term after hearing it first in "not the red one, the chromium one." But even after several months with occasional exposure to the word, half of the children's definitions of the word were still too general to permit them to correctly determine which color it was.

Subsequent encounters with a word, especially in different contexts, elaborate the child's knowledge of the word and its referent. Lexical elaboration includes having different exemplars named by the word, making associations with it, and integrating it into a web of relationships with other words; for example, determining what category it belongs to, such as *furniture* or *hat*, and delineating how it differs from similar words, a *bench* versus a *chair*, a *cap* versus a *sombrero*. A number of studies indicate that children learning a second language have less elaborated information about L2 words than their monolingual age mates (Ordóñez, Carlo, Snow, & McLaughlin, 2002). Verhallen and Schoonen (1993) found that Turkish 9- and 11-year-olds who were learning Dutch as a second language gave less elaborated answers to a Dutch word definition task than did a comparison group of Dutch monolingual children.

Lexical elaboration is related to word retrieval accuracy. Among monolingual children (with and without language impairments), knowing more about a word or having more elaborated knowledge about its referent is associated with greater naming accuracy (McGregor & Leonard, 1989; McGregor, Newman, Reilly, & Capone, 2002).

Bilingual Processes in Lexical Acquisition

A general question in bilingual lexical acquisition is how the two languages will interact in the process: Are there paths for facilitation (or possibly interference) across languages? Research on bilingual preschool children's application of a principle of mutual exclusivity indicates that they use the strategy in the same way as monolingual children within languages, but young bilingual children do not apply the strategy across languages. In a study by Rhemtulla and Nicoladis (2003), French-English bilingual and monolingual English 2- and 3-year-old children were presented with "English" nonwords and "Chinese" nonwords in two different sessions with two different speakers. When given a choice of a familiar object or an unfamiliar one, both the bilingual and monolingual children chose the unfamiliar object as the referent for the English words, a strategy consistent with the mutual exclusivity principle. When presented with the Chinese non-words, the monolingual children continued to choose the unfamiliar object most of the time; in contrast, the bilingual children chose the familiar object one half of the time. The interpretation of this finding was that these bilingual children knew that when they heard a word in one language, it might or might not refer to something they had a word for in the other language. This finding indicates that the strategy is flexible and adaptable to the bilingual child's experience. In fact, both monolingual and bilingual preschool children apply the mutual exclusivity strategy within, but not across, languages when they are specifically told that two sets of nonsense words that are presented to them are in different languages (Au & Glusman, 1990).

Children's use of a mutual exclusivity strategy within, but not across, languages is consistent with evidence that from an early age, bilingual children are able to use each language in appropriate contexts. For example, toddlers from bilingual homes use each parent's native language more with that parent (Genesee, Nicoladis, & Paradis, 1995). Young bilingual children may use a word in the "wrong" language (i.e., the language that is not used by the parent with whom the child is speaking) when they do not know the word in both languages; however, this seems to be a special type of overextension motivated by gaps in the lexicon that is parallel to overextensions of words by monolingual children. In summary, knowing words in one language does not interfere with learning and using words in another language.

Several pieces of indirect evidence indicate whether knowing a word in one language will make it easier to learn it in a second language. Pearson and Fernández (1994) examined the vocabulary growth in each language and in both languages combined in 18 bilingual toddlers, with special attention paid to the growth of TEs across the languages. No child showed faster growth in learning words already known in the other language (TEs, or *doublets*) over words not represented in their other language (*singlets*). In fact, one toddler clearly illustrated slower growth when adding the second language labels for concepts already known in the first language (doublets) than he had in learning them in the first language (Pearson & Fernández, 1994, p. 638). Most of the bilingual children Pearson and Fernández observed permitted TEs across their languages, but no more than two separate monolingual children were expected to share words in their vocabularies. Pearson and colleagues (1995) compared the number of words that appeared in the vocabularies listed for two different monolingual children with the number of words that co-occurred as TEs in the two vocabularies of a single bilingual child. The average values were almost identical. The bilinguals' two vocabularies did not share any more, or any fewer, words than did the vocabularies of the monolingual children (Pearson et al., 1995). The authors interpreted this finding to mean that there was no facilitation (or preference) for learning L2 words that corresponded to words already known in L1.

One might suppose that cognate words that are spelled similarly in both languages (e.g., president/*presidente*) and words that are direct segment-by-segment phonological translations of each other (e.g., "Emily" or "Arnold" with an English accent and stress pattern contrasted with the same name spoken with Spanish vowels and a Spanish accent and stress pattern) (Oller & Eilers, 2002) might give learners more immediate access to those words when learning their second language. Meara (1993) reported estimates of 3,000 cognate pairs between English and Spanish. These cognate pairs may help older learners in building their recognition vocabularies. Spanish-English bilingual children in fourth through sixth grades can recognize cognate relationships (although not as well as adults), and their recognition of cognates is positively related to their reading comprehension performance (Nagy, Garcia, Durgunoglu, & Hancin-Bhatt, 1993). In addition to their value for recognition in context, cognates may also aid in remembering the words as part of the "elaborated" meanings (here cross-linguistically) that McGregor and Leonard (1989) pointed to as aids to retrieval for monolinguals. As Meara pointed out, however, the occurrence of cognates is too unpredictable and the fit of meanings across languages too unreliable for them to be helpful as initial learning strategies.

No research (to our knowledge) has been done on the use of grammatical structures as cues to the meanings of lexical items in early simultaneous bilinguals, but no strong indications are given that basic syntactic bootstrapping processes would differ from bilingual children and those used by monolingual children within a language. As Peña and Kester point out in Chapter 5, however, when grammatical structures of two languages differ, children encounter different types of cues in the surface structures of the input they hear. For example, Spanish-English bilingual children experience input in which adjectives precede nouns in English, but adjectives most often follow the noun in Spanish. Therefore, how bilingual children make use of syntactic bootstrapping when cues for two languages are the same and when they differ may be a promising area of research for increasing our understanding of bilingual lexical acquisition as well as promoting understanding of syntactic bootstrapping processes.

The following section discusses clinical implications of lexical acquisition processes. Recommendations for assessment and intervention are made based on general lexical acquisition processes that occur among monolingual and bilingual children and considerations that apply specifically to bilingual children.

IMPLICATIONS FOR ASSESSMENT AND INTERVENTION

Assessment

Two types of information are essential in compiling any case history for a bilingual child. First, information on the languages with which the child has had significant experience should be obtained from parents and teachers. A complete assessment must address the child's lexical development in each language that the child hears and uses. In other words, selecting one language of assessment based on whether a child is "dominant" in Spanish or English is insufficient. The bilingual child's lexical development (and other aspects of language development) must be assessed in both languages. In addition, the child's history of exposure to each language should include past and present experiences to address potential issues of language loss (see Chapter 8).

Second, the SLP must determine the purpose of the assessment. If the purpose is to identify language impairment, the assessment should be designed to compare a child's lexical development in both languages combined with that of peers—bilingual children in similar circumstances. In contrast, if the primary purpose involves intervention design—how best to foster lexical acquisition (and other aspects of language) for a child with a previously identified language impairment—the issue is not comparing the child with peers. Instead, the focus would be on determining how the child uses and understands words already in his or her lexicon and how he or she links form and meaning when learning new words.

Identification and evaluation of language impairment requires the use of tools that compare a bilingual child's lexical development to peers. Because of the problems inherent in measuring two vocabularies, it is not possible at present to make definitive judgments about the standard milestones of bilingual lexical development. In Chapter 5, Peña and Kester provide an overview of the limited range of tests currently available and then discuss the pros and cons of adaptations of monolingual measures when bilingual measures are not available. Whether a child is tested using a bilingual test or an adapted version of monolingual tests, difficult measurement issues must be confronted. These issues include determining

1) what to treat as the unit of knowledge when a child has equivalent terms in the two languages, and 2) the proper reference group for comparisons of the child's performance.

Consider the issue of what a word "counts for" in a system of measurement. For each word (i.e., each sound–meaning pairing) a monolingual child gets credit for 1) a sound, 2) a meaning, and 3) a link between the sound and the meaning. So, each word has a minimum of three subunits. The sound is like the "label" for the meaning. It tells what word it is, but by itself says nothing about what it refers to. In a bilingual individual's vocabulary, the words that are known in only one language will have at least those three elements, and perhaps a "tag" telling which language it is in (e.g., *dog* might have an "English" tag to identify it as an English word, while *perro* would be tagged as "Spanish").

For words known in two languages, at least two possibilities exist. The word in Language A might be completely distinct from the word in Language B; for example, a child might call a toy animal "cat" but use the word "gato" to refer to live cats. Although they might mean the same things to bilingual adults, there is no reason to assume that the child realizes that the words are equivalent. In this case, the Spanish word has three subunits, and the English word has three subunits, so it represents six units of knowledge plus the language tags that have no counterpart in the monolingual lexical entry. Alternately, the child may store a single meaning but have two labels (*dog* and *perro*), two links, and two language tags for it, one for each language. Here, we would consider a translation equivalent to consist of seven subunits. In either case, knowing a word in two languages represents considerably more mental machinery than knowing a word in just one.

Some test authors have suggested using the child's TCV, that is, crediting the bilingual child with words known in both languages, but counting translation equivalents only once (see Chapter 5). When the goal is to estimate how much conceptual knowledge a child can have access to, TCV may be quite appropriate. For estimates of more specific lexical knowledge, in which both sounds and meanings and their pairings are more crucial, TCV will underestimate the bilingual child's knowledge, and TV will be more appropriate.

The choice of measure may also change at different stages of language acquisition. In the early stages, when individual word meanings are generally less elaborated, the word label (its sound shape) represents a larger proportion of the knowledge of the word than it will later when the meaning is more complex. At later stages, the meaning may reasonably represent a larger "chunk" of knowledge than the word label it is paired with. It may make sense on early vocabulary measures of infants and toddlers to count TV, recognizing each sound–meaning pairing as a separate achievement, and later on at school age to count TCV, giving more weight to the child's conceptual knowledge.

Most commonly used standardized measures (see Chapter 5) were derived from observations of groups of monolingual children, so standard estimates of how many words every 2- or 5- or 15-year-old should know are not appropriate for children who have their vocabulary knowledge distributed across two languages. Even children with very little knowledge of one of their languages have been shown in most cases to know some words in their weaker language that they do not know in their stronger language (Umbel, Pearson, Fernández, & Oller, 1992). That knowledge in the second language is not taken into account in the implied comparison of a bilingual child to the norming groups for tests in a single language.

Efforts are underway to create norms for several language behaviors based on standardization research on bilingual children (Iglesias et al., 1999), and some tests have included bilingual groups in their norming processes (e.g., *Expressive One-Word Picture Vocabulary Test: 2000 Edition* [EOWPVT]; Brownell, 1999). These tests will no doubt be an improvement over the misapplication of monolingual norms to bilinguals. The wide spectrum of bilingual knowledge and experience, however, complicates the task of constructing bilingual norms. The proper reference group for an individual should be composed of children as much like the individual and *each other* as possible. The many avenues of typical bilingual development and the constant change over time in the relation between the languages used by a single individual make assembling a proper reference group problematic at best. It would be as misleading to compare a bilingual child with the "wrong" bilingual group as it would be to compare him or her with a monolingual group (or even two monolingual groups, one in each language). The expectations for the contribution of each language to the TV of a 6-year-old bilingual child who has been learning a language since birth are very different than those for a bilingual 6-year-old with only 1 year of experience in that language. Furthermore, no consensus has been reached on a way to combine the information from both languages.

The expectations for children with different experience and talents at the start of a school year are also different than expectations for the children midway through the first, second, or even third year as the children experience different levels of intensity of exposure to the second language. In summary, good evidence from many sources indicates that current measures are inadequate, but determining how to count units of knowledge and identifying the proper reference groups for bilingual norms are still significant obstacles that must be addressed in developing new language measures for bilingual children.

Quantitative measures such as vocabulary tests obtain estimates of children's vocabulary size in contexts quite different than most occasions of daily communication. Therefore, a complete evaluation must also include samples of the child's use of communication in daily life, or at least in naturalistic situations that are similar to the child's experiences to ensure authenticity of evaluation findings. (See Chapter 2 for cultural considerations of daily activities and appropriate methods of selecting sampling contexts.) For example, a 3-year-old who is typically developing may perform poorly on a standardized vocabulary test but may show strong vocabulary skills by using a wide variety of nouns, verbs, and descriptive terms in a language sample while playing with a sibling. In contrast, a 3-year-old with language impairment might perform poorly on a standardized vocabulary test and use very few specific nouns, action terms, and descriptive terms during a language sample with a peer. Cross-validation of findings from testing and language sampling is key in addressing the question of whether a child has language impairment.

In addition to providing quantitative measures of number of words used, language sampling in naturalistic or daily life contexts allows us to see how the child uses words in communicative interactions, with co-occurring cognitive, social, and other linguistic demands and cues. In order to collect samples with maximum authenticity, the language sampling contexts will need to include situations that are consistent with the child's experiences. For example, if the child's parents usually use both languages with him or her throughout the day, a bilingual language sample with one or both parents should be obtained. If the child primarily has had experience with the two languages in different domains (e.g., a child from a Spanish-speaking home is just beginning to attend a mostly English-speaking preschool), a Spanish sample with the parent should be a major sampling context and the English sample might consist of a classroom observation. Finally, in addition to language samples designed to examine the child's use of lexical items and other aspects of language in daily activities, probes and dynamic assessment procedures can be used. In order to determine the extent of a child's knowledge about a specific word, clinicians can use picture drawing and definition tasks with preschool and elementary school-age children (see McGregor et al., 2002). Definition tasks can be supplemented with a series of questions designed to obtain maximally elaborated responses (Verhallen & Schoonen, 1993). Dynamic assessment procedures can be used to determine what types of contexts facilitate a child's use of words and learning of new words. (See Chapter 5.)

Intervention Implications

Language(s) of Intervention

In what language(s) should intervention take place? In order to answer this question, it is important to keep in mind that both languages are essential for the bilingual child—as de Houwer (2002) has said, a second language is not a luxury for the bilingual child. Therefore, the question is how to provide effective intervention that fosters lexical development (and other aspects of language development) in both languages. It appears that the answer as to when to introduce words in each language may vary depending on the overall timing of the child's exposure to the two languages and the type of lexical skill to be taught.

Among sequential Spanish-speaking learners who are just beginning to acquire English, some evidence suggests that starting with teaching words in L1 and later teaching them in English is more efficient for teaching English vocabulary (and, of course, Spanish vocabulary development) than starting to teach words in L2 (Perozzi, 1985; Perozzi & Sanchez, 1992). Among adult learners with limited L2 proficiency, form–meaning mappings appear to be mediated by relating an L2 word to an equivalent word in L1 (Kroll 1993). If this is also true for monolingual children who are just beginning to learn a second language, the most efficient combination may be to introduce words in L1 followed by teaching the words in L2. This may be especially helpful for conceptually difficult words and those with more abstract meanings, such as *behave, mixture, recycle*, and the higher numerals. Starting with L1 also may be helpful in teaching children more advanced metalinguistic and decontextualized lexical-semantic skills, based on evidence that some word definition strategies are transferred from L1 to L2. In a study of sequential bilingual fourth- and fifth-grade children, use of superordinate category terms (e.g., *A dog is a kind of animal*) when defining words in L1 predicted use of superordinate terms in L2 definitions (Ordóñez et al., 2002).

For sequential learners who are beyond the initial stages of L2 acquisition and for simultaneous bilinguals, however, it may be more effective to simply introduce new lexical items as needed in each language when the goal is initial teaching of new words, rather than elaboration of lexical items. Kroll (1993) reported that adults with more advanced L2 proficiency appear to establish and access meanings of L2 words independently of L1; this may also be true of school-age children with some L2 proficiency, and, as Peña and Kester suggest in Chapter 5, simultaneous bilingual children may also tend to establish independent form–meaning links for equivalent words in the two languages. In fact, as noted, for bilingual toddlers, knowing a word in one language does not appear to result in quicker learning of the equivalent word in the other language (Pearson & Fernández, 1994). Given these findings, it may be best to simply teach a young bilingual child the words he or she needs in each language as the need arises.

Fostering Lexical Learning

The literature on lexical acquisition has implications for intervention strategies for monolinguals and bilinguals alike. These implications should be heeded when providing intervention in any language(s), while taking the child and family cultural context into account (see Chapter 2 and Crowley & Valenti, 2002).

Research on typical children's lexical acquisition provides evidence that children make use of multiple cues when learning new words. Young children make use of nonlinguistic contextual information, social-pragmatic contexts, grammatical cues, and some general principles to form initial hypotheses about word meanings. Therefore, teaching new vocabulary to young children may be most effective in naturalistic contexts, not only for fostering generalization but also because naturalistic contexts provide many cues to meaning. Because joint book reading is particularly facilitative for lexical development, this type of activity should be included among intervention activities for both languages.

The literature on early language intervention and on typical lexical acquisition indicates that a balance of adult-initiated and child-initiated interactions may be ideal for fostering early lexical development. Responsive styles of interaction, in which adults provide language models that pertain to the child's focus of interest (i.e., "child-initiated" interactions), are an important element in lexical acquisition among language-delayed toddlers (Girolametto, Weitzman, Wiigs, & Pearce, 1999). The effectiveness of following the child's lead in this way is consistent with Bloom's (2000) focus on children's learning word meanings as a way to make their own intentions known. At the same time, Akhtar and Tomasello (2000) reviewed research documenting that toddlers attend to and learn meanings of words used to refer to objects and actions that adults introduce in the context of interesting activities with toys. A combination of following the child's lead and introducing new activities and objects would take advantage of children's interest in expressing their own intentions and in understanding others' intentions and meanings.

Research on children's learning of verb meanings provides some guidance on ways to introduce new verbs to young children. First, it appears that referring to an action just before it happens (in the context of an interesting activity) is a particularly potent context—more so than simultaneous modeling of the word as the action occurs (Tomasello, 1995). Furthermore, using the word in sentences, rather than solely in single-word models (e.g., "Let's chew our gum" or "The dog is chewing the shoe!") will give the child with some grammatical knowledge further cues to meaning (e.g., that chewing is an action that someone does to something).

Although the research on lexical acquisition strategies reviewed in this chapter focused primarily on toddlers and preschool children, some limited implications for language intervention with school-age children can be discussed. A combination of learning words from contextual cues in everyday reading and other activities and direct teaching of selected words has been recommended for school-age children who are typically developing (Stahl, 1999). Most words are learned incidentally as children listen to and read texts on a variety of topics. Children with language impairment affecting reading will have fewer opportunities for incidental vocabulary learning during independent reading. Reading aloud to children who with limited reading skills is recommended in order to provide them with a wider range of vocabulary than they would experience independently (Stahl, 1999). For a bilingual child with language impairment, a comprehensive language intervention plan should provide opportunities to listen to texts in both languages that he or she currently is unable to read independently, taking into account the child's level of auditory comprehension in each language. In addition to adults reading aloud to children, some children may benefit from listening to books on audiotape or CD (these are available for all ages, through commercial sources and also through Recording for the Blind and Dyslexic). Because children with limited reading ability often draw erroneous conclusions about meaning compared to good readers (McKeown, 1985), it will be important to teach children with language impairment how to use contextual cues to infer meaning, if they do not do so independently. Norris and Hoffman (1993) and Paul (2001) provided several examples of ways to teach children and adolescents to use contextual cues.

Children who are typically developing learn many new words; however, it is not possible to directly teach a child who has language impairment all of the words he or she will need to know (Stahl, 1999). Therefore, the bases for selecting vocabulary items to teach directly are particularly important. For typical adult L2 learners, Nation (1993) recommended teaching high-frequency words first to provide a basis for understanding most written texts. He cited research indicating that if an individual is familiar with more than 95% of the words in a text, the remaining word meanings can be inferred; this means the reader can understand the text (and, at the same time, presumably the reader can learn new words through inferences when overall comprehension of the text is adequate). Assuming this is also true for school-age bilingual children with language impairments, high-frequency words a child does not know would be particularly important intervention targets. (See Carroll, Davies, & Richman, 1971, for lists of the most frequently used English words in school texts for grades 3 through 9.)

In addition to high-frequency words, subject-specific terms in school texts are other important words to teach second language learners (Nation, 1993). Direct teaching with active engagement of children (Stahl, 1999) and use of visualization and mnemonic strategies such as keyword techniques (Pressley, Levin, & McDaniel, 1987) may be especially important in helping children learn to recall word meanings rather than just to recognize them. For example, to memorize and define 10 words for a science test, direct teaching is likely to be more effective than simply exposing the child to multiple instances of use of the terms. When working with children with language impairments, clinicians can make curriculum-based choices of lexical targets for direct teaching for school-age children (see, e.g., Nelson, 1992). A wide range of teaching techniques, from semantic mapping to analyzing word roots and derivational morphology can be used with children with language impairments as well as with those who are typically developing. For two brief monographs on vocabulary teaching methods that are based on research on reading and vocabulary development in school-age children, see Nagy (1988) and Stahl (1999).

Children with language impairment also may need help to increase the efficiency of storing and retrieving the words they know (see Chapter 3). The work of McGregor and colleagues (McGregor & Leonard, 1989; McGregor et al., 2002) indicated that retrieval processes may be enhanced by more elaborated knowledge of word meanings. Therefore, it is possible that enriching children's understanding of word meanings may be as important as the amount of rehearsal in fostering more efficient access. This may be accomplished in school contexts by a combination of direct teaching and exposure to multiple activities and texts involving vocabulary that will be in classroom texts and activities.

Although multiple implications for intervention can be inferred from the literature on lexical acquisition, professionals must keep in mind that the effectiveness of the strategies chosen must be substantiated in research and experiences as they are used with individual children. This is particularly true when working with bilingual children; in addition to the interacting spheres of social, cognitive, and language development that all children experience, bilingual children come to us with a wide range of cultural and linguistic experiences. Surely one strategy will not fit everyone, and the same strategy may not even fit the same child in both languages or at different points in time.

REFERENCES

Akhtar, N., & Tomasello, M. (2000). The social nature of words and word learning. In R. Golinkoff, K. Hirsh-Pasek, L. Bloom, L.B. Smith, A. Woodward, N. Akhtar, M. Tomasello, & G. Hollich (Eds.), *Becoming a word learner: A debate on lexical acquisition* (pp. 115–135). Oxford, UK: Oxford University Press.

Au, T.K., & Glusman, M. (1990). The principle of mutual exclusivity in word learning: To honor or not to honor? *Child Development, 61*, 1474–1490.

Bloom, L. (2000). The intentionality model of word learning: How to learn a word, any word. In R. Golinkoff, K. Hirsh-Pasek, L. Bloom, L.B. Smith, A. Woodward, N. Akhtar, M. Tomasello, & G. Hollich (Eds.), *Becoming a word learner: A debate on lexical acquisition* (pp. 19–50). Oxford, UK: Oxford University Press.

Brownell, R. (1999). *Expressive One-Word Picture Vocabulary Test: 2000 Edition*. Novato, CA: Academic Therapy Publications.

Bus, A.G., van IJzendoorn, M.H., & Pellegrini, A.D. (1995). Joint book reading makes for success in learning to read: A meta-analysis on intergenerational transmission of literacy. *Review of Educational Research, 65*, 1–21.

Carey, S. (1978). The child as word learner. In J. Bresnan, G. Miller, & M. Halle (Eds.), *Linguistic theory and psychological reality* (pp. 264–293). Cambridge, MA: MIT Press.

Carroll, J., Davies, P., & Richman, B. (1971). *Word frequency book*. Boston: Houghton Mifflin.

Choi, S., & Gopnik, A. (1995). Early acquisition of verbs in Korean: A cross-linguistic study. *Journal of Child Language, 22*, 497–529.

Clark, E. (1993). *The lexicon in acquisition*. Cambridge, UK: Cambridge University Press.

Cobo-Lewis, A., Eilers, R., Pearson, B., & Umbel, V. (2002). Interdependence of Spanish and English knowledge in language and literacy among bilingual children. In D.K. Oller & R. Eilers (Eds.), *Language and literacy in bilingual children* (pp. 118–132). Clevedon, UK: Multilingual Matters.

Crowley, C.J., & Valenti, D.M. (2002). Vocabulary development with students who are culturally and linguistically diverse. *Perspectives on Language Learning and Education, 9*(3), 25–29.

Cummins, J. (1984). *Bilingualism and special education: Issues in assessment and pedagogy.* Clevedon, UK: Multilingual Matters.

Dale, P., Dionne, G., Eley, T. & Plomin, R. (2000). Lexical and grammatical development: A behavioral genetic perspective. *Journal of Child Language, 27,* 619–642.

de Houwer, A. (1995). Bilingual language acquisition. In P. Fletcher & B. Mac-Whinney (Eds.), *The handbook of child language* (pp. 217–250). Oxford, UK: Blackwell.

de Houwer, A. (2002, July). *Uneven development in bilingual acquisition.* Plenary session at the International Association for the Study of Child Language and the Symposium for Research in Child Language Disorders, Madison, WI.

Fisher, C. (1996). Structural limits on verb mapping: The role of analogy in children's interpretations of sentences. *Cognitive Psychology, 31,* 41–81.

García, E. (1983). *Bilingualism in early childhood.* Albuquerque, NM: University of New Mexico Press.

Gathercole, V.M. (2002). Grammatical gender in bilingual and monolingual children: A Spanish morphosyntactic distinction. In D.K. Oller & R.E. Eilers (Eds.), *Language and literacy in bilingual children* (pp. 207–219). Clevedon, UK: Multilingual Matters.

Gathercole, V.M., & Whitfield, L. (2001). Function as a criterion for the extension of new words. *Journal of Child Language, 28,* 87–125.

Genesee, F., Nicoladis, E., & Paradis, J. (1995). Language differentiation in early bilingual development. *Journal of Child Language, 22,* 611–631.

Girolametto, L., Weitzman, E., Wiigs, M., & Pearce, P. (1999). The relationship between maternal language measures and language development in toddlers with expressive language delays. *American Journal of Speech-Language Pathology, 8,* 364–374.

Gleitman, L. (1990). The structural sources of verb meanings. *Language Acquisition, 1,* 1–27.

Golinkoff, R., Hirsh-Pasek, K., Bloom, L., Smith L.B., Woodward, A., Akhtar, N., Tomasello, M., & Hollich, G. (Eds.). (2000). *Becoming a word learner: A debate on lexical acquisition* (pp. 19–50). Oxford, UK: Oxford University Press.

Harley, B., Hart, D., & Lapkin, S. (1986). The effects of early bilingual schooling on first language skills. *Applied Psycholinguistics, 7,* 295–322.

Hart, B., & Risley, T.R. (1995). *Meaningful differences in the everyday lives of young American children.* Baltimore: Paul H. Brookes Publishing Co.

Hoff, E. (2003, May). *Phonological memory skill in monolingual and bilingual 23-month-olds.* Paper presented at the 4th International Symposium on Bilingualism, Tempe AZ.

Iglesias, A., Peña E., Gutiérrez-Clellen V., Bedore L., & Goldstein B. (1999). *Development of a language test for bilingual Spanish-English speaking children* (The Bilingual English/Spanish Assessment, BESA). Paper presented at the American Speech-Language-Hearing Association Convention, San Francisco, CA.

Kroll, J.F. (1993). Accessing conceptual representations for words in a second language. In R. Schrueder, & B. Weltens (Eds.), *The bilingual lexicon* (pp. 53–81). Amsterdam: John Benjamins.

Lambert, W. (1977). Effects of bilingualism on the individual: Cognitive and socio-cultural consequences. In P.A. Hornby (Ed.) *Bilingualism: Psychological, social, and educational implications* (pp. 15–28). New York: Academic Press.

Lambert, W., & Tucker, G. (1972). *Bilingual education of children: The St. Lambert experiment.* Rowley, MA: Newbury House.

Landau, B., Smith, L., & Jones, S. (1988). The importance of shape in early lexical learning. *Cognitive Development, 3,* 299–321.

Macnamara, J.T. (1982). *Names for things: A study of human learning.* Cambridge, MA: MIT Press.

Marchman, V.A., & Martínez-Sussman, C. (2002). Concurrent validity of caregiver/parent report measures of language for children who are learning both English and Spanish. *Journal of Speech, Language, and Hearing Research, 45,* 983–997.

Markman, E., & Wachtel, G. (1988). Children's use of mutual exclusivity to constrain the meanings of words. *Cognitive Psychology, 20,* 121–157.

McGregor, K., & Leonard, L. (1989). Facilitating word-finding skills of language-impaired children. *Journal of Speech and Hearing Disorders, 54,* 141–147.

McGregor, K., Newman, R., Reilly, R., & Capone, N. (2002). Semantic representation and naming in children with specific language impairment. *Journal of Speech, Language, and Hearing Research, 45,* 998–1014.

McKeown, M. (1985). The acquisition of word meaning from context by children of high and low ability. *Reading Research Quarterly, 20,* 482–496.

Meara, P. (1993). The bilingual lexicon and the teaching of vocabulary. In R. Schrueder & B. Weltens (Eds.), *The bilingual lexicon* (pp. 280–297). Amsterdam: John Benjamins.

Nagy, W. (1988). *Teaching vocabulary to improve reading comprehension.* Urbana, IL: National Council of Teachers of English and International Reading Association.

Nagy, W., Garcia, G., Durgunoglu, A., & Hancin-Bhatt, B. (1993). Spanish–English bilingual students' use of cognates in English reading. *Journal of Reading Behavior, 25,* 241–259.

Naigles, L. (1990). Children use syntax to learn verb meanings. *Journal of Child Language, 17,* 357–374.

Nation, P. (1993). Vocabulary size, growth, and use. In R. Schreuder & B. Weltens (Eds.), *The bilingual lexicon* (pp. 115–134). Amsterdam: John Benjamins.

Navarro, A.M., Pearson, B.Z., Cobo-Lewis, A.B., & Oller, D.K. (1995, December). *Assessment of phonological development in bilingual children at age 36 months: Comparison to monolinguals in each language.* Paper presented at the annual meeting of the American Speech-Language-Hearing Association, Orlando FL.

Nelson, K. (1985). *Making sense: The acquisition of shared meaning.* Orlando, FL: Academic Press.

Nelson, N. (1992). Targets of curriculum-based language assessment. In W. Secord & J. Damico (Eds.), *Best practices in school speech-language pathology: Descriptive/nonstandardized language assessment* (pp. 73–85). San Antonio, TX: The Psychological Corporation.

Norris, J., & Hoffman, P. (1993). *Whole language intervention for school-age children.* San Diego: Singular.

Oller, D.K., & Eilers, R.E. (Eds.). (2002). *Language and literacy in bilingual children.* Clevedon, UK: Multilingual Matters.

Ordóñez, C., Carlo, M., Snow, C., & McLaughlin, B. (2002). Depth and breadth of vocabulary in two languages: Which vocabulary skills transfer? *Journal of Educational Psychology, 94*, 719–728.

Owens, R. (2001). *Language development* (5th ed.). Boston: Allyn & Bacon.

Patterson, J.L. (1998). Expressive vocabulary development and word combinations of Spanish-English bilingual toddlers. *American Journal of Speech-Language Pathology, 7*(4), 46–56.

Patterson, J.L. (1999). What bilingual toddlers hear and say: Language input and word combinations. *Communication Disorders Quarterly, 21*, 32–38.

Patterson, J.L. (2002). Relationships of expressive vocabulary to frequency of reading and television experience among bilingual toddlers. *Applied Psycholinguistics, 23*, 493–508.

Paul, R. (2001). *Language disorders from infancy through adolescence* (2nd ed.). St. Louis: Mosby.

Pearson, B.Z. (1998). Assessing lexical development in bilingual babies and toddlers. *International Journal of Bilingualism, 2*, 347–372.

Pearson, B.Z. (2002). Narrative competence among monolingual and bilingual school children in Miami. In D.K. Oller & R.E. Eilers (Eds.), *Language and literacy in bilingual children* (pp. 135–174). Clevedon, UK: Multilingual Matters.

Pearson, B.Z., & Fernández, S.C. (1994). Patterns of interaction in the lexical growth in two languages of bilingual infants and toddlers. *Language Learning, 44*, 617–653.

Pearson, B.Z., Fernández, S.C., Lewedeg, V., & Oller, D.K. (1997). The relation of input factors to lexical learning by bilingual infants. *Applied Psycholinguistics, 18*, 41–58.

Pearson, B.Z., Fernández, S.C., & Oller, D.K. (1993). Lexical development in bilingual infants and toddlers: Comparison to monolingual norms. *Language Learning, 43*, 93–120.

Pearson, B.Z., Fernández, S., & Oller, D.K. (1995). Cross-language synonyms in the lexicons of bilingual infants: One language or two? *Journal of Child Language, 22*, 345–368.

Pearson, B.Z., Navarro, A.M., & Gathercole, V.M. (1995, March). Assessment of phonetic differentiation in bilingual learning infants, 18 to 30 months. Paper presented at the Boston University Conference of Child Language Development, Boston. In D. MacLaughlin & S. McEwen (Eds). *Proceedings of the 19th Annual Boston University Conference on Language Development* (pp. 427–438). Somerville, MA: Cascadilla Press.

Perozzi, J. (1985). A pilot study of language facilitation for bilingual, language-handicapped children: Theoretical and intervention implications. *Journal of Speech and Hearing Disorders, 50*, 403–406.

Perozzi, J., & Sanchez, M. (1992). The effect of instruction in L1 on receptive acquisition of L2 for bilingual children with language delay. *Language, Speech, and Hearing Services in Schools, 23*, 348–352.

Pressley, M., Levin, J., & McDaniel, M. (1987). Remembering versus inferring what a word means: Mnemonic and contextual approaches. In M. McKeown & M. Curtis (Eds.), *The nature of vocabulary acquisition* (pp. 107–127). Mahwah, NJ: Lawrence Erlbaum Associates.

Rhemtulla, M., & Nicoladis, E. (2003, May). *Is mutual exclusivity a pragmatic principle? Evidence from bilingual children.* Paper presented at the 4th International Symposium on Bilingualism, Tempe, AZ.

Romaine, S. (1995). *Bilingualism* (2nd ed.). Oxford, UK: Blackwell.

Scarborough, H.S., & Dobrich, W. (1994). On the efficacy of reading to preschoolers. *Developmental Review, 14,* 245–302.

Stahl, S. (1999). *Vocabulary development.* Cambridge, MA: Brookline.

Sternberg, R. (1987). Most vocabulary is learned from context. In M. McKeown & M. Curtis (Eds.), *The nature of vocabulary acquisition* (pp. 89–105). Mahwah, NJ: Lawrence Erlbaum Associates.

Swain, M., & Weschle, M. (1975). Linguistic interaction: Case study of a bilingual child. *Language Sciences, 37,* 17–22.

Tomasello, M. (1995). Pragmatic contexts for early verb learning. In M. Tomasello & W. Merriman (Eds.), *Beyond names for things: Young children's acquisition of verbs* (pp. 115–146). Mahwah, NJ: Lawrence Erlbaum Associates.

Umbel, V.M., Pearson, B.Z., Fernández, M.C., & Oller, D.K. (1992). Measuring bilingual children's receptive vocabularies. *Child Development, 63,* 1012–1020.

Verhallen, M., & Schoonen, R. (1993). Lexical knowledge of monolingual and bilingual children. *Applied Linguistics, 14,* 344–363.

CHAPTER 5

Semantic Development in Spanish-English Bilinguals

Theory, Assessment, and Intervention

ELIZABETH D. PEÑA AND ELLEN STUBBE KESTER

T he study of semantic development in children learning English as a second language (*sequential bilinguals*) as well as in those who are learning Spanish and English at the same time (*simultaneous bilinguals*) is of interest for both clinicians and researchers. Clinically, the issues of expected vocabulary growth, semantic knowledge, and the language(s) of assessment have implications for accurate identification of children who have language impairment. Furthermore, specific information about these issues has implications for the development of interventions that are specifically tailored to children exposed to two languages, considering both their home language and the school language, English.

In this chapter, we briefly review theoretical accounts that may provide predictions with respect to dual language acquisition in general and semantic development in bilinguals in particular. Next, we examine some of the available research on semantic development in bilingual children. We then examine assessment alternatives and their advantages and disadvantages. Finally, we provide guidelines for intervention with this growing population of bilingual children. The examples we provide are specific to Spanish and English because Spanish-English bilingual children represent one of the most rapidly growing populations in U.S. schools. Although specific information about Spanish-English semantic learning may not be applicable to other bilingual groups, the general principles of examining both languages and considering their interaction should guide application of this information to other language groups in the United States. Examination of some of the theoretical accounts of bilingual lexical acquisition provides guidelines for interpretation of current findings discussed further in the following sections.

THEORIES OF BILINGUAL LEXICAL ACQUISITION

Research in the area of bilingual language processing and use suggests that bilinguals may have different patterns of language development than do monolinguals of either language. Some researchers have proposed that bilinguals use an amalgamation of the strategies, drawing from the cues and strategies used in each of their two languages (Hernandez, Bates, & Avila, 1994; Kroll & de Groot, 1997). For example, the Competition Model proposes that language development is driven by input. In order to learn a given language, children rely on cues in the input (MacWhinney, 1997). These cues are used to learn the rules of the target language. Cues that work consistently in a language have high validity and are used more often. Cue validity is different in different languages, however (MacWhinney, 1987; MacWhinney & Bates, 1989). An example of a cue with high validity in English is preverbal position for identification of the subject. In contrast, the subject is placed in front of the verb less often in Spanish because of the pro-drop nature of the language, which minimizes the information provided by such a cue. For example, in the following Spanish sentences, the subject is established in the first sentence, and it is not necessary to repeat it or substitute a pronoun for it in the second sentence because the subject is implied in the verb, in this case, *compró* (bought): *Maria fue a la tienda. Compró uvas.* (Maria went to the store. She [implied] bought grapes.) Spanish speakers may look to cues of animacy or verb agreement for subject identification. For example, in the sentence *Tiró la pelota Juan* (Threw the ball Juan [or] Juan threw the ball), a Spanish speaker might use animacy cues to make the interpretation that Juan was the subject (actor) and the ball was the object. In the sentence *Los pescados Juan comió* (The fish Juan ate [or] Juan ate the fish), verb agreement provides a good cue about the subjects because the verb (*comió*) agrees with the subject (*Juan*) but not the object (*los pescados*). When cues (e.g., word order or agreement) are similar in two languages, positive transfer can occur. In other words, the cues learned in one language can be applied effectively in another language, such as using the plural -*s*, which occurs in both English and Spanish.

When cue validity differs across languages, however, negative transfer can occur. Negative transfer involves the application of cues that have high validity in one language to a language in which they have low validity. For example, if a word order cue were applied to the Spanish sentence

Los pescados comió Juan, the interpretation would be "The fish ate Juan," but verb agreement tells us "Juan ate the fish." Bilingual children must learn how cues work within and between their two languages, thereby creating a unique system that is an amalgamation of the cues in two languages. Thus, children learning both Spanish and English might make errors in comprehension and production when relevant L1 cues are applied to L2 (and vice versa), as demonstrated in the preceding examples. Applied to word learning, the Competition Model may predict that categories of words that have high cue validity in both languages may be learned earlier in comparison with those categories of words that have high cue validity in only one language. Words with high cue validity might include those that occur frequently and categories of words that are useful in contexts in which both languages are used. Thus, bilingual acquisition of the lexicon may have a different developmental pattern than that seen in children acquiring one language. In addition, timing in acquisition of the second language may also affect the developmental patterns and use of the cues of L1 and L2. For example, sequential and simultaneous bilinguals may demonstrate different patterns of semantic development.

Models of lexical access and production also predict different patterns of semantic development for bilinguals at different points in the acquisition process (Altarriba & Mathis, 1997; Kroll & Stewart, 1994). Two prominent models of lexical and conceptual representation in bilinguals that consider timing of L2 acquisition and language proficiency are the Word Association Model and the Concept Mediation Model (de Groot & Hoeks, 1995; Kroll & Stewart, 1994) (see Figure 5.1). These two models operate under the assumption that there are independent levels of representation

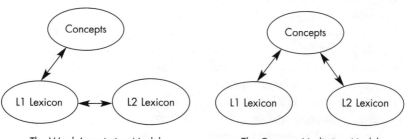

The Word Association Model   The Concept Mediation Model

Figure 5.1.   Schematic of Word Association and Concept Mediation Models. The Word Association Model proposes that individuals gain access to concepts through the L1 lexicon, whereas the Concept Mediation Model theorizes direct links between each lexicon and concepts, eliminating the need to mediate through L1. (Reprinted from *Journal of Verbal Learning and Verbal Behavior, 23*[1]; Potter, M.C., K.-f So, et al. [1984]. Lexical and conceptual representation in beginning and proficient bilinguals, 23–38; copyright © [1984], with permission from Elsevier.)

for word form (lexicon) and word meaning (concepts). In bilinguals, the different levels of representation are theorized as two different lexicons and one area of conceptual representation. The Word Association Model proposes that individuals gain access to concepts through the L1 lexicon. Thus, the L2 lexicon is mediated through the L1 lexicon to access concepts. This process might be seen in those who predominantly use one language and/or who are in the process of acquiring L2 sequentially. The Concept Mediation Model theorizes direct links between each lexicon and concepts, eliminating the need to mediate through L1. Both L1 and L2 lexical forms are directly linked to their concepts. In the Concept Mediation Model, lexical forms in L2 are thought to be tied more directly to their concepts rather than through the stronger language, as in the Word Association Model. This type of learning might be seen in "balanced" bilinguals who are learning two languages simultaneously or in sequential bilinguals who have achieved comparable performance in their two languages.

A number of language tasks performed with adults have indicated that as bilinguals become more proficient in their second language (and their L2 lexicon increases), they move from a Word Association approach, using the L1 to mediate L2 lexicon, to a Concept Mediation approach, in which concepts attach directly to the L2 lexicon without mediation through L1 (Dufour & Kroll, 1995; McLeod & McLaughlin, 1986). This shift in strategies is known as the Developmental Hypothesis (Kroll & de Groot, 1997). For example, in a translation recognition task, visual word pairs were presented to Spanish-English bilingual participants who were asked to determine whether these word pairs were translation equivalents (Kroll & de Groot, 1997; Talamas, Kroll, & Dufour, 1995). These word pairs were similar and dissimilar, varying by form (e.g., *hombre* versus *hambre, man* versus *hunger*) or meaning (e.g., *mujer* versus *hombre, woman* versus *man*). For the nontranslation word pairs (as in the previous examples) more fluent bilinguals exhibited more interference as a result of meaning similarities in the word pairs; whereas for a less fluent group of bilinguals, similarity in form resulted in greater interference (Dufour & Kroll, 1995; Kroll & de Groot, 1997). In a bilingual Stroop color word task, the names of colors were presented on a screen in different colors (e.g., *red* or *rojo* in red text versus blue text) to examine the influence of the color of the text on lexical recognition (Altarriba & Mathis, 1997). More fluent bilinguals demonstrated greater interference as a result of the color of the text than less fluent bilinguals, suggesting a greater reliance on a concept-mediation approach than less fluent bilinguals (Altarriba & Mathis, 1997; Chen & Ho, 1986; Mägiste, 1984; Tzelgow, Henik, & Leiser, 1990). Kroll and de Groot (1997) reported that in a translation study of true cognates (i.e., words with the similar form and meaning across languages, such as *panoramic* [English] and *panoramico/a* [Spanish]), less fluent bilinguals were found to translate cognates more rapidly than more fluent bilinguals, suggesting that less fluent bilinguals relied more on a lexical translation strategy (Dufour & Kroll, 1995).

Similarly, in a categorization task, less fluent bilinguals were found to be less accurate and slower in a between-language condition compared with bilinguals and compared with their own performance on a within-language condition (Dufour & Kroll, 1995). The participants heard a category name followed by the names of objects that either were a member of the category or not. Conditions included within-language, in which the category name and stimulus word were in the same language, and between-language, in which the category name and stimulus words were in different languages. Results suggested that less fluent bilinguals used a less efficient system than did the more fluent bilinguals, consistent with the Word Association Model and Concept Mediation Model, respectively.

Though these studies focused on adult bilinguals, they provide insight into the process of semantic development in bilingual children. As predicted by the Competition Model, the Developmental Hypothesis could be used to predict that children who are less proficient in their second language will experience greater difficulty on tasks presented in the second language because they are required to go through the extra step in that language of mediating through their first language. In addition, as they gain proficiency in both languages, it might be expected that they exhibit great variability in their language production as they shift from the use of a word association strategy to a concept mediation strategy. This change in strategies may result in differential performance on language tasks at different proficiency levels.

These studies highlight the importance of considering the developmental trajectories of both the first and second languages as well as how the two languages may influence each other during the acquisition process. Furthermore, the timing and stability of acquisition is seen as critical for describing how individuals access their lexicons. In a study with adults, Grosjean (1998), for example, discussed the importance of considering when a person learned a second language, as well as whether the person had attained a level of stability in acquisition of that language or whether they were still in the process of organization. He argued that an individual still in the process of learning and accommodating a second language might demonstrate more variability in performance in *both* languages, in comparison with someone who has reached relative stability. These findings have implications for how we interpret current findings of semantic learning, particularly in bilingual children who are most likely still in the process of acquiring language.

SEMANTIC LEARNING IN BILINGUALS

A number of studies and instruments have been used to examine semantic learning in bilingual Spanish- and English-speaking children. For young children, a number of diary studies (Leopold, 1939) as well as detailed case studies (Deuchar & Quay, 2000) have been conducted that examine language development in very young children. For toddlers, studies utilizing parental report have been used to obtain information about children's use and understanding of targeted vocabulary items (Jackson-Maldonado, Thal, Marchman, Bates, & Gutiérrez-Clellen, 1993). Studies of preschool and school-age bilingual children have examined vocabulary knowledge, mainly through the use of single word receptive and expressive vocabulary tests (Umbel, Pearson, Fernández, & Oller, 1992).

Generally, studies have documented that vocabulary growth across languages is very similar. For example, Jackson-Maldonado and colleagues (1993) found that Spanish-speaking infants' and toddlers' vocabulary development generally followed similar developmental trajectories as those documented for speakers of English. Thal, Jackson-Maldonado, and Acosta (2000) found that the Spanish version of the CDI (Fenson et al., 1993), when used with 20- and 28-month-old Spanish-speaking children, yielded raw scores comparable to those reported for other languages. Furthermore, vocabulary growth in bilinguals is generally similar to that of monolingual speakers when both languages are considered together. Specifically, for monolingual speakers of English, research shows that by approximately 16–17 months, on average, children's expressive vocabularies contain 50 words; by 18–20 months, children have approximately 100 words in their vocabularies. By age 2, the expectation is that children have approximately 200 words, and by age 3, they have 3,000–4,000 words (Hulit & Howard, 1997). During the preschool years, children further expand their knowledge of words and word meanings. For example, they begin to realize that words can have more than one meaning, or that a person, object, or event can have more than one name. During this age span, children add words through grammatical morphology such as adding -s to indicate plurality, or -ing and -ed to indicate tense. They also refine word relationships through categorization and description. Finally, during the preschool years children begin to organize their conceptual entries, adding words to conceptual categories such as kinship terms, color words, size, shape, and number. The organizational process of creating and refining mental categories allows for efficient and continued acquisition of new terms and concepts.

During the school-age years, children further add to their vocabulary knowledge. They learn both formal and informal definitions of vocabulary words, and they learn more about the relationships among words, such as those expressed by synonyms and antonyms. They develop formal rules that govern grammatical morphology and add words to their vocabulary through derivational morphology. For example, in English, children learn to add -er to a verb to form a noun (e.g., "run" + -er = "runner"). Likewise, in Spanish, children learn to add the morpheme *ador* to verbs to form nouns (e.g., "pescar" [fish] + *ador* = "pescador" [fisherman]) (Auza, 2002).

With respect to children learning vocabulary in a dual-language environment, studies generally find similar developmental trajectories for bilinguals in comparison with their monolingual counterparts. For example, Patterson (1998) developed a bilingual checklist based on the Language Development Survey (LDS; Rescorla, 1989) and related studies (Rescorla & Alley, 2001; Rescorla, Mirak, & Singh, 2000). Results of field-testing with children whose bilingual environment varied widely indicated developmental milestones to be similar to those reported in the literature for monolingual children. Pearson and Fernández (1994) reported that simultaneous bilingual (Spanish-English) children, ages 10–30 months old, demonstrated that the number of words in their repertoire was similar to that of monolinguals. Furthermore, Pearson and Fernández found that a similar proportion of children experienced lexical spurts in at least one language or in the two languages combined as that reported for monolingual children. Individual children, however, may present different patterns of lexical spurts in each language. Generally, children who are bilingual demonstrate similarities in vocabulary learning and performance in comparison with their monolingual counterparts, with some differing patterns. These different patterns of lexical development, discussed in more detail later in the chapter, have additional implications for assessment and intervention of children learning language in bilingual environments.

Bilingualism and Vocabulary Learning: Toddlers to Young Adults

Pearson and colleagues have studied the acquisition of vocabulary in children between the ages of 9 and 30 months who were acquiring language in a simultaneous bilingual Spanish-English-speaking environment. In one study, Pearson, Fernández, Lewedeg, and Oller (1997) studied the relationship between exposure to Spanish and English to the percentage of words known in each language. Their findings indicated a strong significant correlation between language exposure and vocabulary production. Children who had higher exposure to English produced more words in English, whereas those who had greater exposure to Spanish produced more words in Spanish. Using the CDI (Fenson et al., 1993), the proportion of translation equivalents (e.g., "dog" and "perro" [dog]—was reported to be an average of 30% for these toddlers (Pearson, Fernández, & Oller, 1995). This finding is consistent with Deuchar and Quay's (2000) in-depth report of a child learning English and Spanish simultaneously.

Studies of bilingual (Spanish-English) preschool children in the United States demonstrate lexical growth in L1 and L2, as well as interactions between L1 and L2. Overall, these studies demonstrate that vocabulary knowledge increases with age. Furthermore, for the children studied, early sequential bilinguals (those who started to learn English by 6 years of age), patterns of task performance depended in part on the language of testing. Peña, Bedore, and Zlatic (2002) examined how preschool and early school-age children generated items in categories in Spanish and English. Their participants were early sequential bilinguals who spoke Spanish in the home, and were learning or had learned English through their preschool and/or school program. Findings indicated effects for age. In other words, older children produced more correct items for given categories (e.g., animals, clothing, food) in comparison with younger children regardless of language. Thus, vocabulary growth continued to increase with age in both languages. The study also revealed that although children produced approximately the same number of items in each language, most of the items produced across the two languages were unique items (68.4%), whereas 31.6% of the items were translation equivalents, consistent with the results of Pearson and colleagues (1995) and Deuchar and Quay (2000). In addition, younger children produced fewer translation equivalents than older children for the categorization task. Finally, cultural experience associated with language appeared to play a role in patterns of task performance. For example, the most frequent response to the question, "What food do you eat at a birthday party?" was "cake" or "pastel" in both Spanish and English. When participants were responding in English, they frequently cited "hamburger" and "hot dogs," whereas participants speaking in Spanish frequently cited "arroz" (rice) and "frijoles" (beans).

In another study of early sequential bilingual preschool and school-age children (ages 4–6), Peña, Bedore, and Rappazzo (2003) studied how children performed on different semantic tasks (e.g., analogies, functions, linguistic concepts). The children in the study were subdivided into three groups according to language proficiency: predominantly Spanish-speaking, bilingual, and predominantly English-speaking. Findings indicated similar overall patterns within Spanish and within English. Specifically, both the predominantly Spanish speakers and bilingual speakers performed best on expressive functions in Spanish, whereas predominantly English speakers and bilingual speakers performed best on receptive similarities and differences in English. Furthermore, the bilingual children performed differently in each of their two languages. That is, the bilingual children did not mirror task performance in Spanish and English. Instead, they performed better on some tasks in English and other tasks in Spanish. It is important to note that there were small performance differences between the bilingual and the predominantly Spanish-speaking and predominantly English-speaking groups as well. Specifically, the bilingual speakers did not perform exactly the same as speakers in the predominantly English speaking and predominantly Spanish speaking groups. When performance on all of the tasks was added together to calculate a total score for each child, there were no total score differences among the groups either between or within language(s). Instead, different tasks contributed to the total score in different ways depending on the group (bilingual, predominantly English, predominantly Spanish) and language (English, Spanish).

Studies of vocabulary learning in bilingual individuals from school-age to young adulthood provide further information about development. Kohnert, Bates, and Hernandez (1999) and Kohnert (see Chapter 3) have studied vocabulary performance using a picture-naming task that evaluates both accuracy and response time. Their findings indicate vocabulary growth in early sequential bilinguals from kindergarten to college age. They found greater gains in English over time in comparison with growth in Spanish. Furthermore, they found a shift in language dominance from L1 (Spanish) to L2 (English) by the time children reached older adolescence (14–16 years old). Interestingly, accuracy versus reaction-time trade-offs were found for the 8- to 10-year-old group. This group named more items accurately in Spanish but was faster in English. On the other hand, the 11- to 13-year-old group showed no clear advantage in either language. The authors propose that while there was no "language loss" in either language, there was a shift in dominance from L1 to L2.

Kohnert and Bates (2002) found similar results on a follow-up picture-word verification study. In this task, participants confirmed whether a word presented verbally (through headphones) matched the picture with which it was presented. As before, this experiment was done in both a single-language condition and a mixed-language condition. Kohnert and Bates (2002) found no language differences in the younger groups (5–10 years old) for accuracy or reaction time. By the time the children were 11–13 years old, they performed better in English. This shift to better performance in English is slightly earlier than the findings on the production task (Kohnert et al., 1999).

IMPLICATIONS FOR BILINGUAL SEMANTIC TEST DEVELOPMENT

The limited availability of assessment tools designed for bilinguals makes vocabulary assessment challenging. An efficient way to improve vocabulary assessment with bilinguals would be to develop tools that take into consideration the developmental patterns of bilinguals. Specifically, this consideration would involve examining tasks that work best for that language in identifying semantic deficits, as well as examining how frequency of occurrence in the target language may affect vocabulary knowledge and acquisition. In this section, we first discuss issues related to the development of vocabulary assessment tools for the bilingual population and then discuss ways to assess vocabulary skills in bilinguals using tools already available.

In creating a valid test for measuring vocabulary skills in bilingual children, thorough exploration of the factors that contribute to vocabulary development in each language will foster tests that are appropriate for bilingual children. As noted, Peña and colleagues (Peña, 2001; Peña et al., 2003) found that children were better at performing some tasks in English than other tasks in Spanish. In terms of semantic test development, these results highlight the importance of selecting items based on the information they contribute to an overall score rather than trying to balance the items by type across the two languages. Tests of vocabulary skills in preschool and school-age children might explore performance in each language on a wide variety of semantic concepts, such as similarities and differences in objects, functions of objects, categorization, physical descriptors, and associations between words (Peña, 2001; Peña et al., 2003). This type of broad-based test would function to assess performance on various tasks across more than one language without favoring any one task that may be highly salient in one, but not the other, language. For example, in the Peña and colleagues (2003) study, children performed better on "function" tasks (requiring children to name or identify the functions of items) in Spanish, but they performed higher on "similarities and differences" tasks (requiring children to name and identify similarities and differences between two objects) in English.

In addition to task type, the frequency of occurrence of words is another important issue in the assessment of semantic skills. When creating a test in two languages for bilinguals, items that are representative of the two languages should be of equivalent difficulty. Because the difficulty level of a vocabulary item is primarily determined by the difficulty level of the word (especially with single word tests that minimize contextual cues), matching words on their frequency of occurrence in a language helps equate the difficulty level of the items (Tamayo, 1987). Many published materials on word frequency in different contexts are available in both Spanish and English that can be used to ensure that equivalent terms are not only equivalent in meaning but also are controlled for frequency (or difficulty).

Although a number of vocabulary tests have been developed for Spanish speakers, it is unclear whether they are equally appropriate for Spanish-English bilinguals in the United States. Many test developers have relied on translated assessment tasks or tests in English that have been adapted to Spanish. When test items are merely translated, however, item properties such as item difficulty may not be retained. Furthermore, tasks may not be equally relevant or have the same level of discriminant accuracy in L2 as in L1. One example of differences in item difficulty comes from Restrepo and Silverman (2001), who conducted a validity study on the Spanish version of the Preschool Language Scale–3 (Zimmerman, Steiner, & Pond, 1993). Using item analysis, they found that the Spanish version of the test did not follow a progression of increasing item difficulty. That is, items in what was supposed to be the "easier" portion of the test were too difficult for the Spanish speakers who responded to the test, and items in the "more difficult" portion of the test were answered correctly by many of the children.

The Test de Vocabulario en Imágenes Peabody (TVIP) (Dunn, Padilla, Lugo, & Dunn, 1986), the Spanish version of the Peabody Picture Vocabulary Test–Revised (PPVT-R) (Dunn & Dunn, 1981), illustrates how frequency of occurrence in the target language or language dialect needs to be taken into consideration. The Latin American version of the TVIP was developed for speakers in Spain, and items were ordered by difficulty based on those results. When the test was administered to Spanish speakers in Puerto Rico and Mexico, those speakers scored approximately one standard deviation below the norm developed for speakers in Spain (Dunn, 1987). As vocabulary knowledge is highly related to frequency, it is very possible that words have different frequencies of occurrence in various dialects of Spanish. Vocabulary knowledge is also highly regional; thus, it is possible that a word used in Spain to identify a concept may be unfamiliar to Spanish speakers in Puerto Rico and Mexico.

Obviously, we cannot wait until more tests that appropriately assess semantics in bilingual children become available to assess the skills of bilinguals. Based on current research on semantic development and task performance in Spanish-English bilinguals as well as findings from studies of available tests, however, a number of suggestions can be implemented. These applications will potentially improve the accuracy of assessment for bilinguals using semantic measures that are currently available.

IMPLICATIONS FOR ASSESSMENT AND INTERVENTION

Drawing from the research literature, guidelines on *how* to assess the vocabulary of bilinguals as well as *what* to assess may be developed. How to assess semantic knowledge involves making decisions about the language(s), context, and nature of assessment. What to assess involves the content of the test task itself.

Assessment

Assess Vocabulary in Both Languages Together

The work of Pearson and her colleagues has implications for how the bilingual lexicon should be calculated. In their experiments, they calculated different scores to evaluate children's vocabularies on the CDI (Fenson et al., 1993). In Pearson and colleagues' 1993 study, vocabulary development of Spanish bilinguals on the CDI was compared with monolingual norms. Specifically, they used a monolingual score in which they counted only the Spanish items or the English items. In addition, they used a total score—the sum total of the Spanish and English words produced, and a conceptual score—calculated as the total number of concepts produced. In other words, they counted translation equivalents (e.g., *pato*, duck) only once to obtain the conceptual score. In comparing production scores, when the better of the two monolingual scores (e.g., Spanish only or English only) were compared with scores of monolingual children, no significant differences were found in percentile scores. Pearson and colleagues (1993) reported that in each language the bilingual children produced fewer total words in comparison with the monolingual children, however. When raw scores were compared by age, the bilingual total score and the bilingual conceptual scores were comparable with the monolingual scores for production.

Studies by Pearson and colleagues (1995) and Peña and colleagues (2002) suggested that for young bilingual children, vocabulary items are divided among the two languages with some overlap (about 30%). Thus, in order to best capture young children's vocabulary, it is recommended that both languages be considered together, rather than separately, using conceptual scoring to account for items known in one language but not the other. In addition, Pearson and Fernández (1994) pointed out that exposure to a language strongly correlates with vocabulary production in that language, so whether children use translation equivalents depends in part on who speaks what language. Specifically, children whose caregivers use both languages are more likely to have translation equivalents in their vocabularies in comparison with children who are exposed to two different languages across two situations (e.g., home and school). This observation suggests that for assessment, it is important to conduct a detailed inventory to determine who interacts with the child and the language(s) in which such interactions occur (Gutiérrez-Clellen & Kreiter, 2003). For children who are sequential bilinguals and are learning Spanish at home and English at school, it may not be unusual for them to have fewer translation equivalents overall than simultaneous bilinguals. This finding highlights the importance of understanding the bilingual's language experiences. Experience with a language will influence the type of vocabulary used in each language. Information about language experience also can be obtained using a detailed inventory such as the CDI (Fenson et al., 1993) and the LDS (Rescorla, 1989). Typical language experiences of sequential bilinguals may account for some of the findings with preschool children learning English as a second language that indicate they often perform differently across languages depending on the nature of the task (Peña & Quinn, 1997; Peña et al., 2003).

Although there are no bilingual norms as of yet for the CDI, the research suggests that vocabulary development in bilinguals is similar (in terms of number of words produced and understood at milestone stages) to monolinguals. Thus, a conceptual score can be calculated and compared with the monolingual norms for an estimate of development. For older children, tests such as the Expressive One Word Vocabulary Test–Revised (EOWPVT-R) (Gardner, 1990) were only normed on monolingual English speakers. Studies of this test with bilingual children demonstrated that they performed significantly below the norm even when conceptual scoring was used, and that performance of children with and without language impairment was similar on the 1980 and 1990 versions of this test (Gardner, 1980; Peña, Iglesias, & Lidz, 2001; Peña & Quinn, 1997). The most recent revision of this test (Brownell, 2000) was normed with bilinguals in the United States, although it is still primarily a translation of the English version. Thus, it may not take into account the differences in frequency of occurrence of the words, differences in tasks children generally encounter in each language, or the possible need for basal and ceiling changes. Responses are accepted in either language, which improves estimates of vocabulary skills. The test publisher reported that for four groups of bilingual children: 1) speaks predominantly Spanish, 2) speaks predominantly Spanish with some knowledge of English, 3) speaks both languages with equal ease, and 4) speaks predominantly English with knowledge of Spanish, test score variance between groups did not exceed 3%. Based on those results, these groups were combined into one set of norms. These are significant improvements over older versions of the test; however, there are no current studies that examine the test's ability to discriminate between bilingual children with and without language impairment.

The TVIP (Dunn et al., 1986), the Spanish adaptation of the PPVT-R (Dunn & Dunn, 1981), another assessment tool described earlier in this chapter, may have applications with children learning Spanish in a monolingual environment or with recently arrived Spanish-speaking immigrants; however, because it was not normed with bilingual Spanish-English speakers and does not consider English vocabulary learning, it is not applicable to U.S. Spanish-English bilinguals. Umbel and colleagues (1992) compared 5-year-old bilingual children's vocabulary scores on the TVIP, with those of 8-year-old bilingual children (Dunn & Dunn, 1981; Dunn et al., 1986). They found that, on average, children responded correctly to 67% of the items in their age range on each language version, and responded correctly to an additional 8%–12% of the items in only one language. Some of the additional items included those in their nondominant language. Dunn (1987, 1988) reported that for bilingual children living in the United States, TVIP scores (Spanish alone), over time, were increasingly lower in comparison with the norm. These results suggest that for bilinguals, vocabulary testing in only their dominant language is not sufficient and potentially underestimates vocabulary knowledge, especially during the school-age years when bilingual children often experience a shift in their dominant language.

When using any standardized test instrument with bilingual children, it is important to test beyond the ceiling in both languages. Assessing beyond test ceilings will reduce problems caused by translated tests in which easier concepts appear first and more difficult appear concepts later.

Consider the Context of Assessment Tasks

The context and familiarity of the task also need to be taken into account. Some tasks may be highly unfamiliar to children. Providing a familiar context may help them to demonstrate what they know. For example, Fagundes, Haynes, Haak and Moran (1998) found that African American preschoolers scored higher on the Preschool Language Assessment Instrument (PLAI) (Blank, Rose, & Berlin, 1978) when the items were organized thematically. With respect to assessment of semantic knowledge, Peña and Quinn (1997) found that task familiarity influenced scores on two tasks. The more unfamiliar task, single-word naming, resulted in lower scores overall for both the Puerto Rican and African American children participating in the study. (Children with typical language development and those with suspected language impairment were not differentiated in this study.) The more familiar task of description of functions resulted in higher scores and significant differences between children with and without language impairment, however. Thus, for children from diverse language and cultural backgrounds, assessing vocabulary across contexts may reveal true knowledge and control for possible lack of task familiarity.

Semantic knowledge can be probed using techniques from interactive models such as dynamic assessment (test–teach–retest) and/or clinical interviewing (see Peña et al., 2001, and Peña, 2001, for more information about how to apply these techniques). These interactive methods of assessment have been proposed for testing bilinguals because they allow more insight into how children perform with varying amounts of examiner assistance. Dynamic assessment procedures often involve the use a test–teach–retest procedure to examine how quickly the child can learn and apply concepts. Clinical interviewing involves further probing of a child's answers in order to gain insight about their understanding of the task and of their own responses. These follow-up probes may provide information about how a child arrived at an answer. The examiner may ask a child why given answers were selected or rejected after administering the TVIP. For example, for músico (musician), a child might incorrectly select the ballerina, explaining that ballerinas dance to music. This demonstrates the child's general understanding of music even though there is a misunderstanding of the specific target.

Estimate Semantic Knowledge through Language Sampling

A number of language sampling measures have been used to explore semantic complexity in English-speaking children, including the number of different words used (NDW), the total number of words (TNW), and a value derived from NDW and TNW called the type–token ratio (TTR), which is the number of different words divided by the total number of words in a sample. As a rough guideline, in English, the higher the TTR value the more complex the semantic skills (Leadholm & Miller, 1992). There are certainly problems with the TTR measure and its components (NDW and TNW) that have been acknowledged. For example, TTR is highly dependent on sample length, though this can be controlled for; it does not evaluate the complexity of the relationships between words; and children who use a low TNW can end up with a high TTR simply because the smaller the denominator of an equation, the larger the result. With respect to the components of TTR, the familiarity of the topic, the type of language sample (e.g., narrative, picture description, conversation) and the child's rapport with the examiner are some of the variables that will affect those measures. These measures can be effectively used as a general indicator of word knowledge, organization, and use, however.

In Spanish, the same language sampling measures can be (and are) used. The same cautions apply, and it is important to note that such measures should only be used on a within-language basis. Often, when examiners have the same measure in two different languages, the initial response is to compare across languages. Because the structures of English and Spanish are different, however, different values for NDW, TNW, or TTR are likely, even for utterances or language samples that are of the same semantic complexity. As a simple illustration of the problems that can be encountered using these measures across languages, the sentences "They called me from the café" and "Me llamaron del café" are semantically equivalent but the English TNW is six, whereas the Spanish TNW is four. This type of difference across an entire language sample can produce very different numeric values in English and Spanish.

For collection of the language sample, it is important that materials and elicitation procedures used to elicit the sample are familiar to the child. Younger children may be very familiar with home routines of cooking, playing games with siblings, or going to a party. Older children with more school experience may converse better about situations they have read about, but not experienced. Narrative samples are another way that vocabulary use can be observed. Clinicians can observe selection of words as well as their use. For example, observing how children identify characters and their actions provides insight about the child's word knowledge. Possible word-finding difficulties can be observed during elicitation of a narrative sample as well.

Consider the Content of Semantic Assessment

Vocabulary testing alone may not adequately discriminate between children with and without language impairment (Gray, Plante, Vance, & Henrichsen, 1999; Peña et al., 2001), particularly for preschool and school-age children. For children from bilingual backgrounds, single word vocabulary may not demonstrate their semantic knowledge or ability (Peña & Quinn, 1997). The actual vocabulary used in the various tasks may influence how children from bilingual backgrounds perform on semantic assessment tasks. Children are not exposed to the same vocabulary across cultures. Children who are exposed to two languages may be exposed to different vocabulary as well as to different uses for that vocabulary in each of their languages. Thus, vocabulary testing should be broader, testing different types of semantic demands as well as different vocabulary sets. Semantic tasks such as categorization (Peña et al., 2002) or functions (Peña & Quinn, 1997) may be more indicative of how children organize and use vocabulary. Both home vocabulary and school vocabulary and the language in which a particular item is more likely to occur should be taken into account when testing semantic knowledge and use. In order to probe semantic knowledge more broadly, use of follow-up tests and teaching tasks in addition to single word vocabulary may help clinicians to better evaluate children's semantic knowledge. Some examples of tasks include those already discussed, such as linguistic concepts, categorization, functions, analogies, description, part–whole relationships, and definitions. For example, the use of Spanish and English single-word expressive and/or receptive vocabulary tests combined with a Spanish and English test of word associations and a language sample appropriate to each language would give a more accurate profile of a school-age child's semantic skills and knowledge.

Intervention

Intervention approaches for bilingual children should consider the contexts in which children learn L1 and L2. In addition, intervention plans should consider developmental milestones of each of the target languages as well as how the two languages might interact (e.g., forward and/or backward transfer) in language development and performance.

With respect to language development, as indicated previously, the current literature indicates that Spanish-speaking children follow many of the same developmental milestones for lexical development as that which has been reported in the literature on English language development. Differences in the structures of the two languages might affect specific developmental milestones. For example, the frequency and saliency of nouns as compared with verbs may differ based on grammatical structure and grammatical cues. Whereas word order in English is typically subject–verb–object, Spanish word order can vary greatly and carries the same meaning. For example, the English sentence *Miguel bought the book* could be expressed in Spanish as *Miguel compró el libro, El libro compró Miguel,* or *Compró el libro Miguel.* Furthermore, Spanish is a pro-drop language, in which the noun or pronoun is optional, even awkward after the reference has been established. In English, pronoun omission is considered a hallmark of language impairment (McGregor & Leonard, 1994). Thus, bilinguals who are tested in English may appear to have language impairments based on a test designed for monolingual English speakers.

Another example of a structural difference in English and Spanish is with prepositions. Both action and direction are encoded in the Spanish verb, whereas in English, the action is encoded in the verb while the direction (preposition) is frequently encoded in a verb satellite. An example of this is *"Se bajó* por la escalera" ("He *went down* the stairs"). As a result, bilingual children have been found to have much more difficulty with prepositions in Spanish than in English (Restrepo & Silverman, 2001). This again illustrates the importance of testing bilinguals in both languages.

Slobin (1985) suggested that information that occurs in the initial or final position of sentences may be more salient. Possible differences in frequency as well as position of nouns versus verbs in Spanish and English conversation may affect what children attend to as they learn the vocabulary of the target language. In their study of 10- to 30-month-old bilingual children, Pearson and Fernández (1994) reported that verbs developed once children had a large inventory of words. Yet, there were exceptions. Of the total number of children, 22% of the children had learned a high percentage of verbs in Spanish in their early vocabulary. Indeed, Spanish-speaking mothers are reported to use a higher number of verbs than nouns in their speech to toddlers (age 28 months) (Peña, Thal, Jackson-Maldonado, & Greenblatt, in preparation).

Other differences such as use of grammatical gender may also affect vocabulary learning. For example, Spanish marks grammatical gender (masculine and feminine) using articles (*el* and *la* and their plural counterparts), whereas English does not mark gender. In studies of Spanish-speaking children with language impairment, Bedore and Leonard (2001) found that noun-related morphology was a predictor of language impairment for Spanish. Similarly, Restrepo and Gutiérrez-Clellen (2001) found that

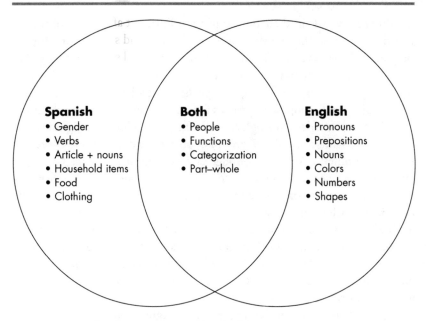

Figure 5.2.   Examples of intervention targets: Semantic learning.

Spanish-speaking children with language impairment made significantly more article omissions and gender agreement substitutions than children with typical language development. These findings have implications for teaching vocabulary in Spanish and are discussed further subsequently.

Based on both similarities and differences in Spanish and English language acquisition, we advocate both monolingual and bilingual approaches be used in designing intervention approaches for children. Generally, the monolingual approaches that we encourage target the kinds of vocabulary needed for each language independently and consider the structure and pragmatic uses of each language independently. In addition, a bilingual approach would be used to target the kinds of vocabulary that are needed for both languages, and that would maximize learning in each language (see Figure 5.2 for some of the areas of particular intervention need in each language and of overlap in both languages).

Monolingual Approaches

For children in bilingual environments, we have seen that the often-advocated testing and intervening in the language of dominance may not be the most appropriate approach. Bilingual children, although they may have a stronger language, learn vocabulary in both languages, often acquiring different words in their two languages. Furthermore, some of the semantic uses across the two languages may be different because of differing pragmatic demands and syntactic structure. Nonetheless, monolingual approaches that consider the unique configurations of each language may be appropriate for specific language goals in each language. These goals should take the developmental stages for that language into consideration.

First, with respect to English, goals for young children might include learning the names of objects, grouping objects, and describing objects in their environment. For preschool-age children, linguistic concepts such as color, number, shape, and size need to be incorporated into English language intervention goals. In addition, prepositions are learned relatively early in English (in comparison with Spanish), so they should be targeted in English first. For school-age children, goals in English might focus on analogies, multiple meanings, and definitions. All of these goals need to be targeted in the context of rich language input through use of scripts, narratives, and literature that will further expose children to the different ways that words are used and understood.

For Spanish, goals for young children might include learning names of objects with their appropriate article. As Spanish marks grammatical gender, learning the noun morphology will be important for Spanish syntax in addition to vocabulary learning. Furthermore, exposure to different verbs and their various forms may be critical because Spanish is a morphologically rich language. For preschool-age children, home language demands must also be taken into account; learning words to express kinship relationships, object functions, location, and names of extended family members may be important for interaction at home. For school-age children, vocabulary related to current events, literature, and popular television programs might be appropriate.

Bilingual Approaches

In addition to considering the unique aspects of each language, it is also important to maximize carryover between the two target languages whenever possible. Although the unique aspects of each language may not carry over to the other (e.g., grammatical gender in Spanish), certain semantic concepts need to be expressed in both languages.

Although the goal is not necessarily to learn translation equivalents of every word in the child's repertoire, words that are functional in both languages should be targeted. Recall that for young children, nouns may be more of a focus in English, whereas verbs may be more prominent for Spanish. As children master these semantic types in each language, it may be appropriate to target at least some of those types in the other language as well.

Tasks such as categorization and description of object functions might be targeted in both languages, but in contexts that match the communicative demands of each language. For example, categorization, functions, and part–whole relationships with respect to manipulatives, art supplies, and blocks might be highly relevant for school (and thus targeted in English), whereas categorization of kitchen tools, toys, and clothing might be applicable for home uses (and thus targeted initially in Spanish). Some areas, such as food, people, and colors, likely are relevant for both school and home settings (and thus targeted in both languages).

Information from a detailed inventory can be used to identify common activities that take place in the home, who participates in the activities, and the language used during the activities. Consulting parents about the types of vocabulary that their child needs and the contexts in which they will use such vocabulary will also lead to a productive intervention plan.

As more is learned about bilingual acquisition and the specific influences that English and Spanish have on each other, more specific guidelines will become available. Nevertheless, the current literature has yielded information that is applicable to clinical practice with children who have language impairment and who are learning both English and Spanish.

REFERENCES

Altarriba, J., & Mathis, K.M. (1997). Conceptual and lexical development in second language acquisition. *Journal of Memory and Language, 36*, 550–568.

Auza, A. (2002, June). *Derivational morphology and vocabulary growth in Mexican children.* Paper presented at the Joint Conference of the IX International Congress for the Study of Child Language and the Symposium on Research in Child Language Disorders, Madison, WI.

Bedore, L.M., & Leonard, L.B. (2001). Grammatical morphology deficits in Spanish-speaking children with specific language impairment. *Journal of Speech, Language, and Hearing Research, 44*, 905–924.

Blank, M., Rose, S., & Berlin, L. (1978). *Preschool Language Assessment Instrument.* San Antonio, TX: Psychological Corporation.

Brownell, R. (2000). *Expressive One Word Picture Vocabulary Test–2000 Edition.* Novato, CA: Academic Therapy Publications.

Chen, H.-C., & Ho, C. (1986). Development of Stroop interference in Chinese-English bilinguals. *Journal of Experimental Psychology: Learning, Memory, and Cognition, 12*, 397–401.

de Groot, A.M.B., & Hoeks, J.C.C. (1995). The development of bilingual memory: Evidence from word translation by trilinguals. *Language Learning, 45*(4), 683–724.

Deuchar, M., & Quay, S. (2000). *Bilingual acquisition: Theoretical implications of a case study.* New York: Oxford University Press.

Dufour, R., & Kroll, J.F. (1995). Matching words to concepts in two languages: A test of the concept mediation model of bilingual representation. *Memory & Cognition, 23,* 166–180.

Dunn, L.M. (1987). *Bilingual Hispanic children on the U.S. mainland: A review of research on their cognitive, linguistic, and scholastic development.* Circle Pines, MN: American Guidance Service.

Dunn, L.M. (1988). *Bilingual Hispanic children on the U.S. mainland: A review of research on their cognitive, linguistic, and scholastic development.* Honolulu, HI: Dunn Educational Services International.

Dunn, L., & Dunn, L. (1981). *Peabody Picture Vocabulary Test–Revised.* Circle Pines, MN: American Guidance Service.

Dunn, L., Padilla, R., Lugo, S., & Dunn, L. (1986). *Test de Vocabulario en Imágenes Peabody* (TVIP). Circle Pines, NM: American Guidance Service.

Fagundes, D., Haynes, W., Haak, N., & Moran, M. (1998). Task variability effects on the language test performance of Southern lower socioeconomic class African American and Caucasian five-year-olds. *Language, Speech, & Hearing Services in Schools, 29*(3), 148–157.

Fenson, L., Dale, P.S., Reznick, J.S., Thal, D., Bates, E., Hartung, J.P., Pethick, S., & Reilly, J.S. (1993). *MacArthur Communicative Development Inventories: User's guide and technical manual.* Baltimore: Paul H. Brookes Publishing Co. (Original copyright assigned 1992)

Gardner, M.F. (1980). *Expressive One-Word Picture Vocabulary Test.* Novato, CA: Academic Therapy Publications.

Gardner, M.F. (1990). *Expressive One-Word Picture Vocabulary Test–Revised.* Novato, CA: Academic Therapy Publications.

Gray, S., Plante, E., Vance, R., & Henrichsen, M. (1999). The diagnostic accuracy of four vocabulary tests administered to preschool-age children. *Language, Speech, and Hearing Services in Schools, 30,* 196–206.

Grosjean, F. (1998). Studying bilinguals: Methodological and conceptual issues. *Language and Cognition, 1,* 131–149.

Gutiérrez-Clellen, V.F., & Kreiter, J. (2003). Understanding child bilingual acquisition using parent and teacher reports. *Applied Psycholinguistics.*

Hernandez, A., Bates, E., & Avila, L. (1994). On-line sentence interpretation in Spanish-English bilinguals: What does it mean to be "in between"? *Applied Psycholinguistics, 15,* 417–446.

Hulit, L.M., & Howard, M.R. (1997). *Born to talk: An introduction to speech and language development.* Boston: Allyn & Bacon.

Jackson-Maldonado, D., Thal, D., Marchman, V., Bates, E., & Gutiérrez-Clellen, V. (1993). Early lexical development in Spanish-speaking infants and toddlers. *Journal of Child Language, 20*(3), 523–549.

Kohnert, K., & Bates, E. (2002). Balancing bilinguals, II: Lexical comprehension and cognitive processing in children learning Spanish and English. *Journal of Speech, Language, and Hearing Research, 45,* 347–359.

Kohnert, K., Bates, E., & Hernandez, A. (1999). Balancing bilinguals: Lexical-semantic production and cognitive processing in children learning Spanish and English. *Journal of Speech, Language, and Hearing Research, 42*(6), 1400–1413.

Kroll, J.F., & de Groot, A.M.B. (1997). Lexical and conceptual memory in the bilingual: Mapping form to meaning in two languages. In J.F. Kroll & A.M.B. de

Groot (Eds.), *Tutorials in bilingualism: Psycholinguistic perspectives* (pp. 169–199). Mahwah, NJ: Lawrence Erlbaum Associates.

Kroll, J.F., & Stewart, E. (1994). Category interference in a word-translation variant of the Stroop task. *Canadian Journal of Psychology, 44,* 76–83.

Leadholm, B., & Miller, J. (1992). *Language sample analysis: The Wisconsin guide.* Madison, WI: Bureau for Exceptional Children, Wisconsin Department of Public Instruction.

Leopold, W.F. (1939). *Speech development of a bilingual child: A linguist's record, I. Vocabulary growth in the first two years.* Evanston, IL: Northwestern University Press.

MacWhinney, B. (1987). Applying the competition model to bilingualism. *Applied Psycholinguistics, 8,* 315–327.

MacWhinney, B. (1997). Second language acquisition and the competition model. In J.F. Kroll & A.M.B. de Groot (Eds.), *Tutorials in bilingualism: Psycholinguistic perspectives* (pp. 113–142). Mahwah, NJ: Lawrence Erlbaum Associates.

MacWhinney, B., & Bates, E. (1989). *The crosslinguistic study of sentence processing.* New York: Cambridge University Press.

Mägiste, E. (1984). Stroop tasks and dichotic translation: The development of interference patterns in bilinguals. *Journal of Experimental Psychology: Learning, Memory, and Cognition, 10,* 304–315.

McGregor, K.K., & Leonard, L.B. (1994). Subject pronoun and article omissions in the speech of children with specific language impairment: A phonological interpretation. *Journal of Speech & Hearing Research, 37,* 171–181.

McLeod, B., & McLaughlin, B. (1986). Restructuring or automaticity? Reading in a second language. *Language Learning, 36,* 109–123.

Patterson, J. (1998). Expressive vocabulary development and word combinations of Spanish-English bilingual toddlers. *American Journal of Speech-Language Pathology, 7,* 46–56.

Pearson, B.Z., & Fernandez, S.C. (1994). Patterns of interaction in the lexical growth in two languages of bilingual infants and toddlers. *Language Learning, 44,* 617–653.

Pearson, B.Z., Fernández, S.C., Lewedeg, V., & Oller, D.K. (1997). The relation of input factors to lexical learning by bilingual infants. *Applied Psycholinguistics, 18,* 41–58.

Pearson, B.Z., Fernández, S.C., & Oller, D.K. (1993). Lexical development in bilingual infants and toddlers: Comparison to monolingual norms. *Language Learning, 43,* 93–120.

Pearson, B.Z., Fernández, S., & Oller, D. (1995). Cross-language synonyms in the lexicons of bilingual infants: One language or two? *Journal of Child Language, 22,* 345–368.

Peña, E. (2001). Assessment of semantic knowledge: Use of feedback and clinical interviewing. *Seminars in Speech and Language, 22,* 51–63.

Peña, E., Bedore, L.M., & Rappazzo, C. (2003). Comparison of Spanish, English, and bilingual children's performance across semantic tasks. *Language, Speech & Hearing Services in the Schools, 34,* 5–16.

Peña, E., Bedore, L.M., & Zlatic, R. (2002). Category generation performance of young bilingual children: The influence of condition, category, and language. *Journal of Speech, Language, and Hearing Research, 41,* 938–947.

Peña, E., Iglesias, A., & Lidz, C. (2001). Reducing test bias through dynamic assessment of children's word learning ability. *American Journal of Speech-Language Pathology, 10*, 138–154.

Peña, E., & Quinn, R. (1997). Task familiarity: Effects on the test performance of Puerto Rican and African American children. *Language, Speech, and Hearing Services in Schools, 28*, 323–332.

Peña, E., Thal, D., Jackson-Maldonado, D., & Greenblatt, R. (in preparation). *Characteristics of Latino mother speech to children in Mexico and the U.S.* Austin, TX.

Potter, M.C., So, K-f., et al. (1984). Lexical and conceptual representation in beginning and proficient bilinguals, *Journal of Verbal Learning and Verbal Behavior, 23*(1), 23–38.

Rescorla, L. (1989). The Language Development Survey: A screening tool for delayed language in toddlers. *Journal of Speech & Hearing Disorders, 54*, 587–599.

Rescorla, L., & Alley, A. (2001). Validation of the Language Development Survey (LDS): A parent report tool for identifying language delay in toddlers. *Journal of Speech Language & Hearing Research, 44*, 434–445.

Rescorla, L., Mirak, J., & Singh, L. (2000). Vocabulary growth in late talkers: Lexical development from 2;0 to 3;0. *Journal of Child Language, 27*(2), 293–311.

Restrepo, M.A., & Gutiérrez-Clellen, V.F. (2001). Article use in Spanish-speaking children with specific language impairment. *Journal of Child Language, 28*, 433–452.

Restrepo, M.A., & Silverman, S.W. (2001). Validity of the Spanish Preschool Language Scale-3 for use with bilingual children. *American Journal of Speech-Language Pathology, 10*, 382–393.

Slobin, D.I. (1985). Crosslinguistic evidence for the language-making capacity. In D.I. Slobin (Ed.), *The crosslinguistic study of language acquisition: Theoretical issues* (Vol. 2; pp. 1157–1256). Mahwah, NJ: Lawrence Erlbaum Associates.

Talamas, A., Kroll, J.F., & Dufour, R. (1999). Form-related errors in second language learning: A preliminary stage in the acquisition of L2 vocabulary. *Bilingualism: Language and cognition, 2*, 45–58.

Tamayo, J. (1987). Frequency of use as a measure of word difficulty in bilingual vocabulary test construction and translation. *Educational & Psychological Measurement, 47*, 893–902.

Thal, D., Jackson-Maldonado, D., & Acosta, D. (2000). Validity of a parent report measure of vocabulary and grammar for Spanish-speaking toddlers. *Journal of Speech-Language-Hearing Research, 5*, 1087–1100.

Tzelgow, J., Henik, A., & Leiser, D. (1990). Controlling Stroop interference: Evidence from a bilingual task. *Journal of Experimental Psychology, 16*, 760–771.

Umbel, V., Pearson, B.Z., Fernández, M.C., & Oller, D.K. (1992). Measuring bilingual children's receptive vocabularies. *Child Development, 63*, 1012–1020.

Zimmerman, I., Steiner, V., & Pond, R. (1993). *Preschool Language Scale-3, Spanish Edition.* San Antonio, TX: The Psychological Corporation.

SECTION III

From Grammar
to Discourse

CHAPTER 6

Verbal Morphology and Vocabulary in Monolinguals and Emergent Bilinguals

DONNA JACKSON-MALDONADO

I n the United States, bilingualism is now more prevalent than ever. Because of the influx of immigrants to the United States, more non-mainstream English-speaking children are entering the schools every day. According to the U.S. Bureau of the Census (2000), the Hispanic population in the United States has increased to a total of 38.8 million people. Thus, a larger segment of the U.S. population is now Spanish-English bilingual, and knowledge of language acquisition of both monolingual and bilingual children is necessary in order to effectively treat children with language disorders. The purpose of this chapter is to examine verb acquisition in monolingual and bilingual children.

First, I give a brief overview of studies in verb acquisition in monolingual and bilingual Spanish speakers. Then, I present theoretical perspectives that aid in the understanding of the acquisition of the verbal system. A description of the Spanish verbal system from a perspective of both tense and verb semantic aspect is provided. Based on this information, I describe two studies of verbal acquisition in groups of 20- and 28-month-old children. Data from the language of these two groups will be analyzed in terms of assessment and intervention issues.

This work was supported, in part, by a grant from the Consejo Nacional de Ciencia y Tecnología (CONACYT) to the author and a grant from the John D. and Catherine T. MacArthur Foundation to Donna Thal, San Diego State University. I would like to thank Donna Thal for the use of some of the data of this study, Ricardo Maldonado for his help, and all of the research assistants and students who helped collect and transcribe the data, especially Martha Beatriz Soto, Rosa Patricia Bárcenas, Gabriela Carrillo, Rocío Jaime, María del Rosario Mejorada González, and Mariana Hernández Hernández.

In most of the early studies of language acquisition, little attention was paid to morphological issues. As more work is now being done on languages with rich morphology, studies of verb inflection have become of interest. This has been further emphasized because morphology is one of the areas of language most affected in English-speaking children with specific language impairment (SLI) (Conti-Ramsden & Jones, 1997; Dromi, Leonard, Adam, & Zadunaisky-Ehrlich, 1999; Leonard, 1998; Leonard & Bortolini, 1998; Restrepo, 1998). For example, Leonard (1998) has shown that English-speaking children with SLI use fewer verb auxiliaries and past-tense markers (i.e., suffixes). In more inflected languages such as Spanish, Italian, and Hebrew, verb and/or noun inflections may be more complex depending on multiple language-specific principles (Bedore & Leonard, 2001; Dromi et al., 1999; Leonard & Bortolini, 1998; Restrepo & Kruth, 2000; Sanz-Torrent, Aguilar, Serrat, & Serra, 2001).

Moreover, children with SLI who are acquiring inflectionally rich languages have more difficulty acquiring particles (e.g., clitics) and arguments that are linked to the verb system rather than inflectional markers. Thus, they may have errors such as omissions of clitics (e.g., *peino* for *me peino*, *[I] comb* for *[I] comb myself*), but the verb inflection remains intact. Some aspects of verbal inflection are acquired differently in children with SLI. Restrepo and Kruth (2000) reported fewer verb errors than noun errors committed by bilingual (Spanish-English) children with SLI. The verb errors that the children exhibited consisted of person–verb agreement errors or failure to use imperfect and subjunctive forms in obligatory contexts. Bedore and Leonard (2001) contrasted the language skills of participants with SLI and typical controls and found significant differences between groups mostly on noun morphology. There was, however, a high percentage of infinitive substitutions for finite forms in SLI and MLU controls (e.g., the form *a comer [let's eat*, literally, *to eat]* was used instead of finite forms like *como ([I] eat)*.

Sanz-Torrent and colleagues (2001) compared monolingual Catalan and Spanish SLI children with monolingual and bilingual age and mean length of utterance–words (MLU-w) controls. They analyzed verb productivity by dividing verbs in different classes based on verb typology and verb arguments, using the Sebastián, Martí, Cuetos, and Carreiras (1996) categories. Verb typology consisted of (general-all-purpose) GAP verbs, concreteness, familiarity, and imaginability. Argument structure was described as the number of arguments and the semantic/syntactic structure of the following categories: external activity, self-activity, locatives, attention, temporality, and state of possession. No differences were found within groups except that children with SLI used fewer verbs of external activity or verbs in which the entity is external to the action, such as *romper* (to break) or *poner* (to put). Thus, they avoided verbs that have more arguments. It is worth noting, though, that participants in these studies were not separated for language preference, so monolinguals and bilinguals were grouped together.

Dromi and colleagues (1999) reported more errors in past tense than in present tense inflections in Hebrew-speaking children with SLI. Leonard and Bortolini (1998) found that Italian-speaking children with SLI used similar inflections but had difficulty with articles and certain pronouns or clitics, such as those that substitute objects, such as "Monica li ha visti" (Monica [them] saw).

Most of the research on Spanish-speaking children with SLI shows that the verb morphology is less vulnerable to error than noun morphology. Still, language disorders do not occur in children with SLI only. Research is lacking in other areas of language disorders such as focal lesion, hearing impairment, Down syndrome, and so forth. Other areas of morphology may be affected in these populations. Children with Down syndrome, for example, may exhibit difficulty with verb agreement or tense/aspect. Children with hearing impairment who use oral language also may omit tense/ person markers. Little, if any, systematic research in Spanish is available in this area. Furthermore, in order to make intervention more appropriate, information about typical language development in the target language or languages is necessary. As Spanish is a highly inflected language, developmental data about verb inflectional morphology need to be collected. Verb morphology still needs further research, both to identify differences between normal and disordered language development and to determine how the system is acquired in monolingual and bilingual children.

RELEVANT ISSUES IN BILINGUAL LANGUAGE ACQUISITION

One of the many issues now prevalent in the bilingual acquisition literature is whether language mixing and/or interference take place in verbal morphology at the first stages of simultaneous bilingualism. In order to understand the relationship between two languages, a brief definition of interference, mixing, and transfer is in order. The terms *interference, mixing,* and *transfer* often may be interchangeable. This chapter refers to mixing and transfer as interchangeable concepts and refrains from using the term *interference* because it would entail research that considers processing times in which there is an imposition of one structure over another (Lanza, 1997).

Mixing does not usually imply a processing limitation. Language mixing implies that two systems interact, and then the structure of one language or words used in that language are applied or used within the other. Reports on the amount and type of mixing vary considerably across all studies (de Houwer, 1995; Lanza, 1997). In language *transfer,* structures from one language are borrowed into the other temporarily (Paradis, Crago, Genesee, & Rice, 2003). Further details on these distinctions can be found in Hammers and Blanc (2000), Paradis and colleagues (2003), and Paradis and Genesee (1996).

Language mixing in bilingual children is an important issue because it lends support or rebuttal to two opposing positions of language representation in the brain: whether the two languages being acquired co-exist and interact as one system, also known as the holistic view, or whether bilinguals are like two monolinguals in one with two systems, also known as *the fractionated system* (Kohnert & Bates, 2002; Kohnert et al., 1999; Lanza (1997). Most of this discussion has pertained to simultaneous bilinguals (acquiring both languages at the same time from birth), but research with sequential bilinguals has shown that both languages are processed in a similar to way to simultaneous bilinguals, depending on the years of second language contact (Kohnert & Bates, 2002; Kohnert et al., 1999). Both Vihman (1999) and Kohnert and Bates (2002) added interesting proposals to the discussion, stating that what is important is not *whether* mixing occurs, but rather *what* is mixed or undifferentiated.

Language transfer is viewed by Kohnert, Bates, and Hernández (1999) from an interactive–activation account of language. Bilingualism is seen as a dynamic process in which transfer from one language to the other occurs. This transfer may be positive or negative (e.g., there may be interference that slows down the processing when cognitive demands are high).

The issues of mixing and transfer are relevant in understanding the research presented later in this chapter. We examine whether a linguistic component that is quite different in English and Spanish—verb morphology—may be particularly susceptible to mixing or transfer when the two languages are in contact during early stages of language acquisition.

Swain and Wesche (1975) and Vihman (1999) found that simultaneous bilinguals mixed morphological forms from one language to another. Based on the many proposals that mixing may be context and person oriented (see Lanza, 1997), language mixing in *emergent bilinguals* (i.e., individuals who speak primarily one language but are acquiring another) may add important information about the influence of one system on the other based on language-specific items.

VERB MORPHOLOGY ACQUISITION
WITH SPECIAL REFERENCE TO SPANISH

Most studies of verb acquisition that are based not solely on English have addressed the development of the morphology of the verbal system, most specifically on person and tense, or on the use of irregular forms. In Spanish language acquisition, for example, multiple studies have shown that children as young as 20 months begin using the present and preterit with first- and third-person markings, as well as the imperative (Ezeizabarrena Segurola, 1997a, 1997b; Fernández Martínez, 1994; Gathercole, Sebastián, & Soto, 1999; Gili Gaya, 1972; González, 1975, 1980, 1983; Hernández Pina, 1984; Maez, 1983; Montes Giraldo, 1974; 1976; Sebastián, Soto, & Gathercole, 2001). The early appearance of these morphological markers is followed by the present progressive, negative imperative, periphrastic future, and sparsely by other forms (see Anderson, 1995, and Bedore, 1999, for a brief review of the literature).

Several other studies on Spanish have supported the perspective that the acquisition of the verbal system is gradual. The influential work of Tomasello (1992), among others, has laid the groundwork for many researchers examining Spanish language development. A number of researchers have shown that in the early acquisition of Spanish verbal inflections, children acquire mostly one form for each verb at the initial stages of acquisition (Childers, Fernández, Echols, & Tomasello, 2001; Gathercole, Sebastián, & Soto, 1999, 2000; Sanz-Torrent et al., 2001; Sebastián, Soto, & Gathercole, 2001; Serrat, 1997; Serrat & Aparici, 2001). Later, these children exhibit gradual increases in verb complexity, forming contrasts both for person and tense. Data from Italian, a closely related Romance language, have also supported this perspective (Pizzuto & Caselli, 1992, 1994).

Verbal inflection has also been addressed by observing the relationship between tense and lexical aspect. Researchers have suggested that, in English, impending verbs have no marking, ongoing and action verbs use -*ing*, and completion or result verbs preferably are produced with an -*ed* ending (Behrend, 1990, 1995; Behrend, Harris, & Cartwright, 1995; Dowty, 1979; Tomasello, 1992; Tomasello & Kruger, 1992). Moreover, Slobin and colleagues (Sebastián & Slobin, 1994; Slobin, 1996; Slobin & Bocaz, 1988) have shown that the tense/aspect distinction is acquired early, and it guides the acquisition of verbal forms in Spanish.

In other Romance languages, the contrasts between impending and result verbs have been found, as well. Antinucci and Miller (1976) and Pizzutto and Caselli (1992, 1994), proposed that in Italian, the development of the verbal inflectional system is influenced by different linguistic components. Thus, tense/aspect and person may be acquired differently depending on input, pragmatic and cognitive contrasts, and language-specific restrictions. Similar results have been found for French (Bronckart & Sinclair, 1973). These researchers found that the *imparfait* (imperfect) (e.g., *elle marchait* [she walked] marked an ongoing action, whereas the *passé composé* (perfect) (e.g., *elle a marché* [she walked]), even with the same verb, gave a resultative meaning. Bassano (2000), also studying French speakers, showed that nonaction verbs were produced mostly in the present, whereas action verbs were inflected with a diversity of forms. In contrast, Cortés and Vila (1991) did not find a tense/aspect relation in Spanish-speaking children. Thus, most studies have shown a relation between specific morphological forms and tense/aspect relations. Only Cortés and Vila (1991) have shown conflicting results, but those results may be a product of methodological issues.

In previous research, my colleagues and I suggested that inflection is not applied in an across-the-board manner (Jackson-Maldonado & Maldonado, 2002). Rather, we found that forms appeared gradually and with specific inflections related to verb semantic aspect depending on MLU-w or verb vocabulary levels. Following a cognitive paradigm for the description of verbal morphology, we suggested that lexical verbal aspect pulls inflection in monolingual Spanish-speaking toddlers (Jackson-Maldonado & Maldonado, 2002; Jackson-Maldonado & Maldonado, in preparation). We proposed a classification of verbal content based on Dowty (1979), Mourelatos (1981), Talmy (1985, 1991), and Vendler (1967), and extending Shirai and Anderson (1995), Smiley and Huttenlocher (1995), and Tomasello (1992) (also see the section called Lexical Aspect Categories).

Verb Morphology Acquisition in Bilingual Children

Studies of verb morphology in bilingual children primarily have examined either each language separately or the amount of contact between languages. Bedore and Leonard (2001) studied Spanish-speaking children from monolingual Spanish families living in Southern California who had minimal contact with English. Thus, those children are what I call in this chapter *emergent bilinguals* (e–bilinguals). Using a morphology elicitation method, Bedore and Leonard observed the children's productions of nine verb morphemes and five nominal morphemes. Although their study included children with specific language impairment (SLI), the data from their MLU-matched controls are pertinent for this discussion. Their controls were between the ages of 2;4 and 3;10—the age of appearance of many verbal inflections. The children showed greatest accuracy for present, past, and infinitive forms both in number and person markings. They were accurate in their use of the singular and plural with the first and third person inflections. Other inflections were not studied.

Childers and colleagues (2001) studied two monolingual groups: English- and Spanish-speaking children. The study contrasted patterns of verb morphology in both languages using an experimental technique of novel and familiar verbs. They proposed that third-person singular forms were understood by age 3, with little or mostly incorrect use of plural forms. They also suggested that highly inflected languages such as Spanish do not present an advantage for acquiring the verb system. Thus, their data support a gradual development of verb morphology.

Another series of studies (Ezeizabarrena Segurola, 1997a, 1997b, 1998) addressed the acquisition of the verbal system in bilingual children, looking independently at each language. Specifically, Ezeizabarrena Segurola studied two Euskera- and Castilian Spanish–speaking children starting from when these children were 19 months old. She proposed that the children developed language-specific structures using two learning models. In Spanish, her findings showed that the first- and third-person singular were the first to appear and that singular forms were substituted for plural ones.

Types of Errors in Verbal Morphology

Bedore and Leonard (2001) completed an extensive study of errors of Spanish-speaking children with SLI in an experimental task using grammatical probes. MLU-matched controls between 2;4 and 3;10 were included in the study. All children were dominant Spanish speakers being brought up in an English environment (as were our subjects). The error data from their MLU controls are relevant to the types of productions observed in this study. Monolingual MLU controls had several verbal response patterns of person and number (Bedore & Leonard, 2001). Third person was mostly substituted for first person, and singular form was substituted for plural forms. Infinitives seldom replaced finite forms. Most frequent tense/aspect errors included using past for present tense or vice versa and present progressive (mostly) for third-person present, but also for past-tense forms.

Monolingual data may aid in determining whether errors are a product of second language contact or part of the typical developmental process. Serrat and Aparici (2001) studied verb errors in 10 children who spoke Spanish and/or Catalan (a related Romance language), whose ages ranged from 1;7 to 2;11. They found a low frequency of errors (7.2%) of several types. Errors included overgeneralizations of irregular forms, auxiliary omissions, and agreement (third person for first person) and tense errors. Overall, there were more agreement errors than tense errors. One curious fact was the substitution of infinitive forms for other inflections, mostly the present. Most of these substitutions disappeared with age. From the way data are presented, it is not possible to infer whether those errors were an effect of second language contact or related to first language acquisition. For the purpose of this discussion, the types of errors they described, independently of language contact, are relevant.

Most monolingual studies that have tangentially addressed error production were based on case studies (Ezeizabarrena Segurola, 1997b; Fernández Martínez, 1994; Gathercole et al., 1999; Hernández Pina, 1984) of one or two speakers of Spanish from Spain. Most authors reported that typically developing bilinguals commit errors such as using third-person singular for third-person plural, regularizing irregular forms, using infinitives for negative imperatives, and incorrectly using the two *to be* forms: *ser* and *estar*. Data from Gathercole and colleagues (1999), based on natural language samples of two children, reported a high percentage of errors in the first appearance of a verb. Errors were reduced considerably, however, once a form became productive. Most frequent errors were using first-person singular for third-person singular; imperatives and infinitives for presents, infinitives for imperatives, negative imperatives for imperatives, and over-regularizations. Data on regular–irregular overgeneralizations are one of the most frequently addressed forms in English acquisition (Marchman & Bates, 1994). Thus, substitutions within these types of verbs are, most probably, an effect of maturation in either monolinguals or bilinguals.

Most of the errors described were one-time errors. Errors occurring more than once were person errors and use of infinitives for finite forms (including imperatives). It must be noted, though, that even the errors occurring more than once occurred less frequently in the subsequent session with each of the two children observed.

The errors that have been described from all of the studies concur. There are overgeneralizations from regular to irregular verbs, person substitutions that create agreement errors (mostly third person for first or second and singular for plural forms), and infinitives occasionally replacing finite forms. Tense errors are mostly a mutual substitution of present and past.

The Critical Mass Hypothesis

As the previous discussion illustrates, most of the recent literature has stressed verbal inflectional stages and the relation between morphological markers and the semantic aspect of the verb. A different perspective, the interactionist/functional approach, stresses the relationship between grammar, specifically verb inflection, and the lexicon. The Critical Mass Hypothesis poses that the development within morphological items is triggered by an expansion or explosion of the lexicon (Bates & Goodman, 1997; Marchman & Bates, 1994). In Marchman and Bates's study, the use of regular and irregular verb markings was a product of the size of the verb vocabulary. Bassano (2000), using French data, augmented the hypothesis by showing that not only the size of the lexicon but also its structure and content explained morphological development. Thus, verb inflection may be a product of vocabulary growth rather than an independent form emerging solely within grammar.

Jackson-Maldonado and Maldonado (in preparation) showed that verb inflection increases over verb types as a product of verb vocabulary in 20- and 28-month-old monolingual Spanish speakers. They found a clear pattern of inflection types by the semantic aspects of verbs independent of the child's linguistic level. Past tense markers were applied to change-of-state verbs, whereas activity and state verbs were marked with the present, future, and progressive forms. A further analysis showed that the variety of verbs that were inflected (a means of determining productivity) increased with the children's verbal vocabulary. These findings are consistent with the Critical Mass Hypothesis whereby a relationship between grammar and the lexicon is shown.

The remainder of this chapter analyzes the use of the Spanish verb system in emerging bilingual children (Jackson-Maldonado & Maldonado, 2002; Jackson-Maldonado & Maldonado, in preparation). In order to fully understand how the system works, we give a brief description of the Spanish verb system and the lexical-semantic description of verbs before presenting the data from emergent bilinguals, which we define in this chapter as potential bilingual children whose parents report that they only speak the home language, Spanish.

Spanish Verbal Forms and Inflections

In Spanish, three verb classes correspond to an equal number of thematic vowels: root + -*ar* (e.g., *caminar*, to walk); root + -*er* (e.g., *comer*, to eat); and

Table 6.1.   Example of verb stem inflected for person and
number for the Spanish -ar conjugation in present indicative

Person	Number	Verb amar (to love)
First	Singular	am<u>o</u>
Second	Singular	am<u>as</u>
Third	Singular	am<u>a</u>
First	Plural	am<u>amos</u>
Third	Plural	am<u>an</u>

root + *ir* (e.g., *subir,* to go up). These verb classes are inflected for person, number, mood, tense, and aspect. Each person and number has a different form. Table 6.1 shows one verb stem inflected for person and number for the *-ar* conjugation in present indicative.

Lexical Aspect Categories

As is well known, lexical aspect is distinguished from morphological aspect. Whereas the former is part of the semantic composition of the verb, the latter is a marker indicating a perfective, imperfective, or progressive configuration of a specific event. This chapter assumes a three-way contrast based on the lexical aspect categories of verbs: states, activities, and changes of state (see Table 6.2).

- States are homogeneous temporal processes that endure or persist over unbounded stretches of time. They cannot be qualified as actions because they involve no dynamics and the state does not constitute a change.

- Activities express actions with no culmination or clear anticipated result. Every part of the process is of the same nature as the whole event. Most activities take present, future, and progressive tenses.

- Changes-of-state verbs are *telic*—that is, they denote a process with a punctual result or outcome. Changes of state involve heterogeneous

Table 6.2.   Lexical aspect categories

States	Activities	Changes of state
dónde está (where is it)	*duerme* (she sleeps)	*se cayó* (it fell)
cabe (it fits)	*camina* (she walks)	*se fue* (he left)
sirve (it works)	*vamos a buscar* (let's go look)	*para cortar* (to cut)
gusta (like it)	*come* (he eats)	*siéntate* (sit down)

processes that designate some result or outcome within a temporal stretch. The distinction between events is developed in a punctual manner. Verb vocabularies are not extensive enough in early child language development to merit a contrast between accomplishments and achievements. Accomplishments are process actions that end in sudden result whereas achievements are actions that culminate in the actual moment. Both imply a change of state. Thus, this class includes both accomplishments (e.g., *Break a glass*) and achievements (e.g., *Find the keys*).

Tense

All tenses in Spanish are marked by a set of suffixes inflected for number and person. The most frequent forms found in expressive child language are periphrastic future, progressive, present, and past. The imperative, which is a mood rather than a tense, carries the inflection of the third person present (e.g., *bájame*, get me down). The periphrastic future expresses an imminent future action that parallels the functions of the English *gonna* (i.e., a child's or slang version of *going to*). It is composed of the verb *ir* (go) + the main infinitive verb root: for example, *voy a jugar* ([I'm] gonna play).

The present progressive designates actions actually being carried out in the moment of speech. It is formed by the verb *estar* (current *be*) + the main verb root + gerund (*está jugando*, he is playing). The past refers to actions carried out before the moment of speech. It carries a specific inflection by verb class and person: *corrí* (ran), first-person singular; *corrió* (ran), third-person singular.

The present tense is the unmarked form in Spanish (see Jackson-Maldonado, in preparation). Some verbs are inflected with a present form although they only partially coincide with or are relevant to the present moment or the moment to which the utterance makes reference. Thus, although marked with a present morpheme, they may refer to the past, the future, or habitual actions. Only performatives may fully coincide with the moment of speech: "I hereby name you John" (Langacker 1987). Other present inflection forms may denote habitual, future actions: *Corro todas las mañanas* (I run every morning) and *Ahora vengo* (I will be back soon; literally—I come back now). The present is also marked for person: *camino* (walk, first-person singular) and *camina* (walk, third-person singular).

This study presents a comparison of verbal inflection and semantic aspect using the categories outlined. The results of a study with monolingual Spanish speakers (Jackson-Maldonado & Maldonado, 2002; Jackson-Maldonado & Maldonado, in preparation) are described and then these individuals are compared with emergent bilinguals.

METHOD

Participants

This study consisted of two groups of children. The first set was composed of monolingual children being raised in two cities in central Mexico. The monolingual Mexico residents are described in Jackson-Maldonado and Maldonado (2002, in preparation). There were a total of 40 children: 20 children who were 20 months old and 20 children who were 28 months old, divided into two groups based on their verb vocabulary or MLU-w.

The second set was composed of monolingual speakers of Spanish being raised in Southern California who had second language contact through their community (emergent bilinguals). Participants in the emergent bilingual group had limited contact with English through television or the environment in which they were living, and, often, they had school-age siblings who were learning English in the schools. A total of 39 children participated in this group. Nineteen were 20 months old and 20 were 28 months old.

Although U.S. participants were recruited as Spanish speakers, 70% of parents reported that their children had had contact with a second language. Of these, a total of 59% of the children had between one and five English words in their total word vocabularies. This means that the use of English in these children was incipient, and second language contact was already manifested in language use. Most of their vocabularies consisted of Spanish words, yet there was early contact with English that influenced their use of Spanish forms.

Because of the limited amount of English contact, we predicted that the developmental process of morphology of the emergent bilingual children would be quite similar to their monolingual peers in the first group. We also hypothesized that there would be a relationship between tense/aspect and verb inflection in which "aspect pulls tense" and that the process would be directly related to the size of the verb lexicon. We addressed the influence or mixing between languages as we described inflections and verb use that appear to be specific to these emerging bilinguals. This is particularly important both for assessment and intervention because it signals whether the acquisition of the verb system is affected when children have initial contact with two languages.

In this sample, some early language mixing in phrases and vocabulary was evident. A small percentage of children produced mixed Spanish and English phrases, such as "van al byebye" ([They] are going bye-bye), "ten baby" (Take this baby), and "peinar al baby" (Comb the baby's hair; literally, comb the baby]). The English used by the children consisted of words such as *baby, ball, bye, uh oh, cookies, penny, woof, cat, cheese, thank-you, quick, know, penny,* and *toilet.*

Instruments

Children in both groups participated in a larger study addressing the relation between language and cognition. They were observed in a series of eight different tasks or instruments. Data from two of those instruments will be discussed here. One is a parent report measure, MacArthur Inventarios del Desarrollo de Habilidades Comunicativas: Palabras y Enunciados (hereafter Inventario II; Jackson-Maldonado, Bates, & Thal, 2003; Jackson-Maldonado, Thal, et al., 2003). The other is a natural language sample.

MacArthur Inventarios del Desarrollo de Habilidades Comunicativas: Palabras y Enunciados

Inventario II, based on parent report, has been shown to be amply effective, reliable, and valid with children speaking both English and Spanish and with bilingual English-Spanish speakers (Jackson-Maldonado, Bates et al., 2003; Marchman & Martinez-Sussman, 2002; Thal, Jackson-Maldonado, & Acosta, 2000). It uses a checklist format in which parents are asked to *recognize* (rather than *recall*) the words their child uses by marking off the words that correspond to the child's current productions. Only one section requests that the parent write down phrases that the child says. This instrument is a cultural and linguistic adaptation of the Words and Sentences portion of Communicative Development Inventory (CDI; Fenson et al., 1993). Only the vocabulary production section of the Inventario II was used in this study (Jackson-Maldonado, Marchman, Thal, Bates, & Gutiérrez-Clellen, 1993; Jackson-Maldonado et al., 2003). This section is divided into 23 semantic categories of nouns, verbs, adjectives, adverbs, and function and/or grammatical words. The *acciones verbos* (action verbs) category, which was used to define verb vocabulary in this study, contains 103 verbs that are presented in the infinitive form. Instructions are given to the parent about how to recognize these words by giving examples of the verbs with different forms or conjugations. This instruction is given so the parents understand that if the child uses either the finite or infinitive form it should be marked on the form. The total number of *acciones* reported by the parents, regardless of whether they are inflected, was used as the total verb score to determine verb vocabulary levels.

Natural Language Samples

Research assistants and parents interacting with the children in a 35-minute session collected natural language samples in three segments. In the first segment, the children played with food, plates, cups, utensils, cars, colored blocks, a doll, a crib, a bottle, and a farm. In the second sample, they looked at books. In the third segment, the experimenter played with each child with tools, a brush and mirror, a necklace, a purse, farm animals, trucks, and wooden blocks.

RESULTS

Verb Characteristics of Monolinguals and Emergent Bilinguals

In order to determine the effect of second language contact on Spanish verb use, a brief description of the data on the verb characteristics of monolingual children is given. Then, data from both groups, the monolingual children and the emergent bilingual children, are compared to determine whether incipient contact with English affects verbal productions. Types of errors in both groups are also considered. Certain deictic words and conversational markers used by young children were not included in the analysis. Examples include the deictic word *mira* (look) (Clahsen, Aveledo, & Roca, 2002; Jackson-Maldonado, 2000) and *a ver* (let me see), which functions as a conversational marker (Jackson, 1989).

Data on the Monolingual Group

Data from the monolingual group are divided in two groups. Group 1 consisted of children with low verbal vocabularies, and Group 2 of children with high verbal vocabularies. A general description of the appearance of verb inflection in the monolingual group of children is consistent with previous studies of Spanish language development that describe verb types by age of appearance of each form (Beléndez Sotero, 1980; Ezeizabarrena Segurola, 1997a; 1997b; Fernández Martínez, 1994; Gathercole et al., 1999, 2000; Gili Gaya, 1972; Gonzalez, 1975, 1980, 1983; Hernández Pina, 1984; Maez, 1983; Montes Giraldo, 1974, 1976; Sebastián, Soto, & Gathercole, 2001; Serra et al., 2000; Serrat, 1997; see also summaries in Anderson, 1995, and Bedore, 1999). In our study, children in Group 1, who were at the beginning stages of language production (measured by MLU-w of 1.0 to 1.5 or a verb vocabulary of fewer than 50 verbs), typically used first- and third-person present. Examples included "quiere" ([he] wants), and "tengo" ([I] have); imperatives: "sácalo" (take it out) and

Table 6.3.   Number of verb types by aspect and inflection: Group 2

Inflection	States	Activities	Change of state
Imperative	0	5	9
Present	28	31	33
Preterit	3	3	21
Periphrastic future	0	13	14
Progressive	0	16	5
Infinitive	0	10	16
Imperfect	1	0	0
Subjunctive	1	1	3
Negative imperative	0	2	0
Total verbs	33	81	96

"toma" ("have this"); and first- and third-person preterite forms: "cayó" ([it] fell), and "rompí" ([I] broke [it]). There were very few productions of infinitives (by one or two children and one or two verb types only), such as "cortar" ([to] cut), and progressives, such as "está jugando" ([he] is playing). Imperatives appeared early for most children but they did not continue developing across age or language level. Usually, the same verbs appeared inflected with the imperative marker: "dame" (give me), "ten"/"toma" (literally, have this), "siéntate" (sit down), and "bájate" (get down). Moreover, as verb vocabulary size increased, imperative forms decreased.

As children mature linguistically (Group 2), with an increase in MLU-w (1.5 to 3.2) or verb vocabulary (more than 50 verbs), other inflections appeared with more verb types. The present and preterit continued to be produced frequently, but with more verb roots. Whereas at the earlier stage there might have been 10 change-of-state verbs in the present, at the second stage there were 33 (see Table 6.3). Furthermore, person inflections became more common, including first person plural. Examples included "ayudamos" ([we] help), "jugamos" ([we] play), and third-person plural present forms such as "aquí están" (here [they] are) and "suenan" ([they] sound). Person markers also developed in the preterit with third-person plural forms such as "se cayeron" ([they] fell) and first-person plural such as "va quitamos éste" ([we] took this one off).

Other inflections began to appear with more frequency in Group 2, as well. Periphrastic future forms were observed with different person and number inflections, for example, "vamos a buscar" ([we] are going to find), "va a comer" ([he] is going to eat), and "voy a jugar" ([I] am going to play). Progressives were produced mostly with singular inflections: "está llo-

Table 6.4.   Number of verb types by aspect and inflection for emergent bilingual children

Inflection	States	Activities	Change of State
Imperative	0	8	18
Present	26	22	37
Preterit	3	2	33
Periphrastic future	2	12	11
Progressive	0	8	0
Infinitive	0	11	13
Imperfect	2	0	0
Subjunctive	0	2	3
Negative imperative	0	0	0
Total verbs	33	65	115

rando" ([she] is crying) and infinitives were produced with periphrastic structures: "quiero dormir" ([I] want to sleep), "para hacer" (literally, for do). Subjunctives ("para que se despierte," literally, for to wake up), imperfects ("pensaba," [she] thought), and negative imperatives ("no hables," do not talk) appeared, but with only one or two exemplars from one or two children. Thus, inflectional types become more diversified with language maturity.

As illustrated in Jackson-Maldonado and Maldonado (2002, in preparation), a clear relationship exists between the inflectional types and the semantic aspect of the verb. In children with low verb vocabularies (less than 50 verbs), it is clear that verb semantic aspect pulls verb inflection. That is, types of verbs help determine verb inflection. For example, state verbs do not occur in the preterit and are produced mostly in the present ("quiere," [he] wants), and change-of-state verbs are mostly inflected with imperative ("ten/toma," have this; "dame," give me) and preterit forms ("acabó," [it] finished). Activity verbs are produced mostly in the present tense ("peino," I comb). This same pattern is observed as verb vocabulary increases (see Table 6.4). As children acquire more verbs in their vocabulary, tense/aspect inflection is used with more verb types and more person and number markers, although the same pattern of verbal aspect is being paired with distinct inflections.

One interesting finding in the monolingual data is that the present tense is an early acquired and highly productive form. Our data indicate that the form is frequent but the meaning does not relate to a current moment. For example, a child's production of "le cerramos" ([we] close it) means "we habitually close it" (i.e., we closed it before, close it now, and will close it in the future). It does not refer to the single act of closing in the present moment. Most of the present forms (particularly in change-of-state verbs) are produced as answers to questions about the future, relating to habitual actions, announcing future actions, or implying an imperative action rather than referring to the here and now. This is particularly important both for assessment and for intervention because children may use the present form to relate to time frames outside of the here and now. We also found a strong "overuse" of the present tense, suggesting that children might be talking not only about the present but also about future events. Thus, in intervention, present forms should not only be used to refer to current actions but also to the future.

In summary, the monolingual data show that a pattern of inflections is used first, but most importantly, *not all inflections are used with all verbs.* A clear pattern of certain inflections being produced emerges according to the semantic aspect of the verb. Furthermore, the present tense is a more generic tense that covers actions that can occur in the past, present, and future.

Comparisons Between Data on Monolinguals and Emergent Bilinguals

The number of verb types reported on the parental report (from the Acciones [Actions] category on Inventario II) is different between monolinguals and emergent bilinguals. Monolingual parents reported significantly more verb productions than did the parents of emergent bilinguals ($F = 4.52$, $df = 68$, $p = .037$). This frequency difference was only observed on parental report. Types and tokens from language sample scores are not significantly different between groups (see Tables 6.3 and 6.4).

The distribution of tense/aspect types and verb semantic aspect followed similar patterns in both groups. In Figure 6.1, it can be seen that in both groups (monolinguals and emergent bilinguals), change-of-state verbs are much more frequent than activity and state verbs. Whereas activity verbs are more frequent than state verbs in monolinguals, they occur similarly in emergent bilinguals. Only state verbs were significantly higher in monolinguals ($F = 17.15$, $df = 76$, $p = .04$).

The tense/aspect distribution is less similar across groups (see Figure 6.2). As noted on the figure, present tense verbs are, by far, the most frequent. As discussed in Jackson-Maldonado and Maldonado (2002, in preparation), this is because most present-tense forms do not manifest a meaning of ongoing events. In monolinguals, the order of frequency is in-

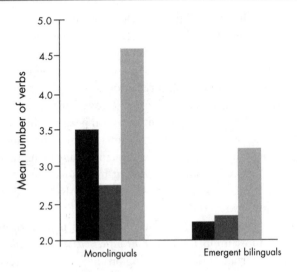

Figure 6.1.   Comparisons by lexical aspect of monolinguals and emergent bilinguals (Key: ■ = state; ■ = activity; ▬ = change of state).

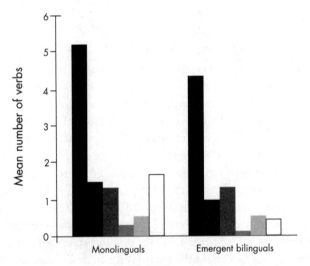

Figure 6.2.   Comparisons by inflection of monolinguals and emergent bilinguals (Key: ■ = present; ■ = past; ■ = imperative; ▬ = progressive; ▬ = future; □ = infinitive).

finitives > past > imperatives, although all forms are quite similar in their mean frequency of occurrence. For the emergent bilinguals, the mean frequency of occurrence is imperatives > past > infinitives. In the case of emergent bilinguals, however, the frequency of occurrence is more uneven. Particularly, infinitives are much less frequent than past tense forms. Still, there are no statistically significant differences for tense/aspect between both groups.

In order to compare the distribution of tense/aspect by semantic aspect of the verb, 28-month-old emergent bilinguals were compared with the data of participants with higher verb vocabularies (Jackson-Maldonado & Maldonado, in preparation). Present tense occurred with all semantic classes, although the forms used with change-of-state verbs were usually not true present tense. Most present tense verbs that represent the ongoing moment appear with state verbs: "no puedo" (I can't) or "tiene cabeza" (it has a head). Activity verbs that appear with a present inflection also refer to the current moment: "come" ([he] eats) or "ayudo" ([I] help). Present tense verbs that occur with change-of-state verbs mostly imply different moments of time: "te lo enseño" (I [will] show it to you) implies a future action or "con éste da golpes" (with this, [you] hit) defines a habitual, or ongoing, action. In clear accordance with the monolingual data, past and imperative forms occur almost exclusively with change-of-state verbs: "mordió" (he bit), "rompió" ([she] broke it), and "ábrele" (open it). Finally, present progressive forms are exhibited almost exclusively with activity verbs: "está comiendo" ([she] is eating).

The information available that shows the relation between tense/aspect and semantic aspect of the verb is quite similar between monolinguals and emergent bilinguals. This suggests that the verb system proposed by Dowty (1979) and Vendler (1967), among others, is supported by early child language data. It further suggests that verbal inflectional acquisition is a process that is highly dependent on the semantics of the verb and is not applied arbitrarily to any verb. What is of interest now is whether children use verbal inflectional rules without errors.

Errors in Verbal Productions

An important issue in the verb morpheme productions is whether all productions were accurate or whether the errors were due to either second language contact or typical developmental tendencies. As Spanish has a highly inflected verbal system with markings for person, number, tense/aspect and mood, and English has very few verbal inflections, we wanted to note if the children had begun to "mix" English with Spanish.

The children described in our study are similar to the children in Bedore and Leonard's study (2001) in terms of initial second language contact. Because of this second language contact, errors that are found could be part of the normal developmental process or a product of the interaction between languages. If they were only developmental errors, we would expect person substitutions (third person for second person, for instance), tense substitutions (present and past changes), and overgeneralizations. These types of errors occurred in the data, but there were also several different types of errors. Furthermore, not all children exhibited errors in their samples. Emergent bilingual children in this study had person or agreement substitutions and present–past changes, as had been found to be true for monolinguals in other reports (Bedore & Leonard, 2001; Fernández Martinez, 1994; Serrat & Aparici, 2001). A commonly stated error, overgeneralizations of irregular forms, was not found in these emergent bilinguals.

The different types of errors observed related to uses of *ser/estar*, mood selection, subject–verb agreement, change of grammatical category, clitic or preposition use, and other tense/aspect confusions. Table 6.5 presents types of verb errors committed by emergent bilingual children and examples with their English translations. The comment column describes the error in more detail. Some errors were consistent with results from previous studies: nonfinite for finite forms and absence of clitics and subject–verb agreement (person substitutions). Finite forms were substituted for infinitives, but the infinitives were also substituted for finite forms: "Voy a enseña una cosa" ([I] will to show you something) for "Voy a enseñar(te) una cosa" ([I] will show you something). In the periphrastic future, where an infinitive accompanies *-ir*, emergent bilinguals used an inflected rather than an infinitive form: "Van mira globo" (They look at the balloon) for "Van *a mirar* el globo" (They are going to look at the balloon). Also, the emergent bilingual children only substituted infinitives for preterits, whereas monolinguals have been reported to substitute infinitives for present forms in some studies (e.g., Bedore & Leonard, 2001) but not in others (e.g., Jackson-Maldonado & Maldonado, 2002, in preparation). Thus, at this point, whether such substitutions follow normal parameters is uncertain.

Other types of errors also seem to be specific to this emergent bilingual group. These children made grammatical category substitutions: "le dio come aquí" (She gave eat here) for "le dio de comer aquí" (She gave to eat here) or "le dio comida aquí" (She gave food here). A very typical type of error in adult learners of Spanish is *ser/estar* substitutions. The emergent bilingual children also produced this error type. Furthermore, emergent bilinguals used the subjunctive in place of the present form, a pattern that has not been reported for monolingual children.

Table 6.5.   Examples of verb errors produced by emergent bilingual children

Type of error	Example	Translation	Comment
Clitic prepositions	"Lo pegaste el carro"	You hit it the car	Redundant direct object, missing preposition
	"No mueven"	(They) don't move	Missing clitic *se*
Grammatical category	"Le dio come aquí"	They gave him eat (sic) here	Verb as a noun
Finite/infinite changes	"Voy a enseña una cosa"	(I) will to show you something	Finite in periphrastic future, missing clitic
	"Ya se llevar esto"	(He) to take this	Infinitive for past
	"Van mira globo"	(They) look the balloon	Finite for periphrastic future, missing preposition
Clitic	"Ese no amarró"	That one not tied	Missing clitic
ser/estar	"Está meter"	Is put in	Overuse *estar*, should be *se metió*
	"Está el peine"	Is a comb	Should be with *estar*
	"Vamos a estar"	We are going to be	*Estar* requires a predicate
Subject–verb disagreement	"Las manos se lava"	Hands is wash	Singular for plural
	"Otro faltan"	Another missing	Plural for singular
	"Yo me sienta"	I sit down	Third person for first person
	"Yo lo encontró"	I found	Third person for first person
Overuse of subjunctive	"Se la ponga"	I would put it on	Subjunctive for present
	"Se duerman"	(They) would fall asleep	Subjunctive for present (both would require a *que* phrase)

Clitics were either misused or omitted in the emergent bilingual group. Although Hernández Pina (1984) reported such omissions, other monolingual data from a larger corpus did not find these types of errors (Granados Velázquez, 1999; Jackson-Maldonado & Maldonado, 1998). Thus, the question of whether these clitic errors are specific to emergent bilinguals remains to be seen.

The error data from Table 6.5 are similar to those found in monolingual groups and may not be a product of monolingual developmental processes. It may be possible that some errors are a manifestation of some interference from English as children begin to adjust the information from two very distinct languages. Both monolinguals and emergent bilinguals make tense/aspect substitutions, subject–verb agreement errors, or person substitutions and, possibly, have clitic omissions. Yet, emergent bilinguals also have tense/aspect substitutions but in the opposite direction: They use finite for infinitive forms. They also have *ser/estar* errors, interchange verbs for nouns, and overuse the subjunctive. The latter type of emergent bilingual errors may be a product of second language contact and not developmental processes.

SUMMARY

This chapter has addressed the acquisition of verbal morphology by monolingual Spanish speakers and emergent bilinguals. More similarities than differences in the developmental patterns of the use of verb semantics and tense/aspect were noted. The striking difference was in the occurrence and types of errors.

Previous studies with monolingual children showed that verbal development could be explained as a slow construction of verb morphology in which verbal semantic aspect "pulls" tense/aspect inflection. Here it has been shown that the semantic aspect pulls tense in the emergent bilingual children. There is a clear picture of past and imperative inflections appearing with change-of-state verbs and true present-tense verbs appearing mostly with state verbs. These findings are consistent both with previous monolingual data and with theoretical considerations of verb morphology (Dowty, 1979; Vendler, 1967).

The use of verb inflection in tense/aspect markings is similar across both samples of children. Both groups show a clear pattern of the tense/aspect relation to semantic aspect and both groups begin producing similar verb inflections. A general pattern emerges that is consistent with what has been reported for most monolingual Spanish-speaking children: the early appearance of the present, preterit, infinitives, and imperatives, with lower frequencies of progressives and periphrastic future. The present-tense inflection form is the most frequent, although we have shown that this form does not always refer to an action that takes place in the present moment. Preterit and imperatives are relatively equally frequent in both groups. Still, the emergent (e-bilingual) sample produced more imperatives than preterits (although not significantly more); the converse was the case for monolingual children.

An important question is whether the incipient second language contact that these children have has somehow influenced their first language verbal system. This influence may be some kind of mixing or transfer phenomena similar to that noted by Vihman (1999), who found "borrowed" morphological forms from one language into the other in her young son's language. In the e-bilingual children, there were no real "borrowed" forms, but more like an adjustment of forms. No -*ed* past morphemes were added to Spanish roots; infinitive forms were not overused; English auxiliaries did not appear; and there were no bare verb roots. Rather, infinitive forms appeared where there should have been finite ones (as is true in monolinguals). In addition, there was an absence or overuse of clitics and prepositions. Adult learners of Spanish as a second language frequently have difficulty with subject–verb agreement and *ser/estar* distinctions. The e-bilinguals, as well, produce errors within these categories, although they are infrequent. Moreover, emergent bilinguals are mostly in control of their verbal use system, but incipient effects of a second language contact begin to appear, because children produce errors that are neither borrowed forms from English nor are they typical monolingual errors.

Errors could be a manifestation of typical development, but most of the children's error types in this sample of e-bilinguals were distinct from those reported for monolinguals. Errors for monolingual children were reported as infrequent and consisting of substitutions of person and number markings and overgeneralizations of irregular verb forms (Bedore & Leonard, 2001; Ezeizabarrena, 1997a, 1998b; Fernández Martínez, 1994; Gathercole et al., 1999; Hernández Pina, 1984; Serrat & Aparici, 2001). The participants described in Jackson-Maldonado and Maldonado's study data (in preparation) did not show evidence of those errors.

IMPLICATIONS FOR ASSESSMENT AND INTERVENTION

What the monolingual and emergent bilingual Spanish verb data have shown is that the relation between tense/aspect and semantics in the acquisition of the verbal system is highly systematic and specific. Children produce specific verbs with specific inflections. Past tense appears with change-of-state verbs, progressive tense appears with activity verbs, and present tense appears with state and activity verbs. Clearly, three inflections appear early on: present, preterit, and imperative. Most language tests or intervention programs do not follow the tense/aspect and semantic aspect relations and do not include the most frequent inflections. In the *Test de Vocabulario en Imágenes Peabody* (TVIP; Dunn, Padilla, Lugo, & Dunn, 1986), verbs appear in the infinitive form. In the *Preschool Language Scale–3* (PLS-3; Zimmerman, Steiner, & Pond, 1993) and Preschool Language Scale–4 (PLS-4; Zimmerman, Steiner, & Pond, 2001), the first test items with verbs are presented in the progressive form, followed by the preterit. In the *Screening Test of Spanish Grammar* (STSG; Toronto, 1973), the change-of-state verb *subir* (to go up) appears in the future tense rather than the preterit tense (Jackson-Maldonado, 1988, 1999). In intervention, usually, stress is placed on the dominance of one verb inflection at a time independently of the semantic type of each verb. The results of our studies would suggest that language tests use more verbal inflections and that they be applied to its specific verb semantic aspect type. In intervention, it is clear that inflections need to be taught in a more diverse way and should relate to verb semantics.

Another result that has implications both for assessment and intervention is that imperatives are forms that are acquired early but they do not develop at the same rate as other inflections. Imperatives are most useful both in comprehension and in production at the *earliest* stages of development. Present- and past-tense markers, rather than the imperative, should be used initially for verb comprehension and production. Subsequently, progressive and periphrastic future tenses should be introduced.

The implication for assessment is that appropriate verb roots need to be selected for testing specific tense forms. Thus, change-of-state verbs should not be used to elicit present forms but should be used specifically with the preterit tense and later with the periphrastic future tense. State verbs should be used to elicit the present tense but not the past tense. Activity verbs are more diverse and appear with the present, present progressive, and periphrastic future tenses. Imperatives first appear with specific change-of-state verbs mostly related to definite actions, such as interchange of objects and movements: *siéntate* (sit down), *párate* (stand up), *tapa* (cover up), and *toca* (touch). Overall, change-of-state verbs are the most frequently used type of verbs in early acquisition. This is true for both monolinguals and emergent bilinguals.

Another important issue is the appearance of production errors. What the literature has shown is that typically developing children produce errors, although less frequently than children with SLI (Restrepo, 1998). Some errors are a result of the ways children manifests their use of the verb system, most specifically by producing overgeneralizations of irregular forms. Other errors may illustrate second language contact but they do not constitute language "deviance." When, or if, a second language begins to influence the first language may depend on the complexity, frequency, salience, and informativeness of the items. It seems that general verb inflection is an area of strength, but when verbs appear with clitics and prepositions, errors such as omissions may be more likely. Furthermore, the *ser/estar* distinction may be affected by contact with a language that does not have such a distinction. The bottom line is that errors should be expected; the frequency and type of the error is what should be considered.

Several other implications are indicated for assessment and intervention. Tests need to be based on Spanish language developmental data in order to determine ages or levels at which verb or verbal argument errors are acquired. Many errors have been considered as a sign of a disorder when they may be a manifestation of a typical developmental process. For intervention, committing many errors may mean that a child is "thinking" about language and beginning to put to practice a set of morphosyntactic rules. This would be a positive process. The types of errors that the child exhibits during intervention should be carefully monitored to determine whether the child is following a rule system that will lead to appropriate verbal morphology or whether he or she is putting together words and forms inadequately. As clitics and prepositions (related to verb arguments) seem to be sensitive items, special attention needs to be paid to the early and frequent introduction of these forms. Sentences in which verbs appear with object clitics could be introduced and monitored frequently. Verbs that are accompanied by prepositions that introduce object arguments should also be a frequent part of intervention. These are elements that are less salient and, thus, can be more affected. By placing attention on them, strategies for working on other less-salient items (e.g., articles) might also be stimulated.

The data from the monolingual children indicated that verb inflection increases in productivity as a result of the increase in verb vocabulary. This means that in order to create a more diverse inflectional system, new verbs need to be taught. It also implies, in assessment, that in order to evaluate verbal inflection, the total number of verbs in a child's lexicon should be considered first. If the child has few verbs in his or her lexicon, few inflections will most probably be produced.

The study of verb morphology has become of interest as languages other than English have become the focus of language researchers' attention. As more bilingual children require services for language intervention, the need for understanding how children's first language (if it is not English) may influence the development of the acquisition of their second language and how they process language in general becomes greater. This information may be applied for both assessment and intervention. The data on verbal inflection development presented in this chapter may aid in the development of better language tests that take into consideration how the Spanish verbal system is acquired. The relation between inflection, the semantic verb system, and verb vocabulary, should be considered. The verbal inflectional system is a window into the relation between words and grammar. This relation may be held constant in the treatment of monolingual and bilingual children.

REFERENCES

Anderson, R. (1995). Spanish morphological and syntactic development. In H. Kayser (Ed.), *Bilingual speech-language pathology: A Hispanic focus* (pp. 41–73). San Diego: Singular Publishing Group.

Antinucci, F., & Miller, R. (1976). How children talk about what happened. *Journal of Child Language, 3*, 167–189

Bassano, D. (2000). Early development of nouns and verbs in French: Exploring the interface between lexicon and grammar. *Journal of Child Language, 27*, 521–560.

Bates, E., & Goodman, J. (1997). On the inseparability of grammar and the lexicon: evidence from acquisition, aphasia and real-time processing. *Language and Cognitive Processes, 12*, 507–584.

Bedore, L. (1999). The acquisition of Spanish. In O.L. Taylor & L. Leonard (Eds), *Language acquisition across North America: Cross-cultural and cross-linguistic perspectives* (pp. 157–207). San Diego: Singular Publishing Group.

Bedore, L., & Leonard, L. (2001). Grammatical morphology deficit in Spanish-speaking children with specific language impairment. *Journal of Speech, Language, and Hearing Research, 44*, 905–924.

Behrend, D.A. (1990). The development of verb concepts: Children's use of verbs to label familiar and novel events. *Child Development, 61*, 681–96.

Behrend, D.A. (1995). Processes involved in the initial mapping of verb meanings. In M. Tomasello & W.E. Merriman (Eds.), *Beyond names for things* (pp. 251–276). Mahwah, NJ: Lawrence Erlbaum Associates.

Behrend, D.A., Harris, L., & Cartwright, K. (1995) Morphological cues to verb meaning: verb inflections and the initial mapping of verb meanings. *Journal of Child Language, 22*, 89–106.

Beléndez Sotero, P. (1980). *Repetitions and the acquisition of the Spanish verb system.* Unpublished doctoral dissertation, Harvard School of Education, Cambridge, MA.

Bronckart, J.P., & Sinclair, H. (1973). Time, tense and aspect. *Cognition, 2*, 107–130.

Childers, J.B., Fernández, A.N., Echols, C.H., & Tomasello, M. (2001). Experimental investigations of children's understanding and use of verb morphology: Spanish and English speaking 2½- and 3-year-old children. In M. Almgren, A. Barreña, M.J. Ezeizabarrena, I. Idiazabal, & B. MacWhinney (Eds.), *Research in child language acquisition: Proceedings of the 8th Conference of the International Association for the Study of Child Language* (pp. 104–127). Somerville, MA: Cascadilla Press.

Clahsen, H., Aveledo, F., & Roca, I. (2002). The development of regular and irregular verb inflection in Spanish child language. *Journal of Child Language, 29*, 591–622.

Conti-Ramsden, G., & Jones, M. (1997). Verb use in specific language impairment. *Journal of Speech, Language, and Hearing Research, 40*, 1298–1313.

Cortés, M., & Vila, I. (1991). Uso y función de las formas temporales en el habla infantil [Use and function of temporal forms in infant speech]. *Infancia y Aprendizaje, 53*, 17–43

de Houwer, A. (1995). Bilingual language acquisition. In P. Fletcher & B. MacWhinney (Eds.), *The handbook of child language* (pp. 219–250). Oxford, UK: Blackwell.

Dowty, D. (1979). *Word meaning and Montague grammar.* Dordrecht, Germany: Reidel.

Dromi, E., Leonard, L.B., Adam, G., & Zadunaisky-Ehrlich, S. (1999). Verb agreement morphology in Hebrew-speaking children with Specific Language Impairment. *Journal of Speech, Language, and Hearing Research, 42*, 1414–1431.

Dunn, L.D., Padilla, E., Lugo, D., & Dunn, L. (1986). *Test de Vocabulario en Imágenes Peabody* (TVIP). Circle Pines, MN: American Guidance Service.

Ezeizabarrena Segurola, M.J. (1997a). *Adquisición de la morfología verbal en euskera y castellano por niños bilingües* [The acquisition of verbal morphology in Euskera and Castillian Spanish bilingual children]. Unpublished doctoral dissertation, University of Hamburg, Germany.

Ezeizabarrena Segurola, M.J. (1997b). Morfemas de concordancia con el sujeto y con los objetos en el castellano infantil [Subject and object agreement morphemes in Castilian Spanish speaking children]. In A.T. Pérez-Leroux & W.R. Glass (Eds.), *Contemporary perspectives on the acquisition of Spanish: Developing grammars* (Vol. 1) (pp. 21–36). Somerville, MA: Cascadilla Press.

Ezeizabarrena Segurola, M.J. (1998). *Dos sistemas de finitud verbal, dos modos de aprendizaje: Euskera y castellano* [Two finite verbal systems, two ways to learn: Euskera and Castilian Spanish]. Seminar presented at the II Mexican Language Acquisition Annual Meeting. Guadalajara, Mexico.

Fenson, L., Dale, P., Reznick, J.S., Thal, D., Bates, E., Hartung, J., Pethick, S., & Reilly, J. (1993). *The MacArthur Communicative Development Inventories: User's Guide and Technical Manual.* San Diego: Singular Publishing Group.

Fernández Martínez, A. (1994). El aprendizaje de los morfemas verbales. Datos de un estudio longitudinal. La adquisición de la lengua española. [The learning of verbal morphemes: Data from a longitudinal study]. In S. López-Ornat (Ed.), *La adquisición de la lengua española* [The acquisition of Spanish] (pp. 29–46). Madrid: Siglo XXI.

Gathercole, V.M., Sebastián, E., & Soto, P. (1999). The early acquisition of Spanish verbal morphology: across-the-board or piecemeal knowledge? *International Journal of Bilingualism, 2*, 72–89.

Gathercole, V.M., Sebastián, E., & Soto, P. (2000). *The acquisition of linguistic person by Spanish-speaking children.* Presentation at the International Conference on Infant Studies, Brighton, England.

Gili Gaya, S. (1972). *Estudios de lenguaje infantil* [Studies of child language]. Barcelona: Vox.

González, G. (1975). The acquisition of grammatical structures by Mexican-American children. In E. Hernández-Chavez, A. Cohen, & A. Beltram. (Eds.), *El lenguaje de los chicanos* [The language of the Chicanos] (pp. 221–237). Washington, DC: Center for Applied Linguistics.

González, G. (1980). The acquisition of verb tenses and temporal expressions in Spanish: Age 2.0–4.6. *Bilingual Education Papers Series, 4*, 3–40.

González, G. (1983). Expressing time through verb tenses and temporal expressions in Spanish: Age 2.0–4.6. *NABE Journal, 7*, 69–82.

Granados Velázquez, J.L. (1999). *Adquisición temprana del clítico de objeto en español* [The early acquisition of object clitics in Spanish]. Unpublished master's thesis, Universidad Autónoma de Querétaro, México.

Hammers, J.F., & Blanc, J.H.A. (2000). *Bilinguality and bilingualism* (2nd ed.). Cambridge, UK: Cambridge University Press.

Hernández Pina, F. (1984). *Teorías psico-sociolingüísticas y su aplicación a la adquisición del español como lengua materna* [Psych-sociolinguistic theories and their application to the acquisition of Spanish as a first language]. Madrid: Siglo XXI.

Jackson-Maldonado, D. (1988). Evaluación del lenguaje infantil: Enfoque transcultural [The assessment of child language: A transcultural focus]. In A. Ardila & F. Ostrosky-Solis (Eds.), *Lenguaje oral y escrito* [Oral and written language] (pp. 92–118). México D.F., México: Trillas.

Jackson, D. (1989). *Una palabra: Multiplicidad de funciones e intenciones* [One word: Multiple functions and intentions]. Unpublished doctoral dissertation, El Colegio de México, México.

Jackson-Maldonado, D. (1999). Early language assessment for Spanish-speaking children: Border realities. In T. Fletcher & C. Bos (Eds.), Helping individuals with disabilities and their families. *The Bilingual Review Special Issue, 25*(1 & 2), 35–52.

Jackson-Maldonado, D. (2000). *Verbal deixis: The case of "mira" in Spanish-speaking infants.* Poster presented at the International Conference on Infant Studies. Brighton, England.

Jackson-Maldonado, D., Bates, E., & Thal, D.J. (2003). *MacArthur Inventarios del Desarrollo de Habilidades Comunicativas.* Baltimore: Paul H. Brookes Publishing Co.

Jackson-Maldonado, D., & Maldonado, R. (1998). Reflexive and middle markers in early child language acquisition: Evidence from Mexican Spanish. *First Language, 18*, 403–429.

Jackson-Maldonado, D., & Maldonado, R. (2002). Determinaciones semánticas de la flexión verbal en la adquisición temprana del español [Semantic determinants of verbal inflexion in the early acquisition of Spanish]. In C. Rojas & L. de León (Eds.), *Estudios de adquisición del lenguaje. Español y lenguas indígenas* [Studies in the acquisition of language: Spanish and indigenous languages] (pp. 165–200). México: CIESAS-IIF UNAM.

Jackson-Maldonado, D., & Maldonado, R. (2004). *Aspect determinants of the verbal inflection in Spanish-speaking toddlers.*

Jackson-Maldonado, D., Marchman, V., Thal, D., Bates, E., & Gutiérrez-Clellen, V. (1993). Early lexical acquisition in Spanish-speaking infants and toddlers. *Journal of Child Language, 20*, 523–550.

Jackson-Maldonado, D., Thal, D.J., Fenson, L., Marchman, V.A., Newton, T., Fenson, L., & Conboy, B. (2003). *MacArthur Inventarios del Desarrollo de Habilidades Comunicativas: User's guide and technical manual.* Baltimore: Paul H. Brookes Publishing Co.

Kohnert, K., & Bates, E. (2002). Balancing bilinguals, II: Lexical comprehension and cognitive processes. *Journal of Speech, Language, and Hearing Research, 45,* 347–359.

Kohnert, K., Bates, E., & Hernández, A. (1999). Balancing bilinguals: Lexical-semantic production and cognitive processing in children learning Spanish and English. *Journal of Speech, Language, and Hearing Research, 42,* 1400–1413.

Langacker, R. (1987). *Foundations of cognitive grammar.* Stanford, CA: Stanford University Press.

Lanza, E. (1997). *Language mixing in infant bilingualism: A sociolinguistic perspective.* Oxford: Oxford University Press.

Leonard, L. (1998). *Children with specific language impairment.* Cambridge: MIT Press.

Leonard, L., & Bortolini, U. (1998). Grammatical morphology and the role of weak syllables in the speech of Italian speaking children with specific language impairment. *Journal of Speech, Language, and Hearing Research, 41,* 1363–1374.

Maez, L. (1983). The acquisition of noun and verb morphology in 18- to 24-month-old Spanish speaking children, *NABE Journal, 7,* 53–68.

Marchman, V., & Bates, E. (1994). Continuity in lexical and morphological development: A test of the critical mass hypothesis. *Journal of Child Language, 21,* 339–366.

Marchman, V., & Martínez-Sussman, C. (2002). Concurrent validity of caregiver/parent report measures of language for children who are learning both English and Spanish. *Journal of Speech, Language, and Hearing Research, 45,* 983–997.

Montes Giraldo, J.J. (1974). Esquema ontogénico del desarrollo del lenguaje y otras cuestiones del habla infantil [An onthogenetic schema of the development of language and other matters of child language]. *Thesaurus: Boletín del Instituto Caro y Cuervo, 29,* 254–270.

Montes Giraldo, J.J. (1976). El sistema, la norma y el aprendizaje de la lengua [Systematicity, normativity and the learning of language]. *Thesaurus: Boletín del Instituto Caro y Cuervo, 31,* 14–40.

Mourelatos, A. (1981). Events, processes and states. In P.J. Tedesci & A. Zaenen (Eds.), *Syntax and semantics: Tense and aspect* (Vol. 14, pp. 191–212). New York: Academic Press.

Paradis, J., Crago, M., Genesee, F., & Rice, M. (2003). French-English bilingual children with SLI: How do they compare with their monolingual peers? *Journal of Speech, Language, and Hearing Research, 46,* 113–127.

Paradis, J., & Genesee, F. (1996). Syntactic acquisition in bilingual children: Autonomous or interdependence? *Studies in Second Language Acquisition, 18,* 1–25.

Pizzuto, E., & Caselli, M.C. (1992). The acquisition of Italian morphology: implication for models of language development. *Journal of Child Language, 19,* 491–557.

Pizzuto, E., & Caselli, M.C. (1994). The acquisition of Italian verb morphology in a cross-linguistic perspective. In Y. Levy (Ed.), *Other children, other languages: Is-*

sues in the theory of language acquisition (pp. 137–187). Mahwah, NJ: Lawrence Erlbaum Associates.

Restrepo, M.A. (1998). Identifiers of predominantly Spanish-speaking children with language impairment. *Journal of Speech, Language, and Hearing Research, 41*, 1398–1411.

Restrepo, M.A., & Kruth, K. (2000). Grammatical characteristics of a Spanish–English bilingual child with specific language impairment. *Communication Disorders Quarterly, 21*, 66–76.

Sanz-Torrent, M., Aguilar, E., Serrat, E., & Serra, M. (2001). Verb type production in Catalan and Spanish children with SLI. In M. Almgren, A. Barreña, M.J. Ezeizabarrena, I. Idiazabal, & B. MacWhinney (Eds.), *Research in child language acquisition: Proceedings of the 8th Conference of the International Association for the Study of Child Language* (pp. 909–922). Somerville, MA: Cascadilla Press.

Sebastián, E., & Slobin, D.I. (1994). Development of linguistic forms: Spanish. In R.A. Berman & D.I. Slobin (Eds.), *Relating events in narrative: A crosslinguistic developmental study* (pp. 239–284). Mahwah, NJ: Lawrence Erlbaum Associates.

Sebastián, E., Soto, P., & Gathercole, V.C.M. (2001). Early verb constructs in Spanish. In M. Almgren, A. Barreña, M.J. Ezeizabarrena, I. Idiazabal, & B. MacWhinney (Eds.), *Research in child language acquisition: Proceedings of the 8th Conference of the International Association for the Study of Child Language* (pp. 1245–1259). Somerville, MA: Cascadilla Press.

Sebastián, N., Martí, M.A., Cuetos, F., & Carreiras, M. (1996). *LEXESP: Base de datos informatizado de la lengua española* [Computarized data base of the Spanish language]. Departamento de Psicología Básica, University of Barcelona.

Serrat, E. (1997). *El procés de gramaticalització en l'adquisició del llenguatge: la categoria formal de verb* [The process of grammaticalization and the acquisition of language: The formal category of verbs]. Doctoral dissertation, Universitat de Girona, Spain.

Serrat, E., & Aparici, M. (2001). Morphological errors in early langugage acquisition: Evidence from Catalan and Spanish. In M. Almgren, A. Barreña, M.J. Ezeizabarrena, I. Idiazabal, & B. MacWhinney (Eds.), *Research in child language acquisition: Proceedings of the 8th Conference of the International Association for the Study of Child Language* (pp. 1260–1277). Somerville, MA: Cascadilla Press.

Shirai, Y., & Andersen, R. (1995). The acquisition of tense-aspect morphology: A prototype account. *Language, 71*, 743–762.

Slobin, D.I. (1996). Aspectos especiales en la adquisición del español: Contribuciones a la teoría [Special aspects of the acquisition of Spanish: Contributions to a theory]. In M. Pérez Pereira (Ed.), *Estudios sobre la adquisición del castellano, catalán, eusquera y gallego. Actas del I encuentro internacional sobre adquisición de las lenguas* [Studies about the acquisition of Castillian Spanish, Catalan, Euskera and Galician. Memoires of the 1st International Meeting of Language Acquisition] (pp. 27–59). Compostela, Spain: Universidad de Santiago de Compostela.

Slobin, D.I., & Bocaz, A. (1988). Learning to talk about movement through time and space: The development of narrative abilities in Spanish and English. *Lenguas Modernas, 15*, 5–24. [Circulated as Berkeley Cognitive Science Report No. 55, Institute of Cognitive Studies, University of California, Berkeley, January 1989.)

Smiley, P., & Huttenlocher, J. (1995). Conceptual development and the child's early words for events, objects and persons. In M. Tomasello & W.E. Merriman (Eds.), *Beyond names for things* (pp. 21–62). Mahwah, NJ: Lawrence Erlbaum Associates.

Swain, M., & Wesche, M. (1975). Linguistic interaction: Case study of a bilingual child. *Language Sciences, 37*, 17–22.

Talmy, L. (1985). Lexicalization patterns: Semantic structure in lexical forms. In T. Shopen (Ed.), *Language typology and semantic description: Grammatical categories and the lexicon* (Vol. 3, pp. 36–149). Cambridge, UK: Cambridge University Press.

Talmy, L. (1991). Path to realization: A typology of event conflation. *Proceedings of the 17th annual meeting of the Berkeley Linguistics Society* (pp. 480–519). Berkeley, CA: Berkeley Linguistics Society.

Thal, D., Jackson-Maldonado, D., & Acosta, D. (2001). Validity of a parent report measure of vocabulary and grammar for Spanish-speaking toddlers. *Journal of Speech, Language, and Hearing Research, 43*, 1087–1100.

Tomasello, M. (1992). *First verbs: A case study of early grammatical development.* Cambridge, UK: Cambridge University Press.

Tomasello, M., & Kruger, A.C. (1992). Joint attention on actions: Acquiring verbs in ostensive and non-ostensive contexts. *Journal of Child Language, 19*, 311–333.

Toronto, A. (1973). *Screening Test of Spanish Grammar* (STSG). Evanston, IL: Northwestern University Press.

U.S. Bureau of the Census. (2000). *Statistical abstract of the United States 2000.* Washington, DC: U.S. Department of Commerce.

Vendler, Z. (1967): *Linguistics in philosophy.* Ithaca, NY: Cornell University Press.

Vihman, M.M. (1999). The transition to grammar in a bilingual child: Positional patterns, model learning, and relational words. *The International Journal of Bilingualism, 3*, 267–301.

Zimmerman, I., Steiner, V., & Pond, R. (1993). *Preschool Language Scale-3* (PLS-3) (Spanish Ed.). San Antonio, TX: The Psychological Corporation.

Zimmerman, I., Steiner, V., & Pond, R. (2001). *Preschool Language Scale-4* (PLS-4) (Spanish Ed.). San Antonio, TX: The Psychological Corporation.

CHAPTER 7

Morphosyntactic Development

LISA M. BEDORE

Q uestions about similarities and differences between monolingual and bilingual acquisition predominate the literature on bilingual language acquisition. In particular, researchers have considered the extent to which the order and rate of acquisition of morphological structures (e.g., past-tense forms [*brincó*, jumped]; plural forms [*sillas*, chairs]) and syntactic structures (e.g., question forms, complex utterances) in bilingual children are comparable with those of monolingual children. Some particular topics of interest to speech-language pathologists (SLPs) and researchers alike are the extent to which morphosyntactic development in early sequential bilinguals (i.e., children who begin to acquire their second language at 3 or 4 years old) resembles that of simultaneous bilinguals (i.e., those who acquire two languages from birth on), the amount of exposure to a language that is needed to support language development, and the long-term grammatical competence of speakers who are exposed to a second language at different points in childhood.

SLPs are likely to see children who vary in the amount of input that they receive in each of their languages, the contexts in which they receive input, and the ages at which they begin to learn their second language. The language profiles of these children are likely to look different from one another. In the United States, children younger than the age of 5 make up one of the largest groups of Spanish speakers. These children, considered *sequential bilinguals*, are expected to acquire English during their first years of school. Other such children growing up in predominantly Spanish-speaking homes learn English at home through interactions with older siblings, cousins, or playmates in the neighborhood; bilingual parents; and external influences such as television. These children may be considered simultaneous bilinguals (or early second language learners), and it is unlikely that their language skills will be equally strong in both of their languages. Both the percentage of time that learners are exposed to each of their languages and the specific knowledge they gain through the experiential contexts in which they learn their languages vary. Yet other children grow up in homes in which English is the primary language, and extended family members such as grandparents speak Spanish. These children may have broad knowledge of English and minimal knowledge of Spanish. Thus, children who are growing up exposed to Spanish and English are distributed across the bilingual continuum (Grosjean, 1989).

Given this variability in language-learning contexts, it may be challenging for SLPs to determine how extensive children's knowledge of Spanish and English should be. Information about the rate and order of morphosyntactic acquisition in bilingual children is needed to establish a model of normal language acquisition that will serve as a backdrop for determining expectations about morphosyntactic development. This information is critical when concerns arise about a child's communicative competence. If it is determined that a child has language-learning difficulties, information on the rate and order of morphosyntactic acquisition (in sequential bilinguals and in simultaneous bilinguals) provides the information needed to select language-learning goals and structure intervention. Some principal issues that must be considered as SLPs determine what constitutes typical morphosyntactic development for bilingual children are 1) what the norm should be used for comparing bilingual children with other children (i.e., with other bilingual children or monolingual children), 2) the relative difficulty of the morphosyntactic structures to be acquired in each of their languages, and 3) how exposure (amount and timing of input) will influence children's acquisition and use of morphosyntactic structures.

The development of morphosyntax in Spanish-English bilinguals is addressed in this chapter, with a special focus on these three issues, to help clinicians begin to form a framework for the evaluation of morphosyntactic development and treatment for language disorders involving morphosyntax. After a brief comparison between morphosyntax in Spanish and English, this chapter focuses on the development of Spanish and English in bilingual children with some brief comparisons with children who are acquiring Spanish or English only. Finally, some implications for language assessment and intervention are considered.

MORPHOSYNTAX IN SPANISH AND ENGLISH

Language is traditionally broken down into three parts: content, form, and use (e.g., Lahey, 1988).

1. *Content,* or a speaker's ideas, is expressed through words or the lexicon and their meanings (semantics).

2. *Form* consists of the morphosyntactic rules for combining sounds into words and words into complete utterances.

3. *Use* refers to a speaker's ability to adapt communication skills to fit his or her intended meaning to the context in which language is being used.

In this three-part model, morphosyntactic rules allow a speaker to re-combine words infinitely to express any idea he or she might wish to, and to provide the range of structures needed for the speaker to use language appropriately. Thus, consideration of morphosyntactic skills cannot be seg-regated from consideration of content and use of language.

At the same time, however, the acquisition of semantics (content) might be expected to look different from the acquisition of morphosyntax (form). Pinker (1999) suggested one key difference between these two sys-tems: Semantics is an open system, and morphsoyntax is a closed system. Learners will continue to add to their semantic knowledge indefinitely, whereas the number of grammatical morphemes and syntactic rules for the bilingual child to learn in each language are finite.

The fact that morphosyntax is a closed system may explain why the patterns of morphosyntactic development of children acquiring two lan-guages simultaneously look like those of monolingual children (Paradis & Genesee, 1997). In contrast, vocabulary development may look different in each of bilingual learners' vocabularies. Vocabulary is acquired in the con-texts in which the language is learned.

Nature of the Languages to Be Acquired

Learners of Spanish and English must accommodate similarities and dif-ferences in morphosyntactic structure in their linguistic systems. Both lan-guages share a preference for subject–verb–object (SVO) word order and have similar movement patterns for forming questions and embedding phrases to form complex sentences. Spanish has greater flexibility in word order, however, allowing for shift in pragmatic focus. A look at the struc-ture of common sentence types highlights some of the similarities between Spanish and English.

1. The little boy ate the big bag of cookies.

2. *El niño chiquito comió la bolsa grande de galletas.* (The boy little ate the bag big of cookies.)

3. *Comió la bolsa grande de galletas.* ([The boy little] ate the bag big of cookies).

4. *Comió la bolsa grande de galletas el niño chiquito.* (Ate the bag big of cookies [the boy little]).

5. *El niño chiquito, él comió todas las galletas.* (The boy little, he ate all the cookies).

6. The little boy, he ate all the cookies.

Sentences 1 and 2 illustrate the predominant basic subject SVO word order in Spanish as well as English. Within the noun phrase, however, Spanish differs from English because the adjective follows the noun rather than precedes it (*bolsa grande, niño chiquito*), as in English. Although pronouns (e.g., *he, él*) can replace the full noun phrase when the subject contains information that is recoverable from the context in both languages, the subject can be further de-emphasized in Spanish through the deletion of the subject noun phrase (shown in sentence 3). In such cases, the speakers must use the appropriate form of the verb (i.e., with person and number marking) so that the subject information is recoverable from context. When a shift in word order occurs, such as that seen in sentence 4, it is used to emphasize new or critical information. For example, the subject could be shifted to sentence final position to emphasize that it was the little boy who ate the cookies. In English, such variation in focus is conveyed mainly through prosodic changes. Following this principle, Spanish speakers can use a topic phrase to highlight the subject, as in sentence 5. Bilingual children often use analogous constructions when speaking English, as in sentence 6. This is a relatively common way in which Spanish-English bilinguals demonstrate an amalgamated linguistic system.

As sentence complexity increases, the basic ordering of elements remains similar.

7. What did the little boy eat?

8. *¿Qué comió el niño chiquito?* (What ate the boy little?)

9. The little boy who was at the table ate the big bag of cookies.

10. *El niño chiquito que estaba en la mesa comió la bolsa grande de galletas.* (The boy little that was at the table ate the bag big of cookies.)

In question forms 7 and 8, the structure of both sentences requires the interrogative to be moved to sentence initial position. While the English question form has an additional level of complexity with the insertion of the auxiliary *do* and no movement of the verb itself, the Spanish forms require the inversion of the noun and the verb. In English and Spanish, complex sentence forms can be achieved by adding phrases to modify the subject, as seen in the sentence pair 9 and 10. Syntactic information may involve minimal changes in word order when bilingual speakers are speaking English or Spanish.

In spite of these similarities, some important differences exist in the semantic–syntactic interface in Spanish and English that bilingual learners must accommodate. In Spanish, grammatical morphemes mark number and gender agreement within noun phrases and tense, mood, and aspect as well as number and gender agreement within verb phrases. In comparison, English is a morphologically sparse language with strict word order. A number of concepts in English, such as conditionality and modality, are expressed through words or phrases (e.g., *could, might*) and through morphological markers (e.g., conditional forms) in Spanish. Table 7.1 compares the morphology of several grammatical constructions in English and Spanish. These differences also yield differences in sentence structures, which are illustrated below.

11. The friends went to the store every day after school.

12. *Los amigos siempre iban a la tienda después de la escuela.* (The friends always went [imperfect] to the store after school.)

13. He said he could go to the movies if he got home before 10:00.

14. *Dijó que podría ir a cine si llegara antes de las 10:00.* ([He] said [preterit] that he can [conditional] go to the movie if [he] arrived [subjunctive] before 10:00.)

15. I want a car that doesn't need batteries.

16. *Quiero un carro que no necesite pilas.* (I want a car that no need [subjunctive] batteries).

17. *Quiero el carro que no necesita pilas.* (I want the car that no need [indicative] batteries.

Just as the structures of the English and Spanish can be compared, one can also compare predictions about what is likely to be easy or difficult to acquire in each language in order to make predictions about bilingual language acquisition. Factors that are thought to influence the acquisition of grammatical structures include the phonetic salience of the forms as well as the transparency of their meaning (Leonard, 1998; Slobin, 1985). Phonetic salience is primarily a function of the relative duration of the form to

Table 7.1.   A comparison of English and Spanish morphology

Grammatical construction	English example	Spanish example	Relevant contrast
Noun plural	The boys	Los niños	Marked on nouns only in English, but on all elements of the noun phrase in Spanish
Possessive	The boy's shoe	El zapato del niño	Grammatical notion in English; expressed syntactically in Spanish
Articles	The boy/a boy	El niño/un niño	Same distinction between definite and indefinite articles. However, articles are considered to be obligatory in all contexts except when referring to mass nouns in Spanish; thus, they are used more often in Spanish.
Clitic pronouns	I like it	La come Le dio un regalo Se lo dio or se le dio	Post verbal in English More extensive range of arguments can be expressed through the clitic system
Gender agreement	The broken tables	Las mesas rotas	Gender agreement only marked in Spanish. No grammatical gender in English
Number agreement for nouns	The broken tables	Las mesas rotas	Number agreement is needed across NP only in Spanish; articles and adjectives agree in number with the noun
Number agreement for verbs	I jump [versus] we jump He jumps [versus] They jump	Yo brinco [versus] nosotros brincamos El brinca [versus] ellos brincan	Limited number marking in English—third person only and only in present tense. First and third person for all tenses and moods
Tense marking	He jumps He jumped He will jump He (always) jumped	Brinca Brincó Brincaré Brincaba	A greater range of notions are expressed morphologically in Spanish relative to English. For example, present and past tense (the Spanish preterit) are similar in meaning. In addition, Spanish employs an imperfect form that expresses continuing past action.

Grammatical construction	English example	Spanish example	Relevant contrast
Tense marking (continued)			Spanish morphemes are not low salience relative to English. The challenge in English may be that they are low in phonetic salience while in Spanish the challenge is the complexity across the system.
Aspect (perfective versus progressive)	I have jumped [versus] I am jumping I was always jumping	Ya he brincado [versus] estoy brincando [versus] siempre brincaba	Expressed syntactically in English; analogous structures are used in Spanish. Spanish also uses an imperfect form for continuous or customary past actions.
Mood/ Modality	If he had some money, he would go to the movies	Si tuviera dinero iría al cine	Mood in English is conveyed with modal verbs such as would should, or may. In Spanish, these notions are conveyed.

be learned. For example, a form such as the -ed in *walked* [wakt] is very brief, whereas the -ing in *walking* is of greater duration. The -ing can be realized as a full syllable, although it will not always be lengthened in connected speech. Some factors that influence phonetic salience are its position in the utterance and whether it can be stressed (Leonard, 1998). Phonetic salience can interact with factors influencing the transparency of a form. Forms that have a concrete meaning in context (e.g., plural marking) will be easier to learn than those that do not (e.g., tense marking) (Slobin, 1985).

One example of the ways that these factors interact can be seen in the order of acquisition of the plural -s, possessive -s, and the third person present tense form, which is also marked with an -s. The plural, which has a concrete correlate in a language learning context, is the earliest to be acquired. The possessive form, which is also relatively concrete, follows. Children learn the third person present tense form last. All three of these forms can occur in sentence final position, where they can be lengthened. The plural -s is much more likely to occur there, however, whereas the present tense -s is less likely to occur in that sentence position.

These factors play out differently in Spanish. Conceptually, the plural, possessive, and present tense are quite similar across English and Spanish; however, a syllabic or multisyllabic form marks the present tense. Omitting this form would result in an incomplete word form in Spanish (e.g., *corr* instead of *corrieron*). This would be more like an English-speaking child saying "ru" for "runs." Predictably, this is among the earliest forms to be produced by children acquiring Spanish. The plural and possessive forms follow.

A comparison of the past tense in English and Spanish also illustrates this point. Past tense can be predicted to be a much earlier acquisition in Spanish than in English. Past tense *-ed* is quite low in phonetic salience in English because it often is realized as a final consonant cluster (e.g., *he walked* [wakt]). In contrast, in Spanish the past tense form is stressed and may be a multisyllabic form (*él caminó* or *ellos caminaron*).

Functional models, such as the competition model, indicate that learners will perform similarly on those elements that work similarly across the languages and that there may be competition across those forms that differ across languages, resulting in those forms being more difficult to learn (MacWhinney, 1997). The language acquisition patterns of young second language learners illustrate some of these influences. For example, articles have similar functions in English and Spanish but are required in more contexts in Spanish. Thus, a child may use articles in a context, such as "I like the doggies," when the child means, "I like doggies," referring to dogs in general. Plurals are similar in form and meaning in Spanish and English and may show no influence; they may be correctly produced in both languages.

Finally, although a child is quite likely to demonstrate knowledge of past tense forms in Spanish if they start to acquire English at 4 or 5 years old, this knowledge may not transfer readily to English. Thus, they may say phrases like, "Yesterday I play in the park." This omission of past tense suffixes such as *-ed* may be attributed to low phonetic salience (which also influences children's acquisition of past tense forms in English as a first language) rather than lack of knowledge of the grammatical notion of tense. Such patterns of acquisition may be the result of interaction between the predicted sequence of acquisition in each language and cross-language influence.

Dialectal Variation

Dialectal variation also influences the morphosyntactic forms that children can be expected to learn. Predominant dialectal patterns in Spanish can generally be grouped into two sets of patterns: *conservative* and *Caribbean*. Conservative dialects, in which syllable final consonants are retained, are representative of the dialects spoken by speakers of Mexican dialects and many interior regions of Latin American countries. For example, words such as *escuela* (school) and *arroz* (rice) are pronounced with their syllable final consonants: "eskuela" and "aros." In the United States, these speakers have traditionally been found in areas such as California, Texas, and Chicago. More recently, speakers of conservative dialects have begun to form communities in areas throughout the Midwest and in large cities such as New York City.

Speakers of Caribbean dialects, in which syllable final consonants may be deleted or aspirated (e.g., <u>escuela</u> is pronounced as "ehkuela" and *arroz* as "aro"), include individuals from Puerto Rico, Cuba, the Dominican Republic, and other parts of Central America. In the United States, many of these speakers are found on both coasts, in communities in Miami, Philadelphia, and New York as well as in Houston and Los Angeles, to name a few. Thus, it is important to consider the dialect that children are exposed to rather than the area in which they live when determining what dialect a child speaks. In the domain of morphosyntax, these dialects influence the marking of grammatical morphemes. Final consonant deletion, for example, affects the singular plural distinction for nouns and verbs. Deletion of final /s/ for example, affects noun pluralization (e.g., "las manos" as "la mano") as well as subject–verb agreement ("corres" as "corre"). When final /n/ is not overtly realized, the distinction between "(él) corre" and "(ellos) corren" (realized as "corre") is lost. When these distinctions are not marked morphologically, children may make greater use of overt subjects because the information will not be recoverable from context (Poplack, 1986).

By the same token, children from bilingual backgrounds learn the dialect of English to which they are exposed. Some children hear a variety of Standard English and use grammatical forms (e.g., articles, plural forms, regular past tense) in the way that would be expected given their level of development (Gregory & Bedore, 2002). Other children may acquire African American English and demonstrate forms such as zero *-ing* (e.g., "The girl is wash"), zero plural *-s* (e.g., "I see two dog"), or invariant *be* (e.g., "He be goin' to school") (Washington, 1996; Zentella, 1997). Still other children acquire Chicano English or Spanish-influenced English. Features that are common in this dialect include zero forms such as the regular past (e.g., "Yesterday I walk"), third-person present (e.g., "He always eat"), and article (e.g., "I go store") (Bayley, 1994; Cronnell, 1985).

Although some researchers (Santa Ana, 1993) indicated that these features are primarily phonological, they will, nonetheless, affect children's production of grammatical forms.

MORPHOSYNTACTIC DEVELOPMENT

Studies of morphosyntactic acquisition can be grouped into those that focus on both of a child's languages and those that focus on only one. Studies of both are referred to here as studies of bilingual acquisition. The goals of such studies have been to document aspects of the acquisition of each language. Some very young children have been included in these studies, so these will be described first.

Bilingual Acquisition

Children who are acquiring two languages simultaneously appear to acquire morphosyntactic constructions at approximately the same rate and in the same order as children acquiring one language. Patterson (2000) collected parent report data on vocabulary development and word combinations in a group of 21- to 27-month-old children who were acquiring Spanish and English simultaneously and compared parent report data with data obtained through language samples collected with a parent. In the surveys, as well in spontaneous language samples, 10 of the 12 children were producing word combinations. The children who did not yet produce word combinations were among the younger children; both were 22-month-olds.

Padilla and Liebman (1975) followed three typically developing children who were learning Spanish and English in their home environments for a period of 3–6 months. One of the children was 1;5 at the outset of the study; the other two were 2;1 and 2;2, respectively. Language sample data and elicited imitations were employed to evaluate the length and the morphological complexity of the children's utterances (i.e., mean length of utterances [MLUs]). When compared with normative data for English (Miller, 1981), each of the children demonstrated English MLUs and morphosyntactic constructions within the expected range for their ages. The older children produced verbs with the progressive marker (e.g, "man watching"), verbs with missing present or past tense markers (e.g, "man do that"), and articles (e.g., "a baby horsie") (Padilla & Liebman, 1975, p. 46). These are all forms that corresponded to the children's level of language development. In Spanish, developmental norms are not available for MLU or grammatical structures. Data comparisons between Spanish-learning children in the United States (González, 1978, 1983) and children in or from Spanish-speaking countries (Hernández Pina, 1984; Morales, 1989; Vivas, 1979) indicate both groups of children were acquiring the same structures in the same time frame and order.

In comparing these studies, one structure of interest was question forms. Like the participants in González's study, these children produced primarily *wh-* type (e.g., who, what, where) questions. The children also produced copula forms (e.g., "Daddy está" [Daddy is here]; "Es un baby pony?" [Is it a baby pony?]) and third person present tense forms (e.g., "baila Mommy" [Mommy dances]). The youngest child in this study began by producing one- and two-word utterances with a variety of semantic functions; again, this was within the developmental expectations for her age in English and in Spanish. In the latter half of the study, she began to use more Spanish than English and produced only single-word utterances in English.

García (1978) documented some aspects of Spanish and English development in a group of children who were participating in a bilingual preschool program. All of the children's parents reported speaking English and Spanish. All 12 children were described as hearing more Spanish than English based on parental input, though all interacted with siblings in English at least part of the time; 11 of the 12 children demonstrated English language complexity within the expected range (when compared with data reported by Miller, 1981). Grammatical structures of interest included plural forms, articles, prepositions, and conjunctions. One child in the group of 12 demonstrated greater use of Spanish than English. The other 11 children used the majority of the target structures but produced somewhat short utterances in Spanish. Only conjunctions were absent (though this may have been related to the use of relatively short and simple utterances). This pattern of findings seems to reflect the ability to learn basic English structures via interactions with children. Both parental and sibling input should be considered when describing the bilingual environment of the child.

Fantini (1985) documented some aspects of morphosyntactic development in Spanish and English acquisition in a child, M, who was acquiring Spanish and English in a multilingual environment. Overall, M was exposed to more Spanish than English early on, and it appears that he spoke more Spanish than English. M progressed from the use of single words (primarily nouns or names for objects) to word combinations by approximately 2½ years of age. Reflecting his predominantly Spanish input, the majority of M's utterances were in Spanish. The pattern of morphological development, based on examples of his utterances, was generally similar to that described for monolingual Spanish-speaking children. For example, M began to attempt to produce articles with nouns in phrases such as "la tasina" for "la cocina" (the kitchen) or "el gatito" (the kitten) with some use of forms such as "a peta" instead of "la puerta" for "the door," which contained a filler syllable rather than a full article such as has been discussed by López Ornat (1997) for children acquiring Spanish. Verbs emerged in third-person singular in the present tense first, and stems were sometimes overgeneralized. By the time he was 5 years old, M produced at least some forms from all of the morpheme classes that are reported for Spanish speakers of the same age. In his acquisition strategies or error patterns (e.g., over-regularization, use of filler syllables), he seems much like children of the same age described in the literature. English forms gradually appeared as M was exposed to more English input via experiences in school and traveling.

Acquisition of Spanish in a Bilingual Environment

Several investigators have described the Spanish of children who are growing up in the United States and acquiring Spanish against a backdrop of English. These are children who will presumably become bilingual, although the amount of English to which they are exposed has not been documented. Such children were described by González (1978) and Kvaal, Shipstead-Cox, Nevitt, Hodson, and Launer (1988), and they have also been included in control groups in studies of children with language impairment (Jacobsen & Schwartz, 2002; Merino, 1992).

González (1978) documented the acquisition of Spanish grammar in a group of preschool- and early school-age children in Texas. Cross sectional samples were used to identify structures that were common at each 3-month interval between 2½ and 6 years of age. By 2½ years, children used some verb marking such as first and third person singular present tense marking. Several verbs were also produced in the past tense. Gender agreement was also evident; children used forms such as *un carro* (a car), which is masculine, and *la casa* (the house), which is feminine. Complexity of verb forms emerged systematically. Children progressed from frequent use of third person singular forms to frequent use of first and third person plural forms by age 3 to 4 years old. It should be noted that some high frequency verbs such as *vamos* (we go) and *están* (they are) were reported at earlier ages. Thus, by age 4 years old, if not earlier, children have the basic elements in place to establish a referent in discourse based on verb marking. The range of verb tenses and aspect expressed also increased system-

Table 7.2.   Examples of grammatical forms in Spanish occurring in children ages 3, 4, and 5 years old

Age	Form	Example	Gloss
3 years old	Preterit	*Me resbalé.*	I slipped.
	Imperfect	*Caminaba así.*	(He) walked like that.
	Progressive	*Está comprando dulces.*	(She) is buying sweets.
	Periphrastic future	*Voy a jugar con los muñecos.*	I am going to play with the dolls.
4 years old	Future	*Iré al cine.*	(I) will go the movies.
5 years old	Present subjunctive	*Quiero que mi mami me compre uno.*	I want my mommy to buy me one.
	Conditional forms	*Me gustaría una galleta.*	I would like a cookie.

Source: González (1978).

atically. At age 3, children produced preterit forms, imperfect progressive forms, and periphrastic future forms. By age 4 they had begun to use the future tense, and by 5 years old they had added present subjunctive and conditional forms in clauses with *si* (if). (See Table 7.2 for examples of these grammatical forms occurring in children of these three age groups.) In general, the patterns described by González are comparable with what has been observed for children acquiring Spanish in other contexts, for example, children growing up in monolingual or bilingual environments such as those described by Hernández Pina (1984), Pérez-Pereira (1989), and Radford and Ploennig-Pacheco (1995). The complexity of syntactic forms also gradually increased. Some rote forms such as *¿Qué es esto?* (What is this?) were also observed. By age 3, children demonstrated full negative forms, more complex questions forms, increased imperatives, and early complex forms consisting of verbs plus infinitive constructions, such as *quiere comer* (he/she wants to eat), or sentences with conjoined noun phrases. Between the ages of 3 and 5, children continued to add to the range of complex sentence forms under their control using many compound sentences, relative clauses, and some compound complex sentences.

The work of Kvaal and colleagues (1988) focused exclusively on morphology. Children were divided into three groups based on the overall MLU in morphemes. At each level, the children's use of the Spanish equivalents of the 14 earliest emerging morphemes in young English language learners as identified by Brown (1973). Children with the shortest utterances (ages 2;0–2;8) used articles, copula forms, and past-tense forms, and demonstrated emerging use of plural forms. Children in the middle range (ages 2;9–4;1) used plurals, the preposition *de* (of) to indicate possession, and the preposition *en* which expresses the notion of *in* as well as *on*. The children with the longest utterances (ages 2;11–4;8) used these same forms with greater frequency and also demonstrated knowledge of irregular preterit forms. A comparison of regular and irregular verbs suggested that unlike English, in which irregular past tense forms emerge early as memorized forms, regular forms were acquired first. This work does not include as wide a range of forms as addressed by González (1978). These studies do provide converging evidence regarding grammatical development, however. The children with the lowest MLUs used all of the forms at the same ages as the participants in González's study. One feature of Spanish language acquisition this study highlights is that at relatively young ages (when English-learning children may still omit or overgeneralize grammatical markers for present or past tense), Spanish learners may be producing a wide range of grammatical structures. By age 2;11, children in the middle and high MLU groups demonstrated accurate production of grammatical features (i.e., the ability to differentiate person, tense, and number distinctions via the use of verb morphology) that are critical to communicative competence in Spanish (Bedore, 2001).

A comparison of 4- to 8-year-old monolingual children in Mexico and children acquiring Spanish in the United States revealed some differences in the order of acquisition (Merino, 1992). As compared with their monolingual peers, the Spanish-speaking children in the United States used number in verb phrases, active sentence order, and plurals accurately at a younger age. Other forms such as passives, indirect objects, and other conditional forms were acquired late by both groups, however. Because the youngest participants were 4 years of age, it is not clear to what extent these findings represent sampling context versus age of acquisition given that many of these forms might have been expected to emerge before age 4 years.

Jacobsen and Schwartz (2002) evaluated the grammatical production skills of a group of incipient bilingual children between the ages of 4;2 and 5;4 years. These children were classified as incipient bilinguals because they were just beginning to learn English. They used Spanish at least 75% of the time and were exposed to English informally (e.g., through television). Some children were beginning to use English at school. Based on elicited descriptions of picture cards and spontaneous language samples, verb tense use and clitic pronoun (e.g., direct object pronouns *lo, la, los,* and *las*) production were evaluated. These preschool-age children used pronouns with 84% accuracy. They demonstrated higher accuracy when masculine agreement was called for than when feminine agreement was required. Analysis of verb tense suggested that the children produced present indicative, preterit, periphrastic future, progressive, imperfect, and present subjunctive forms. They also demonstrated minimal use of the present perfect (i.e., the auxiliary *haber* [have] with the participle in the phrase "Ya han comido" [They have eaten]) and the past subjunctive, "Yo quería que corriera" (I wished [imperfect] that he run [third person singular past subjunctive]).

English Acquisition

Studies of bilingual language development distinguish between language for communicative purposes and language for academic purposes. Longitudinal studies suggest that children acquire communicative skills in a relatively short period of time but that it can take up to 7 years to acquire academic language skills needed to succeed in school (Collier, 1989; Hakuta, Goto Butler, & Witt, 2000). A child's ability to acquire academic language implicates strong morphosyntactic skills in addition to academic vocabulary. Morphosyntax in particular is important to the development of metalinguistic skills needed for reading acquisition. These data are useful for considering the amount of time needed for acquisition of a second language, but they tell little about the interim phases of acquisition.

Several studies have detailed Spanish-speaking children's acquisition of English. Bland-Stewart and Fitzgerald (2001) evaluated the acquisition of Brown's morphemes in a group of children who ranged in age from 2;6 to 5;0 years of age who had been learning English for approximately 1 year. These children spoke Spanish at home and were exposed to English and Spanish in the community. The teachers indicated that the children were all able to converse in English. Based on MLU-morpheme levels (as in Brown, 1973), children produced the majority of the forms expected. Most forms were not produced accurately enough to consider them "achieved," however. For example, the only forms that exceeded 80% accuracy were the progressive *-ing* and the plural *-s* for the group with the highest MLU (4.0–4.4). Some of the forms that children used did not appear to follow the expected developmental pattern based on Brown's stages. *In* and *on*, for example, continued to be used with 50% or less accuracy for all groups. This was attributed to the overlap with the Spanish form *en* that shares some aspects of the meanings of *in* and *on*. Previously, this had been described as a feature of Spanish-influenced English (Cronnell, 1985). Similarities between forms in English and Spanish seemed to facilitate the

production of other forms. For example, the use of articles was more accurate relative to other forms. Although this study is cross-sectional in
nature, the findings suggest that sequential bilinguals who already have
knowledge of their first language may demonstrate some influence in their
acquisition of a second language.

English-speaking children growing up with a bilingual background
who speak minimal amounts of Spanish demonstrate minimally influenced
patterns of morphological acquisition. Gregory and Bedore (2002) evaluated the production of articles, past tense -*ed*, irregular past, third person
singular present tense, auxiliary *be* and *do* forms, and subject pronouns in a
group of children who were between 4 and 6 years old and who spoke little Spanish, although they were exposed to Spanish anywhere from 9% to
50% of the time. These are forms that may be influenced in the production of Spanish-influenced English and also tend to be difficult for children
with language impairment. These children demonstrated accuracy levels
within the expected range for monolingual children (based on their age and
MLU norms according to Miller, 1981) for all of the morphemes under
consideration. These participants represent two distinct points along the
bilingual continuum. The children in the Bland-Stewart and Fitzgerald
(2001) study were typical Spanish learners who were exposed to English
and were actively attempting to communicate in English and Spanish. The
children in the Gregory and Bedore (2002) study were exposed to Spanish
but only attempted to communicate in English. Thus, one key difference
between these two groups of children was the extent to which they were attempting to accommodate knowledge from both languages. For the group
that was actively using English and Spanish, there might have been competition between the grammatical systems that exerted an influence on
their language production.

These studies are limited in scope; however, the findings indicate that
when children have the opportunity to learn and use both of their languages
simultaneously, linguistic milestones are generally met in the same time
frame as might be expected in for monolingual children. The information
is not detailed enough to determine specific information about the rate and
order of acquisition given the limited range of structures studied in these
children. The other insight to be gained from these studies is the role of
input. At least at these early stages it is evident that children's proficiency is
related to their input. Finally, although these findings are indicative of similar patterns of development of early major linguistic milestones, the possibility of cross-language differences between a bilingual's languages cannot
be discarded. Older bilinguals (who are school age or older) may demon-

strate differences in the use of impersonal forms with *se*, substitute conditional for subjunctive forms, and use imperfect progressive forms when simple imperfect forms might be used (Morales, 1995; Silva-Corvolán, 1994; Zentella, 1997). Thus it is logical to continue to explore the possibility of subtle differences between monolingual and bilingual learners early on that are not evident in the major developmental milestones.

IMPLICATIONS FOR ASSESSMENT AND INTERVENTION

Developmental literature on English and Spanish of bilingual children is, as of yet, limited, as can be seen in the review above. Thus, SLPs may not have as much information at their disposal as they might like in order to make clinical decisions. The available body of literature does provide some clinical direction, however. In this section, applications of the developmental literature, which has been discussed here, are considered. This discussion centers on the three questions proposed at the beginning of the chapter.

Rate and Order of Acquisition: Can We Have Norms for Bilingual Children?

SLPs frequently compare children's performance on language tests and conversational samples to those of a normative sample of typically developing children. When we work with bilingual children, we often ask questions about how these children compare with speakers of the same language. Do these children acquire language at the same rate and in the same order as do monolingual children? Are there norms for bilingual children?

The overall pattern of morphosyntactic acquisition in Spanish and English in bilingual children appears to be similar to that of the patterns observed in monolingual children. When evaluating language production of bilingual children, morphological structures may be acquired in a similar order as observed in monolingual children. Thus, early developing forms in Spanish—such as singular present and past markers, articles, and language-specific syntactic structures—should be expected when children are simultaneous bilinguals or have minimal exposure to English. Similarly, children who are acquiring English and have minimal exposure to Spanish or who are simultaneous bilinguals can be expected to learn early acquired forms such as *-ing* and *in* or *on* in the same sequence as monolingual English speaking children. Thus at early phases of development, information from studies of monolingual development may inform us about the kinds of things that children should know.

Another question related to the use of developmental norms is that of rate of acquisition. Will bilingual children acquire morphosyntactic structures at the same rate as their monolingual peers? Studies of Spanish-English bilinguals have not directly addressed this issue. A look at the results of a study such as that reported by García (1978), however, suggested that in the language that children use the most, they will achieve MLU levels that are in the average to low average range as compared with their monolingual peers. This is a broad indicator that rate is comparable. This is consistent with the findings for simultaneous bilingual children. Paradis and Genesee (1997) reported that young French-English bilingual children were in the low average range for their age. The potential problem, of course, is how to interpret below average performance; it is not clear what the normal range for bilingual children is. Thus, information about the range of structures exhibited in a young child's language is probably more useful and reliable than information about rate.

Are the Same Forms Difficult in Both Languages?

Are the same forms difficult in each of a child's languages? Can second language acquisition be expected to follow the same patterns as first language acquisition? As mentioned earlier, one common pattern among U.S. Spanish-English bilinguals is the onset of English language learning at preschool or early school age. Clearly, it would be helpful to know about the expected rate and order of acquisition for these children. Basic communicative skills are acquired quickly, but acquisition of academic language skills is a long-term process. More work is needed in this area that would describe the rate and order of acquisition of English language patterns and what changes are seen in Spanish language development as English is acquired. The work of Bland-Stewart and Fitzgerald (2001) suggested that there may be a mismatch between the complexity of children's utterances and the grammatical forms that children use; thus monolingual norms may not be informative in this case. Studies of older school-age children suggest that bilingual children might use alternative constructions to express grammatical notions in Spanish. For example, conditional forms may replace subjunctive forms and the notion expressed by the imperfect may be expressed only through the imperfect progressive form. Again, monolingual norms may not be informative for older children because monolingual children may be using different forms than bilingual children.

For the purposes of planning intervention, a key piece of information that should be taken away from acquisition studies is the kinds of information that children can be expected to demonstrate in each of their languages. When planning for intervention, one question we can pose is this: What morphosyntactic rules do children need to have acquired to be competent communicators in each of their languages? The developmental literature is helpful in highlighting the forms that are needed for English and Spanish and that can be expected to occur in the repertoire of young children. Some structures that are important in English include syntactic forms for generating a variety of sentence types (e.g., statements, question forms, complex sentences) as well as grammatical forms needed to differentiate old and new information (definite and indefinite articles) as well as the ability to mark tense; these all contribute to communicative competence. In Spanish, the ability to generate a variety of sentence types is important, as well. Goals for grammatical morphology might focus on the inclusion of forms to differentiate person and number marking within tense distinctions (e.g., first- versus third-person past tense or third-person singular versus plural present tense) because this can play a role in establishing reference. Direct and indirect object clitics also play an important role in sentence structure and reference and would also be important for effective communication in Spanish. The developmental literature provides evidence that all of these forms are acquired early and might be reasonable targets for a child at preschool or early school age if these forms were troublesome.

The Role of Input

Most studies have focused on one of the bilingual child's languages and do not necessarily provide detailed information about how much the child was exposed to the language in question. More recent studies such as those of Bland-Stewart and Fitzgerald (2001) and Jacobsen and Schwartz (2002) have quantified the amount of input that children have received in their second language. When considering to whom results might be generalized, such estimates are helpful. Several developmental studies (described in this chapter) that addressed Spanish and English for the purpose of examining children's knowledge of structures have also provided insight into the role of input. In Fantini's (1985) case study, M demonstrated periods of growth in Spanish that accompanied periods of intense input in Spanish, and growth in English accelerated the most after M began to attend school in English. In Padilla and Liebman's (1975) study, the youngest child demonstrated similar language skills in English and Spanish, but her knowledge of Spanish was significantly greater in Spanish by the end of the study. This matched increases in input in Spanish during the latter half of the study.

Information about input can guide decisions about the language of assessment for children from bilingual backgrounds. Children who primarily use one language will most likely benefit from assessment in that language only. The results from studies such as Bland-Stewart and Fitzgerald (2001), whose participants had been using English in school for approximately 1 year, and Jacobsen and Schwartz (2002), who had participants who were exposed to English about 25% of the time, suggested that children will begin to use their second language for some purposes with a relatively small amount of input provided that they have occasion to use the language. At the point that a child can communicate in each of his or her languages, it will be beneficial to assess morphosyntactic knowledge in each language.

Another decision that clinicians will make is about the language of intervention. Information about input and children's communicative needs in each of their languages will help determine intervention needs. For a child who communicates in English or Spanish only, few would question that the most logical language for service provision would be the child's primary language. For a child who has basic communicative skills in a second language (English, for example) it may be beneficial to provide service in the second language. Increased input may serve to reinforce learning in that language and can be directed toward the development of the forms that most increase the child's effectiveness in that language and support communicative effectiveness overall. Where forms have similar underlying meaning, transfer of knowledge from one language to the other should be facilitated. For example, knowledge of the notion of definiteness expressed via articles might transfer easily. Particular instruction about gender agreement (a feature not shared by English) might be necessary, however. Gender agreement could be taught by emphasis on article–noun agreement or by adjective–noun agreement.

In summary, studies of Spanish-English language development provide data that SLPs can use to guide their decisions regarding evaluation and treatment of language disorders in young bilingual children. Current data suggest that major developmental milestones are the same for young Spanish-English bilinguals as they are for monolingual children acquiring Spanish or English. Major milestones in the acquisition of English morphology include the acquisition of rules for forming different types of sentences (e.g., questions or negative forms that require children to learn about adding the verb *do* to the sentence) and learning about grammatical morphology. In Spanish, children also learn about a variety of sentence types, but a more significant challenge is acquiring the complexity of the grammatical system. Children need to learn the forms corresponding to a range of tense, aspect, and mood distinctions (e.g., present, past, future, imperfect, subjunctive) as well as person and number distinctions. Future work that focuses on both languages of children who are acquiring Spanish and English simultaneously and that evaluates how children acquire English at preschool age and early school age will help us refine this picture.

REFERENCES

Bayley, R. (1994). Consonant cluster reduction in Tejano English. *Language Variation and Change, 6,* 303–326.

Bedore, L.M. (2001). Assessing morphosyntax in Spanish-speaking children. *Seminars in Speech and Language, 22*(1), 65–77.

Bland-Stewart, L.M., & Fitzgerald, S.M. (2001). Use of Brown's 14 grammatical morphemes by bilingual Hispanic preschoolers: A pilot study. *Communication Disorders Quarterly, 22*(4), 171–186.

Brown, R. (1973). *A first language: The early stages.* Cambridge, MA: Harvard University Press.

Collier, V.P. (1989). How long? A synthesis of research on academic achievement in a second language. *TESOL Quarterly, 23*(3), 509–531.

Cronnell, B. (1985). Language influences in the English writing of third- and sixth-grade Mexican American students. *Journal of Educational Research, 78*(3), 168–173.

Fantini, A. (1985). *Language acquisition of a bilingual child.* San Diego: College-Hill Press.

Garcia, E.E. (1978). *Early childhood bilingualism with special reference to the Mexican-American child.* Albuquerque, NM: University of New Mexico Press.

González, G. (1978). *The acquisition of Spanish grammar by native Spanish speaking children.* Rosslyn, VA: National Clearinghouse for Bilingual Education.

González, G. (1983). Expressing time through verb tenses and temporal expressions in Spanish: Age 2.0–4.6. *NABE Journal, 7*(2), 69–82.

Gregory, L., & Bedore, L. (2002, July). *English grammatical morphology in children from Spanish-speaking environments: A descriptive analysis.* Paper presented at the International Conference for the Study of Child Language and Symposium for Research on Child Language Disorders, Madison, WI.

Grosjean, F. (1989). Neurolinguists, beware! The bilingual is not two monolinguals in one person. *Brain and Language, 36*(1), 3–36.

Hakuta, K., Goto Butler, Y., & Witt, D. (2000). *How long does it take English learners to attain proficiency?* (Policy Report 2000-1.) Davis, CA: University of California Linguistic Minority Research Institute.

Hernández Pina, F. (1984). *Teorías psicosociolingüísticas y su aplicación a la adquisición del español como lengua materna* [Psychosociolinguistic theory and its application to the acquisition of Spanish as a first language]. Madrid, Spain: Siglo XXI de España.

Jacobsen, P.F., & Schwartz, R.G. (2002). Morphology in incipient bilingual Spanish-speaking preschool children with specific language impairment. *Applied Psycholinguistics, 23,* 23–42.

Kvaal, J.T., Shipstead-Cox, N., Nevitt, S.G., Hodson, B.W., & Launer, P.B. (1988). The acquisition of 10 Spanish morphemes by Spanish-speaking children. *Language, Speech, and Hearing Services in Schools, 19,* 384–394.

Lahey, M. (1988). *Language disorders and language development.* New York: Macmillan.

Leonard, L. (1998). *Children with specific language impairment.* Cambridge, MA: Bradford Books.

López Ornat, S. (1997). What lies between a pre-grammatical and a grammatical representation? Evidence on nominal and verb form-function mapping in Spanish from 1;7 to 2;1. In A. Peréz-Leroux & W. Glass (Eds.), *Contemporary perspectives on the acquisition of Spanish: Developing grammars* (Vol. 1, pp. 3–20). Somerville, MA: Cascadilla Press.

MacWhinney, B. (1997). Second language acquisition and the competition model. In A. De Groot & J. Kroll (Eds.), *Tutorials in bilingualism* (pp. 113–142). Mahwah, NJ: Lawrence Erlbaum Associates.

Merino, B.J. (1992). Acquisition of syntactic and phonological features in Spanish. In H.W. Langdon & L.-R. Cheng (Eds.), *Hispanic children and adults with communication disorders: Assessment and intervention* (pp. 57–98). Gaithersburg, MD: Aspen Publishers.

Miller, J.F. (1981). *Assessing language production in children.* Boston: Allyn & Bacon.

Morales, A. (1989). Manifestaciones de pasado en niños Puertorriqueños de 2–6 años [Use of past tense by Puerto Rican children aged 2–6 years]. *Revista de Linguistica Teórica y Aplicada, 27,* 115–131.

Morales, A. (1995). The loss of the Spanish impersonal particle se among bilinguals: a descriptive profile. In C. Silva-Corvalan (Ed.), *Spanish in four continents: Studies in language contact and bilingualism* (pp. 149–162). Washington, DC: Georgetown University Press.

Padilla, A., & Liebman, E. (1975). Language acquisition in the bilingual child. *The Bilingual Review, 2,* 34–55.

Paradis, J., & Genesee, F. (1997). On continuity and the emergence of functional categories in bilingual first-language acquisition. *Language Acquisition, 62,* 91–124.

Patterson, J.L. (2000). Observed and reported expressive vocabulary and word combinations in bilingual toddlers. *Journal of Speech, Language and Hearing Research, 43,* 121–128.

Pérez-Pereira, M. (1989). The acquisition of morphemes: Some evidence from Spanish. *Journal of Psycholinguistic Research, 18,* 289–312.

Pinker, S. (1999). *Words and rules: The ingredients of language.* New York: Basic Books.

Poplack, S. (1986). Acondicionamiento gramatical de la variación fonológica en un dialecto Puertorriqueño [Grammatical conditions for phonological variation in a Puerto Rican dialect]. In R. Nuñez-Cedeño, L.P. Urdanetes, & J. Guitart (Eds.), *Estudios sobre la fonología del Español del Caribe* [Studies on Caribbean Spanish phonology] (pp. 95–107). Caracas, Venezuela: La Casa de Bello.

Radford, A., & Ploennig-Pacheco, I. (1995). The morphosyntax of subjects and verbs in child Spanish: A case study. *Essex Research Reports in Linguistics, 5,* 23–67.

Santa Ana, O. (1993). Chicano English and the nature of the Chicano language setting. *Hispanic Journal of Behavioral Sciences, 15*(1), 3–35.

Slobin, D.I. (1985). Cross-linguistic evidence for the language making capacity. In D.I. Slobin (Ed.), *The cross-linguistic study of language acquisition: Theoretical issues* (Vol. 2, pp. 1157–1249). Mahwah, NJ: Lawrence Erlbaum Associates.

Silva-Corvolán, C. (1994). The gradual loss of mood distinctions in Los Angeles Spanish. *Language Variation and Change, 6,* 255–272.

Vivas, D.M. (1979). Order of acquisition of Spanish grammatical morphemes: Comparison to English and some cross-linguistic methodological problems. *Kansas Working Papers in Linguistics, 4*(1), 77–105.

Washington, J.A. (1996). Issues in assessing the language abilities in African American children. In A.G. Kahmi, K.E. Pollock, & J.L. Harris (Eds.), *Communication development and disorders in African American children: Research, assessment, and intervention* (pp. 35–54). Baltimore: Paul H. Brookes Publishing Co.

Zentella, A.C. (1997). *Growing up bilingual: Puerto Rican children in New York.* Malden, MA: Blackwell Publishers.

CHAPTER 8

First Language Loss in Spanish-Speaking Children

Patterns of Loss and Implications for Clinical Practice

RAQUEL T. ANDERSON

O ne of the most salient linguistic characteristics of immigrant populations across the world is that in language contact situations, first language (L1) skills will be affected. How these are changed in terms of structure and degree is dependent on a myriad of variables. Latino children living in the United States are not immune to this phenomenon, and practitioners coping with the complexities of assessing and treating children from dual language environments need to understand the phenomenon and how it is manifested in the children's use of Spanish, which is often their L1. Not understanding L1 loss may result in incorrect interpretation of performance, thus increasing the potential for misdiagnosis of language ability/disability.

The purpose of this chapter is to describe Spanish-speaking children's patterns of use of their L1 as they begin to learn to use their second language (L2), which, in the United States, is usually English. In particular, the phenomenon of first language loss in children is described, with particular emphasis on Spanish. By presenting what is known about L1 loss and how it is manifested in the Spanish-speaking child, speech-language pathologists (SLPs) will be able to interpret L1 skill in the context of L1 loss and, thus, discern true disability in this population.

The chapter is divided into four major sections:[1] 1) definition of terms and concepts as they are used throughout the chapter; 2) discussion of sociolinguistic factors that affect L1 skill; 3) description of patterns of use of the first language, focusing mainly on productive (i.e., expressive) skills; and 4) clinical implications for assessment and intervention.

DEFINING LANGUAGE LOSS AND RELATED TERMS

Researchers in the field of bilingualism and second language acquisition are well aware of the many factors that affect L1 skills in immigrant communities. These factors interact in a variety of ways, resulting in various patterns of language use in communities characterized by language contact situations. Of particular interest are immigrant communities of people who speak a language different from that of the host country. Within this social context, it is usually the case that if the immigrant group's language is not considered high status by the host country, and if the country's policies—either covertly or overtly—foster monolingualism or use of the country's dominant language, various linguistic phenomena within the immigrant community typically emerge. Of course, the end result of this "linguistic" relationship between the immigrant community and the host nation varies greatly even across groups from a similar linguistic background within the same country. For example, in communities in which a large Latino population resides and to which Spanish speakers continue to emigrate, the minority language—Spanish—will be better maintained within and across generations than it will be in a community that is small and isolated, with little, if any, continued immigration. Nevertheless, certain general patterns of language use have been noted in instances in which the languages in contact do not share equal status in the dominant society (Petrovic, 1997).

Language Shift

A common phenomenon reported in minority–majority language contact situations is that of *language shift*. This is a pattern of language use in which the relative prominence or use of the two languages changes across time and generations (Gutiérrez, 1990; Petrovic, 1997; Silva-Corvalán, 1986, 1991). The process is one in which, during the initial stages, the immigrant

---

[1]Because the main focus of the chapter is on presenting data that will aid clinicians in distinguishing between true disability and language contact phenomena, the discussions are more descriptive than explanatory in nature, although theoretical explanations are provided. If the reader would like to learn more about the current theoretical models proposed, it is suggested that he or she read the original sources cited in the chapter.

community's native language has prominence across various contexts. In short, it is the language of communication across situations. As community members increase contact with the majority language, especially in the areas of work and education, a movement grows toward adopting this language as the main means for communication. The majority language thus becomes used more frequently in contexts in which the native language was central for communication. As the population of native-born individuals increases, the use of the native language decreases while that of the host nation's increases. The end result is a shift from the use of one language to the use of another, with a loss of skill—both expressive and receptive—of the native language. Language shift is usually reported across generations, and is characterized by a pattern whereby members of the immigrant population are fluent in their native language with limited skill in the host country's language. The offspring of this generation (i.e., second generation) become proficient in both the native language and the community's second language, usually resulting in higher proficiency or skill in the second language. Further movement toward monolingualism in the host country's language is evidenced when the third generation becomes fluent only in the host country's language, thus replacing the minority language as the first language for this population.

Language shift has been reported in many immigrant populations across the globe—for example, Turkish immigrants in the Netherlands (Boeschoten, 1992; Verhoeven, 1997) and Italian immigrants in Australia (Bettoni, 1986). It is a common phenomenon in the United States experienced by many immigrant Spanish-speaking groups (as well as other language-minority groups) in which there is a cross-generational movement toward English monolingualism (Fillmore, 1991; Orellana, 1994; Veltman, 1988; Zentella, 1997).

L1 LOSS AND ATTRITION

Language shift results in changes in native language use with an eventual erosion of abilities in the language. The process usually occurs across generations and is more gradual in nature. *L1 loss*, however, refers to a more rapid shift from first language prominence to second language prominence. L1 loss has been defined as a process in which a person's L1 abilities, usually measured expressively, are reduced or diminished (Anderson, 1999a, 1999b, 2001; Fillmore, 1991; Kaufman & Aronoff, 1991; Orellana, 1994; Pfaff, 1991; Schiff-Myers, 1992; Silva-Corvalán, 1991; Turian & Altenberg, 1991). Although L1 loss has been described in the adult immigrant population, it is much more readily apparent in the children of this population. When it occurs in children, L1 loss can be described as a language shift phenomenon that occurs within—rather than across—generations. In this context, L1 loss describes patterns in L1 use in which there is a change toward earlier linguistic forms; in other words, the child evidences reduction in linguistic skill in the L1 relative to his or her skill at a previous time.

In concordance with L1 loss, a second phenomenon can also be observed—*L1 attrition*. L1 attrition describes patterns of language use in which an individual does not lose his or her ability in the L1, but does not advance in its use either (Schiff-Myers, 1992). It co-occurs with L1 loss whereby demonstrated skill in certain aspects of the language is reduced across time. Simultaneously, certain patterns are also present in which characteristics of the language do not continue to develop as noted in monolingual speakers of the target language.

As clinicians working with children who are either bilingual or learning English as a second (or other) language, the phenomena of language shift and L1 loss/attrition is of great relevance. This is especially salient when working with Latino populations in the United States. Research on the status of Spanish in many Latino communities suggests that there is cross-generational language shift with concomitant structural changes to the Spanish language. Some examples include the use of the Spanish copulas *ser* and *estar* (Silva-Corvalán, 1986), mood distinctions (Morales, 1993; Silva-Corvalán, 1993), and the imperfect/perfect tenses within narrative discourse (Silva-Corvalán, 1991). In addition, it is often the case that English becomes the dominant language of many individuals who began their lives as primarily Spanish speakers (Anderson, 1999a, 1999b, 2001; Veltman, 1988; Zentella, 1997). Language shift and L1 loss have both been reported in many Latino communities. Studies focusing on the Spanish language skills of children in various Latino groups have reported a pattern whereby these expressive skills in Spanish are reduced across time (detailed in the section called Why Does Language Loss Occur?) (Anderson, 1999a, 1999b, 2001; Fillmore, 1991; Pueyo, 1992).

When assessing children who may be in a situation in which a language shift process is occurring, whereby Spanish structural changes are evident in the community's speakers, and when assessing children who are experiencing L1 loss, the main concern is differentiating between language difference and language disability. Because some of the patterns that are observed in language shift/loss situations may mimic what has been noted in children with true language disabilities, correctly diagnosing language impairment in this population is not a trivial matter. Relying on Spanish monolingual norms during Spanish language assessment procedures would provide inaccurate information. Understanding the factors that affect L1 ability and having information about the observed patterns in L1 loss will aid clinicians in correctly identifying language disorders in Latino children in this country.

Why Does Language Loss Occur? Factors that Affect L1 Skill

Language loss occurs primarily in a context in which minimal support is given for the use and maintenance of the L1. Thus, the sociolinguistic environment plays a critical role in the emergence of L1 loss (and language shift). Most often, L1 occurs in a context in which there is a minority-majority language dichotomy and in which different values are placed, either overtly or covertly, on each of these languages. This is the case of many immigrant communities who speak a language other than that of the host country. Two examples of this pattern have been reported in the literature: Turkish speakers in the Netherlands (cf. Boeschoten, 1992; Verhoeven, 1997), and Spanish speakers in the United States (cf. Fillmore, 1991; Silva-Corvalán, 1991; Veltman, 1989). In both contexts, the majority language—Dutch in the Netherlands and English in the United States—can be described as having higher status than the two minority languages in question. Higher status in this case means that it is the language of education and one that must be mastered in order for the individual to obtain a better paying job (Petrovic, 1997). A sociolinguistic "imbalance" results, then, in a movement within the community toward the more prestigious language (language shift), as well as a movement to a reduction in productive skill in the L1 within a generation (language loss/attrition).

The disparity between the L1 and L2 results in a concomitant reduction in the domains of L1 use. As children leave their immediate home environment, they begin interacting within other contexts in which the majority language is used for communication, especially in educational settings. As a result, the L1 is relegated to restricted contexts, primarily those of the home (Chávez, 1993; Petrovic, 1997). For example, in the United States, most language minority children, including children from Latino communities, attend schools in which English is the language of instruction. Only 16% of Latino children that are eligible to attend bilingual programs are actually enrolled in them (Petrovic, 1997). Although bilingual programs are sometimes offered, most of these are transitional in nature; that is, they do not have as a goal the maintenance of the L1, but rather, focus on the use of the L1 to support learning of English. Thus, as Latino children enter school in the United States, the environment or domains for speaking English increase while those for speaking Spanish diminish.

How does this shift in relative use and exposure from the L1 to English affect maintenance of the L1? Changes in relative input and, in turn, in a child's actual use of the L1 results in a reduction of instances in which he or she hears the L1, in this case, Spanish. Thus, the opportunities to use the language are also diminished. These patterns in turn have an impact on the child's L1 skill, especially in the context of a more dominant language. This is because reduction in use and in input (i.e., listening to the language) hampers the furthering of skills in the language as well as the maintenance of acquired skills, especially at the productive level (Anderson, 1999a, 1999b, 2001; Fillmore, 1991). In addition, the limited domains of use also bring forth a narrower range of use of certain linguistic forms and concepts in the minority language. Specific vocabulary used for different topics or contexts will be limited to that which is used within the domains in which the L1 is spoken, whereas the vocabulary used in contexts in which the language of interaction is the L2 will tend to be known only in that language. For example, on the one hand, if the child only uses the L1 within the home environment, only concepts and terms that are used in that context will be known in that language. On the other hand, if the child only uses the L2 in a school setting, then concepts and terms within that context will be known in that language and not in the L1.

It appears, then, that changes in the relative use of each language, with a movement toward the greater use of the L2—English—across domains (e.g., situations and topics) affects children's skill in their L1. The main sociolinguistic variable that appears to affect this process is that of relative status of the minority language and, thus, of the minority language speakers within the greater context of the host nation. As mentioned previously, this relative status of each language is readily identified within the society by the importance placed on speaking each of the languages in securing better jobs and thus economic opportunities. Language status is also a factor in educational advancement.

Although this pattern is what appears to guide language shift and loss, the reality is much more complex. The relative status variable interacts with other demographic, social, and individual variables, which results in differing degrees of loss across communities and individual families. Thus, people working with Spanish-speaking children in a context such as that common to the United States must consider the myriad of factors that influence maintenance and loss of the L1. Factors that tend to foster L1 loss are summarized in Table 8.1.

Table 8.1.   Some examples of factors that foster first language (L1) loss

1. Gender (females tend to experience L1 loss more than males)
2. Early immersion in English preschool programs
3. Low status of the minority language for
     Vocational advancement
     Educational advancement
4. Limited bilingual programs that foster maintenance of L1
5. Lack of L1 peer interactions
6. Younger siblings with whom English is spoken
7. Perception (and reality) that general status of the L1 is low relative to the L2
8. Limited contact with L1 speakers outside the home environment
9. Parents who are bilingual
10. Community has small minority population
11. Lack of L1 monolingual speakers in the community
12. Diminished use of the L1 across domains

Certain demographic variables appear to affect the occurrence of language shift and loss in immigrant communities. In a study of various Mexican American populations that included elementary and middle school students from New Mexico, factors such as gender, rurality, socioeconomic status, and employment patterns influenced the individual's perceived Spanish language skills as well as tests scores measuring Spanish proficiency (Chávez, 1993). Females, in general, tended to have lower Spanish expressive skills, with concomitant higher English skills, than males. This was especially noted in more rural communities, where there is a tendency toward higher Spanish maintenance than in urban communities. In addition, higher educational levels and higher paying jobs also tended to correlate with lower Spanish skills and greater English proficiency.

The observed patterns can be explained in various ways. As Chávez (1993) noted, women in these communities (as well as in other immigrant communities) obtain jobs in which it is necessary for them to speak English. Some examples are domestic services and white-collar jobs. In addition, in the communities studied by Chávez (1993), Spanish was used as a group marker, and males were more prone to use it as a symbol of their ethnicity. As expected, higher education resulted in higher English skills with concomitant loss of Spanish skills because English is the primary language of instruction and of vocational attainment.

Language use within the home and in the larger community (including school) also affects the occurrence of L1 loss. Most studies that have looked at groups of immigrant children in which the use of the L1 is restricted to the home environment have found that L1 loss tends to occur rapidly (Anderson, 1999b, 2001). This is especially true if the parents can speak the L2 because the children can, in turn, use the L2 and still be understood by the parents. L1 loss has also been reported in studies of families whose children were immersed in an English-speaking environment in school or child care at a young age. A survey study conducted by Fillmore (1991) of a large group of immigrant families indicated that L1 loss was evident in children who attended English-only preschools, even in families in which parents had limited English skills. On the one hand, Fillmore (1991) suggested that the younger a child is immersed in English, the more dramatic will be the child's L1 loss. On the other hand, other studies have followed children who are raised in contexts in which Spanish is an integral part of the community and in which the children attend bilingual preschools or stay at home until elementary school with a Spanish speaking parent, and they have found that these children tend to maintain their Spanish language with no apparent loss of skill (Winsler, Díaz, Espinosa, & Rodríguez, 1999). This maintenance has been reported for children between the ages of 3 and 5; changes after age 5 in skill from exposure to educational experiences and through interactions outside of the community have not been studied. Nevertheless, loss of Spanish skill is lessened in communities where there is strong support for the L1 through specific educational programs, and where the language has a strong presence in the media, church, and commerce, in contrast with communities in which there is no such support.

Other factors that have been reported to affect L1 skills include peer interactions in the language and the child's role within the family. In consonance with Fillmore's (1991) observation of the rapid L1 loss in contexts of preschool English immersion programs, the lack of input from peers can also affect L1 skill (Kravin, 1992). In case studies in which children are only exposed to a language via parental input, the tendency is for that language to be attrited or to not be acquired at the level of skill expected for a child's age. It appears that having peers and siblings who continue to speak the L1 is a positive factor for L1 maintenance (Anderson, 1999b, 2001; Kravin, 1992). Within the home environment, the level of L1 skill can vary from sibling to sibling. This is due to a variety of factors, including some that were mentioned previously, such as a child's gender and age when he or she was immersed in the L2. In addition, the role the child plays within the family may affect the level of L1 skill. For example, some children within the family serve as the parents' translators, thus these children need to maintain a certain level of L1 skill in order to be able to function in this capacity. As this is usually relegated to the firstborn or older children, it has been noted that birth order may correlate with L1 skill. This correlation may also be due to the fact that firstborn children, unlike later-born children, do not have English input from other siblings and thus their exposure to English occurs later (Anderson, 1999b, 2001). Older siblings often provide English input to the younger siblings early on, thus giving their brothers and sisters earlier exposure to the L2.

The factors that influence L1 maintenance and loss are varied and complex. It is the intermingling of macrosocial, microsocial, and individual variables that create an environment that does or does not support L1 maintenance. The clinician's responsibility, then, is to understand these factors and how they may be evidenced in the Latino population with whom he or she is working. In this way, a more comprehensive picture of what should be expected relative to L1 and L2 skill can be established, and thus better identification of true language learning disability will result.

Patterns of L1 Loss in Spanish-Speaking Children

Most research in the area of L1 loss has indicated that the lexicon and the grammatical system are the areas most affected by the phenomenon. As mentioned in the previous section, reduction in frequency of use of the language and in the domains of use results in a narrowing of the lexicon that is actually produced during conversation. This, in turn, affects the individual's ability to access the lexicon quickly and may even result in loss of vocabulary across time (Kravin, 1992).

Reduction in input and output also has an impact on grammatical skill. Several patterns of loss have been identified. These can be summarized as 1) a progressive reduction in inflectional morphology (Anderson, 1999b, 2001; Bayley, Alvarez-Calderón, & Schechter, 1998; Bettoni, 1986; Dressler, 1991; Maher, 1991; Schmidt, 1991; Silva-Corvalán, 1991), 2) a leveling of grammatical distinctions with a resulting regularization of irregular forms (Maher, 1991; Martínez, 1993; Silva-Corvalán, 1991), 3) a tendency to use coordinated sentences with a reduction in the use of embedding (Maher, 1991), and 4) the transfer of L2 syntactic structure to the L1 (Anderson, 1999a; Turian & Altenberg, 1991).

Lexical Patterns

Various researchers in the field of L1 (and L2) language loss have indicated that lexical knowledge is particularly vulnerable to loss (Gal, 1989; Smith, 1989; Weltens & Grendel, 1993). This is due to the already mentioned phenomena in many bilingual communities where individuals experience a reduction in the domains of use of the L1. This reduction in use and input has, as a consequence, the attenuation of the speaker's access to the L1 lexicon. Thus, if input and output are critical for maintaining lexical connections and the strength of lexical items, it would be expected that rapid access or even loss of the lexical item at the storage level will occur. Patterns noted in children experiencing L1 loss suggest simultaneous lexical loss. This may translate to an individual's ability to retrieve items or to actually lose items, and may also include reduction in L1 productive vocabulary with a concomitant use of general terms and lexical innovation.

Lexical loss appears to occur, at the earliest stages of L1 loss, in the production of nouns, followed by a reduction in verb lexemes. In a longitudinal case study of a Spanish-English bilingual child who was experiencing L1 loss, Anderson (1999a) reported a significant decline in the use of different nouns and verbs across time. This was attested by the child's use of fewer noun and verb types and an increase in the use of general terms, especially when the target form was a noun. For example, across time, the child expanded her use of general terms such as demonstrative pronouns (e.g. *éste*, this one; *eso*, that one; *esa*, that one/feminine). The range of verb forms was also reduced, with the child experiencing a tendency to use fewer action words across time. It appears, then, that lexical loss or access is apparent in L1 loss and that nouns appear to be affected the most by this phenomenon, as well as some verb forms.

Another pattern that suggests that L1 vocabulary loss or at least rapid access to the lexicon has diminished is the increase of L2 vocabulary items in the child's L1 productions. This is what is commonly called *language mixing* in the bilingual development literature (e.g., Zentella, 1997). This increase in language mixing at the lexical level has been reported in children who are evidencing a shift to the L2 (Kravin, 1992). Although language mixing by itself is not necessarily an indication of L1 loss, as this is typical of vibrant bilingual communities, it should nevertheless be considered in children for which L1 loss is suspected.

In consonance with these patterns described, children who are experiencing L1 loss may also present a pattern of lexical innovation, that is, of using words in the L1 in a way that is distinct from what is typical of speakers of the language. This phenomena is, again, not limited to L1 loss, but also is observed in bilingual individuals who are competent speakers of the L1. As a result, lexical innovation by itself is not an identifier of L1 loss, but it occurs in this context. Rather, a change in use of particular words across time as well as the presence of other patterns associated with L1 loss suggests that L1 loss is occurring. A pattern of lexical innovation noted in L1 loss (and in bilingual communities) is *meaning extension*. Meaning extensions refer to changes in the meaning of a particular word. A word's meaning is extended to include the range of meanings present in the L2. For example, a word in Spanish may be used in contexts that seem incorrect when analyzing the Spanish meaning of the word, but are substituted where a similar word in the L2—English—would be used. One example would be the Spanish word *vaso*, which in English is *glass*, or a receptacle from which you drink. In English, *glass* describes not only glasses from which you drink a variety of beverages but also the special glass that is used to serve wine or similar drinks. In Spanish, there is another word for this particular type of glass, *copa*, which is used instead. An individual would be practicing a meaning extension if he or she used "vaso" to describe a particular type of glass instead of using the word *copa*.

Another pattern of lexical innovation that occurs in child L1 loss (as well as in bilingual communities) is lexical borrowing or assimilation of words from the L2 to the L1. Unlike code-mixing, the individual incorporates a word into the L1 with a change in the phonology, and sometimes the morphology, that is in consonance with the rules of the L1. For example, a Spanish-speaking child experiencing L1 loss may produce a phrase such as "Dame un break" (Give me a break) with the English word following Spanish phonology (e.g., use of a tap or trilled [r]). The child may also use words such as "taquear" for the Spanish word "hablar" (to talk), evidencing use of an English form that has been incorporated to his or her Spanish lexicon by the addition of morphological markers to indicate a verb form (e.g., [ar] ending and person conjugation, such as "taqueo"/I talk). What is interesting about this pattern is that it demonstrates that the child has knowledge of Spanish grammar and phonology as he or she modifies these English words to fit the Spanish grammatical rules. Although not verified in the research, it is possible that this type of lexical innovation may diminish in use as the child becomes less fluent in the L1.

Grammatical Patterns in L1 Loss

Studies of Spanish grammar in language contact situations have mainly focused on cross-generational studies conducted to identify aspects of Spanish that change as a result of language shift. Although a discussion of these studies is beyond the scope of this chapter, these patterns of language shift need to be considered when evaluating the Spanish language abilities of children. The community's use of Spanish should be used as the norm, not the language of monolingual speakers or speakers of other Spanish-English bilingual communities. The studies that have addressed grammatical patterns of L1 loss in Spanish do point to specific aspects as being particularly vulnerable to loss. These include features of the noun phrase, verbal morphology, and word order.

The most significant pattern of L1 loss noted in Spanish-speaking children at the noun phrase is that of errors in gender agreement (Anderson, 1999a, 1999b). In Spanish, both the article and the adjective (in most instances) have to agree with the noun with respect to its grammatical gender. Each noun is ascribed a gender that is arbitrary in nature (Gariano, 1984). Although general rules apply (e.g., words ending in -*o* tend to be masculine and words ending in -*a* or *é* tend to be feminine), exceptions abound to this rule. For example, the word *café* (coffee) is masculine (*el café negro*, the black coffee), while the word *mano* (hand) is feminine (*la mano negra*, the black hand). The exception to this arbitrariness is words that describe concepts that have a defined gender, such as mother (*la mamá bonita*, the pretty mother) and brother (*el hermano favorito*, the favorite brother).

Research by Anderson (1999a, 1999b) on the Spanish skills of two children who were experiencing L1 loss indicated that the main error observed was that of gender agreement. Limited problems were noted on the actual production of articles in that these were generally not omitted, and indefinite/definite (i.e., *un/el, una/la*, a/the) distinctions were maintained. When omission occurred, it was in instances in which the neutral *lo* was used with more abstract terms such as *lo bueno* (the good). Although the incidence of gender errors varied, these were evident in both children, with greater increase in one of the children across time. The most common gender error noted was the use of a masculine article for a feminine article (e.g., "el mesa/la mesa," the table [masculine and feminine]). Of note, this trend toward gender errors and the use of masculine forms for feminine forms has also been noted in adult Spanish-English bilinguals who demonstrate good Spanish comprehension skills but who have difficulty speaking Spanish and individuals who have been described as passive bilinguals (Lipski, 1993). Use of the plural forms was maintained across the two children, thus suggesting that grammatical gender is the form that appears to be most vulnerable to L1 loss in Spanish-speaking children (Anderson, 1999b).

Data on Spanish verb morphology changes in children experiencing L1 loss, as well as data on the use of verb phrases, indicate interesting patterns. As noted in the children's use of noun phrases, certain aspects of verb morphology and of the verb phrase appear to be more vulnerable to loss. These include the use of mood, aspect, person and number distinctions, and the production of clitics or object pronouns. With respect to verb morphology, the following characteristics have been reported: 1) diminished use of aspectual distinctions across time (i.e., perfect/imperfect tense) (Anderson, 2001; Bayley et al., 1998), 2) reduction and lack of use of the Spanish subjunctive (Anderson, 2002), 3) loss of person and number distinctions across time (Anderson, 2001), and 4) regularization of irregular verbs (Anderson, 2001).

Bayley and colleagues (1998) used narrative tasks and Anderson (2001) used conversational samples to examine Spanish-speaking children's use of aspect distinctions. Both types of data revealed a movement toward the use of the perfect tense (e.g., "Yo comí," I ate) for the imperfect tense (e.g., "Yo comía," I was eating) in instances in which the imperfect form was obligatory. Children did use the imperfect tense, but mainly in stative verbs such as *gustar* (to like), *estar* (to be), and *ir* (to go). These verbs are frequently used in imperfect tense in Spanish, as they denote actions with no clear beginning or end and thus have an inherent "imperfective" bias. This particular pattern suggests that factors such as frequency of use as well as the semantic relevancy of the morphological marker for the particular verbal lexeme affect the pattern of maintenance and loss in children. Tense distinctions, such as present, future, and past, tend to be maintained in children who are experiencing L1 loss, at least during the initial stages of language contact (Anderson, 1999a, 2001). The pattern of tense distinctions noted is one in which those forms that are acquired early by Spanish-speaking children are maintained (Anderson, 1995); for example, the present indicative (e.g., "Yo camino," I walk), the present progressive (e.g., "Yo estoy caminando," I am walking), and the simple past (e.g., "Yo caminé," I walked).

Anderson (1999a, 2001) reported on mood errors, which are characterized by a tendency to use indicative mood for the subjunctive mood (e.g., "Yo no sé que ibas a ir," I do not know you were going to go; "Yo no sabía que ibas a ir," I did not know you were going to go). Interestingly, the shift toward the use of the indicative for the subjunctive mood has been reported in adult speakers of Spanish in language contact situations in the United States, with third generation speakers utilizing fewer mood distinctions than first generation speakers of the same community (Ocampo, 1990). With the Spanish-speaking children, especially if the L1 loss occurs early or in the preschool years, mood distinction errors may be due not only to loss in L1 skill but also to incomplete acquisition. The acquisition of the subjunctive mood occurs for a protracted period of time, usually beginning when the child is 3 years old and continuing up to his or her 9th birthday (Pérez-Leroux, 1998), and its use across contexts is related to cognitive as well as linguistic maturity. It is plausible, then, that difficulties in the use of mood distinctions are related more to incomplete learning than to actual loss of skill.

Verb person and number distinctions appear to be aspects of morphology that are particularly vulnerable to L1 loss in Spanish-speaking children. Analysis of the verb forms used by the two children studied by Anderson (2001) indicated that most of the nontarget responses or errors occurred in the use of the correct person and/or number. Thus, subject-verb agreement is affected by L1 loss. Both children evidenced agreement errors in their productions, with one of them showing a consistent trend toward an increase in such errors. Most frequently, the direction of the errors was one of use of singular for plural forms (e.g., "él/ella camina," he or she walks; "ellos/ellas caminan," they walk), and the use of the third-person singular form for all other persons (e.g., "él/ella camina," he or she walks; "Yo camino," I walk). The pattern thus noted in the use of verb agreement morphology is toward a reduction of the person/number paradigm in the language with a tendency to collapse forms to one general form, in this case the third person singular form.

Anderson (2001) reported one final pattern of verb use. This pertains to the use of irregular verb forms; that is, verbs that do not follow the general rules for the formation of tense and person/number distinctions. For example, a regular verb in English would be *walk*, for which the past tense is the form *walked*. The verb *eat* is irregular; its past tense form (*ate*) does not follow the general rules for English. The data collected by Anderson (2001), in consonance with data from other studies on language shift and attrition with other L1s (cf. Kravin, 1992; Seliger, 1989), indicate that the children participating in these studies tended to regularize irregular forms in Spanish. For example, the verb *saber* (to know) is irregular for some person distinctions in present tense, in particular, the first person. If regular, it would be *yo sabo*. The actual form is *yo sé*. A child who is regularizing verbs forms may produce "yo sabo" and not "yo sé." Of interest is that this pattern tended to be inconsistent, or not used all of the time, and tended to be evidenced in certain, but not all, irregular verbs. Inconsistency in production suggests that perhaps it is rapid lexical access to the form that is affected in L1 loss, at least for particular forms and at the beginning stages of loss. The fact that regularization occurred with certain, and not all, irregular verbs indicates that some forms are more vulnerable to loss, and factors such as frequency of occurrence in the input and output may be responsible for this pattern. For example, irregular verbs such as *estar* (to be), *ser* (to be), and *ir* (to go), which were very frequent in the children's output and which have been identified as frequently occurring verbs in the language (Alameda & Cuetos, 1993) were not produced in error.

Clitic production, or the use of object pronouns, has also been reported as being affected in language contact situations. Of note, the pattern of error most frequently observed was one of substitution, with errors of omission occurring less frequently. In a study of bilingual children in Los Angeles by Pueyo (1992), the most frequent error observed in the children's corpora was that of gender and/or number error in the use of the third person direct object pronouns *la* (her/it [feminine]), *lo* (him/it [masculine]), *las* (them [feminine]), and *los* (them [masculine]). As noted in the noun phrase data from Anderson (1999b), the direction of the error was one toward the use of the masculine form in contexts in which the referent was feminine. The least frequently occurring errors of omission tended to occur in instances in which Spanish requires marking the object twice; for example, "Lo ví a él" (Him I saw him). In these cases, the children tended to omit the object pronoun and maintain the prepositional phrase, as in "Ví a él" (I saw him).

The last grammatical pattern noted in Spanish L1 loss in children is the tendency to apply L2 (English) word order rules to Spanish. This results in a more restricted word order configuration in Spanish, in which such order is much more flexible than in English. Yet, more inflexible word order in the manner of subject–verb–object aids the communication process when other aspects of the language, such as agreement morphology, may be compromised. Anderson (1999a) reported two examples of word order changes influenced by English word order—one affecting the noun phrase and another affecting question formation with prepositions. One of the children studied by Anderson (1999a) exhibited a change in word order in Spanish noun phrases that contained an adjective corresponding to the English noun phrase word order. Instead of producing a noun phrase with the typical Spanish order of article + noun + adjective, she began using the order of article + adjective + noun in instances in which it was inappropriate (e.g., "la grande casa," the big house, instead of "la casa grande," the house big). A second pattern noted was one in which the preposition in questions was used in clause final position, as is acceptable in English (e.g., "Who do you want to play with?"). In Spanish, this construction is unacceptable, and such a clause would be considered ungrammatical (e.g., "¿Qué estás hablando de?" What are you talking about?; "¿De qué estás hablando?" instead of About what are you talking?). L1 word order may thus be influenced by the L2, and this influence may be manifested in different ways and in different children who are native speakers of the same language.

Table 8.2.   Patterns of L1 loss reported in Spanish-speaking children

Patterns	Example
Lexical	
Code-mixing at the word level (mainly nouns)	*un dog* (a dog)
Use of general terms in Spanish	*Yo quiero esto.* (I want this.)
Lexical innovations	
Meaning extensions	Use of the word *embarazada* (pregnant) to include the English meaning embarrassed
Lexical borrowing/assimilation	*Emtiar/vaciar* (made-up word using English word to *empty*)
Morphology	
Noun phrase	
Gender agreement errors	*el casa rojo/la casa roja* (the red house [masculine]; the red house [feminine])
Verbal morphology/verb phrase	
Person/number errors	*Yo camina/Yo camino* (I walk [third person singular]/I walk [first person singular])
Use of third-person singular default form	*Ellos come/Ellos comen* (they eat)
Aspectual errors	(see above examples)
(perfect/imperfect substitution)	*Yo fui/yo iba* (I went/I used to go [implying habitual action]
	Yo lo hago/Yo lo haría (I do it/I would do it)
Mood errors	
(indicative/subjunctive substitution)	*lo busqué/la busqué* (referent: la pluma;
Gender errors in the use of third-person object pronouns	I looked for it)
Regularization of irregular verbal forms	*Yo no sabo/Yo no sé* (I don't know)
Syntax	
More rigid word order (subject–verb–object	Consistent use of subject–verb–object forms
Transfer of English word order	*el grande vaso/el vaso grande* (the large glass/the glass large)

SUMMARY

A summary of the main patterns noted in the Spanish of children who are experiencing L1 loss is presented in Table 8.2. As was described in the previous sections, both the lexical and grammatical skills of the children are affected. Grammatical skill is differentially affected in that some aspects of the language are more vulnerable to loss than others. It is important that clinicians not lose sight of the fact that some of the characteristics present in L1 loss also are part of many vibrant and strong bilingual communities. It is also important to remember that because language shift is part of the linguistic reality of the Latino population in this country, any comparison of skill in the L1 will have to rely on what is typical of a child's community in the United States and not of a particular country of origin.

One final caveat concerning Spanish L1 loss needs to be made. Only a limited amount of research exists specifically on L1 loss/attrition of Latino children. The data presented in this section, although in agreement with what has been reported in other language contact situations, are based on a limited number of children. Nevertheless, the data do provide information concerning possible patterns of loss and which structural aspects are more vulnerable to loss.

IMPLICATIONS FOR ASSESSMENT AND INTERVENTION

Assessment

The possible presence of L1 loss makes it important for clinicians to develop dynamic models of assessment—models that do not rely only on comparison of performance with an ideal Spanish norm. These models must be based on intimate knowledge of a child's linguistic community, be it one family or a large group of families and individuals. They must also be based on the realization that in language contact situations, the relationship between the L1 and L2 is not static but is one in which change is constant. Thus, clinicians need to move from a view that each language has to be assessed separately (i.e., L1 assessment and L2 assessment) to a more encompassing approach that answers the question of what a child knows about language and not what the child knows about language X and language Y separately (Backus, 1999).

Professionals' understanding of the sociolinguistic reality of the community is of primary importance. This includes knowledge of how both languages are used across settings and situations (i.e., domains of use); the presence of code-switching and code-mixing; and how the Spanish spoken deviates from the standard forms, especially in the area of morphosyntax. Clinicians should thus gain knowledge about the Spanish variant spoken in the community and not necessarily the variant spoken in the community's home country because the patterns may be different as a result of the language contact situation.

Such information can be obtained through various means. A cultural informant who is fluent or familiar with the Spanish variant spoken in the community can provide useful input as to the patterns that are similar and those that deviate from the expected norms of the home country. In addition, the informant can help in identifying the patterns noted in children that may

Table 8.3.   Areas of inquiry when interviewing parents and teachers

Areas of inquiry when interviewing parents	Areas of inquiry when interviewing teachers
Language use by the child 　At home 　At school 　With peers	Present educational placement
Use of language across topics, contexts and situations	Changes in educational placement across time
Language used with the child 　At home by each family member 　At school 　By peers	
Changes in use of Spanish and English across time by the child	Instruction in each language Time spent using each language during class work Areas taught in each language
Changes in language input for Spanish and English across time	Literacy (and preliteracy) skills in each language
Parental concern about the child's language learning ability	Academic concerns
Parental attitude toward maintenance of Spanish skill	Language use by the child within the school setting Language input to the child within the school setting

deviate from the community's norm, including how child speakers in the community use Spanish. Obtaining speech samples from vari-ous community members may also be helpful for discerning morphosyntactic patterns of the Spanish variant. Information concerning L1 and L2 use across domains and the particular Spanish variant spoken by a variety of community members can thus be used to identify expected patterns of performance.

Because each child will have unique experiences concerning language input in Spanish and in English, careful scrutiny of each child's linguistic background needs to be made. Interviews with family members and educators familiar with a child's background will provide the necessary information on L1 and L2 use and changes in use across time (Anderson, 2002). A summary of topic areas to cover in interviews with both the family and teachers is presented in Table 8.3. As can be observed, questions need to be asked regarding both language input and output (i.e., use by the child), and changes in both areas across time. Parents should also be asked to indicate if they have noticed changes in a child's relative ability in Spanish and English across time, and if changes have occurred, to explain how these are manifested. It is important to inquire as to the parents' perceptions regarding their child's skills in each language as well as their concerns about their child's language ability because parents have been noted to be good judges of their children's linguistic skills (Restrepo, 1998). Teachers should be asked about a child's educational experience in each language. If the child has been in a bilingual program, detailed information concerning how such a program was run and how each language was used is essential for understanding what should be expected in terms of the child's academic skills in each language. The data gathered from both parents and teachers will provide a detailed view of a child's previous and current language experiences. These data will also point to the possibility of L1 loss as being part of the child's linguistic reality. Reports from parents and teachers that indicate an increase in a child's use of English with a reduction of Spanish, as well as parental reports that the child's Spanish skill appears to have decreased, point to the possibility of L1 loss.

If there is the possibility that a child who was referred for assessment is experiencing language loss, it is essential for the clinician to consider alternatives to traditional testing. In addition to obtaining information concerning actual performance in the areas of lexical, morphological, and syntactic skill, the clinician will need to address other areas such as pragmatic abilities, strategies used to communicate in each language and in bilingual contexts, comprehension of both Spanish and English, language processing skills, and learning potential. Having obtained the necessary information concerning the Spanish variant spoken in the community, as well as L1 and L2 use patterns, language samples across settings and listeners can be collected and analyzed. Language samples should incorporate a variety of linguistic tasks, such as narratives and conversations, because different tasks result in the use of different linguistic structures (Anderson, 2002).

Because the language used may be dependent on aspects such as topic and listener, more than one sample needs to be collected. This, in turn, will provide a more panoramic view of the child's linguistic skill. With knowledge of the child's language experiences, the clinician can then choose the topics, activities, and interactants that will provide a more comprehensive view of the child's linguistic skill. These samples need not be long, but they need to be comprehensive enough to encompass the child's varied language environments. The particular environments chosen will be child dependent, but should be those in which the child interacts most frequently. Speech samples should be at least 15 minutes in length.

Analyses of the obtained samples should address a child's morphosyntactic skill as contrasted with the community norms as well as the various communicative strategies that the child uses and their effectiveness within each context sampled. Strategies that suggest that the child is being innovative in his or her use of language include lexical innovations, lexical borrowings and assimilations, use of code-mixing with bilingual speakers, and nonverbal strategies for supporting communication. Thus, although the main purpose of language samples is that of assessing productive use of structural aspects of the language, it can also aid the clinician in assessing how effective the child is communicating across contexts.

In addition to language samples that provide information on the child's present level of performance, other procedures can be used, mainly to identify a possible language learning disorder. These include dynamic assessment and processing tasks. Because these do not rely on present linguistic performance for identifying language disability but instead, address areas that affect language skill, they are particularly relevant for assessing a child who may be experiencing L1 loss. As these tasks have been effective in differentiating between language impairment and language difference, they have the potential for distinguishing a child who may be presenting patterns that mimic language disability but who may in fact be experiencing L1 loss from a child with a true language learning disability. Dynamic assessment measures such as those described by Gutiérrez-Clellen and Peña (2001), which consist of a test–teach–retest methodology, are particularly applicable to children in bilingual environments who may be experiencing L1 loss. Process-dependent measures such as those that focus on processing nonlinguistic information and include tasks that address aspects such as attention and memory may be particularly adequate for differential diagnosis in this population. Although most of the studies in the area of processing tasks with diverse populations have not looked at second language learners (cf. Campbell, Dollaghan, Needleman, & Janoski, 1997; Rodekohr & Haynes, 2001), recent studies with bilingual children seem to suggest that this area of testing may potentially serve as a reliable means for identifying language disability in bilingual children (Kohnert & Windsor, 2002). Of course, these two procedures are used for differentiating between difference and disorder and are not effective for describing regularities in linguistic performance. Such regularities in performance need to be identified through language sample analyses and child-specific language probes.

A final area that needs to be considered during the assessment of children who may be experiencing L1 loss is comprehension skills. Recall that most of the patterns noted in L1 loss occur at the productive or expressive level. Evaluating the child's ability to understand Spanish, using both informal (i.e., conversational and observational data) and formal (i.e., comprehension probes, grammaticality judgment tasks), will provide additional information concerning the child's language skills. In fact, comprehension should be a salient component of the assessment of children who are experiencing language loss (Anderson, 1999a). As with spontaneous speech, the comprehension tasks need to conform to expected patterns noted in the community's use of Spanish (and English), especially if the comprehension tasks are probing morphosyntactic skill and if grammaticality judgments are being used as an assessment tool. An example of a comprehension probe may be one in which the person distinctions noted in the verb are presented without the use of the subject (e.g., *como* [*eat*, subject understood] versus *yo como* [*I eat*]) and a child has to indicate which participant is performing the activity. A grammaticality judgment task would include providing a child with correct and incorrect productions of certain morphosyntactic features, such as perfect/imperfect tense; then he or she would be asked to identify the productions that are said correctly.

In conclusion, assessment needs to consider the possibility of L1 loss in the population of Spanish-speaking children in the United States. A summary of characteristics typical of language loss during assessment is presented in Table 8.4. Because some of these characteristics may also be

Table 8.4.   Expected performance of typical language learners experiencing language loss during assessment

Type of assessment	Expected performance
Parent/teacher report	Noted decrease in productive use of Spanish across domains
	Perceived decrease in expressive Spanish language skill
	No parental concern regarding language development
Language sample	Presence of morphosyntactic errors typical of Spanish L1 loss
	Presence of lexical innovations and assimilations
	Code-mixing at the lexical level
	Use of general terms
	Reduced sentence complexity (e.g., use of embedding)
	Ability to choose language according to speaker and context characteristics
Comprehension tasks	Generally good comprehension skills in Spanish conversational situations
	Comprehension skill noticeably better than expressive skills
Pragmatic skills	Adequate conversational skills
	Efficient use of nonverbal communication to facilitate interaction
Dynamic and processing assessment tasks	Expected performance of a typical learner

noted in children with language learning disorders, especially in the area of morphosyntactic skill, diagnosis should consider performance across all areas assessed. Spanish language performance should be evaluated using the child's linguistic community as the yardstick. It is essential that clinicians gain insight as to the linguistic characteristics of the child's community because these—and not monolingual norms—should be used for comparison. In addition, clinicians need to obtain pertinent information concerning the child's use of both languages and changes in relative proficiency across time. Actual assessment instruments should include language sampling across a variety of settings as well as evaluation of the child's comprehension and pragmatic skills. Dynamic and processing tasks should be used in addition to parental input for distinguishing difference from disorder in this child population.

Intervention

When working with children who are experiencing L1 loss, the main issue concerns language of intervention. A comprehensive discussion on this topic is beyond the scope of this chapter (cf. Gutiérrez-Clellen, 1999), but certain aspects of this choice within the contexts of L1 loss are presented briefly. First and foremost, it is important for the clinician to consider the parents' attitudes toward the child's maintenance of Spanish skills. It is also essential to be cognizant of the parents' English skills because parent–child interactions will be negatively affected in situations of L1 loss because the parents and the child will not have a shared language for conversation (Fillmore, 1991). If the parents want the child to maintain and improve his or her Spanish skills and if there is a concern for maintaining Spanish as a necessary tool for parent–child interaction, every effort should be made to incorporate Spanish as a language of intervention. This can be done in a variety of ways: 1) providing intervention primarily in Spanish, either by a bilingual clinician or through the use of a paraprofessional (cf. Langdon & Cheng, 2002); 2) providing services in both English and Spanish; and 3) incorporating the parents as essential members of the intervention team and providing them with activities that will enhance their child's use of Spanish. Obviously, these three alternatives are not mutually exclusive, and parents should be part of any intervention program that considers both cultural and linguistic diversity in its implementation. Incorporation of Spanish into intervention will provide the child opportunities to use this language in contexts in which perhaps it is covertly (or overtly) viewed as less acceptable than English, thus raising its perceived status for the child and the family. It will also aid in maintaining the linguistic ties between the child and the family. As a consequence, it may also enhance the positive perception of being bilingual for the child, the family, and the community. As with assessment, the intervention goals in Spanish should reflect what is known about Spanish language development and expected performance should be that which parallels the child's community. Such an intervention will, in addition to aiding the child in developing language skills, help in the maintenance of his or her native tongue.

REFERENCES

Alameda, J.R., & Cuetos, F. (1993). *Diccionario de frecuencias de las unidades lingüísticas del castellano* [Dictionary of frequency counts of linguistic units in Castilian Spanish]. Oviedo, Spain: Universidad de Oviedo.

Anderson, R. (1995). Spanish morphological and syntactic development. In H. Kayser (Ed.), *Bilingual speech-language pathology: An Hispanic focus* (pps. 41–74). San Diego: Singular Publishing Group.

Anderson, R. (1999a). First language loss: A case study of a bilingual child's productive skills in her first language. *Communication Disorders Quarterly, 21,* 4–16.

Anderson, R. (1999b). Noun phrase gender agreement in language attrition: Preliminary results. *Bilingual Research Journal, 23*(4) 318–337.

Anderson, R.T. (2001). Lexical morphology and verb use in child first language loss: A preliminary case study investigation. *International Journal of Bilingualism, 5,* 377–401.

Anderson, R.T. (2002). Practical assessment strategies with Hispanic students. In A.E. Brice (Ed.), *The Hispanic child* (pp. 143–184). Boston: Allyn & Bacon.

Backus, A. (1999). Mixed native languages: A challenge to the monolithic view of language. *Topics in Language Disorders, 19,* 11–22.

Bayley, R., Alvarez-Calderón, A., & Schechter, S.R. (1998). Tense and aspect in Mexican-origin children's Spanish narratives. In E.V. Clark (Ed.), *The proceedings of the twenty-ninth annual child language research forum* (pp. 221–230). Stanford, CA: Center for the Study of Language and Information.

Bettoni, C. (1986). *Altro polo: Italian abroad.* Australia: University of Sydney.

Boeschoten, H. (1992). On misunderstandings in a non-stabilised bilingual situation. In W. Fase, K. Jaspaert, & S. Kroon (Eds.), *Maintenance and loss of minority languages* (pp. 83–97). Amsterdam: John Benjamins.

Campbell, T., Dollaghan, C., Needleman, H., & Janoski, J. (1997). Reducing bias in language assessment: Processing-dependent measures. *Journal of Speech, Language, and Hearing Research, 40,* 519–525.

Chávez, E. (1993). Gender differentiation in minority language loss among Hispanic children in northern New Mexico. *Southwest Journal of Linguistics, 12,* 39–53.

Dressler, W.U. (1991). The sociolinguistic and patholinguistic attrition of Breton phonology, morphology, and morphophonology. In H.W. Seliger & R.M. Vago (Eds.), *First language attrition* (pp. 99–112). New York: Cambridge University Press.

Fillmore, L.W. (1991). When learning a second language means losing the first. *Early Childhood Research Quarterly, 6,* 323–346.

Gal, S. (1989). Lexical innovation and loss: The use and value of restricted Hungarian. In N.C. Dorian (Ed.), *Investigating obsolescence: Studies in language contraction and death* (pp. 313–331). Cambridge, UK: Cambridge University Press.

Gariano, C. (1984). El aprendizaje del género en español [The learning of gender in Spanish]. *Hispania, 67,* 609–613.

Gutiérrez, M. (1990). Sobre el mantenimiento de las cláusulas subordinadas en el español de Los Angeles [The maintenance of subordinate clauses in Los Angeles Spanish]. In J.J. Bergen (Ed.), *Spanish in the United States: Sociolinguistic issues* (pp. 31–38). Washington, DC: Georgetown University Press.

Gutiérrez-Clellen, V.F. (1999). Language choice in intervention with bilingual children. *American Journal of Speech-Language Pathology, 8,* 291–302.

Gutiérrez-Clellen, V.F., & Peña, E. (2001). Dynamic assessment of diverse children: A tutorial. *Language, Speech, and Hearing Services in Schools, 32,* 212–224.

Kaufman, D., & Aronoff, M. (1991). Morphological disintegration and reconstruction in first language attrition. In H.W. Seliger & R.M. Vago (Eds.), *First language attrition* (pp. 175–188). New York: Cambridge University Press.

Kohnert, K., & Windsor, J. (2002, July). *Separating children with SLI from typical second language learners: Insights from non-linguistic processing measures.* Paper presented at the Joint Conference of the IX International Congress for the Study of Child Language and the Symposium on Research in Child Language Disorders, Madison, Wisconsin.

Kravin, H. (1992). Erosion of a language in bilingual development. *Journal of Multilingual and Multicultural Development, 8,* 138–154.

Langdon, H.W., & Cheng, L.L. (2002). *Collaborating with interpreters and translators.* Eau Claire, WI: Thinking Publications.

Lipski, J.M. (1993). Creolid phenomena in the Spanish of transitional bilinguals. In A. Roca & J.M. Lipski (Eds.), *Spanish in the United States: Linguistic contact and diversity* (pp. 155–182). New York: Mouton de Gruyter.

Maher, J. (1991). A crosslinguistic study of first language contact and language attrition. In H.W. Seliger & R.M. Vago (Eds.), *First language attrition* (pp. 67–84). Cambridge, UK: Cambridge University Press.

Martínez, E.A. (1993). *Morphosyntactic erosion between two generational groups of Spanish-speakers in the United States.* New York: Peter Lang.

Ocampo, F. (1990). El subjuntivo en tres generaciones de hablantes bilingües [The subjunctive in three generations of bilingual speakers]. In J.J. Bergen (Ed.), *Spanish in the United States: Sociolinguistic issues* (pp. 39–48). Washington, DC: Georgetown University Press.

Orellana, M.F. (1994). *Superhuman forces: Young children's English language acquisition and Spanish language loss.* Paper presented at the annual meeting of the American Educational Research Association, New Orleans.

Pérez-Leroux, A.T. (1998). The acquisition of mood selection in Spanish relative clauses. *Journal of Child Language, 25,* 585–604.

Petrovic, J.E. (1997). Balkanization, bilingualism, and comparisons of language situations at home and abroad. *Bilingual Research Journal, 21,* 103–124.

Pfaff, C.W. (1991). Turkish contact with German: Language maintenance and loss among immigrant children in Berlin (West). *International Journal of the Sociology of Language, 90,* 97–129.

Pueyo, F.J. (1992). El sistema de clíticos en niños bilingües de Los Angeles: Transferencia lingüística y motivación social [The clitic system in bilingual children from Los Angeles: Linguistic transfer and social motivation]. In H.U. Cárdenas & C. Silva-Corvalán (Eds.), *Bilingüismo y adquisición del español* [Bilingualism and the acquisition of Spanish] (pp. 255–273). Bilbao, Spain: Instituto Horizonte.

Restrepo, M.A. (1998). Identifiers of predominantly Spanish-speaking children with language impairment. *Journal of Speech, Language, and Hearing Research, 41,* 1398–1412.

Rodekohr, R.K., & Haynes, W.O. (2001). Differentiating dialect from disorder: A comparison of two language processing tasks and a standardized language test. *Journal of Communication Disorders, 34,* 255–272.

Schiff-Myers, N.B. (1992). Considering arrested language development and language loss in the assessment of second language learners. *Language, Speech, and Hearing Services in Schools, 25,* 156–164.

Schmidt, A. (1991). Language attrition in Boumaa Fijian and Drybal. In H.W. Seliger & R.M. Vago (Eds.), *First language attrition* (pp. 113–124). Cambridge, UK: Cambridge University Press.

Seliger, H. (1989). Deterioration and creativity in childhood bilingualism. In K. Hyltenstam & L.K. Obler (Eds.), *Bilingualism across the lifespan* (pp. 173–184). Cambridge, UK: Cambridge University Press.

Silva-Corvalán, C. (1986). Bilingualism and language change: The extension of *estar* in Los Angeles Spanish. *Language, 62,* 587–608.

Silva-Corvalán, C. (1991). Spanish language attrition in a contact situation with English. In H.W. Seliger & R.M. Vago (Eds.), *First language attrition* (pp. 151–171). New York: Cambridge University Press.

Smith, M.A.S. (1989). Crosslinguistic influence in language loss. In K. Hyltenstam & L.K. Obler (Eds.), *Bilingualism across the lifespan* (pp. 185–201). Cambridge, UK: Cambridge University Press.

Turian, D., & Altenberg, E.P. (1991). Compensatory strategies of child first language attrition. In H.W. Seliger & R.M. Vago (Eds.), *First language attrition* (pp. 207–226). New York: Cambridge University Press.

Weltens, B., & Grendel, M. (1993). Attrition of vocabulary knowledge. In R. Schreuder & B. Weltens (Eds.), *The bilingual lexicon* (pp. 135–156). Amsterdam: John Benjamins.

Veltman, C. (1988). *The future of the Spanish language in the United States.* New York: Hispanic Policy Development Project.

Verhoeven, L. (1997). Acquisition of literacy by immigrant children. In C. Pontecorvo (Ed.), *Writing development: An interdisciplinary view* (pp. 219–240). Amsterdam: John Benjamins.

Winsler, A., Díaz, R.M., Espinosa, L., & Rodríguez, J.L. (1999). When learning a second language does not mean losing the first: Bilingual language development in low-income, Spanish-speaking children attending bilingual preschool. *Child Development, 70,* 349–362.

Zentella, A.C. (1997). *Growing up bilingual.* Malden, MA: Blackwell.

CHAPTER 9

Grammatical Impairments in Spanish-English Bilingual Children

MARÍA ADELAIDA RESTREPO AND VERA F. GUTIÉRREZ-CLELLEN

S
pecific language impairment (SLI) is a developmental language disorder that affects a child's ability to acquire language, even when the
child has typical intelligence, typical hearing, and no gross neurological impairment. Children with SLI present with significant language
learning difficulties that are not only heterogeneous but also may manifest
in language-specific ways cross-linguistically. Despite this variability, evidence exists that children with SLI have significant grammatical difficulties across languages (Leonard, 1998). Although the great majority of research on children with SLI is based on English-speaking children, this
chapter summarizes the characteristics of Spanish-speaking bilingual children with SLI based on available research with this population. Research
findings are used to provide directions for the appropriate identification
and clinical management of the disorder in this population.

SLI affects approximately 7% of the English-speaking population in
the United States (Leonard, 1998; Tomblin et al., 1997). These prevalence
estimates come from studies that systematically exclude children who do not
speak English or who come from homes in which another language is spoken. According to Serra (2002), in Spain, the prevalence of SLI is about 3%.
To our knowledge, however, no prevalence studies have been conducted in
the United States specific to children who speak Spanish as their native language, and thus, the true prevalence of SLI in Spanish-speaking children living in the United States has not been established. Yet, these children can be
over- or underrepresented in the caseloads of speech-language pathologists
(SLPs) and as a result, they may not receive appropriate speech or language

services (Gutiérrez-Clellen, Restrepo, Peña, Bedore, & Anderson, 2000; Restrepo, 1998; Roseberry-McKibbin & Eicholtz, 1994).

The misdiagnosis of SLI in Spanish-speaking children in the United States is related to several inappropriate clinical practices: 1) the reliance on English language features and translated measures to identify SLI (specifically, grammatical features found deficient in English but not necessarily in Spanish); 2) the use of language norms based on monolingual speakers to identify impairments in bilingual children; and 3) the use of language measures that do not address the frequency of occurrence of specific forms across Spanish dialects or English dialects. For example, the use of past tense in Spanish is not an appropriate measure for identifying language impairment in these children, although it is appropriate for English-speaking children.

In the sections to come, we discuss the language-specific manifestations of SLI in the area of morphosyntax across English and Spanish languages in monolingual and bilingual Spanish-speaking children. Dialectal differences within languages that may affect the identification of the disorder are described. Available research with both monolingual and bilingual children are used to show shared and unshared patterns of grammatical impairment across groups that can provide a basis for the development of appropriate assessment protocols and intervention plans.

GRAMMATICAL IMPAIRMENTS IN CHILDREN WITH LANGUAGE-SPECIFIC DEFICITS

Given that the cross-linguistic literature on monolingual children indicates that language impairment affects languages differently (Leonard, 1998), one should not expect that Spanish-English bilingual children would exhibit the same deficits from one language to the other. One reason for these differences is the grammatical characteristics of the languages; English is a language with a sparse morphology, whereas Spanish is a language with a rich morphology. Developmentally, this linguistic difference has an impact on the rates at which different morphological aspects of the languages are acquired cross-linguistically. For example, past tense, a form frequently discussed in the developmental literature, is a form that children acquire in English relatively late—as late as 48 months (Brown, 1973)—in comparison with monolingual children learning Spanish, who acquire past tense before age 2 (Hernández Pina, 1984), and bilingual children, who acquire it at approximately 2½ years of age (Eziezabarrena, 1996). Past tense in English takes longer to learn and seems to cause significant difficulty for children with SLI who speak English as their native language (Leonard, 1998). Yet, this form does not appear to be affected to the same extent in Spanish speakers with SLI (Bedore & Leonard, 2001; Restrepo, 2003; Restrepo & Gutiérrez-Clellen, 2001; Restrepo & Kruth, 2000).

Children with SLI demonstrate significant difficulties with morphemes that have limited perceptual salience. For English, these forms include third-person singular, copula *be*, auxiliary *be*, past *-ed*, pronoun use, and article use when compared with mean length of utterance (MLU) controls (e.g., Leonard, Bortolini, Caselli, McGregor, & Sabbadini, 1992; Leonard, Eyer, Bedore, & Grela, 1997; Rice, Wexler, & Cleave, 1995). Conversely, children with SLI who speak languages with a rich morphology, such as Spanish, which offers highly marked grammatical features, tend to have different linguistic profiles. Errors in inflectional morphology such as use of past tense, a frequent error in English speakers with SLI, are not as common in Spanish-speaking children with SLI, probably because Spanish verbs also are marked for person, number, mood, and aspect. Spanish verb forms also have greater perceptual salience than English verbs and are highly reliable. In contrast to English, Spanish-speaking children with SLI tend to have most difficulty with article and clitic pronoun use, perhaps because they are less perceptually salient and because they require gender agreement with regular (*la casa*, the house) and irregular (*la nariz*, the nose) nouns (Bedore & Leonard, 2001; Eng & O'Connor, 2000; Restrepo, 2003; Restrepo & Gutiérrez-Clellen, 2001; Restrepo & Kruth, 2000).

Because of these differences across the two languages, it is not surprising to find cross-linguistic differences in the overall grammatical error rates. Grammatical error rates do not appear to be as preponderant in Spanish SLI as in English SLI. For example, Rice and colleagues (1995) reported that the English-speaking children with SLI who participated in their study produced third-person verbs correctly 34% of the time and past tense verbs 18% of the time. In contrast, Bosch and Serra (1997) reported a very low incidence of errors on verb phrases. The Spanish-speaking children with SLI in their study produced 91.7% of the verbs correctly, despite the fact that the production errors were significantly different from controls.

Spanish SLI: Article Errors

Research findings indicate that Spanish-speaking children with SLI demonstrate significant difficulties with article production in spontaneous language (Restrepo & Gutiérrez-Clellen, 2001) and elicited tasks (Bedore & Leonard, 2001; Eng & O'Connor, 2000; Torrens & Wexler, 2001). Restrepo and Gutiérrez-Clellen (2001) found that a group of 5- to 7-year-old (mean age of 6 years) Spanish-speaking children with SLI matched by age, grade, gender, and school who were engaged in spontaneous tasks had specific problems using definite articles correctly compared with age controls, even when MLU in words was covaried. For example, the children made errors such as saying "la sapo" (feminine article *the* + toad) when they should have said "el sapo" (masculine article *the* + toad). The researchers' results indicated that this definite article form is affected beyond what is expected in younger children.

Available studies with Spanish speakers have underscored the significance of article errors as a characteristic of SLI in Spanish. Differences exist across studies in the types of article errors reported, however, which may be related to methodological differences in how the forms were elicited or the criteria used to identify Spanish-speaking participants with SLI. Some investigators, for example, have used spontaneous language sample analyses, whereas others have used structured language elicitation tasks. When investigators use spontaneous language samples, children may not use the same number and types of forms as in structured probes. Using spontaneous language samples, Restrepo and Gutiérrez-Clellen (2001) found that Spanish-speaking children with SLI demonstrated the greatest difficulty with gender agreement, especially with the singular masculine definite article *el*. The next most common error they found was that of omission of this article. Furthermore, they found that most (65%) of the errors occurred when the article was preceded by weak syllables, such as in the phrase "estaba en la trabajo" (was at the work). Similarly, in a longitudinal study, Torrens and Wexler (2001) found that two Spanish-speaking children between 4 and 5 years of age—one Spanish- and Catalan-speaking child and one Catalan-speaking child, each with SLI—acquired gender agreement later than did the children in the MLU control group. In contrast, Bosch and Serra (1997) found that the spontaneous language samples of their children with SLI exhibited article omission, especially of the singular feminine definite article *la*. The children with SLI made errors in both definite and indefinite articles and had the most difficulty with number agreement. Bosch and Serra's (1997) study included children with phonological disorders, however, which may have confounded their error analysis.

In studies that used language probes, article difficulties were significantly different from controls, but the patterns of errors were not consistent with those from studies that used spontaneous language samples. Bedore and Leonard (2001) found that their Spanish-speaking participants scored significantly below age controls in definite and indefinite article use. These results differ from those of Restrepo and Gutiérrez-Clellen, who did not find significant differences across groups in indefinite article use. It is important to note that Bedore and Leonard based their results on 14 statistical analyses with no correction for alpha. Bedore and Leonard (2001) reported that number agreement errors were the most frequent type of error. Unfortunately, Bedore and Leonard did not test these errors statistically, although they did multiple tests in other areas without alpha correction. Restrepo and Gutiérrez-Clellen (2000) found that the percentage of number agreement errors did not differ statistically between the SLI and typical language groups. Additional research using structured probes indicates that the majority of article errors of Spanish-speaking children with SLI are of gender agreement. Eng and O'Connor (2000) found that preschool children with SLI had gender agreement difficulties for *el* and *la* articles; in particular, they had problems using *el* correctly before regular nouns (e.g., those nouns that end in masculine *-o*), and using *el* or *la* correctly before irregular nouns as in *el agua* (masculine article + noun ending in *-a*, typically a marker of feminine gender) or nouns ending in a consonant (e.g., nouns with no vowel cue for gender). These results corroborate Restrepo and Gutiérrez-Clellen's (2000) results based on spontaneous language samples, in which most of the participants' difficulties surrounded use of the singular masculine definite form *el*.

Discrepancies between studies may be due to differences in children's ages, tasks, severity of SLI, and other characteristics of the samples. Bedore and Leonard (2001), for example, tested children with SLI who were younger (range 3;11–5;6, no mean provided by authors) than the children in Restrepo and Gutiérrez-Clellen's (2000) (range 5;0–7;1 mean 5;9) and Bosch and Serra's (1997) (7-year-olds) studies. Furthermore, severity differences between the SLI groups across studies may also relate to discrepancies in the error patterns found. Restrepo and Gutiérrez-Clellen (2000) evaluated children considered to have moderate to severe language deficits, whereas in the other studies, severity was not controlled. In addition, differences in sociolinguistic backgrounds may affect the amount of language use and maintenance, the types of errors the children produce, and the relative level of difficulty for each child and task. Restrepo and Gutiérrez-Clellen (2000) and Bedore and Leonard (2001) primarily studied children from Mexican backgrounds who had exposure to English and were receiving Spanish instruction. Eng and O'Connor (2000) tested children in New York City, mostly of Puerto Rican heritage. Neither level of exposure to each language nor the language of instruction was described for these children. Bosch and Serra's (1997) study was based on Spanish children with

Catalan influence. Therefore, it is difficult to draw a definite conclusion about error pattern differences across the studies because of the different methods and populations used.

Spanish SLI: Verb Errors

Although children with SLI appear to show difficulties primarily with articles and clitic pronouns, these children also exhibit verb errors. Sanz Torrent (2002) investigated verb use in 5-year-old bilingual (Spanish-Catalan) children with SLI who were living in Spain. She found that the children with SLI produced fewer verbs per utterance than language- and age-matched children in control groups. Sanz Torrent did not provide information regarding the types of errors, except to state that the majority (20%) of the errors were on verb inflections, and a small percentage (4.18%) of the errors involved verb omissions. Although these percentages in the Spanish-speaking children with SLI are small compared with English-speaking children with SLI, the percentages differed significantly from age and MLU controls. Furthermore, Sanz Torrent found that the three groups of children produced similar percentages of general-all-purpose or GAP verbs, which are highly frequent and not specific semantically (e.g., *do, go, get*), a result that is contrary to some of the findings with English-speaking children with SLI (e.g., Rice & Bode, 1993; Watkins, Rice, & Moltz, 1993). In contrast, no differences were found on the verb type/token ratios and the number of verbs produced, although the groups differed on the number of verbs per number of utterances. Unfortunately, these results are not presented by either language (monolingual or bilingual) or types of errors, so it is unclear whether these results apply equally to both languages and how they compare to other studies cross-linguistically. In addition to the errors and verb frequencies, Sanz Torrent (2002) analyzed the children's verb productions by the number of arguments (complements to the verb such as "hit the ball on the wall"). The children with SLI produced significantly fewer verbs with three arguments compared with the language- and age-matched children. Sanz Torrent's (2002) results leave multiple questions unanswered given that this study gave no clear description of what characterizes the verb system in Spanish-speaking children with SLI except that they produce fewer arguments than controls.

Torrens and Wexler (2001) examined the development of verb morphology in four Spanish-Catalan bilingual children with SLI and compared them with MLU controls. Based on spontaneous language samples, they found that these children took longer to acquire subject–verb agreement than did the MLU controls. Unfortunately, the authors did not describe the types of errors the children produced, although they stated that the children did not use nonfinite forms, which is a frequent type of error in English. Restrepo and Gutiérrez-Clellen (2000) found statistical differences in verb use between SLI and control groups, although the differences were not clinically significant. The children with SLI produced more errors in the subjunctive verbs, which they substituted with the indicative, than did children in the age control group, indicating that the children with SLI had difficulty with more complex sentence structures.

When Spanish-speaking children with SLI make verb phrase errors, they seem to use incorrect person or number agreement. For example, Bosch and Serra (1997) found that the only significant difference across their age-matched controls and SLI groups was with number agreement, in that the children preferred to use third person singular for third person plural. Although the differences between groups were significant, the mean number of errors was only 5.42% for the children with SLI and 1.93% for the control group, indicating that these types of errors are not clinical markers of SLI. The studies conducted with English monolinguals with SLI indicate that these children may make errors in about 50% of their verb productions, a clinically significant problem (for a review, see Leonard, 1998). Using a verb elicitation task, Bedore and Leonard (2001) found that their Spanish-speaking children with SLI used third-person singular present for first-person singular present and third-person singular past (4.7% errors of the total verbs). Furthermore, they used third-person plural present for first-person singular past and third-person plural past (4.1% errors of the total verbs). The children with SLI differed from age controls only on use of third person singular, plural preterit, and third person singular present verb forms. Bedore and Leonard (2001) found that the children's error types were very similar between groups; thus, these tenuous differences between groups in the verb system may be strictly due to performance errors and not to specific difficulties with the verb system. If alpha had been controlled for all the different statistical tests, two of the verb measures would not have been significantly different between groups.

Bedore and Leonard (2001) also reported that compared with controls, the children with SLI used more infinitives (2.4%) in contexts in which they should have used finite verbs. These findings do not indicate clearly that this feature is a marker of SLI, however, given the high percentage of correct productions and the limited number of infinitives produced. In addition, the statistical significance of this finding is unknown because the results are described but not tested between groups. Furthermore, the use of infinitives was an appropriate pragmatic response given the task used to elicit verbs. For example, the child was asked to say what he or she did today in school; the use of infinitives equivalent to "to play" in that specific context is pragmatically appropriate for Spanish. Thus, the preference for infinitives does not seem to have clinical or practical relevance for the identification of SLI in Spanish speakers.

Spanish SLI: Clitic Pronouns and Other Errors

In addition to specific difficulties with articles, children with SLI may exhibit specific deficits in the production of clitic pronouns, plural nouns, and adjective agreement. Bedore and Leonard (2001) found that these children differed from MLU and age controls on direct object clitics, noun plural inflections, and adjective number and gender agreement. Similarly, Bosch and Serra (1997) found significant differences between MLU and age controls and children with SLI in clitic pronoun use, with most errors being omissions. Gutiérrez-Clellen, Restrepo, and colleagues (2000) further supported these results in their finding that Spanish-speaking children with SLI presented with omission of clitic pronouns. Furthermore, they found that the difference in performance between spontaneous language samples and elicited tasks affected the total percentages to a great degree. That is, the performance of children with SLI during the spontaneous task did not differ from controls (the production of both groups was above 96%), whereas performance was shown to differ during elicited tasks (37% correct for the SLI group and 80% correct for the control groups).

GRAMMATICAL IMPAIRMENTS IN CHILDREN WITH SLI IN CONTEXTS OF SUBTRACTIVE BILINGUALISM

Many children who are speakers of Spanish as a first language may not have the opportunity to achieve a high level of proficiency in their home language because they are being raised or exposed to language contexts in which the focus is to teach English without support of the first language. For these children, learning English implies suppression of the native language; in other words, the family and the children are discouraged from using their native language and the children are not taught literacy skills in their native language. This language-learning condition, also described as subtractive bilingualism (for a review, see Valdés & Figueroa, 1994), may have serious consequences for language development in children with SLI. These children may not have access to mediation or systematic intervention in their native language. For these children, there is some indication, although limited, that their grammatical skills may be affected to a

greater extent and/or differently from their peers with SLI who are growing up in additive language contexts or contexts in which the two languages
are encouraged.

Research with typically developing bilingual children (Anderson, 1999,
2002) and bilingual children with SLI in the United States (Restrepo, 2003;
Restrepo & Kruth, 2000) has shown that lack of opportunities to use and
improve the Spanish language may relate to limited development in that
language. For example, Restrepo (2003) found that Spanish use in two
Spanish-speaking children with SLI in English-only schools significantly
deteriorated in just 1 year. Although the children showed changes in their
grammatical system, the patterns of change were different for both children. Child 1 went from 0.15 grammatical errors per sentence in Spanish
to 0.59 errors per sentence, as his MLU increased from 3.5 to 4.9. In other
words, while his MLU increased, his grammatical errors increased, contrary to developmental expectations. In contrast, Child 2 went from 0.78
grammatical errors per sentence to 0.08, while her MLU went from 3.8 to
1.94. That is, while the child decreased the number of grammatical errors,
her sentence length also decreased to one- to two-word utterances in spontaneous conversations with her mother. Interestingly, both children received Spanish language intervention twice weekly for a period of 1 year,
although this treatment was outside of school, where the English-only language intervention occurred. Despite clinical efforts to help these children
in their native language, 2 hours per week were not sufficient to improve
grammaticality or utterance length (depending on the child). In studies
of Spanish-speaking children with typical language, the deterioration and
change within 1 year is not as significant as is documented with these children with SLI (Anderson, 1999, 2002). Therefore, children with SLI in
contexts of subtractive bilingualism may be at a higher risk for language
loss than their peers in additive contexts.

In Restrepo's (2003) study, an analysis of the children's difficulties revealed several patterns of error. Whereas Child 2 improved Spanish article
production from 6% correct initially to 33% correct at the second testing
point, her errors were mostly characterized by the substitution of the form
le for all of the different articles. In contrast, Child 1 used articles correctly
79% of the time at the initial testing and 15% correctly at the last testing
point, with most of the errors on gender agreement on the articles *el* and
la. This pattern of error is consistent with the idea that those forms with
the least saliency or reliability would be the most difficult for these children. During the last testing point, however, Child 2 also substituted the
Spanish articles with the English article *the*, using expressions such as "the

perro" (the dog). Although both children exhibited different error patterns, they seemed to resort to the use of only one form (i.e., "le perro," "the casa"), rather than the different Spanish articles, possibly reflecting the influence of English grammar (Restrepo, 2003). In addition, these children are likely to show errors characteristic of second language learners that may not be found in monolingual SLI children (e.g., subject ellipsis as in "looked for the frog"). Thus, although the grammatical deficits of bilingual children with SLI are consistent with the vulnerable areas described in SLI research with monolingual children, they may also show errors that reflect transfer from English to Spanish, greater first language (Spanish) loss, and errors common to learners of English as a second language.

The children in Restrepo's study (2003) also demonstrated difficulty in producing prepositions, and most of their errors were omissions. Furthermore, in clitic pronoun use, they mostly omitted the forms, even though Child 2 exhibited some substitution errors at the first time of the testing. Although these data are preliminary, they provide support for a comprehensive bilingual intervention program to ensure that both languages develop appropriately. These findings also suggest that bilingual children with SLI have significant difficulty maintaining one of the two languages unless they receive sufficient input in both languages, as has been shown in additive educational contexts (Bruck, 1982).

Grammatical Impairments in Children with SLI in Contexts of Additive Bilingualism

Preliminary language data collected in California from 75 children ranging in age from 4 to 5;9 years suggested that bilingual children with SLI make the same types of grammatical errors as monolingual children with SLI (Gutiérrez-Clellen, 2001; Gutiérrez-Clellen, Restrepo, Silva, & Del Castillo, 2000). Based on their narrative samples, Spanish-speaking children with SLI differed significantly from controls in the number of noun phrase errors, specifically articles, with few errors in the verb phrase. In contrast, English-speaking children with SLI differed significantly from controls in the number of verb phrase errors, specifically omissions of verbs and third person singular. These trends were corroborated when sentence completion tasks were used to elicit specific grammatical targets (i.e., for Spanish: articles, auxiliary *be* + gerund, preterite, clitic pronouns, and subjunctive mood; for English: possessive nouns, third person singular, past tense -*ed*, auxiliary *be*, copula *be*, plural nouns, auxiliary *do*, and passives). Children with SLI had most difficulty in Spanish with articles and clitic pronouns. In English, they showed difficulty with possessives, third person singular, past tense -*ed*, auxiliary *be*, copula, auxiliary *do*, and passives. These patterns resembled those of monolinguals with SLI and were consistent regardless of level of English exposure. Bilingual grammatical performance may not differ from monolingual grammatical performance if children have sufficient exposure to and use of the two languages. Preliminary findings indicated no differences on the grammatical areas described between typical language (TL) children with limited English proficiency and TL children with high use and exposure to the two languages. Assessments need to ensure that children who are bilingual are tested in the two languages, however, because children who are not proficient enough in one of the two languages will show limited grammatical skills in that language.

Characteristics of Code-Switching in SLI Children

Code-switching refers to the alternation between two languages within the same conversational event. Although an individual's use of code-switching may vary depending on different sociolinguistic factors (e.g., the characteristics of language contact within communities, the language attitudes of the members of the speech community), it is commonly found in bilingual children and adults. Yet, SLPs and teachers frequently avoid the use of code-switching in their intervention or in their teaching of a second language because they believe that it would affect the child's proficient learning of the two languages. This has led some professionals to recommend the use of a *one-parent/one-language* approach at home. The question of whether code-switching represents an undeveloped language system has been the subject of great debate in the bilingual literature (for a review, see Lanza, 1997). Furthermore, it is unclear whether code-switching has different grammatical characteristics in SLI children.

If there are specific code-switching features that occur more frequently in the speech of SLI children, it should be possible to document these features in the assessment protocols of bilingual children. Gutiérrez-Clellen and Erickson (in preparation) compared the code-switching patterns of children with and without SLI across different levels of bilingualism in terms of the type of code-switching and locus of code-switching in the sentence. Their results indicated no significant differences in the percentages of code-switches produced across groups for any of the variables, or any interaction effects. Children with SLI did not exhibit code-switching that violated grammatical constraints, such as saying "the casa" (versus grammatically acceptable noun switches as in "la house"). This finding is in contrast with one of the two children with SLI reported by Restrepo

(2003), who code-switched to the English form *the* with a Spanish noun. For this child, these forms increased in use from 15% in the initial sample to 59% of the total articles in the final sample, evaluated in a post-test 1 year later. The majority of the children in the group study were learning English in bilingual additive contexts, whereas in the case studies reported by Restrepo, the children were learning English in a subtractive language environment (Gutiérrez-Clellen & Erickson, in preparation). Clearly, more research with bilingual children with SLI is needed in order to understand how children with SLI develop their code-switching skills across additive and subtractive bilingual environments. The studies reported so far do not provide evidence that suppressing the native language would reduce code-switching or would facilitate second language acquisition.

In summary, Spanish-speaking children with SLI present with difficulties in both noun and verb phrases. Problems with the article system, clitic pronouns, and, possibly, prepositions seem to be more preponderant than verb difficulties. The significant difficulties these children have with these forms, compared with age and language controls, indicate that these structures should be evaluated carefully in the language assessment of Spanish-speaking children. In contrast, although language assessments in English should focus on the production of verb forms, available research indicates that Spanish verb production is generally well preserved due to the high frequency of inflections in the language, and that only deficits may be apparent when children are tested using complex verb forms such as subjunctive verbs.

IMPLICATIONS FOR ASSESSMENT AND INTERVENTION

Assessment

The lack of research in the characterization and identification of Spanish-speaking children with SLI has increased the risk of misdiagnosis of SLI in Spanish-speaking children. SLPs often complain that there are no tools available to assess these children appropriately (Roseberry-McKibbin & Eicholtz, 1994). As of 2004, assessment instruments were not normed on appropriate reference groups and lacked diagnostic accuracy. Some of the tests, therefore, lead to the overidentification of language disorders, whereas others lead to underidentification. For example, an early study designed to obtain normative data for the *Test of Auditory Comprehension of Language–Spanish Version* (TACL, SP; Carrow, 1973) from 60 monolingual and bilingual native Mexican children found that their language age equivalent scores fell significantly below language norms derived from English-speaking children (Wilcox & McGuinn Aasby, 1988). If English norms were used in the diagnosis of Spanish SLI, children with TL would have been identified incorrectly as having a language disorder.

In another study, Restrepo and Silverman (2001) found that the use of the *Preschool Language Scale–3: Spanish Edition* (SPLS; Zimmerman, Steiner, & Pond, 1993) had the potential to lead to gross overidentification of typically developing Spanish-speaking children presenting with language disorders. Restrepo and Silverman studied 37 Spanish-speaking children between 4;4 and 6;6 years of age in subtractive language environments. The children were given the SPLS, language samples were obtained from the children, and their parents participated in interviews. The children in the study scored an average of 1.5 standard deviations below the mean, which reflected problems with the test rather than indicating that the children had a true disorder. Children scored lower on questions that had obvious answers, such as "When do you eat?" or on ones focusing on spatial concepts that were not as critical for path description as in English (Slobin & Bocaz, 1988). Furthermore, based on the experimenters' experience with the children, questions asked to identify vocabulary such as *stamps*, a *wagon*, and *parachutes* that families of low-income Latino children do not typically use with their children. Also, the SPLS evaluates pre-academic concepts and vocabulary development appropriate for monolingual English-speaking children (Restrepo & Silverman, 2001). Although the participants in Restrepo and Silverman's study were learning English in a subtractive language environment, it is likely that their findings extend to other groups given the characteristics of the normative sample and the linguistic/cultural bias of this test.

The problem with these translated or adapted tests such as the SPLS and the TACL, SP, which are designed to identify language disorders in children, is that the tests are not designed to assess the specific language skills that are sensitive to the identification of the disorder in Spanish. In these two tests, a majority of the children would qualify as having impaired language based on the tests' cut-off score. The under-representation problem is also possible with current language tests, however. The lack of diagnostic accuracy is directly related to the structures and items selected for inclusion in these tests. An example of this problem is illustrated in the items of the *Spanish Test for Assessing Morphologic Production* (Nuget, Shipley, & Provencio, 1991). A review of this test indicates that 20 items involve adjectives or nouns, and 85 items assess Spanish verbs. The test items do not address article or clitic pronoun use, which have been found to be specifically problematic for Spanish-speaking children with SLI. The focus on verbs may not have diagnostic sensitivity given that Spanish-speaking children with SLI appear to have less difficulty with verb phrases than with noun phrases. Thus, this test may have limited clinical significance for the identification of children with grammatical impairments.

Another possible reason for under-representation with current language measures is the lack of consideration of the language and sociolinguistic variables in the norming of the bilingual population. For example, the *Clinical Evaluation of Language Fundamentals–3: Spanish Edition* (CELF-3 SP) (Semel, Wiig, & Secord, 1997) reports in its manual that the test correctly classified 71.6% of the children. It misdiagnosed 11% of the children with normal language and underdiagnosed 17.4% of Spanish-speaking children with SLI. In addition to the limited validity of the items selected for testing, the unacceptable diagnostic accuracy of this test is probably related to the lack of consistent or appropriate criteria to determine the language proficiency of the normative sample. The manual in this test did not provide information regarding the children's Spanish language proficiency levels or how Spanish proficiency was determined in the development of the Spanish norms. Children who are losing their Spanish may perform as poorly as their SLI peers in that language. Therefore, failure to consider these variables significantly affects tests' sensitivity and specificity (e.g., Restrepo & Silverman, 2001; Torres, Simon-Cerrejido, & Rosas, 2000).

These concerns motivated a significant project funded by the National Institute of Deafness and Other Communicative Disorders (NIDCD) to develop and validate a language test for bilingual Hispanic children (Iglesias, Peña, Gutiérrez-Clellen, Bedore, & Goldstein, 1999). First, Spanish grammatical targets with diagnostic potential should include article + noun phrases (i.e., gender and number agreement), clitics (i.e., *la, lo, las, los*), and complex verb forms such as the subjunctive. The clitic pronoun *le/les*, present perfect verb forms, and simple future forms vary across Spanish dialects and may not be reliable diagnostic markers in assessment (Alvar, 1996; Varela, 1992). Further research with these forms and with prepositions is needed to determine their clinical significance for the identification of grammatical impairments. Dialectal differences in the production of plurals should be considered in assessment because speakers of Caribbean dialects may omit them. English grammatical forms in assessment should include possessive nouns, plural nouns, third person singular, past tense *-ed*, and copula and auxiliary *be* (see Leonard, 1998, for a review of the English characteristics of English-speaking children with SLI). Spanish-speaking children learning English in African American communities may exhibit differences in their use of most of these features. For these children, alternative scoring procedures that do not penalize dialectal differences will be needed. For example, such a procedure might stipulate that the use of copulas and the marking of past tense is optional for these children and therefore, the omission of these practices would not be considered an error.

Second, it has been repeatedly documented that the elicitation tasks selected may have an effect on the use or misuse of specific forms (e.g., Anderson, 1996). Children with limited experience in responding to tasks such as those used in tests may not do well on the test unless enough practice items and demonstration or modeling is provided. Gutiérrez-Clellen's (2001) work on the development of probes for the assessment of morphosyntax indicates that sentence completion and cloze tasks can elicit specific grammatical forms across age groups, socioeconomic levels, and parent education. These observations are consistent with findings by Anderson (1996). She compared two tasks to identify production of target grammatical forms in children with normal language: *Spanish Structured Photographic Expressive Language Test—Preschool* (Werner & Kresheck, 1989), in which the child is asked a series of questions based on pictures and a spontaneous structured probe in which the clinician played with the child and encouraged the child to describe what was happening. Results indicated that when using the structured probe, children were more apt to demonstrate their grammatical skills than they were on the test.

Clinical Criteria for Identification of SLI

The variables investigated by Restrepo (1998), and discussed further by Gutiérrez-Clellen, Restrepo, and colleagues (2000), can be used to outline a protocol for the identification of children with SLI using spontaneous language sampling as well as parent and teacher questionnaires. Restrepo (1998) investigated a group of 62 4- to 7-year-old Spanish-speaking children from the southwest United States. Of these children, 31 had been identified with moderate to severe SLI and 31 had been identified with typical language, matched by age, grade, language use, and school. On a series of measures, Restrepo found that parent interviews (regarding family history of speech and language problems and parental concerns regarding speech and language problems) and language sample measures (mean length of terminable unit/sentence and number of grammatical errors per terminable unit) identified children with SLI with more than 90% accuracy. Of these measures, parental concern regarding the child's speech and language problems and number of grammatical errors per sentence *combined* were the best predictors of group membership. Children with typical language scored with a mean of 0.09 (*SD* = 0.05) grammatical errors per sentence, and children with SLI scored with a mean of .39 (*SD* = 0.21) grammatical errors per sentence. Therefore, for Spanish-speaking children with limited English input, the cut-off score for grammatical errors per sentence may be .09 plus 2 *SD*, which leads to score of 0.18 errors per sentence. That is, children who score above this cut-off are at risk of presenting with a language disorder.

Gutiérrez-Clellen, Restrepo, and colleagues (2000) showed that there is not one accepted and validated method to perform morphological analyses in Spanish and, thus, different analyses may yield different results. The use of MLU in morphemes may be problematic across dialects because in some Caribbean Spanish dialects, the plural form may be deleted, and the third person plural form may not be used contrastively (e.g., "lah casah" and "la casa" for "las casas"). Therefore, Gutiérrez-Clellen and colleagues recommended the use of MLU in words in order to achieve some level of comparison in utterance length across the two languages. Furthermore, the clinician must look for converging evidence that a child has a language problem from a variety of sources: parent interview, teacher interview, spontaneous language analyses of grammatical errors per sentence, MLU, and structured tasks and dynamic assessment procedures. The use of only one measure to make this kind of decision is insufficient in the absence of standardized, normed, and validated measures. In fact, the use of invalid measures only leads to misdiagnosis about the child's language skills (Restrepo & Silverman, 2001).

Several issues need to be addressed when applying these criteria to the grammatical assessment of bilingual speakers. First, it is critical to document the child's language history. Limited grammatical performance in English may simply reflect limited use and exposure, not a language deficit. Spanish grammatical performance may be affected by language loss. Research suggests that parent and teacher estimates of language use and proficiency may be useful to determine bilingual status because they correlate with the child's grammatical performance in the target language (Gutiérrez-Clellen & Kreiter, 2003; Restrepo, 1998). Language histories will be useful to explain differences across the two languages and to differentiate language differences from disorders. Furthermore, it is clear that children developing two languages should demonstrate, at least grammatically, a strong language. That is, they would not present grammatical errors that are not expected for their age. The presence of grammatical errors in both languages places the child at risk for speech and language difficulties.

Second, language sample transcribers should not penalize utterances containing code-switching because there is no evidence that children with SLI tend to code-switch more than their typical language peers. For children who exhibit frequent code-switching in their spontaneous language, it is extremely difficult to differentiate the matrix language from the embedded language, and no guidelines are yet available to determine the grammaticality of forms within code-switched utterances. Thus, lengthier samples will be needed for grammatical analysis because utterances with code-switching may need to be excluded from the error analysis or considered within the whole linguistic context of the speakers and topics.

Finally, evidence exists that diagnostic accuracy may improve when sentence recall or sentence repetition tasks are included in assessment (Conti-Ramsden, Botting, Simkin, & Knox, 2001). These tasks require the elicitation of complex forms, and the ability to process and store incoming information. Preliminary results with bilingual children indicate that these children can be trained to repeat words and sentences with sufficient practice and demonstration items. Processing measures such as the Competing Language Processing Task, in which participants are asked to listen to sets of unrelated sentences while simultaneously attempting to retain the last word of each sentence, and nonword repetition tasks, have been found to be sensitive measures to identify children with SLI in monolingual English speakers (Campbell, Dollaghan, Needleman, & Janosky, 1997; Ellis Weismer, Tomblin, Zhang, Chynoweth, & Jones, 2000) as well as in Spanish-speaking bilingual children (Calderón & Gutierrez-Clellen, 2000; Gutiérrez-Clellen & Calderón, 2000; Gutiérrez-Clellen, Calderón, & Ellis Weismer, in press). When these measures are used together with parent–teacher reports of concern and evidence of ungrammatical performance based on spontaneous language data and structured probes, SLPs may be likely to limit the misdiagnosis of these children. Further research is still needed with these processing measures across different groups of bilingual children before clinicians can use them clinically, however.

Intervention

In a review of the literature on the language of intervention, Gutiérrez-Clellen (1999) concluded the following: No evidence exists that bilingual input retards first or second language development. Learning a first or second language involves shared cognitive processes and interrelated linguistic processes, and children's ability to transfer skills to a second language with limited English proficiency can be facilitated by mediation in the native language. To our knowledge, no published reports document the efficacy of grammatical treatment with monolingual Spanish speakers or with bilingual children with SLI who attend programs in which their native language is not stimulated. Based on findings from Restrepo (2003) and Restrepo and Kruth (2000), however, children in subtractive language environments seem to be at risk of losing their native language ability. Their results suggest that two sessions of Spanish intervention a week may not be sufficient to produce language maintenance, let alone to promote language gains in these children, if there is not enough language stimulation in the home. These results indicate a need for more structured first language input to help develop the home language, which, in many cases, is the only language spoken by the family. Furthermore, it is likely that Spanish-speaking children with SLI may demonstrate difficulty acquiring the second language given that they have a language-learning disability. As a result, these children may show a significant rate of transfer errors (i.e., errors based on their knowledge of Spanish). Thus, clinicians should explicitly mediate the second language by providing direct instruction on features that are shared and unshared across the two languages. Examples include use of word order and obligatory subjects in English. Spanish does not require a strict word order, and subject ellipsis is grammatical. This work should be done in addition to the focused treatment of English grammar typical of monolinguals with SLI.

Based on the issues discussed above, it is clear that bilingual children should receive bilingual intervention (Gutiérrez-Clellen, 1999; Restrepo, 2003) to ensure that both languages develop well. Intervention goals for morphosyntax should be based on evidence of significant grammatical deficits in the two languages. The selection of grammatical areas to target should first address variability across dialects. For example, when focusing on Spanish clitic pronouns, clinicians should consider whether *le(s)/la(s)* or *lo(s)* is optional in the Spanish dialect used by the family or speech community. Target forms should be those that are obligatory in the language variant spoken by the family. Second, intervention strategies should be based on a variety of elicitation tasks—from spontaneous language to structured probes—and less naturalistic tasks. Certain forms such as articles may not be easy to elicit using structured probes compared to spontaneous narratives or conversation. Clitic pronouns may require directly elicited probes because they are not obligatory when children choose to use a full noun phrase to mark direct objects. For example the child can say "Dámelo" (Give it to me) or "Dame el carro" (Give me the car). Complex verb forms will require structured scripts because they would not be used in play activities.

Although there is no research available on the efficacy of grammatical treatment with Spanish-speaking children with SLI in the United States, and longitudinal studies are needed to determine language change cross-linguistically and over time, targeting the grammatical areas that seem to be most vulnerable in the manifestations of the disorder should provide a preliminary framework for intervention. Furthermore, intervention research should address groups with different bilingual experiences as well as factors such as school language policies and language outcomes across families with various educational and socioeconomic levels to determine the amount of language stimulation needed across the different contexts in order to improve, not just maintain, language skills.

SUMMARY

This chapter has reviewed the characteristics of Spanish-speaking and Spanish-English bilingual children with SLI that are important areas for the identification of these children. Understanding these characteristics leads to less biased assessments because the grammatical aspects discussed are not subject to cultural differences or differences in literacy experience. Although these measures of grammatical skills hold promise for accurate identification, clinicians are always in search of more efficient methods. Processing methods for identification have clinical potential; however, no measures are yet available for clinical purposes.

In terms of intervention, this chapter underscores how important it is for bilingual children to receive bilingual services so that both languages can grow to mature levels. To recommend English-only intervention for children with SLI whose homes are Spanish-speaking is detrimental not only to their language development but also to their overall communication in the home. These types of recommendations may have significant social and emotional consequences that can lead to serious communication problems in the children's homes.

REFERENCES

Alvar, M. (1996). *Manual de dialectología Hispánica: El español de América* [Manual of Hispanic Dialectology: The Spanish of America.] Barcelona, Spain: Ariel.

Anderson, R. (1996). Assessing the Grammar of Spanish-speaking children: A comparison of two procedures. *Language, Speech, and Hearing Services in the Schools, 27,* 333–344.

Anderson, R. (1999). Impact of first language loss on grammar in a bilingual child. *Communication Disorders Quarterly, 21,* 4–16.

Anderson, R. (2002). Lexical morphology and verb use in child first language loss: A preliminary case study investigation. *International Journal of Bilingualism, 5,* 377–401.

Bedore, L., & Leonard, L.B. (2001). Grammatical morphology deficits in Spanish-speaking children with specific language impairment. *Journal of Speech and Hearing Research, 44*, 905–924.

Bosch, L., & Serra, M. (1997). Grammatical morphology deficits of Spanish-speaking children with specific language impairment. In A. Baker, M. Beers, G. Bol, J. de Jong, & G. Leemans (Eds.), *Child language disorders in a cross linguistic perspective: Proceedings of the Fourth Symposium of the European Group on Child Language Disorders* (Vol 6.) Amsterdam: University of Amsterdam, Institute for General Linguistics.

Brown, R. (1973). *A first language: The early stages.* Cambridge, MA: Harvard University Press.

Bruck, M. (1982). Language impaired children's performance in an additive bilingual education program. *Applied Psycholinguistics, 3*, 45–60.

Calderón, J., & Gutiérrez-Clellen, V.F. (1999). Language choice in intervention with bilingual children. *American Journal of Speech-Language Pathology, 8*, 291–302.

Campbell, T., Dollaghan, C., Needleman, H., & Janosky, J. (1997). Reducing bias in language assessment: Processing-dependent measures. *Journal of Speech, Language, and Hearing Research, 40*, 519–525.

Carrow, E. (1973). *Test for Auditory Comprehension of Language.* Austin, TX: Learning Concepts.

Conti-Ramsden, G., Botting, N., Simkin, Z., & Knox, E. (2001, April–June); Follow-up of children attending infant language units: Outcomes at 11 years of age. *International Journal of Language and Communication Disorders, 36*(2), 207–219.

Ellis Weismer, S., Tomblin, J.B., Zhang, X., Chynoweth, J.G., & Jones, M. (2000). Nonword repetition performance in school-age children with and without language impairment. *Journal of Speech, Language, and Hearing Research, 43*, 865–878.

Eng, N., & O'Connor, B. (2000). Acquisition of definite articles + noun agreement of Spanish-English bilingual children with specific language impairment. *Communication Disorders Quarterly, 21*, 114–124.

Eziezabarrena, M.J. (1996). *Adquisición de la morfología verbal en euskera y castellano por niños bilingües* [The acquisition of verbal morphology in euskera and spanish for bilingual children]. Bilbao, Spain: Universidad del País Vasco: Servicio Editorial.

Eziezabarrena, M.J. (2001, October). *Deletion of finiteness: An avoid error-strategy in early child language?* Paper presented at the Fourth Conference on the Acquisition of Spanish and Portuguese as First and Second Languages, University of Illinois, Urbana-Champaign.

Gutiérrez-Clellen, V.F. (1999). Language choice in intervention with bilingual children. *American Journal of Speech-Language Pathology, 8*, 291–302.

Gutiérrez-Clellen, V.F. (2000, June). *Development of a Spanish nonword repetition task: Preliminary results.* Paper presented to the 2000 Symposium on Research in Child Language Disorders, Madison, WI.

Gutiérrez-Clellen, V.F. (2001). *Morpho-syntactic development of bilingual children with and without language disorders.* Paper presented at the Third International Symposium on Bilingualism, Bristol, UK.

Gutiérrez-Clellen, V.F., & Calderón, J. (2000, November). *Nonword repetition in Latino children with language impairment: Preliminary results.* Paper presented at the American Speech-Language-Hearing Association national convention, Washington, DC.

Gutiérrez-Clellen, V.F., Calderón, J., & Ellis Weismer, S. (in press). Verbal working memory in bilingual children. *Journal of Speech, Language, and Hearing Research*.

Gutiérrez-Clellen, V.F., & Erickson, A.B. (in press). *Codeswitching in SLI children*. Manuscript submitted for publication.

Gutiérrez-Clellen, V.F., & Kreiter, J. (2003). Understanding child bilingual acquisition using parent and teacher reports. *Applied Psycholinguistics, 24,* 267–288.

Gutiérrez-Clellen, V.F., Restrepo, M.A., Bedore, L., Peña, L., & Anderson, R. (2000). Language sample analysis: Methodological considerations. *Language, Speech, and Hearing Services in the Schools, 31,* 88–98.

Gutiérrez-Clellen, V.F., Restrepo, M.A., Silva, M.R., & Del Castillo, T.S. (2000, June). *Cross-linguistic profiles of Latino children exposed to a second language*. Paper presented to the 2000 Symposium on Research in Child Language Disorders. Madison, WI.

Hernández Pina, F. (1984). *Teorías psicolingüísticas y su aplicación a la adquisición del español* [Psycholinguistyic theories and their application to Spanish acquisition]. Madrid: Siglo XXI.

Iglesias A., Peña E., Gutiérrez-Clellen V., Bedore L., & Goldstein B. (1999). *Development of a language test for bilingual Spanish-English speaking children: The Bilingual English/Spanish Assessment (BESA)*. Paper presented at the American Speech-Language-Hearing Association Convention, San Francisco, CA.

Lanza, E. (1997). Language contact in bilingual two-year-olds and code-switching: Language encounters of a different kind? *International Journal of Bilingualism, 1,* 135–162.

Leonard, L.B. (1998). *Children with specific language impairment*. Cambridge, MA: The MIT Press.

Leonard, L.B., Bortolini, U., Caselli, M. C., McGregor, K., & Sabbadini, L. (1992). Morphological deficits in children with specific language impairment: The status of features in the underlying grammar. *Language Acquisition, 2,* 151–179.

Leonard, L., Eyer, J., Bedore, L., & Grela, B. (1997). Three accounts of grammatical morpheme difficulties of English-speaking children with specific language impairment. *Journal of Speech and Hearing Research, 40,* 741–753.

Nuget, T.M., Shipley, K.G., & Provencio, D.O. (1991). *Spanish Test for Assessing Morphologic Production*. Oceanside, CA: Academic Communication Associates.

Restrepo, M.A. (1998). Identifiers of predominantly Spanish-speaking children with language impairment. *Journal of Speech, Language, and Hearing Research, 41,* 1398–1411.

Restrepo, M.A. (2003). Spanish language skills in bilingual children with specific language impairment. In S. Montrul & F. Ordóñez (Eds.), *Linguistic theory and language development in Hispanic languages. Papers from the 5th Hispanic Linguistics Symposium and the 2001 Acquisition of Spanish and Portuguese Conference* (pp. 365–374). Somerville, MA: Cascadilla Press.

Restrepo, M.A., & Gutiérrez-Clellen, V.F. (2000, June). *Cross linguistic profiles of Latino children exposed to a second language*. Poster presentation at the Symposium on Research in Child Language Disorder, Madison, WI.

Restrepo, M.A., & Gutiérrez-Clellen, V.F. (2001). Article production in bilingual children with specific language impairment. *Journal of Child Language, 28,* 433–452.

Restrepo, M.A., & Kruth, K. (2000). Grammatical characteristics of a bilingual student with specific language impairment. *Disorders Quarterly Communication Journal, 21,* 66–76.

Restrepo, M.A., & Silverman, S. (2001). The validity of the Spanish Preschool-Language Scale for use with bilingual children. *American Journal of Speech-Language Pathology, 10,* 382–393.

Rice, M., & Bode, J. (1993). GAPS in the lexicon of children with specific language impairment. *First Language, 13,* 113–131.

Rice, M., Wexler, K., & Cleave, P. (1995). Specific language impairment as a period of extended optional infinitive. *Journal of Speech and Hearing Research, 38,* 850–863.

Roseberry-McKibbin, C.A., & Eicholtz, G.E. (1994). Serving children with limited English proficiency in the schools: A national survey. *Language, Speech, and Hearing Services in Schools, 25,* 156–164.

Sanz Torrent, M. (2002). Los verbos en niños con trastorno de lenguaje [Verbs in children with language disorders]. *Revista de Logopedia, Foniatría y Audiología, XXII,* 100–110.

Semel, E., Wiig, E.H., & Secord, W.A. (1997). *Clinical Evaluation of Language Fundamentals–3: Spanish Edition. Manual del examinador.* San Antonio, TX: The Psychological Corporation.

Serra, M. (2002). Trastornos del lenguaje: Preguntas pendientes en investigación e intervención [Language disorders: Pending questions in research and intervention]. *Revista de Logopedia, Foniatría y Audiología, XXII*(2), 63–76.

Slobin, D., & Bocaz, A. (1988). Learning to talk about movement through time and space: The development of narrative abilities in Spanish and English. *Lenguas Modernas, 15,* 5–24.

Tomblin, J.B., Records, N., Buckwalter, P., Zhang, X., Smith, E., & O'Brien, M. (1997). Prevalence of specific language impairment in kindergarten children. *Journal of Speech and Hearing Research, 40,* 1245–1260.

Torrens, V., & Wexler, K. (2001). El retraso del lenguaje en la adquisición del castellano y el catalán [Language delay in the acquisition of Castillian and Catalan]. *Aloma, 9,* 131–148.

Torres, A., Simon-Cerrejido, G., & Rosas, J. (2000, November). *The validity and reliability of the CELF-3 Spanish.* Poster session presented at the American Speech-Language-Hearing Association annual convention, Washington, DC.

Valdés, G., & Figueroa, R.A. (1994). *Bilingualism and testing: A special case of bias.* Norwood, NJ: Ablex.

Varela, B. (1992). *El español cubano-americano* [Cuban-American Spanish]. Coral Gables, FL: Senda Nueva de Ediciones, Inc.

Watkins, R., Rice, M., & Molz, C. (1993). Verb use by language impaired and normally developing children. *First Language, 37,* 133–143.

Werner, E.O., & Kresheck, J.D. (1989). *Spanish Structured Photographic Expressive Language Test—Preschool.* Sandwich, IL: Janelle Publications.

Wilcox, K.A., & McGuinn Aasby, S. (1988). The performance of monolingual and bilingual Mexican children on the TACL. *Language, Speech, and Hearing Services in Schools, 19,* 34–40.

Zimmerman, I.L., Steiner, V.G., & Pond, R.E. (1993). *Preschool Language Scale–3: Spanish Edition.* San Antonio, TX: Psychological Corporation.

CHAPTER 10

Narrative Development and Disorders in Bilingual Children

VERA F. GUTIÉRREZ-CLELLEN

N arratives can provide significant information about a child's ability to represent and organize past experiences beyond the level of the sentence or conversational turn. In narrative production tasks, children are asked to organize narrative events while linking story statements with appropriate linguistic means to maintain coherence. In narrative comprehension activities, such as listening to or reading stories, children are required to integrate grammatical and semantic knowledge as they mentally represent the sequence of events in the original story. Children need to keep track of contextual clues across stretches of discourse at the same time that they process new narrative information. Because of the greater processing demands posed by these narrative tasks, children with language disorders have specific difficulties in the production and comprehension of narrative discourse, which may not be apparent in their performance on sentences in isolation.

Developmentally, children show significant differences in narrative proficiency during the earlier school years. Although most preschool children are capable of retelling a past event, it is during a child's school years that use of specific narrative features and appropriate story interpretations have clinical and educational significance. The first section of this chapter summarizes the literature on narrative development in Spanish-speaking children with various levels of English proficiency. Contextual variables and typological differences that may influence narrative performance in bilingual speakers are discussed, based on available crosslinguistic research. Then, features that may be useful for the clinical assessment of narratives in children during the early school years are presented.

THE ACQUISITION OF NARRATIVE PROFICIENCY

Developmental Trends in Overall Narrative Structure

The developmental literature based on children from monolingual Spanish-speaking backgrounds indicates that their overall narrative structure is similar to that of children from other linguistic backgrounds. Early narrative studies based on story recall tasks conducted in Chile and Argentina used a story grammar approach based on research with English-speaking monolingual children (e.g., Stein & Glenn, 1979). Within this framework, it was found that a narrative episode is expected to contain specific narrative elements or components (i.e., a setting, an initiating event, an internal response, an attempt, a consequence, and a reaction). Developmental comparisons indicated great variability in children's use of these categories across narrative episodes within stories (Bocaz, 1986; Signorini & Monzone de Manrique, 1988). Yet, there were some developmental trends. Children at age 6 appeared to focus only on providing sequences of actions (e.g., "John opened the door; the dog went after him") and changes in physical state (e.g., "It was raining; he got all dirty"). Motivations or changes in mental state (e.g., "John was angry; he went inside") were not used often at this age. At age 7, children demonstrated an increase in the use of causal and temporal markers such as *entonces* (so), but narratives still lacked explicit relationships between the characters' actions and goals or mental states. It was not until children reached the ages of 8–12 years old that they showed greater use of mental states and goals in their stories. At these ages, children also included detailed contextual information and interpretive inferences about the stories they recalled. These studies were based on monolingual Spanish speakers but they provide a basis for examining the Spanish narratives of bilingual children.

Children's limited use of information about internal responses, goals, or mental states may reveal limitations in their narrative development. Children with language-learning disabilities from monolingual English backgrounds are likely to omit this information in their narratives (Griffith, Ripich, & Dastoli, 1986; Roth & Spekman, 1986). The use of story grammars for assessing narrative competence may not be a useful framework in clinical applications with children from diverse backgrounds, however. Story grammars assume that all stories are composed of a series of invariant informational units. Yet, the amount and type of narrative information provided in stories reflect a child's perspective on the purpose of the task, which is based on previous experiences with similar storytelling contexts (Gutiérrez-Clellen & Quinn, 1993). Because these experiences vary from child to child within groups, one cannot assume that a traditional story grammar approach may provide an accurate estimate of the child's narrative skills.

Developmental Changes in Narrative Coherence

Unlike story grammars, which categorize story statements into specific components to then build a hierarchical representation of the discourse, microstructural models focus on coherence relationships such as causal, referential, spatial, or temporal, at a local level. Using this framework, Gutiérrez-Clellen and Iglesias (1992) examined the causal sequences produced by Spanish-speaking children with limited English proficiency (and from primarily Puerto Rican backgrounds) in their retellings of a short silent film. The analyses showed that 8-year-olds included more actions in their stories than did younger children with similar backgrounds. They also appeared to provide more precise information about properties of objects, people, and locations (e.g., "The frog was in his pocket; she jumped; she fell on his plate") compared with the relatively higher use of unrelated statements by the younger children (e.g., "There was a frog and a boy; and the man came; and went to the house"). Although the 8-year-olds did not show greater use of mental states or motivations overall compared with the 4-year-olds, they produced longer and more explicitly linked sequences of actions that were causally related (e.g., actions result in changes of physical states; physical states enable/disable actions; mental states motivate actions that, in turn, result in changes of physical or mental state), and they showed a decrease in their use of unrelated statements in their stories. Thus, the analysis of causal sequences may be useful in the identification of differences in narrative development.

These developmental trends in causal coherence were also replicated using a referential cohesion analysis. Gutiérrez-Clellen and Heinrichs-Ramos (1993) examined the types of referents and the referential accuracy demonstrated in narratives based on a short film by Spanish-speaking Puerto Rican children ages 4–8 who had limited English proficiency. Children introduced or reintroduced referents using different referents: nominal (e.g., "a boy," "a house," "a frog"), pronominal (e.g., "he," "it," "that," "there"), or elliptical reference (e.g., "The boy had a frog; one day [he] went to a restaurant"). Use of ellipsis was reflective of these children's proficiency with Spanish grammar because in Spanish, sentence subjects may be omitted if the referents are introduced in previous statements. With age, children increasingly used ellipsis to refer to the location of story events. Yet, there were no developmental differences in the frequency of children's use of nominal, pronominal, or demonstrative referents from ages 4 to 8 years.

In contrast, Oudega-Campbell (1985) found that bilingual Mexican American third graders used increasingly more pronominal and demonstrative references in their story retellings than first graders of similar linguistic backgrounds. Although narrative elicitation differences between these studies make it difficult to draw any definitive conclusions, the findings suggest that bilingual children who are increasingly exposed to English-only input may show a greater use of pronominal reference in their Spanish stories due to transfer from English, a language that has obligatory subjects. Referential accuracy seems to be an important indicator of narrative proficiency, with significance for the clinical assessment of narratives in bilingual children.

Developmentally, children appear to become more precise in their introductions or re-introductions of referents in narratives. From 4 to 8 years old, children show changes in the appropriateness of referential markers. Eight-year-olds exhibited increased use of appropriate phrases to introduce new referents and a decreased use of ambiguities when referents were reintroduced (Gutiérrez-Clellen & Heinrichs-Ramos, 1993). These differences were not observed in the study with bilingual children reported by Oudega-Campbell (1985), probably because the story retelling task used in that study may not be as challenging as a film story based on multiple characters and events. Thus, narrative tasks that require the introduction and re-introduction of several characters may be needed in clinical applications of this analysis.

Complex Syntax in the Development of Narrative Discourse

Complex syntax also is important to describe simultaneous events or events that occur at different times in a story (e.g., flashbacks in a movie or book). Complex syntactic constructions are useful means to mark background information about the identity of referents (e.g., "The man who was carrying the tray saw the frog") or to recapitulate previously presented information (e.g., "After he found the frog, he went home"). Gutiérrez-Clellen and Hofstetter (1994) examined the Spanish movie retellings of 46 Puerto Rican and 31 Mexican American children matched by age who were learning English as a second language. Their findings indicated that the 8-year-old children showed a greater use of subordination in their descriptions of events, specifically using nominal clauses as complements to differentiate narrative time from event time (e.g., "It was [about] a boy who had a frog") or to mark a variety of narrative perspectives (e.g., "The mother told him that he had to go to his room") compared with preschool children. Whereas only about one third of preschoolers used relative clauses in their stories, more than one half of the 8-year-olds used them to elaborate on the identity of referents or to specify additional information to disambiguate reference. Thus, the functional use of complex syntax in narrative performance represents another important index of narrative proficiency in school-age children.

In addition, syntactic complexity was found to be a significant measure that distinguished bilingual children with different reading achievement. Gutiérrez-Clellen (1998) compared 57 Spanish-speaking Mexican American children with low school achievement (LA) and average school achievement (AA) from kindergarten to fifth grade matched by grade. All children had limited English proficiency and were attending bilingual classrooms. Oral narratives were elicited with book and film retelling tasks in counterbalanced order of presentation. Group comparisons indicated that approximately 31% of the LA children performed below the cutoff score for complex sentences and approximately 48% demonstrated below-expected performance for sentences containing relative clauses. Interesting differences across the groups were also noted in how children used their syntactic skills to maintain reference. Children with LA tended to use proportionately fewer relative clauses than did their peers with AA, and when they used relative clauses to clarify the identity of characters, they were not able to use complex syntax to convey narrative information in a clear and unambiguous manner.

For children who are bilingual, it is important to note that Spanish and English languages differ in the frequency of use of relative clauses in narratives. Across ages, Spanish speakers are more likely to use relative clauses and to use them with more frequency than do English speakers (Dasinger & Toupin, 1994). Relative clauses to situate a new or an old referent in an ongoing event emerge at an earlier age in Spanish speakers than in English speakers (i.e., at approximately age 3). At 9 years of age, Spanish speakers use relative clauses to provide motivation/psychological state or physical state information of characters more frequently than do English speakers. These trends were also found for adult speakers of the two languages (Dasinger & Topin, 1994).

These differences indicate that subordination should not be expected with similar frequency across the languages of bilingual children. Differences in the use of these constructions across the two languages should not be confused with differences in narrative development or ability. Instead, the relative use of these syntactic forms reflects the consequences of typological differences and rhetorical norms across the two languages (for a detailed discussion, see Dasinger & Topin, 1994).

BILINGUAL NARRATIVE PERFORMANCE

The majority of studies conducted with Spanish-speaking children are based on monolingual children or children with limited English proficiency. As such, they provide a starting point to evaluate the narrative skills of children in the process of learning English as a second language. As was described in the studies reviewed so far, the languages share much in common that can guide the identification of narrative areas for assessment and intervention with bilingual children. Narrative assessments of bilingual children should also consider three critical issues that can explain differences in narrative performance in typical learners: 1) typological differences across the two languages; 2) cross-linguistic transfer; and 3) language dominance. These issues will provide a foundation to recognize differences in narrative performance that are language-specific as well as individual variability related to a child's relative proficiency and use of the two languages.

Typological Differences

Slobin (1996) suggested that typological differences in the grammars of the languages have consequences for the preference of specific rhetorical styles in narratives. The following are some types of typological differences.

Marking Motion Events

According to Slobin (1996), cross-linguistic differences in the characteristics of verbs and motion events have an influence on the development of a rhetorical style to describe movement in stories within a language. This research, based on narratives collected from monolingual children and adults in Argentina and Chile (Slobin & Bocaz, 1988), the United States (Slobin, 1990), and Madrid (Sebastián & Slobin, 1994a), showed that at all ages, English speakers provided twice as much detail in their descriptions of motion events than did Spanish speakers. English verbs of motion such as *fall* (*caerse*) were more likely to be accompanied by a prepositional phrase (e.g., "fall in the water"); a verb particle (e.g., "fall down"); or an adverbial expression to indicate directionality, source, or goal of motion (e.g., "He threw him off over a cliff into the river").

In contrast, Spanish relies on the inherent directionality of the verb itself and as a result, bare verbs of motion are more frequent in descriptions of motion events (e.g., *Se cayeron,* [they] fell). Although Spanish adults provided more elaboration (approximately 64% of adults' motion descriptions added some locative information to the verb compared with approximately 46% of 9-year-olds or preschoolers who added locative information), their descriptions of motion events were likely to differ from those of English speakers. For English speakers, approximately 85% of these verbs were elaborated with path descriptions. Slobin suggested that speakers of the two languages might pay different attention to path information in their narratives because of the different ways the languages mark movement in space. He observed that Spanish speakers might favor use of adverbial constructions in separate clauses to encode manner and use of relative clauses to encode setting information. Thus, for descriptions of motion events, learning to become a proficient narrator in Spanish would mean using appropriate verbs of motion and subordination, and in English, providing sufficient detail on trajectories in space by adding locative information to the verbs. Bilingual learners would need to recognize these differences and use the features provided by each language to indicate expected narrative information in the target language.

Marking Temporal Events

Slobin (1990) and colleagues (Sebastian & Slobin, 1994b) also described cross-linguistic differences in the marking of temporality based on narratives from monolingual children and adults. Location in time is marked by use of tense markers (e.g., "John *opened* the door"). In fact, *tense markers* are the grammatical realizations of location in time (Comrie, 1985). (The acquisition of tense is discussed in Chapter 9 and elsewhere in this book.) In contrast, *aspect* (see examples that follow) refers to the internal temporal structure of a situation and, as such, it involves a viewpoint or the speaker's perspective on the situation (Comrie, 1976). Narrative performance involves proficient use of aspect forms licensed by the languages. Competent narrators use aspect contrasts to mark foreground and background in their narratives. In English, temporal relations are marked through three verbal aspects: progressive (e.g., *running*), perfect (e.g., *has/had run*), and habitual (e.g., *runs*) aspects. In contrast, Spanish aspect forms include progressive (e.g., *está/estaba corriendo*, is/was running), perfect (e.g., *ha/había corrido*, has/had run), imperfective (e.g., *corría*, was running), and perfective (e.g., *corrió*, ran) aspects. Monolingual children as young as 3 years old use the aspect forms their native languages provide. In English they show use of the past, past progressive, present, and present progressive. In Spanish they use six different aspect forms: past perfective, past imperfective, past progressive, present, present progressive, and present perfect. It is important to note that the present perfect is only found in Spanish speakers from Spain, not Latin America, due to dialectal differences within Spanish (Sebastian & Slobin, 1994a).

Both languages have a progressive aspect to differentiate ongoing (e.g., *was flying*) and complete events (e.g., *fell out*) as in "the owl *was flying*" and "the boy *fell out* of the chair." Spanish makes a perfective–imperfective distinction that marks two different perspectives on narrative events, however. To indicate that the events are durative or that they extend in time, individuals mark verbs using imperfective (I) aspect forms (e.g., "Y el niño veía [I] que se caía [I] el perro," And the boy saw [I] that the dog fell [I]). To indicate a completed event, the verbs are marked with perfective (P) forms (e.g., "El niño vio [P] que se cayó [P] el perro," The boy saw [P] that the dog fell [P]). These imperfective/perfective distinctions are made in the simple past tense as in *veía* (I) and *vio* (P) (saw [I] and saw [P], respectively) and in the past progressive forms as in *estaba viendo* (I) and *estuvo viendo* [P], (was seeing [I] and was seeing [P], respectively).

Thus, to tell an English story, children must learn to contrast present tense with present progressive forms (e.g., "The boy looks in a hole and the dog is looking at this beehive"); past tense with past progressive forms (e.g., "They saw a beehive; they were calling the frog"); or past tense with past perfect forms (e.g., "They saw the frog; they had looked for the frog for a long time"). But in Spanish, a richer set of aspect options can be used to mark temporality. Proficient Spanish speakers may shift present tense and progressive forms, past tense with past progressive forms, imperfective and perfective forms in simple past tense verbs, and imperfective and perfective forms in the past progressive. Thus, Spanish narratives are likely to provide more detailed information about the time of events and the overlap of events in time, compared with English narratives.

The cross-linguistic research reported by Slobin and colleagues replicate previous studies with monolingual children in the use of progressive forms. Sebastián and Slobin (1994b) observed that in Spanish, the progressive forms were used infrequently. They elaborated that the use of these forms is more optional in Spanish than in English, perhaps because of the availability of imperfective/perfective contrasts in Spanish. Sebastián and Slobin (1994b) also found that for both children and adult Spanish narratives, the present tense was the dominant tense used to mark temporal events. This may be related to the use of pictures to elicit the narratives. In their elicitation task, speakers were to tell the story as they viewed a picture. The Spanish research cited in this chapter however, did not find a predominant use of present tense when stories were elicited using film retelling, spontaneous stories of personal experience, or narrative recall tasks.

In summary, Spanish temporal markers show frequent shifts between perfective and imperfective forms because these aspectual forms seem to be the preferred choice to mark foreground versus background information. In English, these distinctions are limited to the use of contrastive progressive/nonprogressive or present/past and present/past perfect forms. Bilingual learners need to show knowledge of the tense features licensed by the two languages to mark location in time. In addition, they need to recognize their associated semantic interpretations (e.g., durative/completed; habitual/nonhabitual) in order to mark aspect distinctions within and across the two languages.

Word Order

Available cross-linguistic research has shown that Spanish and English narratives vary greatly in word order, in spite of the fact that both languages are considered subject–verb–object (SVO) languages. Sebastián and Slobin provided multiple examples of Spanish constructions in which the subject follows the verb, as in "y salen las moscas" (and come out the flies) (1994a, p. 267). These and other constructions in which the verb is preceded by temporal and locative adverbs as in "del agujero sale como una especie de ratón" (from the hole comes out a sort of rat) (p. 268) are very frequent in children and adults' Spanish narratives. Other examples include the order used in negative sentences such as "y vio que no estaba la rana" (and saw that not was the frog). These types of word order are not to be considered ungrammatical, as they would be in English. Spanish has a flexible word order because the verb inflections of person and number help identify the subject. Shifts in word order serve pragmatic functions in the production of Spanish discourse. Sebastián and Slobin (1994a) indicated that the postponing of a subject already in the topic of the discourse is done in order to identify the predicate as new information. This type of word order also is very frequent in intransitive clauses, as in "Aquí está gritando el niño" (Here is shouting the boy), in which the postponed subject is considered a continuing topic. In contrast, English has a fixed word order with which narrators at all ages must comply. From very early on, English narrative statements adhere to the SVO word order of major clause constituents followed by manner, place, and time adverbial elements (Berman & Slobin, 1994b). English narrative statements do not reverse word order to mark shifts in perspective or to give more emphasis to information. These cross-linguistic differences should be taken into account when examining the narratives of bilingual children.

Marking Reference and Subject Ellipsis

Markers of reference include indefinite and definite reference. Indefinite reference is expected to introduce new referents (e.g., "There was *a boy* who had *a frog*"), whereas definite references are to reintroduce them or to refer to already known referents in the discourse (e.g., "Then, he went to look for *the frog*"). Both languages mark indefinite/definite reference distinctions; however, Spanish and English differ in the use of obligatory subjects when referents are reintroduced in the discourse. Reference to characters may be maintained in Spanish by the markers of person and number in verbs (e.g., "Luego, se fue a buscar a la rana," Then went to look for the frog). In contrast, in English, subjects are obligatory and referents are typically reintroduced using personal pronouns (e.g., "then, *he* went to look for the frog"). Thus, to learn to tell a story in Spanish, bilingual children must learn to use a null subject (i.e., ellipsis) only when the referent has been introduced with full nominal phrases in previous narrative statements. In turn, in English, these children must learn that subjects are obligatory and that to reinstate referents they may need to use pronouns. Pronouns are very infrequent in the reference markers used by Spanish speakers (Berman & Slobin, 1994a) because referents also are introduced or reinstated using relative clauses.

In summary, proficient speakers of the two languages are expected to use language-specific features distinctively in narratives told in each language. As is discussed in the next section, the cross-linguistic differences described so far may help explain patterns of cross-linguistic influence or language transfer in the narrative performance of bilingual speakers.

IMPLICATIONS FOR ASSESSMENT AND INTERVENTION

Assessment

Language Transfer

Döpke (2000) showed that instances of transfer from one language to the other occur when a particular structure(s) is common to the two languages but is optional in the other. The common structure(s) is reinforced in the input of the two languages, therefore leading to overgeneralization of that form. Researchers such as Döpke have focused on transfer of grammatical structures at the sentence level. Yet, transfer may also occur in narrative discourse.

Based on typological differences across the languages, cross-language transfer may be predicted to occur at points of divergence between the two languages. For example, Spanish-influenced English narratives may not include obligatory subjects, as subjects are optional in Spanish. Similarly, it is possible to predict that English-influenced Spanish narratives will show a greater use of pronouns (as opposed to subject ellipsis) in the reintroductions of referents. Movement events may appear as having little detail in Spanish-influenced English narratives, and English-influenced Spanish narratives may show incorrect use of imperfective/perfective distinctions in the marking of temporal events. These predictions imply sufficient exposure to the two languages in the input environment as well as sufficient opportunities to use the languages in daily routines and activities.

The likelihood of cross-language transfer does not imply that all bilingual children will necessarily produce "accented" narratives. Some evidence indicates that when children have high exposure and use of the two languages, they may not show any significant differences in their production of narratives compared with monolingual children or to children with limited English proficiency if tested in their strong language (Gutiérrez-Clellen, 2002; Silliman, Huntley Bahr, Brea, Hnath-Chisolm, & Mahecha, 2002). Yet, children learning English in contexts of suppression of the first language (L1; i.e., Spanish) may show cross-language transfer from the L1 to the second language (L2; i.e., English) during the early stages of second language acquisition. As these children become fluent English speakers in learning environments that do not promote Spanish exposure or use of the language, it is expected that there may be cross-language transfer in the opposite direction (i.e., from the L2 to the L1).

Thus, in order to examine narratives in clinical practice, it is necessary to analyze narrative performance in the two languages and to interpret differences between the two languages by a careful evaluation of the sociolinguistic contexts available for narrative development in each language. The type and directionality of cross-language transfer can provide useful information about the child's ability to apply linguistic knowledge from one language to the other. Cross-language transfer differences should not be considered narrative deficits.

Language Dominance

Children's spontaneous narratives in the two languages may not show differences in the number of utterances produced, their grammaticality, syntactic complexity, cohesion, or overall structure. Yet, differences may occur across the two languages if narrative tasks that are highly demanding of language processing are used in assessment. Gutiérrez-Clellen (2002) examined the narratives of 33 typically developing bilingual children from mostly Mexican American backgrounds, ages 7;3–8;7 years, using story recall and story comprehension tasks. The bilingual status of the children was determined using parent and teacher questionnaires. All children who received input in each language more than 20% of the time were rated as highly proficient in the two languages, and used the two languages frequently based on parent and teacher reports. In addition, spontaneous narrative samples were obtained using *Frog Goes to Dinner* (Mayer, 1974) for Spanish, and *Frog, Where Are You?* (Mayer, 1969) for English. Comparisons on the proportion of grammatical utterances indicated no significant differences between the two languages. However, large individual differences were found on children's recall of a multiepisodic narrative that was read to them and on the responses to questions about the story.

Story recall requires children to process a long stretch of discourse, to draw inferences while they keep track of old and new information, and to use specific vocabulary, connectives, and complex syntax to establish narrative coherence when they reproduce the story. These narrative demands were able to reveal differences in narrative ability across the two languages. Gutiérrez-Clellen (2002) explained these findings by showing that the poor performance of some children on one of the two languages could have been related to the children's excessive focus on sentence form, lexicon, or prosodic cues, which affected their ability to recall the stories coherently and clearly.

The processing demands of the narrative recall also had an effect on the children's comprehension of the stories in their weaker language. It was interesting to note that the patterns of differential performance varied from child to child. Some children showed better performance in Spanish and some showed exactly the opposite pattern. In order to obtain good estimates of narrative proficiency, it is critical to elicit narratives in the two languages using complex tasks such as narrative recall. Cross-language differences in performance should be evaluated by a careful analysis of the bilingual histories of the children. Children who are bilingual may show differences in performance depending on the frequency of use and type of exposure to the target language. Bilingual speakers who do not have high exposure to Spanish literate language may not show accurate use of imperfective/perfective forms in their temporal events, regardless of when English was first acquired (e.g., simultaneous, early L2 acquisition, late L2 acquisition). Bilingual speakers who had limited exposure to Spanish exhibited less production accuracy in the use of imperfect and preterit/past perfect contrasts, and they showed deficiencies in their semantic interpretations when asked to judge sentences (Montrul, 2002). Thus, it is critical that clinicians consider the contexts of language acquisition available to the child as potential explanations for proficiency discrepancies between the two languages.

These findings have important clinical implications for the appropriate assessment of bilingual speakers. Traditionally, language proficiency tests are used to select the language of assessment or intervention. If children show English proficiency based on these tests, their language skills are only assessed in English. Proficiency or dominance tests are not valid estimates of narrative proficiency, however, because they do not focus on narrative features that have clinical significance for this population. Narratives should be elicited in the two languages and then the languages should be compared to establish the child's true narrative skills.

Narrative Characteristics of Children with Language Disorders

Children with language disorders exhibit specific deficits in the production of narratives. Their stories are likely to omit specific links between events and as a result, they may not show clear causal relationships that would allow the audience to interpret the character's actions or to understand their main points. These children may also show limited referential cohesion. New referents may not be introduced with appropriate noun phrases, and referents already introduced may be ambiguous. In addition, the children's narratives may not provide clear information about when or where the events took place as the narrative evolves from episode to episode.

Children with limited syntactic complexity also have difficulty providing sufficient background information about the actions of a character while recreating a past event. A spontaneous spoken narrative from a Spanish-speaking third grader with SLI, which was elicited using a frog story, illustrates some of these difficulties (see Figure 10.1). This child introduces new referents using definite reference (e.g., "One day, the boy was looking at the frog") rather than indefinite reference (*a boy; a frog*) and it is difficult to follow who does what in the story (e.g., "Over there below is the dog. He didn't see him. And that a deer got him. And then he ran"). No clear information is given about the reasons for the characters' actions, and when the story includes statements about feelings or emotions, they are not connected to the story actions (e.g., "And the dog (he got up) fell on top of the boy looking at the moon. He was happy. And he heard something"). Background and foreground information are not consistently distinguished, and there is no evidence of use of complex imperfective forms needed to differentiate location in time. For example, in "El perro buscó {en una} donde están muchas abejas" (The dog looked [in a] where there are lots of bees), background information is not provided with the imperfect form *estaban* or *habían* (were). The same occurs in "El perro estaba agarrando para que lo deja ir" (The dog was grabbing to let him go), in which the appropriate subjunctive form should have been the imperfective

Spanish narrative	English translation
Un dá el niõ estaba mirando al sapo/	One day the boy was looking at the frog/
y el perro estaba pusiendo la boca a la jarra adonde estaba el sapo/	And the dog was putting the mouth (to the**) to the pitcher where was the frog/
despué el sapo se salió	Then the frog got out/
y el niõ y el perro estaban dormidos/	And the boy and the dog were asleep/
y despué cuando se fijaron en la jarra, el niõ y el perro vieron a la jarra/	And then when they looked in the pitcher, the boy and the dog saw in the pitcher/
y no estaba el sapo/	And the frog was not there/
y despué el niõ buscáen su bota/	And then the boy looked in his boot/
despues el perro buscáen la jarra	Then the dog looked in the pitcher/
y despué el se xx en la ventana/	And then he xx in the window/
el niõ estaba sentado/	The boy was sitting/
estaba dijendo šapo/	he was saying frog/
despué el perro tená la jarra donde estaba/	Then the dog had the jar where it was/
despué el perro se cayácon la jarra arriba/	Then the dog he fell with the jar on top/
el niõ como asustada/	And the dog like scared/
despué el perro se quebrá a jarra/	Then the dog the jar broke/
despues el perro estaba bien/	Then the dog was okay/
despues el niõ estaba enojado/	Then the boy was mad/
y el niõ estaba gritando šapo, donde está/	Then the boy was yelling frog where is it?/
despues el perro estáunas abejas/	Then (the dog) the dog there are some bees/
y despué el niõ se buscáen el tunel {de} de un animal/	And then the boy he looked in the tunnel of an animal/
despué el perro buscá{en una} donde está muchas abejas/	Then the dog looked (in a) where there are lots of bees/
y despué {el niõ, a un niõ} el niõ {les pican} le picó	And then (the boy, to a boy) the boy (it bites him) it bit him/
y depué {la abeja} el perro molestá las abejas/	And then (the bee) the dog bothered (the) the bees/
y despué {el, las abejas} los abejas cuando el niõ estaba la buscando, el perro estaba allí/	And then (he the bees) the bee when the boy was looking at the moon the dog was there/
despué cuando estaban tumbaron {al} el perro corrá/	Then when they were dropped (the) the dog run/
y el niõ se cayáporque los sustaron/	And the boy he fell because they scared him/
y despué el niõ corrián la roca {a que, porque} porque tená mucho miedo/	And then the boy ran in the rock (because) because he was very scared/
despué se subió	Then he got on/
allá abajo estáel perro/	Over there below is the dog/
no lo vio/	He didn't see him/
y despué un venado lo agarró	And then a deer got him/
y despué corrió	And then he ran/
el perro estaba agarrando para que lo deja ir/	The dog was grabbing to let him go/
y tumbáel venado al perro y el niõ/	And the deer dropped the dog and the boy/
y el perro {se subó a} cayáarriba del niõ viendo a la luna/	And the dog (he got up) fell on top of the boy looking at the moon/
estaba feliz/	He was happy/
y oyáalgo/	And he heard something/
el niõ y el perro viendo/	The boy and the dog looking/
despué dice el niõ no hables dijo que se callara porque oyáalgo/	Then says the boy don't talk said to be quiet because he heard something./
despué el niõ y el perro vio a su rana/	Then the boy and the dog saw his frog/
y despué el niõ y el perro está feliz/	And then the boy and the dog were happy/
y las ranas tambié/	And the frogs too/
y el perro y el niõ y el sapo se fueron/	And the dog and the boy and the frog left/
y dijo ádió/	And he said bye/

Figure 10.1.   Narrative based on the storybook *Frog, Where Are You?* (Mayer, 1969) produced by a third grader with specific language impairment (SLI) (*Key:* xx = unintelligible text; ** = repeated text).

dejara. The difficulty with marking time distinctions in the narrative is evidenced further in "Después dice el niño no hables, dijo que se callara porque oyó algo" (Then says the boy don't talk said [past subjunctive] to be quiet because he heard something). Here, the appropriate marker for time before the time of narrative action (in the past) should have been the verb "había oído" (had heard).

Research on the narrative performance of bilingual children with language disorders is limited. The available research suggests that bilingual children's narrative deficits in the two languages are not different from the deficits of monolingual children in the target languages. As the Spanish narrative illustrates, these children may have specific difficulties with establishing coherence relationships (i.e., temporal, causal, referential, spatial) and their limited syntactic skills may not allow them to use the variety of linguistic constructions provided by the languages to provide needed narrative information.

These children may also have problems in the comprehension of narratives. Research with monolingual English speakers with SLI indicated that children showed limitations in integrating sequences of narrative statements and answering story comprehension questions about facts and inferences (Bishop & Adams, 1992). Research with Spanish-speaking children learning English as a second language indicated similar deficits (Gutiérrez-Clellen, 1996; Restrepo & Gutiérrez-Clellen, 1997). For example, the child described previously had difficulties answering questions about facts and inferences based on a story read to him. These difficulties were consistent with limited recall of the story. The child's story recall did not show the main points, and findings suggested that the child might have difficulty suppressing irrelevant material. In brief, comparisons between narrative production and narrative comprehension within children and across languages will be useful to identify specific narrative needs and to provide direction for intervention.

Narrative Assessment Protocols: Qualitative and Dynamic Approaches

Narrative assessments should be based on a variety of elicitation tasks and narrative stimuli. Children from diverse backgrounds may not have similar experiences with specific narrative tasks (e.g., talking about books, retelling stories). Thus, it is critical that narratives be evaluated across different elicitation contexts, with different partners, and with stimuli of different length and complexity (Gutiérrez-Clellen, 2002; Gutiérrez-Clellen, Peña, & Quinn, 1995; Gutiérrez-Clellen & Quinn, 1993). Children may not produce spontaneous narratives during play interactions. Conversational samples during play may elicit simple utterances because children may view the task as "play time," not "discussion time" or storytelling time, based on their previous cultural experiences with play interactions. Likewise, children who have limited exposure to books at home may not produce a detailed story using books as props. For these children, it will be important to provide appropriate modeling and practice.

Gutiérrez-Clellen and Quinn (1993) proposed a narrative assessment protocol that addresses culturally based differences in contextualization processes using a dynamic assessment approach. The protocol focused on describing the child's narrative skills across different narrative contexts to identify areas of weakness across tasks, and then on examining the child's responsivity to examiner cues, modeling, and practice designed to mediate narrative performance. The initial assessment of narrative skills included an analysis of temporal coherence (i.e., a temporal order for the narrative events; temporal connectives to link events and to mark time shifts); causal coherence (i.e., physical or mental states to interconnect story actions; causal connectives to mark cause–effect relationships); referential coherence (appropriate introduction/re-introduction of characters and objects); and spatial coherence (i.e., initial location; changes in location).

Based on the child's initial performance (pre-test phase), the examiner focuses on mediation of specific narrative skills (teaching phase) by describing the contextualization rules expected of a given narrative task (e.g., using explicit referents to introduce a character in a story without assuming the listener knows who the child is talking about). Then, the child is asked to tell a new story and the child's observed changes in performance are used as indicators of narrative ability.

The assessment protocol also includes an estimate of the frequency of cues needed to obtain targeted narrative behaviors during mediation. For example, clarification cues are used to elicit appropriate loudness and speech; information cues are used to elicit unstated information about the setting, motivating events, or consequences/conclusions; relevance cues help a child link narrative statements; and reference cues focus on providing appropriate antecedents or names for the referents in the story. The examiner then evaluates the child's narrative skills by determining the level of change in narrative performance after mediation, the child's ability to transfer learned narrative strategies to other tasks, and the frequency and type of cues needed to facilitate improvements in narrative performance. Within this model, children who have limited exposure to certain narrative activities would show high modifiability when those narrative contexts are appropriately mediated in assessment. In contrast, children with true narrative deficits would show limited modifiability in performance and a continued need for cueing, modeling, and practice. Thus, the assessment addresses differences in narrative experience and provides useful information about the child's narrative needs.

The narrative assessment protocol was later modified to obtain a more detailed estimate of the overall quality of the story (Gutiérrez-Clellen & DeCurtis, 2001). The initial judgment of narrative quality is based on the quality of narrative plot (i.e., sufficient background information, goal-directed actions, problems, resolution, ending), clarity (i.e., a chronology of events with specific connectives), cohesion (i.e., appropriate use of reference to introduce/re-introduce characters), specificity (i.e., use of specific and relevant language and descriptions), and memorable features (e.g., use of reported speech, figurative language, overall charm). These categories were used to obtain story rubrics from Spanish-speaking children from third, fourth, and fifth grade who had no history of language impairment. The rubrics exemplified each category (plot, clarity, cohesion, specificity, and memorable features) at each rank using a four-point rating scale. For example, for plot, a rubric with a rank of 3 indicated that central elements were present and focused on a central theme; a rubric with a rank of 2 indicated that some elements of the story structure were provided but the central theme was lost at times; and a rubric of 1 meant that the overall story structure was confusing or that the events were not focused on a central theme. The protocol and the story rubrics were used by a panel of bilingual student clinicians to rate the narratives of Spanish-speaking children with limited English proficiency with and without language disorders (DeCurtis, 1999). The assessment protocol with the story rubrics was found to identify children with different narrative skills and to provide a structured rating system for assessing narrative gains using a dynamic assessment approach.

The dynamic assessment approach has also been used for assessing narrative recall and story comprehension. Traditional narrative assessment procedures focus on the correctness of the child's answers to questions about stories. Yet, some children may misinterpret the examiner questions based on differences in expectations about the purpose of story questions. In addition, traditional narrative assessment procedures provide limited information about the nature of the child's incorrect answers. Researchers found a dynamic assessment approach designed to mediate story comprehension useful in identifying children's true narrative comprehension needs (Gutiérrez-Clellen, Peña, Conboy, & Pasechnik, 1996).

Gutiérrez-Clellen and her colleagues mediated the story comprehension of bilingual children with and without reading delays as part of a larger reading study. The dynamic assessment followed a test–teach–retest approach. The dynamic assessment included two mediation sessions designed to teach how to use information presented in texts, to differentiate relevant versus irrelevant information, and to express textual knowledge with precision and accuracy. Change was evaluated by posttest gains on the task using different stories and by modifiability ratings based on behavioral observations of the child's responsiveness to the examiner's mediation.

Spanish was used to facilitate comprehension as needed. In each session, the instructor read a targeted passage, asked a comprehension question, and encouraged the child to use a sequence of five strategies or steps in order to learn how to devise an appropriate answer. Specifically, the child was prompted to 1) summarize the story facts (to access text knowledge); 2) derive inferences (to access the child's background knowledge); 3) organize the information and select the "best" inferences for the story facts; 4) evaluate his or her answer to the question; and 5) restate it with increased accuracy and precision.

Cue cards listing the five steps needed to determine appropriate answers to questions were used to teach and promote strategy use. The mediator applied these principles of mediated learning: 1) intentionality (i.e., teach strategy using modeling and explanation), 2) meaning (i.e., teach why strategy should be used), 3) feelings of competence (i.e., teach how to use strategy well using praise and encouragement), 4) transcendence (i.e., teach when/where to use strategy by showing how strategy applies to other situations), and 5) self-regulation (i.e., teach how to evaluate strategy use).

A comparison of children's narrative performance pre- and post-mediation indicated that some children had poor performance on story comprehension questions because they provided vague answers to questions (e.g., using general vocabulary terms and ambiguous referents). Their answers lacked specificity and appeared to have limited relevance to the story. Mediating how to provide answers with accuracy and precision as well as teaching how to evaluate answers to story questions helped children demonstrate their true narrative comprehension abilities.

The dynamic assessment approach described so far has been applied to monolingual English populations, as well (Gillam, Peña, & Miller, 1999; Miller, Gillam, & Peña, 2001). These applications focus on an initial assessment of story productivity (e.g., total number of words, C-units, number of clauses per sentence); episodic structure (how many episodes or parts of an episode are included); story components (setting, character information, temporal order, causal relationships); and story ideas and language (complexity of ideas, vocabulary, dialogue, creativity). In general, the initial assessment applies similar features as the narrative quality categories. Yet, the aspects of narrative analysis included appear to overlap somewhat across categories. Within a dynamic assessment model, these applications focus on the child's ability to form a more complete or coherent story that includes more episodic elements given examiner support, as well as on the level of effort needed to induce change and to transfer newly learned strategies to other story tasks. Together with an error analysis and ratings of modifiability (see Gutiérrez-Clellen & Peña, 2001, for a discussion of modifiability measures), these protocols can help clinicians identify narrative needs and plan intervention for those children who need additional mediation.

Intervention

Narrative Intervention: A Monolingual or Bilingual Approach?
The research reviewed early in this chapter suggests that mediation of narrative skills learned in one language will transfer to the other language. Across the two languages, narrative coherence requires 1) sufficient background information, goal-directed actions, problems, resolutions, and endings; 2) a chronology of events in temporal order or with explicit temporal and causal connectives; 3) appropriate reference to introduce/reintroduce characters; and 4) specific and relevant language in descriptions. Because these skills involve primarily semantic and pragmatic skills, intervention strategies designed to mediate these skills in one language should induce transfer of skills to the other language. The knowledge that stories have a chronology of events that are causally linked is expected to transfer from one language to the other. When a child learns to take into account what the listener knows and what is expected in different contexts, this will help the child to provide sufficient background information and precise reference in any language.

However, the languages have also specific linguistic means to represent narrative information that will require explicit mediation. For example, marking reference in Spanish would have a focus on subject ellipsis and relative clauses, whereas, in English, it would have a focus on the use of appropriate pronouns. Children will not be able to learn to use precise or specific vocabulary if their vocabulary skills in the target language are not sufficiently developed. Thus, one should not expect that a monolingual intervention would facilitate narrative development in the two languages.

For narrative comprehension, one may also predict transfer of skills from one language to the other. For example, narrative comprehension processes such as learning how to differentiate relevant versus irrelevant information presented in narrative texts or how to provide answers to story comprehension questions that are relevant and specific can be expected to generalize to the language not targeted for intervention. A monolingual approach may not induce transfer to the untargeted language if the language selected for intervention (e.g., English) does not have a sufficient level of development, however. Vocabulary or syntactic limitations related to lack of proficiency in the language would not allow the child to integrate factual information or to draw appropriate inferences. In contrast, a bilingual approach to mediate text meanings and to help the child learn strategies for monitoring story comprehension may be more effective. No treatment efficacy studies comparing monolingual with bilingual approaches in narrative intervention have been conducted. Yet, one may predict that a bilingual focus on general narrative strategies would promote faster learning rates than a monolingual approach. A bilingual approach would provide additional opportunities to transfer skills if the child is given access to development of the two languages. Learning how to express textual knowledge with precision and accuracy when answering comprehension questions in the two languages should help children to perform better in both languages, not only in one. Children in situations of suppression of the home language will not have the opportunity to transfer newly learned skills from the language of intervention (i.e., English) to the home language (i.e., Spanish), and as a result, they may not show narrative gains in both languages.

REFERENCES

Berman, R.A., & Slobin, D.I. (1994a). Becoming a native speaker. In R.A. Berman & D.I. Slobin (Eds.), *Relating events in narrative: A crosslinguistic developmental study* (pp. 611–639). Mahwah, NJ: Lawrence Erlbaum Associates.

Berman, R.A., & Slobin, D.I. (1994b). Development of linguistic forms: English. In R.A. Berman & D.I. Slobin (Eds.), *Relating events in narrative: A crosslinguistic developmental study* (pp. 127–187). Mahwah, NJ: Lawrence Erlbaum Associates.

Bishop, D.V.M., & Adams, C. (1992). Comprehension problems in children with specific language impairment: Literal and inferential meaning. *Journal of Speech and Hearing Research, 35*, 119–129.

Bocaz, A. (1986). Comprensión de la estructura narrativa de la gramática de las historias: Estudio preliminario [Comprehension of the grammatical narrative structure of histories: A preliminary study]. *Revista de Lingüística Teórica y Aplicada. Concepción, 24*, 63–79.

Comrie, B. (1976). *Aspect: An introduction to the study of verbal aspect and related problems.* Cambridge, UK: Cambridge University Press.

Comrie, B. (1985). *Tense.* Cambridge, UK: Cambridge University Press.

Dasinger, L., & Toupin, C. (1994). The development of relative clause functions in narrative. In R.A. Berman & D.I. Slobin (Eds.), *Relating events in narrative: A crosslinguistic developmental study* (pp. 457–514). Mahwah, NJ: Lawrence Erlbaum Associates.

DeCurtis, L. (1999). *The quality of Spanish narratives from bilingual children with-normal language and language impairment.* Unpublished master's thesis, San Diego State University, San Diego, CA.

Döpke, S. (2000). Generation of and retraction from cross-linguistically motivated structures in bilingual first language acquisition. *Bilingualism: Language and Cognition, 3*, 209–226.

Englert, C.S., Tarrant, K.L., Mariage, T.V., & Oxer, T. (1994). Lesson talk as the work of reading groups: The effectiveness of two interventions. *Journal of Learning Disabilities, 27*, 165–185.

Gillam, R.B., Peña, E.D., & Miller, L. (1999). Dynamic assessment of narrative and expository discourse. *Topics in Language Disorders, 20*, 33–47.

Griffith, P.L., Ripich, D.N., & Dastoli, S.L. (1986). Story structure, cohesion, and propositions in story recalls by learning-disabled and nondisabled children. *Journal of Psycholinguistic Research, 15*, 539–555.

Gutiérrez-Clellen, V.F. (1996). Language impairment in school-age Latino children. Poster presented at the annual convention of the American Speech-Language-Hearing Association, Seattle, WA.

Gutiérrez-Clellen, V.F. (1998). Syntactic skills of Spanish-speaking children at risk for academic underachievement. *Language, Speech, and Hearing Services in Schools 29*, 207–215.

Gutiérrez-Clellen, V.F. (2002). Narratives in two languages: Assessing performance of bilingual children. *Linguistics and Education, 13*, 175–197.

Gutiérrez-Clellen, V.F., & DeCurtis, L. (2001). Narrative assessment: A qualitative approach. *Seminars in Speech and Language, 22*, 79–89.

Gutiérrez-Clellen, V.F., & Heinrichs-Ramos, L. (1993). Referential cohesion in the narratives of Spanish-speaking children: A developmental study. *Journal of Speech and Hearing Research, 36*, 559–568.

Gutiérrez-Clellen, V.F., & Hoffstetter, R. (1994). Syntactic complexity in Spanish narratives: A developmental study. *Journal of Speech and Hearing Research, 37*, 645–654.

Gutiérrez-Clellen, V.F., & Iglesias, A. (1992). Causal coherence in the oral narratives of Spanish-speaking children. *Journal of Speech and Hearing Research, 35*, 363–372.

Gutiérrez-Clellen, V.F., & Peña, E. (2001) Dynamic assessment of diverse children: A tutorial. *Language, Speech, and Hearing Services in Schools, 32*, 212–224.

Gutiérrez-Clellen, V.F., Peña, E., Conboy, B., & Pasechnik, P. (1996). *Dynamic assessment of language: Research issues and clinical applications across cultures.* Paper presented at California Association of Mediated Learning Conference, San Diego, California.

Gutiérrez-Clellen, V.F., Peña, E., & Quinn, R. (1995). Accomodating cultural differences in narrative style: A bilingual perspective. *Topics in Language Disorders, 15*, 54–67.

Gutiérrez-Clellen, V.F., & Quinn, R. (1993). Assessing narratives in diverse cultural/linguistic populations: Clinical implications. *Language, Speech, and Hearing Services in Schools, 24,* 2–9.

Lidz, C.S. (1991). *Practitioner's guide to dynamic assessment.* New York: Guilford Press.

Mayer, M. (1969). *Frog, where are you?* New York: Puffin Pied Piper.

Mayer, M. (1974). *Frog goes to dinner.* New York: Puffin Pied Piper.

Miller, L., Gillam, R., & Peña, E. (2001). *Dynamic assessment and intervention: Improving children's narrative abilities.* Austin, TX: PRO-ED.

Montrul, S. (2002). Incomplete acquisition and attrition of Spanish tense/aspect distinctions in adult bilinguals. *Bilingualism, Language, and Cognition, 5,* 39–68.

Oudega-Campbell, A.C. (1985). *Cohesion and textual coherence in Spanish and English oral retells produced by Mexican American bilingual children, grades 1–3.* Unpublished doctoral dissertation, The University of Texas at Austin.

Restrepo, M.A., & Gutiérrez-Clellen, V.F. (1997, November). *A data-based approach to the language assessment of Spanish-speaking children.* Paper presented at ASHA National Convention, Boston, MA.

Roth, F.P., & Spekman, N.J. (1986). Narrative discourse: Spontaneously generated stories of LD and normally achieving students. *Journal of Speech and Hearing Disorders, 51,* 8–23.

Sebastián, E., & Slobin, D.I. (1994a). Development of linguistic forms: Spanish. In R.A. Berman & D.I. Slobin (Eds.), *Relating events in narrative: A crosslinguistic developmental study* (pp. 239–284). Mahwah, NJ: Lawrence Erlbaum Associates.

Sebastián, E., & Slobin, D.I. (1994b). Mas allá del aquí y el ahora: El desarrollo de los marcadores temporales en el discurso narrativo en español. [Beyond the here and now: The development of temporal markers in Spanish narrative discourse]. *Substratum II, 5,* 41–68.

Signorini, A., & Borzone de Manrique, A.M. (1988). Incidencia del esquema narrativo en la comprensión y el recuerdo de cuentos [The effect of narrative schemata on narrative comprehension and recall]. *Revista Argentina de Lingüística, 4,* 91–117.

Silliman, E.R., Huntley Bahr, R., Brea, M.R., Hnath-Chisolm, T., & Mahecha, N.R. (2002). Spanish and English proficiency in the linguistic encoding of mental states in narrative retellings. *Linguistics and Education, 13,* 199–234.

Slobin, D.I. (1990). The development from child speaker to native speaker. In J.W. Stigler, R.A. Shweder, & G. Herd (Eds.), *Cultural psychology: Essays on comparative human development* (pp. 233–256). New York: Cambridge University Press.

Slobin, D.I. (1996). Two ways to travel: Verbs of motion in English and Spanish. In M. Shibatani & S.A. Thompson (Eds.), *Grammatical constructions: Their form and meaning* (pp. 195–219). Oxford, UK: Clarendon Press.

Slobin, D.I., & Bocaz, A. (1988). Learning to talk about movement through time and space: The development of narrative abilities in Spanish and English. *Lenguas Modernas, 15,* 5–24.

Stein, N., & Glenn, C.G. (1979). An analysis of story comprehension in elementary school children. In R.O. Freedle (Ed.), *New directions in discourse processing: Advances in discourse processes* (Vol. 2, pp. 53–120). Norwood, NJ: Ablex.

Speech Characteristics

CHAPTER 11

Phonological Development and Disorders

BRIAN A. GOLDSTEIN

Approximately 6.8 million 5- to 17-year-old Spanish speakers live in the United States (U.S. Bureau of the Census, 2000). Some of these children (most of whom will learn English at some point) may be acquiring Spanish and English simultaneously from birth; some may be learning Spanish first and then English; and, in some rare cases, some may be acquiring English first and then Spanish. Thus, most of the children who are Spanish speakers probably will be bilingual to one degree or another. It is likely that they will have exposure to and facility with both languages. That is not to say that children who are bilingual will have equal receptive and expressive skills in both languages; however, it is presumed that "there is knowledge present (to whatever degree) in *more than one* language" (Valdés & Figueroa, 1994, p. 7, emphasis in original).

Despite the relatively large number of bilingual children in the United States, little is known about their language development. The vast majority of existing studies on language development and disorders in bilingual children have focused on either syntactic or lexical development. Far fewer studies have examined phonological[1] development and disorders in bilingual children. As Watson noted,

> [P]honology is to a large extent the Cinderella of bilingual studies. The most immediately obvious aspect of speech is ironically that which has been least

Funded in part by National Institute on Deafness and Other Communication Disorders contract #N01-DC-8-2100.

[1]The terms *phonology* and *phonological* are used throughout this chapter to encompass both segment- and pattern-based aspects of speech sound production.

intensively researched with respect to bilingual speech behavior in general, and bilingual acquisition in particular. (1991, p. 25)

Only recently has there been an increase in research devoted to phonological development and disorders in Spanish-English bilingual children. If, as estimated, the prevalence of phonological disorders is 10% (National Institute on Deafness and Other Communication Disorders, 1994), then approximately 680,000 children in the United States 5–17 years old exhibit some type of phonological disorder in a language other than or in addition to English.

This chapter provides information on three key issues related to phonological development and disorders in Spanish-English bilingual children:

1. How the phonological system might be represented in bilingual children

2. The way in which phonological skills in one language might be affecting phonological production in the other language

3. How phonological development in Spanish-English bilingual children compares with phonological development in monolingual children

These three main issues will be examined in detail so that their impact on the assessment and intervention of phonological disorders in Spanish-English bilingual children can be gauged.

PHONOLOGICAL REPRESENTATION

One of the tasks for children acquiring the phonology of their ambient language is to "deduce the set of oppositions which constitute the phonological structure of the language" (Watson, 1991, p. 27). That is, children must determine, for example, which sounds constitute the segmental inventory of the language (e.g., recognizing that the two affricates in English are /tʃ/ and /dʒ/) and how sounds can be combined in permissible ways in that language (e.g., knowing that word initial clusters contain, at most, two segments in Spanish). Bilingual children must accomplish this task for two languages, of course. Spanish-English bilingual children have to determine, for example, which sounds are those of English and which are those of Spanish, the syllable structure of each language, and the suprasegmental features of each language.

The deduction of the phonological structure of two languages has caused researchers to consider how a bilingual individual's two languages might be represented in the brain. In the bilingual literature, two general models have been posited about the way in which the bilingual's two languages are represented across all language domains (e.g., de Houwer, 1995). Advocates of the Unitary System Model state that individuals initially possess a single storage system of linguistic elements in which links between those elements get stronger with increased use (Vogel, 1975; Volterra & Taeschner, 1978). These advocates maintain that bilingual children, either gradually or in stages, separate their languages over time. Conversely, advocates of the Dual Systems Model argue that separate systems for each language are maintained from the onset of acquisition, with separate sets of phonemes, rules, words, and so forth (e.g., Genesee, 1989; Paradis, 1987, 2001). As Genesee noted

> [Bilingual children] are psycholinguistically able to differentiate two languages from the earliest stages of bilingual development and that they can use their two languages in functionally differentiated ways, thereby providing evidence of differentiated language systems. (1989, pp. 161–162)

Unfortunately, most of the research attempting to provide evidence for one model over the other has come from studies of the lexicon and/or syntax (e.g., Almgren & Barreña, 2001; Meisel, 1989; Volterra & Taeschner, 1978) and, for the most part, has included children acquiring both languages simultaneously from birth, that is, children undergoing Bilingual First Language Acquisition (e.g., Deuchar & Quay, 2000; Meisel, 1989). Given the focus on phonology in this chapter, the reader is referred to Walpole (1999) for a detailed discussion of representation in other language domains.

In studies of bilingual phonology, one primary area of research concerns the extent to which bilingual children combine aspects of each language into a "partially merged system," (i.e., the Unitary System Model) versus the extent to which they keep the phonological system of each language separate (i.e., the Dual Systems Model; Watson, 1991). Any theory attempting to illustrate the way in which phonology is represented in bilinguals must differentiate three key elements in their production[2] that are shaped by the phonological input: 1) cross-linguistic effects (also may be termed *transfer, interference,* or *mixing*) to determine if the rate of bidirectional transfer is evidence of access to both languages or simply reflects amount of mixing in the input, 2) accuracy in the production of

---

[2]Although the focus here is on children's production skills, studies examining areas such as children's input, perceptual abilities (e.g., Bosch & Sebatián-Gallés, 2001; Zampini & Green, 2001), acoustic characteristics (e.g., Deuchar & Clark, 1995), suprasegmental skills (e.g., Paradis, 1996), and language-specific substitutions for segments occurring in both languages (Barlow, 2001; Johnson & Lancaster, 1998) will also have to be accounted for.

phonemes common to both languages and in the production of phonemes unique to each language to determine if children implicitly understand that segments may be common to both languages and different for each language, and 3) developmental patterns in each language to offer insight as to whether bilingual children develop phonology similar to or different from monolingual children of either language. The next sections of the chapter examine each of these three key issues.

Cross-Linguistic Effects and Phonological Representation

Given that bilingual children receive input in more than one language, this input often results in cross-linguistic effects such that each language influences the other in systematic ways (Goldstein, 2001b). These influences likely will come from parents, peers, the dialect emphasized in the school system, and the influence of one phonological system on another (Wolfram & Schilling-Estes, 1998). Factors such as the amount of contact with Spanish and English speakers, the speaker's motivation, a speaker's oral and perceptual abilities, and the prestige of the various dialects may also be influencing factors (Leather & James, 1996). Spanish phonology can influence the production of English in terms of both consonants and vowels. The influence of Spanish on English production at the segmental level is described in Table 11.1. As noted in this table, the phonology of Spanish might influence phonological production in English in many ways, and vice versa. One phonological system may influence the other because phonemes or allophones occur in one language but not the other (Goldstein & Iglesias, 2004). For example, /ʃ/ does not occur in most dialects of Spanish, so a native Spanish speaker might substitute a close relation and thus produce /ʃ/ as [ʧ]; /ʃek/ "shake" → [ʧek]. The influence of one phonological system on another may result from differences in the phonotactic constraints of the two languages. For example, word initial clusters cannot begin with /s/ in Spanish, so Spanish speakers producing clusters of that type in English might exhibit either cluster reduction (e.g., /staɚz/ "stars" → [taɚz]) or epenthesis (e.g., /stet/ "state" → [estet]) (Perez, 1994).

Dialect-specific features in one language might also influence production in the other language. For example, Spanish speakers who exhibit final /s/ deletion in Spanish as a typical dialect feature (e.g., /dos/ "two" → [do]) might also show that feature in English (e.g., /mæs/ "mass" → [mæ]). Finally, the individual's speech community may be an influence. Wolfram (1971) found that native Spanish speakers' English pronunciation was influenced by African American English spoken by members of their speech community. For example, in their English production of word-medial /ð/,

Table 11.1. Potential segmental-level characteristics of Spanish-influenced English by sound class

Sound class	Example
	General American English versus Spanish-influenced English
Stops	
/t/ → [t̪]	/tu/ "two" → [t̪u] (dentalized [t])
/d/ → [d̪]	/du/ "do" → [d̪u] (dentalized [d])
Nasals	
/n/ → [ŋ]	/fæn/ "fan" → [fæŋ]
/n/ → ∅	/fæn/ "fan" → [fæ]
Fricatives	
/s/ → [es]	/stamp/ "stomp" → [estamp]
/s/ → ∅	/pes/ "pace" → [pe]
/z/ → [s]	/piz/ "peas" → [pis]
/ʃ/ → [tʃ]	/ʃi/ "she" → [tʃi]
/z/ → [s]	/hɪz/ "his" → [hɪs]
/v/ → [b]	/ves/ "vase" → [bes]
/θ/ → [t]	/θat/ "thought" → [tat]
/ð/ → [d]	/ðo/ "though" → [do]
Affricates	
/dʒ/ → [tʃ]	/dʒɛl/ "gel" → [tʃɛl]
Liquids	
/ɹ/ → [r]	/ɹod/ "road" → [rod]
/ɹ/ → [ɾ]	/ɹod/ "road" → [ɾod]
Glides	
/j/ → [dʒ]	/jɛlo/ "yellow" → [dʒɛlo]
Vowels	
tense → lax	/ki/ "key" → [kɪ]
lax → tense	/kɪd/ "kid" → [kid]
diphthongs → monophthongs	/hoʊm/ "home" → [hom]
central → [a]	/əwe/ "away" → [awe]
/ɝ/ → [ɛɾ]	/kɝb/ "curb" → [kɛɾb]

From "Transcription of Spanish and Spanish-influenced English" by B. Goldstein, 2001, *Communication Disorders Quarterly, 23*, 54–60; Copyright © 2001 by PRO-ED, Inc. Reprinted with permission.

Spanish speakers most frequently substituted [v] (e.g., /bɹʌðɚ/ "brother" → [bɹʌvɚ]).

Influence of one language on another is not relegated solely to consonants. Vowels also may undergo the types of influence noted for consonants. For example, given that in Spanish there are no phonemic, lax vowels (e.g., /ɪ/), Spanish speakers might substitute tense vowels for them in their English productions (e.g., /ɛ/ → [e]; /bɛt/ "bet" → [bet]). Other vocalic changes might include diphthongs such as /aʊ/ being produced as monophthongs such as [ɑ], (e.g., /kaʊ/ "cow" → [kɑ]; schwa lowering to [a] (e.g., /bəlun/ "balloon" → [balun]); and *r*-colored vowels being produced as a vowel plus a flap (e.g., /kɝtən/ "curtain" → [kɛɾtən]).

A bilingual speaker's production of English also may influence his or her Spanish production (often termed English-influenced Spanish). For example, Goldstein and Iglesias (1999) found that in 4- to 6-year-old bilingual children, the English postvocalic, unstressed *r* substituted for the flap in Spanish words (e.g., /ɾ/ → [ɚ]; /floɾ/ "flower" → [floɚ]). In another example, Fantini (1985) found that his son aspirated voiceless stops in Spanish (/teʧo/ "roof" → [tʰeʧo]) even though stops in Spanish are described typically as unaspirated.

As mentioned previously, cross-linguistic effects specific to phonology encompass not only segmental features of a language (i.e., consonants and vowels) but also suprasegmental aspects (i.e., stress, pitch, and intonation). Spanish and English differ in the ways that these aspects of phonology are produced (remembering, of course, that variations will occur within and across dialects in both languages). Stress in Spanish occurs most frequently on the penultimate syllable (e.g., *elefánte*, elefant); however, it also can occur either on the final syllable (e.g., *jamón*, ham) or on the antepenultimate syllable (e.g., *frígido*, cold) (Hochberg, 1988). Placement of stress in English is more complex and depends on factors such as syntactic category and weight of the syllable (i.e., whether the vowel is long or short and the number of consonants that follow the vowel) (Goodluck, 1991). Thus, a native Spanish speaker who attempts to apply Spanish stress rules to English may stress words in English using Spanish stress rules; for example, /békɪŋ/ "baking" as [bekíŋ] and /ɹəválv/ "revolve" as ɹívalv].

Pitch also varies as a function of language, modulating less in Spanish than it does in English (Hadlich, Holton, & Montes, 1968); that is, the overall pitch range is narrower for Spanish speakers than it is for English speakers. Thus, Spanish speakers acquiring English may use a pitch pattern that may be perceived as less rich or more "monotone" than that used by English speakers. In English, statements, questions, and exclamations start at an overall higher pitch than in Spanish, and a large pitch change occurs on the most-accentuated word (Snow, 2001). In Spanish, utterances generally begin at an overall lower pitch than those in English, and the major pitch change usually takes place on the first stressed syllable (Hadlich et al., 1968). In their production of English, speakers of Spanish-influenced English then may utilize intonational patterns that are more characteristic of Spanish than English.

As evidence for the way in which language may be represented in bilinguals, researchers often examine the rate and types of cross-linguistic effects. The hypothesis is that relatively high rates of cross-linguistic effects indicate that the bilingual child has a unitary system that is not yet differentiated, providing at least partial evidence for the Unitary System Model. On the other hand, relatively low rates of mixing suggest that the bilingual child has a differentiated system for each language, providing support for the Dual Systems Model.

Gildersleeve, von Hapsburg, and Davis (1997) performed an acoustic analysis on the vowels of bilingual English- and Spanish-speaking children, monolingual English-speaking children, and monolingual Spanish-speaking children to determine if and how the vowel system of one language might influence the vowel system of the other language. Children in all three groups showed similarity in vowel quality, although slightly more variability was present in the acoustic features of bilingual children. This variability did not impede intelligibility of the children's vowels, however. Gildersleeve and colleagues also found that the acoustic characteristics for the majority of vowels produced by the bilingual children were between the values for English monolingual and Spanish monolingual children. This group of bilingual children's values tended to be closer to those of monolingual English speakers as opposed to those of the monolingual Spanish speakers. The authors suggested this finding indicated a mild effect of English on their production of Spanish vowels. From the limited number of participants, Gildersleeve and colleagues would not speculate on whether their findings lent support to a differentiated or undifferentiated phonological system, although their finding that the bilingual children exhibited acoustic values between those of monolingual English-speaking and monolingual Spanish-speaking children may show at least some interaction between the two systems.

Amastae (1982) found support for the Unitary System Model in his daughter's speech. At 30 months of age, he noted cross-linguistic effects in her speech; for example, she used the Spanish spirantization rule (i.e., voiced stops /b/, /d/, and /g/ become their spirant counterparts [ß], [ð], and [ɣ], respectively, most commonly in intervocalic position) (Hammond, 2001) in her production of English, /wadɚ/ "water" → [waðɚ]. That type of effect, however, did not occur in all possible environments. Although Amastae argued that this type of effect lent support to the Unitary System Model, the child also showed evidence of phonological separation between languages as demonstrated by the production of her own name "Laura"; [wawa] in English but [laʷwa] in Spanish. "By the time the English [wawa] had developed into [lowa], the Spanish was the correct form [laʷra]" (1982, p. 8). In a longitudinal study of their son who spoke both Spanish and English, conducted from when he was age 1;1 to age 3;9, Schnitzer and Krasinski (1994) found evidence for both a unitary system earlier in the process of phonological acquisition (relatively high rates of cross-linguistic effects) and a separate representational system later during phonological development (relatively low rates of cross-linguistic effects). Major (1977) found the same phenomenon in his study of a bilingual child acquiring Portuguese and English. In a follow-up study on another Spanish-English son from ages 1;6 to 4;6, Schnitzer and Krasinski (1996) found separation of the two phonological systems from the earliest time period with little transfer. In attempting to explain the differences in results between the two studies, Schnitzer and Krasinski speculated whether the phonological system is represented as one system or two, indicating that "the answer appears to be *both*, or perhaps *neither*. It is possible that we are imposing the idea of a system (in terms of mental representation) upon the emerging phonological production" (1994, p. 619, emphasis in original). As Johnson and Lancaster have also pointed out in a case study of a child, Andreas, acquiring Norwegian and English from birth, "The claim that Andreas provided evidence for distinguishing English and Norwegian is different from the claim that he had two separate *systems*" (1998, p. 295, emphasis in original). That is, the fact that children differentiate their two languages in terms of use may not be indicative of the underlying phonological representation.

Most studies of bilingual children's language skills (again, examining mainly the lexicon and syntax) find a low frequency of cross-linguistic effects overall (as measured by overall percentage of utterances containing such tokens) (e.g., Genesee, Nicoladis, & Paradis, 1995; Meisel, 1989; Walpole, 1999). In addition, the cross-linguistic effects that do occur often decrease with age and increased linguistic complexity (Genessee, 1989). Thus, Genessee (1989) argued that measuring cross-linguistic effects might be a rather limited way to look at the underlying representational system. He noted that ". . . most proponents of the unitary-system do not present or analyse [sic] their data by context" (Genesee, 1989, p. 166).

One way in which to examine phonological "context" might be to determine what bilingual children implicitly "know" about the sounds in the two languages they are acquiring (Watson, 1991). That is, do bilingual child understand, to a certain extent, to which language each sound belongs and that the input represents two different languages? The answer to this

Table 11.2.   English versus Spanish: Shared and unshared phonemes

Shared consonants	
Stops	/p/, /b/, /t/, /d/, /k/, /g/
Nasals	/m/, /n/
Fricatives	/f/, /ð/, /s/
Affricate	/tʃ/
Liquid	/l/
Glides	/w/, /j/
Vowels	/i/, /e/, u/, /o/
Unshared consonants	
English	
Nasal	/ŋ/*
Fricatives	/v/,* /θ/,* /z/,* /ʃ/,* /ʒ/*, /h/
Affricate	/dʒ/*
Liquid	/ɹ/
Vowels	/ɪ/,* /ɛ/,* /æ/, /ʊ/, /ɔ/, /ɑ/, /aʊ/, /aɪ/, /ɔɪ/, /ə/, /ʌ/, /ɚ/, /ɝ/
Spanish	
Nasal	/ɲ/*
Spirants	[β], [ɣ]
Flap	/ɾ/**
Trill	/r/
Vowels	/a/

*Produced in some Spanish dialects.
**Not phonemic in English.

question may derive from determining how accurately Spanish-English bilingual children produce shared phonemes (i.e., sounds common to both languages) and unshared phonemes (i.e., sounds unique to each language). Understanding how bilingual children produce shared and unshared consonants may provide another piece of evidence as to how bilinguals represent their phonological system.

Shared and Unshared Phonemes

Shared and unshared English and Spanish phonemes (Hammond, 2001) are represented on Table 11.2. Although shared and unshared vowel phonemes are listed on the table, only consonant phonemes will be discussed here. In addition, it should be noted that the Spanish spirants [β], [ð], and [ɣ] are analyzed separately given their relatively late development in the acquisition process (Goldstein & Washington, 2001).

Spanish and English share 15 phonemes. Nine consonants that are unique to English do not exist in Spanish and five consonants that are unique to Spanish do not exist in English. Goldstein, Iglesias, and Rojas (2001) and Goldstein and Iglesias (2002) examined how accurately Spanish-English bilingual children produced phonemes shared between the two languages and phonemes unique to each language. It should be noted that the results are based on a total of 37 4-, 5-, and 6-year-old children, approximately two thirds of whom were sequential bilinguals (typically beginning to acquire English upon entering school at age 3 or 4) and approximately one third of whom were simultaneous bilinguals (acquiring both languages from birth). Data were collected in English and Spanish from both typically developing children and children with phonological disorders.

The results indicated that for typically developing children and children with phonological disorders, accuracy for shared phonemes was significantly higher than for unshared phonemes (Goldstein & Iglesias, 2002). No significant difference occurred in accuracy between languages for shared phonemes or between languages for unshared phonemes, however. That is, accuracy rates were almost identical for shared phonemes between English and Spanish and for unshared phonemes between English and Spanish.

To control for type of bilingual, Goldstein, Fabiano, and Iglesias (2003) examined accuracy of shared and unshared phonemes in 12 sequential, Spanish-English bilingual children. Of the children, ages 4;8–7;0, six were typically developing and six had phonological disorders. The results indicated that typically developing bilingual children and bilingual children with phonological disorders showed significant differences in production accuracy between shared and unshared phonemes.

Given that some unshared are also later developing (e.g., flap and trill in Spanish and prevocalic *r* in English), Fabiano and Goldstein (2004) analyzed accuracy of early and late developing phonemes in four 4-year-old Spanish-English bilingual children. Of the four, two (one sequential and one simultaneous bilingual) were typically developing and two (again, one sequential and one simultaneous bilingual) exhibited a phonological disorder. In the English and Spanish productions of typically developing children, accuracy for early and late developing shared phonemes was commensurate as was accuracy for early and late developing unshared phonemes. In the English and Spanish productions of children with phonological disorders, accuracy for early shared phonemes was higher than for late shared phonemes as it was for early and late developing unshared phonemes. No significant correlation was found, however, between either early shared and late shared phonemes (although there was a large effect size for English) or early unshared and late unshared phonemes. Overall, these findings indicate that the distinction in accuracy between shared and unshared phonemes is largely nondevelopmental.

These data indicate that typically developing bilingual children and bilingual children with phonological disorders produced shared phonemes more accurately than unshared phonemes, demonstrating that these children distinguished phonemes common to both languages from phonemes occurring in only one language. This finding supports Paradis's (2001) Interactional Dual Systems Model. This differentiation, however, may not indicate how the two languages are represented but rather, how they are used (Johnson & Lancaster, 1998). Additional evidence for representation may come from how phonological development in bilingual children might be similar to and different from monolingual speakers of either language.

Bilingual Phonological Development

Many aspects of phonological development are relatively constant across learners of different languages (Locke, 1983). That is, typically developing monolingual children, regardless of the language they are acquiring, show many of the same tendencies that are exhibited by all children acquiring phonology typically. For example, anterior sounds (e.g., bilabials) tend to be acquired before posterior sounds (e.g., velars), and stops are typically acquired before liquids. This commonality of acquisition, however, must be tempered by the specific constraints of the ambient language. For example, Spanish-English bilinguals must discern that the flap is phonemic in Spanish but allophonic in English.

Given that bilingual children acquire two ambient languages, it is first necessary to provide specific details about phonological development in bilingual children. Then, evidence indicating that phonological acquisition in Spanish-English bilingual speakers is similar to and somewhat different from that of monolingual speakers of either Spanish or English are reviewed. Data from typically developing children and those with phonological disorders are then described to provide a picture of phonological development in Spanish-English bilingual children.

Walters (2000) examined the frequency-of-occurrence of phonological processes in three 2-year-old simultaneous, bilingual (Spanish-English) children. She found that the bilingual children tended to perform similarly in both languages overall: They made greater use of syllabic processes than substitution processes; they experienced similar processes with high (percentage-of-occurrence greater than 50%), moderate (percentage-of-occurrence 26%–50%), and low (percentage-of-occurrence less than

26%) frequencies of occurrence in both languages; their percentages-of-occurrence of phonological processes decreased as their age increased; and similar sound classes were most likely to exhibit errors (e.g., liquids, stridents, velar nasal). Walters also reported that the bilingual children exhibited phonological processes (e.g., consonant sequence reduction/cluster reduction, final consonant deletion) in both languages in frequencies similar to those reported in the literature for monolingual 2-year-olds. Some processes, however, such as liquid gliding, stopping of affricates, vowelization, and final consonant devoicing were frequently exhibited in English only. Differences between bilingual and monolingual children included the following: 1) Unstressed syllable deletion was less frequent in bilinguals, 2) palatal and velar fronting and stopping of fricatives were less frequent in bilinguals than in English monolinguals, 3) medial and initial consonant deletion were less frequent in bilinguals than in monolingual Spanish speakers, and 4) deaffrication and stopping of affricates were used more frequently in bilinguals than in monolingual Spanish speakers.

Gildersleeve, Davis, and Stubbe (1996) analyzed the phonological skills of 29 typically developing 3- and 4-year-old bilingual (English-Spanish) children. The children's phonological skills were measured in English only (the preferred language of all of the children according to parent and teacher report and the language spoken by the children during testing). The results indicated that the bilingual children showed an overall lower intelligibility rating, made more consonant and vowel errors overall, distorted more sounds, and produced more uncommon error patterns than did either the monolingual English or monolingual Spanish speakers in the study. The bilingual children also exhibited error patterns found in both languages (cluster reduction, stopping, and gliding) and evidenced phonological patterns that were exhibited by neither monolingual Spanish speakers (e.g., final consonant devoicing) nor monolingual English speakers (e.g., initial consonant deletion). Gildersleeve and colleagues (1996) and Gildersleeve-Neumann and Davis (1998) also found higher percentages-of-occurrence (7%–10% higher) for typically developing bilingual children (in comparison with their monolingual peers) on a number of phonological processes including cluster reduction, final consonant deletion, and initial voicing.

Goldstein and Washington (2001) examined the English and Spanish phonological skills of 12 typically developing 4-year-old simultaneous bilingual (Spanish-English) children and found that there were no significant differences between the two languages on percent consonants correct (Shriberg & Kwiatkowski, 1982), percent consonants correct for voicing, place of articulation, manner of articulation, or percentage-of-occurrence for phonological processes. With the exception of interdental sounds in English (percent consonants correct of 25%), all other places of articulation either exceeded or approached mastery (greater than or equal to 90% correct) (Smit, Hand, Freilinger, Bernthal, & Bird, 1990). For manner of articulation classes, only two sound classes in English—fricatives and affricates—were exhibited with accuracy rates less than 90%, 83.9%, and 88.9%, respectively). In Spanish, the flap, trill, and spirants ([ß], [ð], and [ɣ]) were produced with accuracy rates of less than 90% (71.8%, 77.3%, and 76.8%, respectively). The relatively low accuracy rate for spirants indicated that the children, in general, did not possess adult-like use of the allophonic rule that changes stops into spirants (most commonly the stops /b/, /d/, /g/ become their spirant counterparts intervocalically) (Hammond, 2001). The results indicated that the phonological skills of these bilingual 4-years-olds were similar overall to monolingual speakers. The bilingual children, however, were much less accurate than monolingual speakers on a few sounds classes (spirants, flap, and trill in Spanish). Decreased accuracy for these few sound classes might mark the bilingual children as having less-advanced phonological skills in comparison with monolingual speakers.

Goldstein and Washington (2001) also found that typically developing, bilingual children's error patterns for two sound classes, the flap and trill in Spanish, were different from those of typically developing, monolingual Spanish-speaking children (Goldstein, 1988). Bilingual children either deleted the flap (approximately half of the time) or substituted [l] for it (about half of the time). Monolingual children, in contrast, rarely deleted the flap (approximately 6% of the time) and only sometimes substituted [l] for it (approximately 20% of the time). For the trill, the bilingual children used a larger number of substitutes for the target. Bilingual children substituted [l], [r], [j], [s], [t], [tj], [dr], and [ld] for the trill, but monolingual children substituted only [l], [r], or [j] for it. More research is needed to determine whether the use of different error patterns by bilingual and monolingual speakers is a widespread effect or limited to a few target phonemes.

Although this book focuses on language development in Spanish-English bilingual children, it is important to review two studies of bilingual children acquiring language pairs other than Spanish-English. Dodd, So, and Li (1996) examined the phonology of 16 typically developing Cantonese-speaking children who were acquiring English in preschool. They found that the children's error patterns were characteristic of children with disorders and were atypical for monolingual speakers of either language. Dodd and colleagues noted a higher number of atypical error patterns in the bilingual children in an amount usually associated with children with phonological disorders. They went on to say that "[d]elayed phonological acquisition might not be surprising given the need to master two phonological systems and, perhaps proportionately less exposure to each language compared to monolingual children" (p. 132).

The term *delayed* in this case is probably not fitting. No evidence exists that the phonological development of these children was delayed in the clinical sense (i.e., none of these children would have been recommended for phonological intervention). Their development, perhaps, may have been slower than monolingual children of either language, but it is still *typical* for bilingual children. In two other studies, Holm and Dodd's (1999) longitudinal study of two Cantonese-English bilingual children and Keshavarz and Ingram's (2002) study of a Farsi-English speaking child, all three children participating acquired their phonology in a similar way to other bilingual children. Also, Gildersleeve-Neumann and Davis (1998) found that even though Spanish-English bilingual children (examined in English only) demonstrated different developmental patterns, exhibited more errors, and were less intelligible initially than their monolingual peers, these differences dissipated over a relatively short period of time (9 months). Thus, over time, the phonological skills of bilingual children were similar to those of monolingual children.

Very few studies have examined the phonological skills of Spanish-English bilingual children with phonological disorders. Goldstein (2000) characterized the phonological patterns in ten 4- to 5-year-old bilingual (Spanish-English) children (mean age = 4;8) with phonological disorders. The results indicated that the bilingual children with phonological disorders exhibited more errors, lower consonant accuracy scores, and higher percentages-of-occurrence for phonological processes than did typically developing bilingual children (Goldstein & Iglesias, 1999) or monolingual Spanish-speaking children with phonological disorders (Goldstein, 1993; Goldstein & Iglesias, 1996). The frequency and types of errors exhibited by the children were similar regardless of target language, however. Specifically, the children, as expected for most children with phonological disorders, showed higher error rates on clusters, fricatives, and liquids than other classes of sounds. They did not show significant quantitative differences between languages on either places or manners of articulation. Finally, bilingual children with phonological disorders had higher overall percentages-of-occurrence for phonological processes than did monolingual, Spanish-speaking children with phonological disorders. This discrepancy between monolingual and bilingual speakers, however, was not absolute across individual phonological processes. In Goldstein's (2000) study, initial consonant deletion and deaffrication were exhibited at somewhat lower rates in bilingual children with phonological disorders than has been reported for monolingual Spanish-speaking children with phonological disorders (Goldstein & Iglesias, 1996). Although the average percentage-of-occurrence difference is not large, the results indicated that bilingual children will not exhibit higher percentages-of-occurrence than monolingual children across all measures. It should be noted finally that the results also indicated that the phonological characteristics of these children were similar to children with phonological disorders acquiring other languages (see Yavas, 1998, for a review). That is, they showed a continued use of processes beyond the expected age for suppression, atypical error patterns, restricted segmental repertoires, and sound or syllable preferences.

In summary, phonological acquisition in bilingual children does seem to be somewhat different than in monolingual children of the same age. That difference, however, may be localized to decreased accuracy of segments within a small set of sound classes rather than a difference affecting the entire phonological system. It also seems to be the case that bilingual children may exhibit different error patterns on at least a few specified phonemes than monolingual children of the same age exhibit. Finally, these data indicate that the acquisition of more than one language may result *temporarily* in a more compromised phonological system compared with children acquiring only one language; however, that difference is short-lived, with typically developing bilingual children acquiring the phonological system of both languages.

IMPLICATIONS FOR ASSESSMENT AND INTERVENTION

Assessment

In assessing the phonological skills of bilingual children, it is likely that modifications will have to be made to the "standard" assessment protocol. For example, it may take twice as long to assess the communication skills of a bilingual child compared with a monolingual child because assessment must take place in both languages (Goldstein, 2001a). The goals of a phonological assessment, however, are likely to be similar for all children being assessed for potential phonological disorders. These goals, as outlined by Bankson and Bernthal (2004), include

- Determining whether the child's phonological system is developing typically

- Describing the child's phonological system and determining if it is different from typically developing speakers of the same dialect/language to require intervention

- Identifying factors that may be related to the presence or maintenance of a phonological disorder

- Determining the intervention approach and initial treatment targets

- Making predictive and prognostic statements in terms of phonological change with or without intervention

- Monitoring change in phonological performance

Based on the main issues of phonological representation and bilingual phonological development described previously, a speech-language pathologist (SLP) must determine how bilingual children exhibit phonological disorders in each of their languages and how the concepts of shared versus unshared phonemes and dialect differences impinge on assessing phonology in bilingual speakers.

In order for a bilingual child to be diagnosed with a phonological disorder, deficits must be evident in both languages (Roseberry-McKibbin, 2001). A diagnosis of language disorder would not be made if deficits were noted in only one language (e.g., Kayser, 2002; Roseberry-McKibbin, 1995). Researchers have found that in bilingual children with phonological disorders, the disorder is present (to one extent or another) in both languages. As Holm, Dodd, and Ozanne have noted,

[I]t would be expected that a bilingual child would have disordered phonology in both languages because the underlying process of developing a phonologically appropriate system requires the ability to abstract the relevant information about that system from the input they receive. It follows therefore that the phonological errors need not necessarily be the same. (1997, p. 67)

Dodd, Holm, and Wi (1997) presented case studies of two sequential bilingual (Cantonese-English) children with phonological disorders. Both children began acquiring Cantonese first and then began speaking English around 3 years old. The results indicated that both children showed characteristics of phonological disorder in both languages and made similar and dissimilar errors in both languages. In a group of 10 Spanish-English bilingual children ages 4;0–5;7 with phonological disorders, Goldstein (2000) found that the children exhibited similar accuracy rates for consonants and vowels in both Spanish and English across a number of dimensions. Overall accuracy rates between the two languages were similar for both consonants (77.9% in Spanish and 80.3% in English) and vowels (96% in English and 96.3% in Spanish). Accuracy rates also were similar between languages for consonants by voicing (87.7% in Spanish; 88.5% in English), place of articulation (81.2% in English; 83.5% in Spanish), and manner of articulation (80.2% in Spanish; 84.3% in English). The three most commonly occurring phonological processes—cluster reduction, liquid simplification, and stopping—were the same in both languages. Moreover, the percentages-of-occurrence for cluster reduction and liquid simplification were similar in both languages. Percentages-of-occurrence for uncommon processes (e.g., backing, initial consonant deletion) were similar between languages, as well.

Because phonological development in bilingual children seems to be both similar to and different from that of monolingual speakers of either language, phonological samples must be collected from both of the bilingual child's languages. It is, therefore, not appropriate to administer and then report the normative data from assessment tools designed for and normed on monolingual speakers. Although these tests might be used in an informal way, the normative data associated with them are not valid for bilingual speakers. Differentially diagnosing a phonological disorder in a child for whom English is not his or her only language requires that the appropriate comparison database be used. As Dodd and colleagues noted, "[C]linicians cannot, therefore, assess sequential bilingual children's need for intervention by comparing their performance, either quantitatively or qualitatively, with monolingual children's performance" (1997, p. 241). Thus, if the child is a monolingual speaker, then data collected from other monolingual children should be used. If the child is a bilingual speaker, however, then data collected from bilingual children should be utilized. The phonological skills of bilingual children should not be judged and compared with their monolingual counterparts. Doing so runs counter to Grosjean's notion of a "whole view" of bilingualism in which the bilingual is a whole whose two languages cannot be artificially separated and examined (Grosjean, 1989, 1992, 1997).

In order to assess phonological development in bilingual speakers, an SLP should analyze a child's phonology as one combined system as well as separately according to the constraints of each language. To determine language-specific qualities about the bilingual child's two languages, the SLP should perform independent analyses (e.g., documenting sounds produced, syllable types used, and number of syllables per word), and relational analyses (e.g., noting number and types of omissions, substitutions, distortions, and additions; percentage-of-occurrence for phonological processes) (Stoel-Gammon & Dunn, 1983). These analyses should be performed separately for each language given that the English phonology is different from Spanish phonology. The child's phonological system also should be analyzed as a whole without reference to each individual language. Given the evidence that bilingual children distinguish between shared and unshared phonemes (recall that typically developing bilingual children and bilingual children with phonological disorders produced shared phonemes with a much higher accuracy rate than phonemes not shared between the two languages), the SLP may want to analyze the child's accuracy of production using that metric. This analysis would give the SLP added information about the phonological system as a whole without regard to specific language.

Analyzing the accuracy of shared and unshared phonemes has been shown to be effective in making differential diagnoses in African American English-speaking children with phonological disorders. In African American English-speaking children, Stockman (1996a) has suggested assessing word- and syllable-initial phonemes—/m/, /n/, /p/, /b/, /t/, /d/, /k/, /g/, /f/, /s/, /h/, /w/, /j/, /l/, /ɹ/—that are shared in both African American English and General American English. Wilcox and Anderson (1998) found that assessing these sounds along with clusters provided enough information to differentiate typical from atypical speech sound development in a group of African American English speakers. Controlled studies will need to be completed with Spanish-English bilingual children to determine the sensitivity and specificity of this analysis for those speakers as well.

Regardless of the types of analyses that are completed, SLPs will need to consider the role that dialect plays in these analyses. In English, dialect differences in phonology are largely defined by changes in vowels. There are, of course, notable exceptions to that generalization. For example, in African American English, a number of consonant changes occur (e.g., f/θ in intervocalic position; /nʌθiŋ/ "nothing" → [nʌfiŋ]) in addition to some vowel changes (Stockman, 1996b). In Spanish, dialect differences largely affect consonants. For comprehensive information on Spanish dialectal features specific to phonology, the reader is referred to Alvar (1996), Cotton and Sharp (1988), Dalbor (1980), Goldstein (1995), Lombardi and de Peters (1981), and Terrell (1981). Guitart (1996) has distinguished two general types of dialects and applied them to Spanish: conservative dialects and radical dialects. Conservative dialects (e.g., the variety of Spanish spoken in many parts of Spain) are those that tend to preserve consonants in the syllable coda; the coda is the sound or sounds that occur after the vowel in a syllable; for example, the /s/ in /mas/ (more.) Radical dialects (e.g., Caribbean varieties such as Puerto Rican or Dominican Spanish) are ones that alter consonants in the coda. Alterations in radical dialects (Guitart, 1996) might include features such as

- Deleting syllable segments (e.g., /dos/ "two" → [do])

- Laryngealizing fricatives (e.g., aspirating /s/–/dos/ "two" → [doʰ],

- Laryngealizing or velarizing stops (e.g., /pɛpsi/ "Pepsi" → [peʔsi] or [peksi]),

- Nasalization of /n/ on the preceding vowel (e.g., /xamon/ "ham" → [xamõ]) or production of /n/ as a velar nasal [ŋ], even before nonvelars (e.g., /xamon/ "ham" → [xamoŋ])

- Neutralization of /r/ and /l/ (e.g., /l/ is rhotacized–/sol/ "sun" → [sor]), /ɾ/ is lateralized–/flol/ "flower" → [flol], or (c) both are realized as a third segment that may be a nonliquid–/kaɾta/"letter" → [katta])

SLPs must be vigilant in differentiating true errors from dialect differences (Yavas & Goldstein, 1998). Failing to account for dialect differences may result in either over- or underidentification of phonological disorders in children. Moreover, not accounting for dialect features might place a child diagnosed with a true phonological disorder in an inappropriate severity category, thus altering the amount and type of intervention that is provided to the child. Fleming and Hartman (1989), Cole and Taylor (1990), and Washington and Craig (1992) examined this issue in groups of African American English-speaking children and found that not accounting for dialect features decreased the overall scores of children on phonological analyses. In a group of typically developing Spanish-speaking children and Spanish-speaking children with phonological disorders, Goldstein and Iglesias (2001) found that the number of consonant errors, the number of errors within individual sound classes, and the percentages-of-occurrence for phonological processes all decreased based on the accounting of Puerto Rican dialect features. In addition, the percentage of consonants correct (Shriberg & Kwiatkowski, 1982) increased after accounting for dialect features. For children with phonological disorders, the accounting of dialect features would not have changed the classification for any child from phonologically disordered to typically developing; however, it would have decreased the severity rating for some children, thus possibly affecting intervention in terms of prognosis, number of goals, and types of goals. Finally, Goldstein and Iglesias (2001) found that taking dialect into account still left enough true errors that would differentiate typically developing children from those with phonological disorders and aid the SLP in planning intervention for bilingual children with true phonological disorders.

Intervention

Providing intervention to bilingual children with phonological disorders is difficult for two main reasons. First, the language of intervention is often not apparent. Second, the general approach to intervention is often arduous to discern. In this section, information on these two issues are addressed. Studies in these areas with Spanish-English bilingual children as participants will be supplemented by other studies of children acquiring other constellations of languages.

SLPs may take two general approaches in planning intervention for bilingual children with phonological disorders. The SLP may base intervention on the child's knowledge of shared and unshared phonemes. Given that bilingual children appear to distinguish between phonemes shared and not shared by the two languages (Goldstein, Fabiano, & Iglesias, 2003; Goldstein & Iglesias, 2002), SLPs may choose to either 1) treat shared phonemes initially and monitor any transfer that takes place between the two languages or 2) treat unshared phonemes initially and monitor the effect on the other phonemes in the child's inventory. Given that in Spanish and English, many, although not all, of the unshared phonemes are later developing (e.g., prevocalic *r*, flap, trill), the second approach might be more appropriate for children with severe to profound phonological disorders who have a number of consonants missing from their phonetic inventory in the same way that a nondevelopmental approach (e.g., maximal opposition) has been shown to be more effective than a developmental approach for monolingual English-speaking children (Gierut, 1989).

The way in which intervention is carried out specifically may rely not only on language choice but also on the types of errors exhibited by the children and the occurrence of those error types in each language. SLPs may choose intervention targets based on the type and rates of error patterns found in both Spanish and English, remembering, of course, that neither cross-linguistic effects nor dialect features should be treated. Cross-linguistic effects and dialect features are part of the expected developmental system for bilingual children and, thus, are not appropriate intervention targets (ASHA, 1983). In terms of treating true error patterns in each language, the SLP may first target true error patterns with high occurrences in both languages (e.g., cluster reduction, unstressed syllable deletion) (Yavas & Goldstein, 1998). After targeting commonly occurring error patterns that are highly evident in both languages, error patterns that are exhibited in both languages with unequal frequency (e.g., final consonant deletion in English; trill errors in Spanish) would be targeted. Finally, error patterns that were exhibited in only one language would be targeted (e.g., final consonant devoicing in English).

This model of intervention necessitates intervening, at some point during the therapeutic process, in both languages. The evidence presented earlier in the chapter on phonological representation and bilingual children's differential accuracy in producing shared versus unshared phonemes also lends support to the requirement of intervention in both languages. The idea of having to intervene in both languages contrasts with the view commonly held by many SLPs that if a bilingual child speaks any English at all, then intervention can be provided in English and that it will "transfer" to the other language. Studies of language (i.e., syntactic) disorders in sequential bilingual children, however, show the benefit of intervention in the home language before the second language. For example, Perozzi and Sanchez (1992) found benefits for intervention in the second language only after sufficient language levels were reached in the first language. Single-subject designs with typically developing children (Kiernan & Swisher, 1990) and those with language delays (Perozzi, 1985) also have shown the benefit of instruction in a child's first language.

Although few studies have examined this issue in bilingual children with phonological disorders, evidence indicates that intervention for phonological disorders will need to take place at some point during the course of treatment in both languages. Holm, Dodd, and Ozanne (1997) found evidence of transfer and nontransfer in a case study of a 5-year-old bilingual (Cantonese-English) child who spoke Cantonese exclusively at home until he went to child care at age 3;3, where English was used exclusively. For example, /s/ (common to both Cantonese and English) was targeted only in English using English words. The authors found that correct production of /s/ in English generalized to correct production in Cantonese. Targeting consonant cluster reduction (again, in English) showed decreased use of consonant cluster reduction in English but *not* in Cantonese. It can be inferred, then, that intervention for cluster reduction would need to take place in Cantonese as well for a similar decrease in that phonological process to occur. Thus, the results from this study indicated that transfer of increased skills from one language to another cannot be expected even if the child exhibited similar patters in both languages. As Dodd,

Holm, and Wi noted for sequential bilingual children, "[A]ppropriate intervention would, then, need to target both languages so that the ways in which the two phonological systems differed could be explicitly taught" (1997, p. 241). For all the intervention approaches discussed in this section, however, future efficacy and effectiveness studies with Spanish-English bilingual children need to be conducted.

SUMMARY

The goal of this chapter has been to highlight several key issues related to phonological development and disorders in bilingual children that inform phonological representation and that demonstrate that bilingual phonological acquisition both similar to and different from acquisition in monolingual speakers of either language. Although the developmental timetable for phonological acquisition is not the same as that for monolingual children, this difference should not be interpreted to mean that phonological acquisition for bilingual children is *delayed* in the clinical sense. Moreover, it should be evident that phonological skill in each language is similar but not identical, and that each language may influence the other in quite systematic ways. Assessment and intervention, then, should take advantage of a child's acquisition of more than one language by taking into account the bilingual child's knowledge of phonemes shared by the two languages and phonemes unique to each language and that thus necessitate evaluation and likely intervention in both languages.

REFERENCES

Almgren, M., & Barreña, A. (2001). Bilingual acquisition and separation of linguistic codes: Ergativity in Basque versus accusativity in Spanish. In K. Nelson, A. Aksu-Koç, & C. Johnson (Eds.), *Children's language* (Vol. 11, pp. 27–48). International Association for the Study of Child Language.

Alvar, M. (Ed.). (1996). *Manual de dialectología Hispánica* [Manual of Hispanic dialectology]. Barcelona, Spain: Ariel.

Amastae, J. (1982). Aspects of the bilingual acquisition of English and Spanish. *Journal of the Linguistic Association of the Southwest, 5*, 5–19.

American Speech-Language-Hearing Association. (1983). Social dialect position paper, *ASHA, 25*, 23–25.

Bankson, N., & Bernthal, J. (2004). Phonological assessment procedures. In J. Bernthal & N. Bankson (Eds.), *Articulation and phonological disorders* (5th ed., pp. 201–267). Boston: Allyn & Bacon.

Barlow, J. (2001, February). *Error patterns and transfer in Spanish-English bilingual phonological production.* Paper presented at the 26th annual Boston University Conference on Language Development, Boston, MA.

Bosch, L., & Sebatián-Gallés, N. (2001). Early language differentiation in bilingual infants. In J. Cenose & F. Genesee (Eds.), *Trends in bilingual acquisition* (pp. 71–93). Amsterdam: John Benjamins.

Cole, P., & Taylor, O. (1990). Performance of working class African-American children on three tests of articulation. *Language, Speech, and Hearing Services in Schools, 21,* 171–176.

Cotton, E., & Sharp, J. (1988). *Spanish in the Americas.* Washington, DC: Georgetown University Press.

Dalbor, J. (1980). *Spanish pronunciation: Theory and practice* (2nd ed.). New York: Holt, Rinehart & Winston.

de Houwer, A. (1995). Bilingual language acquisition. In P. Fletcher & B. MacWhinney (Eds.), *The handbook of child language* (pp. 219–250). Oxford, UK: Blackwell.

Deuchar, M., & Clark, A. (1995). Early bilingual acquisition of the voicing contrast in English and Spanish. *Journal of Phonetics, 24,* 275–305.

Deuchar, M., & Quay, S. (2000). *Bilingual acquisition: Theoretical implications of a case study.* Oxford, UK: Oxford University Press.

Dodd, B., Holm, A., & Wi, L. (1997). Speech disorder in preschool children exposed to Cantonese and English. *Clinical Linguistics and Phonetics, 11,* 229–243.

Dodd, B., So, L., & Li, W. (1996). Symptoms of disorder without impairment: The written and spoken errors of bilinguals. In B. Dodd, R. Campbell, & L. Worrall (Eds.), *Evaluating theories of language: Evidence form disorder* (pp. 119–136). London: Whurr Publishers.

Fabiano, L., & Goldstein, B. (2004, May). *Phonological representation in sequential and simultaneous bilingual Spanish-English speaking children.* Paper presented at the 2004 Child Phonology Conference, Tempe, AZ.

Fantini, A. (1985). *Language acquisition of a bilingual child: A sociolinguistic perspective (to age 10).* San Diego: College Hill Press.

Fleming, K., & Hartman, J. (1989). Establishing cultural validity of the computer analysis of phonological processes. *Florida Educational Research Council Bulletin, 22,* 8–32.

Genesee, F. (1989). Early bilingual development: one language or two? *Journal of Child Language, 16,* 161–179.

Genesee, F., Nicoladis, N., & Paradis, J. (1995). Language differentiation in early bilingual development. *Journal of Child Language, 22,* 611–631.

Gierut, J. (1989). Maximal opposition approach to phonological treatment. *Journal of Speech and Hearing Disorders, 54,* 9–19.

Gildersleeve, C., Davis, B., & Stubbe, E. (1996, November). *When monolingual rules don't apply: Speech development in a bilingual environment.* Paper presented at the annual convention of the American Speech-Language-Hearing Association, Seattle, WA.

Gildersleeve, C., von Hapsburg, D., & Davis, B. (1997). *Speech acquisition in bilinguals: Differences in vowel acoustic quality.* Seminar presented at the 1997 Texas Research Symposium on Language Diversity, Austin, TX.

Gildersleeve-Neumann, C., & Davis, B. (1998, November). *Learning English in a bilingual preschool environment: Change over time.* Paper presented at the annual convention of the American Speech-Language-Hearing Association, San Antonio, TX.

Goldstein, B. (1988). *The evidence of phonological processes in 3- and 4-year-old Spanish speakers.* Unpublished master's theses, Temple University, Philadelphia, PA.

Goldstein, B. (1995). Spanish phonological development. In H. Kayser (Ed.), *Bilingual speech-language pathology: An Hispanic focus* (pp. 17–38). San Diego: Singular Publishing Group.

Goldstein, B. (2000, June). *Phonological disorders in bilingual (Spanish-English) children.* Seminar presented at the 2000 Child Phonology Conference, Cedar Falls, IA.

Goldstein, B. (2001a). Assessing phonological skills in Hispanic/Latino children. *Seminars in Speech and Language, 22,* 39–49.

Goldstein, B. (2001b). Transcription of Spanish and Spanish-influenced English. *Communication Disorders Quarterly, 23,* 54–60.

Goldstein, B., Fabiano, L., & Iglesias, A. (2003, April). *The representation of phonology in sequential Spanish-English bilingual children.* Poster session presented at the International Symposium on Bilingualism 4, Tempe, AZ.

Goldstein, B., & Iglesias, A. (1996). Phonological patterns in Puerto Rican Spanish-speaking children with phonological disorders. *Journal of Communication Disorders, 29*(5), 367–387.

Goldstein, B., & Iglesias, A. (1999, February). *Phonological patterns in bilingual (Spanish-English) children.* Seminar presented at the 1999 Texas Research Symposium on Language Diversity, Austin, TX.

Goldstein, B., & Iglesias, A. (2001). The effect of dialect on phonological analysis: Evidence from Spanish-speaking children. *American Journal of Speech-Language Pathology, 10,* 394–406.

Goldstein, B., & Iglesias, A. (2002, July). *Phonological representation in Spanish-English bilingual children.* Poster session presented at the 23rd annual Symposium on Research in Child Language Disorders/9th Congress of the International Association for the Study of Child Language, Madison, WI.

Goldstein, B., & Iglesias, A. (2004). Language and dialectal variations. In J. Bernthal & N. Bankson (Eds.), *Articulation and phonological disorders* (5th ed., pp. 348–375). Boston: Allyn & Bacon.

Goldstein, B., Iglesias, A., & Rojas, R. (2001, November). *Shared and unshared consonants in Spanish-English bilingual children.* Seminar presented at the Convention of the American Speech-Language-Hearing Association, New Orleans, LA.

Goldstein, B., & Washington, P. (2001). An initial investigation of phonological patterns in 4-year-old typically developing Spanish-English bilingual children. *Language, Speech, & Hearing Services in Schools, 32,* 153–164.

Goodluck, H. (1991). *Language acquisition: A linguistic introduction.* Oxford: Blackwell.

Grosjean, F. (1989). Neurolinguists, beware! The bilingual is not two monolinguals in one person. *Brain and Language, 36,* 3–15.

Grosjean, F. (1992). Another view of bilingualism. In R. Harris (Ed.), *Cognitive processing in bilinguals* (pp. 51-62). Amsterdam: Elsevier.

Grosjean, F. (1997). Processing mixed languages: Issues, findings, and models. In A. de Groot & J. Kroll (Eds.), *Tutorials in bilingualism: Psycholinguistic perspectives* (pp. 225–254). Mahwah, NJ: Lawrence Erlbaum Associates.

Guitart, J. (1996). Spanish in contact with itself and the phonological characterization of conservative and radical styles. In A. Roca & J. Jensen (Eds.), *Spanish in contact: Issues in bilingualism* (pp. 151–157). Somerville, MA: Cascadilla, MA.

Hadlich, R., Holton, J., & Montes, M. (1968). *A drillbook of Spanish pronunciation.* New York: Harper & Row.

Hammond, R. (2001). *The sounds of Spanish: Analysis and application.* Somerville, MA: Cascadilla Press.

Hochberg, J. (1988). First steps in the acquisition of Spanish stress. *Journal of Child Language, 15,* 273–292.

Holm, A., Dodd, B., & Ozanne, A. (1997). Efficacy of intervention for a bilingual child making articulation and phonological errors. *International Journal of Bilingualism, 1,* 55–69.

Johnson, C., & Lancaster, P. (1998). The development of more than one phonology: A case study of a Norwegian-English bilingual child. *International Journal of Bilingualism, 2,* 265–300.

Kayser, H. (1993). Hispanic cultures. In D. Battle (Ed.), *Communication disorders in multicultural populations* (pp. 114–157). Boston: Andover Medical Publishers.

Kayser, H. (2002). Bilingual language development and language disorders. In D. Battle (Ed.), *Communication disorders in multicultural populations* (3rd ed., pp. 205–232). Boston: Butterworth-Heinemann.

Keshavarz, M., & Ingram, D. (2002). The early phonological development of a Farsi-English bilingual child. *International Journal of Bilingualism, 6,* 255–269.

Kiernan, B., & Swisher, L. (1990). The initial learning of novel English words: Two single-subject experiments with minority-language children. *Journal of Speech and Hearing Research, 33,* 707–716.

Leather, J., & James, A. (1996). Second language speech. In W. Ritchie & T. Bhatia (Eds.), *Handbook of second language acquisition* (pp. 269–316). San Diego: Academic Press.

Locke, J. (1983). *Phonological acquisition and change.* New York: Academic Press.

Lombardi, R.P., & de Peters, A.B. (1981). *Modern spoken Spanish: An interdisciplinary perspective.* Washington, DC: University Press of America.

MacDonald, M. (1989). The influence of Spanish phonology on the English spoken by United States Hispanics. In P. Bjarkman & R. Hammond (Eds.), *American Spanish pronunciation: Theoretical and applied perspectives* (pp. 215–236). Washington, DC: Georgetown University Press.

Major, R. (1977). Phonological differentiation of a bilingual child. *Ohio State University Working Papers in Linguistics, 22,* 88–122.

Meisel, J. (1989). Early differentiation of languages in bilingual children. In K. Hyltenstam & L. Obler (Eds.), *Bilingualism across the lifespan* (pp. 13–40). Cambridge: Cambridge University Press.

National Institute on Deafness and Other Communication Disorders. (1994). *National strategic research plan.* Bethesda, MD: Author.

Paradis, J. (1996). Prosodic development and differentiation in bilingual first language acquisition. In A. Stringfellow, D. Cahana-Amitay, E. Hughes, & A. Zukowski (Eds.), *Proceedings of the 20th Annual Boston University Conference on Language Development* (pp. 528–539). Somerville, MA: Cascadilla Press.

Paradis, J. (2001). Do bilingual two-year-olds have separate phonological systems? *International Journal of Bilingualism, 5,* 19–38.

Paradis, M. (1987). *The assessment of bilingual aphasia.* Mahwah, NJ: Lawrence Erlbaum Associates.

Perez, E. (1994). Phonological differences among speakers of Spanish-influenced English. In J. Bernthal & N. Bankson (Eds.), *Child phonology: Characteristics, assessment, and intervention with special populations* (pp. 245–254). New York: Thieme Medical Publishers.

Perozzi, J. (1985). Pilot study of language facilitation for bilingual, language handicapped children: Theoretical and intervention implications. *Journal of Speech and Hearing Disorders, 50,* 403–406.

Perozzi, J., & Sanchez, M. (1992). The effect of instruction in L1 on receptive acquisition of L2 for bilingual students with language delay. *Language, Speech, and Hearing Services in the Schools, 23,* 348–352.

Roseberry-McKibbin, C. (1995). *Multicultural students with special language needs.* Oceanside, CA: Academic Communication Associates.

Roseberry-McKibbin, C. (2001). *The source for bilingual students with language disorders.* East Moline, IL: LinguiSystems.

Schnitzer, M., & Krasinski, E. (1994). The development of segmental phonological production in a bilingual child. *Journal of Child Language, 21,* 585–622.

Schnitzer, M., & Krasinski, E. (1996). The development of segmental phonological production in a bilingual child: A contrasting second case. *Journal of Child Language, 23,* 547–571.

Shriberg, L., & Kwiatkowski, J. (1982). Phonological disorders, III: A procedure for assessing severity of involvement. *Journal of Speech and Hearing Disorders, 47,* 256–270.

Smit, A., Hand, L., Freilinger, J., Bernthal, J., & Bird, A. (1990). The Iowa articulation norms project and its Nebraska replication. *Journal of Speech and Hearing Disorders, 55,* 779–798.

Snow, D. (2001). Transcription of suprasegmentals. *Topics in Language Disorders, 21,* 41–51.

Stockman, I. (1996a). Phonological development and disorders in African American children. In A.G. Kamhi, K.E. Pollock, & J.L. Harris (Eds.), *Communication development and disorders in African American children: Research, assessment, and intervention* (pp. 117–154). Baltimore: Paul H. Brookes Publishing Co.

Stockman, I. (1996b). The promises and pitfalls of language sample analysis as an assessment tool for linguistic minority children. *Language, Speech, and Hearing Services in Schools, 27,* 355–366.

Stoel-Gammon, C., & Dunn, C. (1985). *Normal and disordered phonology in children.* Austin, TX: PRO-ED.

Terrell, T. (1981). Current trends in the investigation of Cuban and Puerto Rican phonology. In J. Amastae & L. Elías-Olivares (Eds.), *Spanish in the United States: Sociolinguistic aspects* (pp. 47–70). Cambridge, UK: Cambridge University Press.

U.S. Bureau of the Census. (2000). *Language use.* Retrieved May 20, 2004, from http://www.census.gov/population/www/ socdemo/lang_use.html

Valdés, G., & Figueroa, R. (1994). *Bilingualism and testing: A special case of bias.* Norwood, NJ: Ablex Publishing.

Vogel, I. (1975). One system or two: An analysis of a two-year-old Romanian-English bilingual's phonology. *Papers and Reports in Child Language Development, 9*, 43–62.

Volterra, V., & Taeschner, T. (1978). The acquisition and development of language by bilingual children. *Journal of Child Language, 5*, 311–326.

Walpole, C. (1999). The bilingual child: One system or two? In E. Clark (Ed.), *The proceedings of the thirtieth annual child language research forum* (pp. 187–194). Stanford, CA: Center for the Study of Language and Information.

Walters, S. (2000, November). *Phonological development in three two-year-old simultaneous bilingual children.* Paper presented at the annual convention of the American Speech-Language-Hearing Association, Washington, DC.

Washington, J., & Craig, H. (1992). Articulation test performances of low-income African American preschoolers with communication impairments. *Language, Speech, and Hearing Services in Schools, 23*, 201–207.

Watson, I. (1991). Phonological processing in two languages. In E. Bialystok (Ed.), *Language processing in bilingual children* (pp. 25–48). Cambridge, UK: Cambridge University Press.

Wilcox, L., & Anderson, R. (1998). Distinguishing between phonological difference and disorder in children who speak African-American vernacular English: An experimental testing instrument. *Journal of Communication Disorders, 31*, 315–335.

Wolfram, W. (1971). *Overlapping influence and linguistic assimilation in second generation Puerto Rican English.* Paper presented at the meeting of the American Anthropological Association, New York. (ERIC Document Reproduction Service No. ED057665).

Wolfram, W., & Schilling-Estes, N. (1998). *American English: Dialects and variation.* Oxford: Blackwell.

Yavas, M. (1998). *Phonology: Development and disorders.* San Diego: Singular Publishing Group.

Yavas, M., & Goldstein, B. (1998). Phonological assessment and treatment of bilingual speakers. *American Journal of Speech-Language Pathology, 7*, 49–60.

Zampini, M., & Green, K. (2001). The voicing contrast in English and Spanish: The relationship between perception and production. In J. Nicol (Ed.), *One mind, two languages: Bilingual language processing* (pp. 23–48). Oxford: Blackwell Publishers.

CHAPTER 12

Fluency and Stuttering in Bilingual Children

NAN BERNSTEIN RATNER

This chapter explores concepts relevant to the assessment and treatment of Latino bilinguals who stutter or have other fluency concerns. To establish a framework for assessment and remediation, the multifaceted dimensions of stuttering as a disorder of speech production are explored. Next, specific concerns that arise in the diagnostic process are discussed, with an emphasis on both those that emerge from bilingualism and those that arise from Spanish language use and acculturation. We then evaluate the impact of these and other issues on appropriate strategies for fluency intervention and counseling.

CLINICAL CONCERNS IN THE ASSESSMENT AND TREATMENT OF STUTTERING

Before addressing the specific challenges posed by working with fluency disorders in the Latino bilingual population, it is important to understand the multifactorial nature of stuttering. Stuttering is much more than the behavior of producing nonfluent speech. In particular, it is the associated psychosocial and cognitive features of the disorder that will require careful consideration when working with members of the Latino community.

Many clinicians and researchers working in the field of fluency disorders characterize stuttering in terms of its "ABCs" (see Figure 12.1). In this model, A stands for *affective components*, which include feelings, emotions, and attitudes that accompany stuttering. B stands for what is usually most obviously in need of therapeutic attention when a person stutters: the overt *behaviors* that characterize stuttering. C stands for the *cognitive components* inherent in stuttering, including strategies, beliefs, and interpreta-

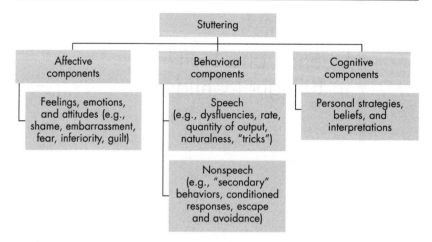

Figure 12.1. The ABCs of stuttering illustrating the complex nature of stuttering behavior, which is composed of three different components and related factors.

tions. Because the B component is the most salient characteristic of stuttering, it is discussed first.

Behaviors in this context include both speech and nonspeech features. Speech features of stuttering include hallmark atypical dysfluency types such as blocking; multiple iterations of sounds, syllables, and monosyllabic words; phonation breaks in the middle of words; and prolongations of sounds (e.g., consonants) not normally prolonged in speech that is perceived to be fluent. A list of the typical dysfluencies that characterize stuttered speech is provided in Table 12.1, along with a comparison listing of speech disfluencies that are considered normal and typical in speech production. As discussed later in this chapter, normal speech disfluencies are an integral and probably necessary component of an individual's spontaneous speech production. They may be more numerous when language formulation skills are weak or challenged, as they can be in cases of unbalanced bilingualism. Some of these more normal disfluencies may also be strategies that stuttering speakers use to mask difficulties in conversation, and they need to be examined carefully when assessing a speaker's conversational fluency. Furthermore, wide cross-linguistic variation occurs in the types of normal disfluencies across language communities, particularly in the use of what are termed *filled pauses* or *fillers* (Montes, 1999; Muñoz-Duston, 1992).

Speech behaviors in stuttering, in contrast to normal disfluencies, are usually accompanied by nonspeech behaviors as well. These features, often called *accessory* or *secondary* behaviors, appear to reflect the generalized ten-

Table 12.1.   Behaviors distinguishing stuttering from normal disfluency

Behavior	Stuttering	Normal disfluency
Sound, syllable, and word repetitions		
Number of iterations	More than two	Less than two
Frequency per 100 words	More than two	Less than two
Tempo	Fast	Normal tempo
Tension	Often apparent	Absent
Intrusion of schwa vowel	Often present	Absent
Prolongations		
Duration	Longer than 1 second	Shorter than 1 second
Accompanying pitch rise	Often present	Absent
Location	May affect all continuents	Only present on vowels and syllabic consonants
Frequency	More than one per 100 words	Less than one per 100 words
Tension	Often present	Absent
Blocks and silent pauses		
Within words	May be present	Absent
Prior to speech onset	May be long	Not obvious
Awareness of speech and disfluency		
Frustration	May be present	Absent
Situational avoidance	May be present	Usually absent
Word avoidance	May be present	Absent
Self-concept as disfluent speaker	Present	Absent
Eye contact during conversation	May be disturbed	Normal
Disability in talking, work performance, and situational coping	Possible	Rare
Occupational, vocational, and social handicap	Possible	Rare

Sources: Van Riper (1982) and Manning (2001).

sion of stuttered speech production and may also reflect learned strategies that the speaker has adopted either to escape the moment of stuttering or to produce speech when difficulty arises or is expected. Such behaviors might include eye blinks, facial grimaces, head or body movements, and so forth.

Most clinicians are readily able to identify such core *behavioral* features of stuttering. In fact, student clinicians often are able to identify moments of stuttering in speakers conversing in languages with which they are not familiar. The rhythm and "look" of stuttered speech appear to supersede the segmental or linguistic components of a speaker's message and are usually judged to have similar characteristics across the languages of a bilingual speaker.

To understand stuttering well enough to effectively treat it, however, the affective and cognitive features of the disorder should also be appreciated. As mentioned previously, affective components of stuttering include how the person who stutters feels about speaking and stuttering. Affective components of stuttering build quickly over childhood, as listeners respond unfavorably to stuttered speech. Fears of speaking and of fluency breakdown soon become evident as children with chronic stuttering confront the task of talking. These may become very specific to particular settings, tasks, or interlocutors. Along with fear and anxiety, many children (and their families) often experience guilt and shame (Murphy, 1997) about their inability to control stuttering, which has an unpredictable effect on speech production. Sometimes speech is fluent, even when the speaker does not try to make it so, and often speech is dysfluent, despite strong efforts to speak fluently.

Cognitive aspects of stuttering include those beliefs or strategies that speakers use to manage speaking tasks and cope with stuttering. Among such beliefs are notions that speech is not acceptable unless it is fluent, that certain words or situations elicit stuttering, or that a person's inability to gain fluency reflects his or her failure to use therapeutic information and techniques that he or she has been given. Strategies may include avoidance of speaking situations, the use of "running starts" or other behaviors thought to improve fluency of speech, and so forth.

This chapter focuses on the affective and cognitive aspects of stuttering and their role in therapy planning. These features are most likely to vary from person to person, family to family, and culture to culture, making them important considerations in the adaptation of stuttering intervention with Latino clients. They may also vary within an individual as a function of sociolinguistic experience, in ways that may affect language therapy planning and generalization in bilingual speakers enrolled in stuttering therapy.

Differences Between the Child and Adult Client

Clinicians face different issues when working with child and adult clients. These differences are important to conceptualize in order to understand the desired outcomes of diagnostic sessions and their implications for culturally sensitive communication and effective therapeutic goal setting.

Stuttering in Children

Stuttering usually has a relatively early onset in childhood; it usually becomes manifest between the ages of 2½ to 3½ years of age (Yairi & Ambrose, 1992). When it first appears and clinical consultation is first sought, parents' questions usually involve those of differential diagnosis and the need for intervention. Does the child stutter, or is he or she merely developmentally disfluent? If the child is thought to stutter, is direct intervention warranted at this time? Parents have a sense, and are often counseled by others such as pediatricians and older relatives, that children frequently "grow out" of stuttering without formal intervention. As a general rule, they are correct: We now know that approximately 80% of children appear to recover from stuttering, apparently spontaneously (Curlee & Yairi, 1997). We also now know that some factors can enable us to predict whether recovery is less likely for a given child (Yairi, Ambrose, Paden, & Throneburg, 1996). Among these are the following:

- *Age of onset of the stuttering.* Onset before 3½ years old is statistically associated with greater likelihood of spontaneous recovery.

- *Gender of the child.* Females are much more likely to experience spontaneous recovery than are males.

- *Family history of chronic and recovered stuttering.* Rather than relying on a simple family history of stuttering, researchers have now determined that children with chronically stuttering relatives are more likely to progress to chronic stuttering themselves, whereas those with relatives who "outgrew" stuttering are more likely to duplicate this pattern.

- *Language ability of the child.* This issue is addressed in more detail later, particularly because of the high degree of bilingualism in the Latino population and its potential impact on stuttering. In the monolingual population, however, evidence is mounting to suggest a link between language proficiency (as measured by scores on standardized language measures) and recovery from stuttering. Children with less than average linguistic ability appear to be less likely to recover spontaneously from stuttering. In the Latino population, making reliable judgments about relative language ability can be a challenging task, as other chapters in this book discuss.

- *Time since onset of symptoms.* Although 80% of children do apparently recover from stuttering, most do so within a relatively confined time frame: 18 months–2 years after symptoms first appear. Spontaneous recovery can be seen after this time; however, it decreases in likelihood quite markedly. Parents who delay treatment for many years hoping for spontaneous recovery must be made aware of such information, particularly because the ABCs of stuttering become more complex as the child continues to cope with stuttering over the course of child-hood. Therapy that is given later in childhood can be very effective, but must often address much more complex attitudes and emotions than therapy given earlier in childhood.

Cultural- and language-specific concerns related to interpretation of the clinical information can be quite important when conveying this informa-tion to parents and caregivers, and are discussed in a later section. In par-ticular, whereas all of these factors appear to play a statistical role in pre-dicting the eventual cohort of older children and adults who stutter, they are imperfect in predicting individual outcomes (Bernstein Ratner, 1997a). Thus, serious and ongoing discussion between the clinician and family needs to acknowledge this fact and to continually re-evaluate the child's current need for services. Relationships between clinicians and the parents of children who stutter should be based on a joint "watch (*not* wait) and see" approach that includes frequent interaction and counseling.

Stuttering in Older Children and Adults

When faced with older children and adult clients, the question, "Does this person stutter?" is rarely an issue. Stuttering is either quite apparent or is reported by the client. In this older population, however, the ABCs of stut-tering become much more important for assessment and therapy planning purposes. Although strictly behavioral treatment of stuttering symptoms may alleviate counterproductive affective or cognitive features of the dis-order, sometimes these very features make the use of behavioral strategies in therapy quite difficult, if not impossible. For example, fear can make it extraordinarily difficult for one to master any skill, be it verbal or athletic. (How many of us have "frozen" in the spotlight?) Likewise, certain strate-gies or beliefs may impede therapy progress. For these reasons, open, in-sightful, and culturally sensitive discussion needs to occur between the client and the clinician. What does the client want from therapy? Al-though most will automatically say "to not stutter," upon closer discussion, other goals do emerge, including the desire to reduce fear and anxiety when required to speak or to say what one intended to say, rather than cir-cumlocuting or code-switching to avoid stuttering. Other goals may in-clude the ability to use the telephone, respond to bullying or teasing, move through the moment of stuttering more easily, or have less conspicuous or tense moments of fluency breakdown. A number of general texts on stut-tering treatment (Conture, 2001; Guitar, 1998; Manning, 2001; and Sha-piro, 1999), as well as video short courses for practicing clinicians (Bern-stein Ratner & Sisskin, 2002), demonstrate how to anticipate and discuss these goals with clients. In this chapter, I address potential concerns that arise when adapting general approaches to the Latino bilingual population as well as culturally sensitive concepts in establishing a therapeutic relationship that enables discussion of such goals.

Overt versus Covert Stuttering

Some clinicians distinguish between stuttering symptoms that are overt (easily observed) and those that are covert (hidden from ready view). Although one popular analogy likens stuttering to an iceberg (Sheehan, 1975), with behavioral symptoms lying above the water line and affective and cognitive components deeply submerged, some people who stutter manage to suppress a very large proportion of their potential speech dysfluencies, usually through situational and word avoidance tactics. Such individuals with so much "below the waterline" are often called *covert* stutterers. They typically come for treatment after years of frustration at the effort involved in speaking, and the degree to which fear of stuttering has defined their everyday lives and limited their ability to say what they want to say. Some evidence indicates that in cultures with less tolerance of stuttering, adults are more likely to present with a covert profile. As discussed later in this chapter, Latino cultures are among those identified as being relatively less tolerant of speech disfluency. Individuals who are covert stutterers may seem relatively more fluent than overt stutterers but they may be extremely unhappy.

The clinician who does not understand the covert stutterer is likely to be confused by what may appear to be unreasonable expectations of speech fluency ("I don't understand your concern; I hear hardly any disfluencies in your speech"), and may be unprepared to utilize the interventions often recommended for this type of stuttering such as approach–avoidance therapy, with its ensuing interim goals of open, deliberate stuttering, desensitization to feared situations and stuttering events, and so forth. Obviously, the use of such approaches also implies great care and insight into how to change deeply ingrained feelings of fear and shame about stuttering. These skills, in turn, rely on culturally sensitive counseling abilities.

GENERAL PRINCIPLES OF CULTURE-SENSITIVE ASSESSMENT, TREATMENT, AND COUNSELING

A number of texts and resources are available to help clinicians understand the impact of cultural and social diversity on clinical assessment, treatment, and counseling. Some are particularly focused on the Latino population and are referenced in other chapters. In this chapter, those principles that are most important to providing intervention to people who stutter and counseling to their families are emphasized (see also Hall, 2000; Watson & Kayser, 1994).

Attitudes Toward Speech and Fluency

As noted, both a client's and his or her family's attitudes toward speech and the importance of speech fluency have a strong impact on the eventual features of the disorder. Bilingualism entails biculturalism, and one of the speaker's cultures is likely to have different impressions of stuttering than the other. Bebout and Arthur (1992) noted that non–North American cultures are more likely to view disordered speech (particularly stuttering) as a symptom of emotional disturbance or punishment by a god or spiritual figure than "mainstream" American cultures. Maestas and Erickson (1992) found that 93% of Mexican immigrant mothers living in the United States considered "God's will" to be a reasonable cause of their children's disabilities. Furthermore, more non–American groups were likely to feel that speech (especially stuttering) can be improved if the speaker simply "tries harder." Such examples are offered to remind clinicians that there may be real but unspoken differences in the assumptions that clients and families make about stuttering and their own knowledge and belief systems. It is also important to recognize that despite the fact that some generalizations have been made about Latino orientation toward various health beliefs and practices, researchers have found high levels of variation among Latino groups from different areas, and those who are residing in different parts of the United States (Pachter et al., 2002). Thus, the only way to recognize and respond to such belief systems and their potential impact on fluency treatment decisions is through careful discussion with the client and/or family as appropriate. Clinicians should be prepared to open a dialogue with clients and families to ascertain their beliefs and feelings about stuttering.

Cultures may also differ in their acceptance of behavioral differences as well as their level of shame in the face of imperfect behavior (Rodriguez Mosquera, Manstead, & Fischer, 2000). These researchers reported that Spanish children and young adults described more intense shame experiences than did Dutch peers when they experienced failure in social situations, for example. As Murphy (1997) noted, shame and guilt are unusually strong emotional responses to stuttering in both those who stutter and their families. Although mainstream American society is not particularly tolerant of stuttered speech, certain Latino subcultures appear even less comfortable with the disorder (Tellis, 2000) and seem only gradually to develop a less stigmatizing but still negative view of stuttering as they become more acculturated. For such clients and their families, the notion that the clinician might view some level of easy, less obtrusive stuttering as success-fully treated speech may not be acceptable. In some situations like these, then, covert stuttering may be more frequently observed.

Vulnerability is another concern in the treatment of stuttering. Stut-tering children are often seen as emotionally vulnerable (Oyler, 1996) and particularly susceptible to the negative impact of teasing, social isolation, and more. Because some Latino children are vulnerable for additional reasons (e.g., linguistic, socioeconomic, or family support limitations; the presence of additional disabilities) (Zambrana & Dorrington, 1998), extra care may need to be taken to understand the cumulative dynamics of chil-dren's social and communicative environment, address these dynamics in functional goal setting, and include proactive counseling on such issues as teasing and bullying.

Bilingualism and Stuttering

As has been repeatedly observed in this book, the rate of bilingualism is high in the Latino population. Bilingualism may exert a number of influ-ences on the diagnosis and treatment of fluency disorders. Among these are the potential for bilingualism to be a risk factor for stuttering or a hin-drance to recovery from stuttering, as well as its potential for complicat-ing the differential diagnosis of stuttering and language formulation diffi-culty. Finally, bilingualism may complicate generalization of therapy skills across languages and settings. Each of these concepts is addressed in turn, beginning with the question, Does bilingualism affect the risk of stutter-ing? Despite many earlier suggestions (primarily derived from case stud-ies, e.g., Karniol, 1992) that bilingualism is a risk factor associated with the onset of stuttering, a recent summary of available data (Van Borsel, Maes, & Foulon, 2001) found little evidence to support this belief. That is, a mixed-language environment *per se* (e.g., a household in which more than one language is spoken, differences between home and school language) is not likely to be a cause of stuttering, nor would removing one of a bilin-gual child or adult's languages necessarily ameliorate stuttering. Stahl and Totten (1995) suggested that limiting the stuttering child to a single lan-guage by removing opportunities for the use of the other(s) (e.g., encour-aging a single home language or congruence between home and school language) is only reasonable to consider if a child is highly at risk for chronic stuttering by family history and, in particular, shows delay in ac-quisition of both the first and second language. In such cases, language formulation difficulties may precipitate fluency breakdown, and use of a single language may reduce the child's processing burden. No empirical tests of such recommendations are known to exist.

Related questions focus on whether bilingualism affects the degree of stuttering and whether stuttering patterns differ in the two or more languages of the person who stutters. Virtually no reliably attested cases exist of stuttering in multilingual speakers that show only one language affected (Van Borsel et al., 2001). Stuttering severity may be similar (Nwokah, 1988) or different (Jayaram, 1983) across the languages of a stuttering speaker, suggesting the value of sampling in both languages to ascertain baseline and therapy outcome measures of fluency. Similarly, the structure of a given language may cause stuttering to emerge on different parts of speech or sounds, suggesting that one cannot make generalizations about easy and difficult targets without sampling across languages (Bernstein Ratner & Benitez, 1985; Jankelowitz & Bortz, 1996). Finally, because truly balanced bilinguals are rare and relative proficiency in a speaker's languages may affect fluency rates, it has been noted that dysfluency is likely to be higher in the less proficient language (Van Borsel et al., 2001). The role of language proficiency in the diagnosis and treatment of fluency disturbance is discussed further subsequently.

Code-Switching and Its Potential Role in Stuttering

Code-switching is very common in bilingual speakers. Although firm data on code-switching and stuttering are not available, stuttering may occur at higher levels during code-switching moments (Cabrera & Bernstein Ratner, 2000), and would be consistent with language processing accounts that support the role that linguistic complexity (e.g., lexical search) plays in precipitating stutter events (Bernstein Ratner, 1997b). For example, research has shown higher levels of cortical activation and slowed response times during language-switching conditions (Hernández, Martínez, & Kohnert, 2000) in bilinguals with typical fluency, as well as speed-accuracy trade-offs during naming tasks (Kohnert, Bates, & Hernandez, 1999).

In all speakers, word retrieval effort has a strong impact on the incidence of stutter-like dysfluencies (Brown & Cullinan, 1981). Therefore, certain situational pressures, such as pressure to retrieve novel or less-accessible lexical items in one of a speaker's languages, may provoke fluency failure. This problem is likely to be exacerbated in cases in which the child cannot demonstrate age-appropriate linguistic skills in either of his or her two languages (so called "semilingualism"). Given known linguistic stressors on fluency (Bernstein Ratner, 1997b), therapists must be especially vigilant in designing fluency therapy tasks that fit comfortably within the bilingual stuttering child's language skills, otherwise, fluency goals may be stalemated by language pressures that provoke fluency breakdown.

Language Dominance and Relative Ability Across Languages

Emerging data on children with delayed or disordered language strongly suggest elevated levels of generalized disfluency and of stutter-like dysfluencies (Boscolo, Bernstein Ratner, & Rescorla, 2002). Mattes and Omark (1984) specifically cautioned against confusing disfluency that results from limited English proficiency with clinical stuttering. As Boscolo and colleagues noted, key differentiating features between these two conditions may include lack of secondary features, lack of self-concept as a stutterer, and locus of disfluency at positions of encoding difficulty in the less proficient language. In other words, as noted, stuttering is more than disfluent speech production. To this list of distinguishing criteria, one can also add lack of stuttering in the stronger or native language. That is, if a child only appears to stutter in his or her less proficient language, he or she is more likely to be experiencing language-formulation disfluency. The use of a native language interlocutor in gathering cross-linguistic samples is therefore useful. Likewise, although the specific role of language loss (Gutiérrez-Clellen et al., 2000) on the fluency of bilingual children in the language undergoing loss has not been explored, it is reasonable to assume that fluency may be affected as much as observed changes in grammatical and lexical proficiency. It is important to consider that typical fluency intervention programs are unlikely to be effective in remediating language-based nonstuttering disfluencies, even when they are numerous and somewhat stutter-like, because they stem from a distinct underlying mechanism, and because stuttering programs do not address these issues. Strengthening an individual's language abilities is most likely to facilitate his or her fluency in such cases.

Generalization Concerns in Bilingual Children Who Stutter

A reasonable assumption is that abstract skills such as those involved in fluency shaping or stuttering modification would transfer and generalize easily across languages, because they are, in a sense, language-independent concepts. However, research exists to call such an assumption into question.

Affective and cognitive responses to stuttering may be linguistically based. Clinically, we experience many anecdotal accounts of individuals who are recovered stutterers but become disfluent in their native language or dialectal environment or with old friends. Recent research suggests that many experiences and concepts are strongly coded in bilinguals by language of exposure (Schrauf & Rubin, 2000). Thus, it should not be surprising if desensitization to feared speaking situations or addressees in one language does not generalize to different situations and interlocutors encountered in the other language. In fact, one unpublished case study specifically noted failure of a client's successful treatment in English to generalize to Spanish (Humphrey, 1999). Such failure should not seem unreasonable if situational or addressee factors appear to play a role in the client's fluency profile or associated affective or cognitive components. Shenker, Conte, Gingras, Courcey, and Polomeno (1998) noted that even in operant programs, parent-administered therapy appeared to be facilitated by having one parent conduct therapy using one language until criteria were met for dismissal and then switching to the other parent and the other language, until both languages were reported to be used fluently.

IMPLICATIONS FOR ASSESSMENT AND INTERVENTION

Stuttering has a peculiar place in most popular cultures. It is more stigmatized than other communicative disorders. Lay theories of its origins abound and are often inconsistent with current scientific findings. In particular, although most current research suggests that stuttering has a neurological basis and a strong genetic component (see recent fluency textbooks referenced previously), which may be shaped by a speaker's adaptive attempts to control speech and fluency over the lifespan, popular views about the underlying cause of stuttering tend to focus on psychological factors, emotional trauma, or parenting behaviors as proximate causes of stuttering onset and maintenance. In some parts of the eastern United States, for example, it is not uncommon to find parents in a number of communities who blame stuttering on switched handedness, unrest in the household caused by travel, moving, a new sibling, or even on an excess of foot tickling in infancy. Many cultures view stuttering as contagious. Still others, including some Latino and non-Latino communities, view the treatment of stuttering as the domain of psychologists or other professionals rather than speech-language pathologists (SLPs) (Gonzales Barbosa, 1998). Such beliefs, when held by either the client or his or her family, may be unspoken barriers to successful attempts by the SLP to treat the disorder. The clinician should try to gently probe for beliefs about stuttering that are counterproductive to client and family progress in graduating to "self-therapy" for the ABCs, and should provide them with easily understood information that responds to such etiological hypotheses. When language facility poses a barrier to communication, a number of web and text resources now enable bilingual clients and families who are more comfortable using Spanish to view information that can confirm and enlarge on the clinician's discussions about the nature and treatment of stuttering. As discussed in a subsequent section, Resources for Spanish- and English-Speaking Clients and Families, however, clinicians should attempt to verify original Spanish language information through translation, or facilitate internet-based translation of preferred information currently available only in English.

Language-Specific Concerns in Evaluation and Treatment

This section focuses on diagnostic and therapeutic concerns that arise from differences in translating English language norms, expectations, and assessment tools into other languages, specifically Spanish. The typology of specific languages may cause changes from patterns of disfluency seen in English monolingual speakers, and appropriate calculations of disfluency rates used in baselining and observations of therapy progress. The validity of translations of commercially available fluency inventories is also discussed.

Linguistic Effects on the Types of Disfluencies Seen

Normal disfluency types can vary from language to language (e.g., Montes, 1999; Muñoz-Duston, 1992). Lexical fillers obviously change in going from English to Spanish and vice versa (e.g., *pues* for *well*), but so do non-lexical fillers (e.g., *eh* for *um*) (Montes, 1999). As indicated, some of these may also be "appropriated" as devices for running starts or avoidance. The core stutter-like disfluencies of sound and syllable repetition, blocks, and prolongations of inappropriate phonemic segments do not appear to differ cross-linguistically, although individual profiles of disfluency can vary tremendously.

Language and Speech Rate Measures

The literature on stuttering has noted on numerous occasions that certain types of dysfluency counts may have poor replicability across speaking conditions. For example, the rate of stuttered words per minute does not allow appreciation of speech rate or number of attempted words. Similarly, differences may be found in proportioned measures across languages (e.g., word versus syllable counts). Kempler, Teng, Dick, Taussig, and Davis (1998) noted that performance on verbal fluency tasks such as rapid naming within categories could be affected by the syllabic structure of Spanish, which has a higher proportion of multisyllabic nouns than do English and some other languages. In this case, a bilingual speaker might score lower on percent stuttered syllables in Spanish than in English because stuttering is typically confined only to initial segments of words. In this case, within-subject comparisons across languages spoken might be best expressed in percent stuttered words.

Validity of Published Severity Measures

Because no evidence exists to suggest cross-cultural or cross-linguistic differences between speech and nonspeech behavioral characteristics of stuttering, there is no reason why existing measures used in English (e.g., the *Stuttering Severity Instrument–3*; SSI-3; Riley, 1994) are not valid baseline measures for this diagnostic and therapeutic construct. For example, the SSI-3 measures behavioral severity by combining measures of percent stuttered words with estimates of the severity of stuttered events and presence of physical concomitants, and it is virtually language- and culture-free. However, any test using a reading or repetition task based on English (including one option on the SSI-3 and a number of tasks on measures such as the *Assessment Digest and Treatment Plan* form; Cooper & Cooper, 1985) cannot be norm-referenced, although it may be adapted for use as a criterion-referenced baseline or progress measure.

Counting stutters is not necessarily the single most reasonable intake method or way to measure progress, although it is a critical and necessary component of diagnosis and treatment efficacy. Assessment of the speaker's reactions to speaking, stuttering, and therapeutic goals are often assessed using additional measures in English, such as the modified *Erickson Scale* (*S-24*; Andrews & Cutler, 1974), Brutten's *Communication Attitude Test* (Brutten & Dunham, 1989), Watson's *Inventory of Communication Attitudes* (Watson, 1988), and Ornstein and Manning's *Self-Efficacy Scale for Adults Who Stutter* (see Manning, 2001, for samples of these and additional measures). To my knowledge, no formal translations of these measures exist for Spanish. Ad hoc translations may be useful clinically if used as criterion-referenced estimates of pre- and post-therapy beliefs; again, care must be taken not to interpret derived scores against English language norms as measures of severity *per se*.

Some work examining the validity of personality inventories translated from English to Spanish suggested no measurable effects of language or culture on obtained scores, and so there is no obvious reason to expect cultural or linguistic bias if similar affective/cognitive measures are translated (Negy, Lachar, & Gruber, 1998). As I often note in my own clinical work, however, many of these devices are well-supplemented by asking the client whether some items are irrelevant to his or her own personal experience, whereas other, very meaningful everyday situations affecting speech and stuttering have not been addressed. Such informal additional information is especially valuable when the client's background and living experiences are likely to differ from those listed on the inventories.

Cultural Trends in Stuttering Treatment

In the United States today, the most common direct treatment approaches for stuttering tend to group into three major philosophical threads: fluency shaping, stuttering modification (with some clinicians and programs combining elements of these approaches), and operant programs. Because this chapter is not meant to review basic therapy approaches, the reader is encouraged to consult the textbooks recommended earlier for details regarding how each of these therapy approaches might be implemented. Cultural differences may play a role in how a client views certain therapy approaches (Gonzales Barbosa, 1998). For example, despite the fact that psychological treatment of fluency disorders is not currently viewed as consistent with American professional practice, it is still typical for stuttering to be viewed as the symptom of psychological maladjustment in other cultures, including Latino cultures.

Kathard (1998) suggested that programs emphasizing fluency shaping and operant programs may have greater acceptance across varied cultural groups than do stuttering modification programs because they are more concrete and direct and do not address affective and cognitive components that vary cross-culturally to any substantial degree. Stuttering modification programs depend critically on helping the person who stutters to develop new attitudes and cognitions toward speaking and stuttering. The belief that fluency shaping and operant programs are more acceptable cross-culturally may or may not be valid; no formal investigation of this hypothesis has been undertaken. Many fluency shaping and operant approaches exist in programmed material format. It is important to consider that even such behaviorally oriented programs do require some adjustments to make them more representative of diverse cultures and socioeconomic groups. Kathard (1998) suggested the following:

- Replacement of original stimulus materials with culturally appropriate stimuli

- Modification of instructions to ensure full understanding by nonnative English speakers/listeners

- Designing and recording speech samples for modeling purposes in a language/dialect familiar to the client

- Structuring the therapy plan to ensure opportunities for application and practice of fluency skills to the contexts most relevant to the client's personal experiences

Indirect Management of Stuttering

American speech-language pathologists still commonly recommend indirect management approaches when a child is viewed as too young for direct fluency intervention or when the stuttering problem is of recent onset and has a high likelihood of remitting spontaneously. Indirect management instructs the child's caretakers in ways to reduce the severity of stuttering symptoms by altering the child's environment and adult–child interaction patterns. Because indirect management strategies require a high degree of parent instruction and support, however, it is important that the clinician be able to relate to the child's parents and everyday caregivers, explain techniques clearly, and support the parents' efforts without implying that improper parenting techniques have caused the child's problems. Madding (1999) noted many differences in parenting styles between "mainstream" American mothers and Latino mothers, which potentially affect the ease with which Latino parents respond to typical indirect fluency management suggestions such as rate modification, recasting, turn-taking adjustments, and language simplification. In general, she observed Latino mothers to be less verbal in interaction with their children and less accepting of the concept that verbal input facilitates the child's development. Many parents in all cultures view suggestions that they slow their rate of speech and change their input and interaction styles to facilitate fluency as an implication that inappropriate input on their part has caused their children's stuttering.

We have found that drawing analogies between stuttering and other childhood disorders such as diabetes or asthma that are not considered environmentally induced can be helpful if parents agree with current thought on the origin of such disorders. For example, diet is not known to cause diabetes, but appropriate diet aids its symptomology, just as inappropriate diet aggravates its symptoms. Similarly, a dusty house does not cause asthma, but removing drapes and carpets and keeping dust levels down may reduce asthma severity experienced by a child. It is critical that clinicians who conduct parent counseling to alter or adjust input and interaction styles with stuttering children understand that such advice is palliative, rather than curative, and that parental language styles are not known to cause stuttering to emerge. Care should be taken to ensure that parents understand these concepts.

Resources for Spanish- and English-Speaking Clients and Families

For English speakers, the Internet has become an increasingly influential source of information and discussion about stuttering. In addition, public service and self-help groups such as American Speech-Language-Hearing Association (ASHA), the Stuttering Foundation of America, and the National Stuttering Association have extremely useful printed and videotaped materials available for clients, clinicians, and families. Less of this information is available in Spanish, and care should be taken in either using or referring to such information, as is discussed next. Service providers are highly likely to find that monolingual Spanish-speaking parents of bilingual stuttering children fall in this category.

Publications and Web Sites in Spanish

A number of organizations offer Spanish-language information and guidance about stuttering that may be of use to clinicians, clients and families. A prime example is the Stuttering Foundation of America (http://www.stuttersfa.org/), which has a number of publications in Spanish in addition to its low-cost Spanish-language videotape for parents of young children who stutter. Clinicians and bilingual speakers with some English language facility can find multiple links that have been filtered to emphasize professionally acceptable information at the Stuttering Home Page (http://www.stutteringhomepage.com), which also contains a few links to specifically Spanish-language materials. These materials and others may be made somewhat available to non- or limited-English readers by use of AltaVista translations (http://babel.altavista.com/tr), which can perform rough-and-ready translations of entire web sites. Other utilities to facilitate translation of websites are emerging rapidly. Thus, if the clinician can identify web sites with information of potential use to Latino patients or families, he or she can either provide instruction in the use of Internet translation of the site or produce materials for distribution. It must be cautioned that the translation algorithms are far from fail-proof, and the clinician may wish to note that a certain amount of ungrammaticality, untranslated terms, or stilted language may result from use of such programs.

The use of such translation capacity in its reverse form (e.g., Spanish to English) may be of substantial use to clinicians in auditing Spanish-language sites about stuttering on the open Internet. (It also allows the clinician to appreciate the general quality of web-based translation from English to Spanish.) Many unrecognized and scientifically unendorsed approaches to stuttering treatment exist on the Internet in all languages. Because increasing numbers of clients and families search for information and guidance about stuttering and therapy independently on the Internet, even while pursuing professional contact, it is wise for the clinician to survey the current Spanish-language materials on the Internet when the client enters therapy to assure themselves of the general utility of various sites. This enables the clinician to recommend some while cautioning against others during counseling because of the concepts embedded in them. For clinicians who are not Spanish-speaking, the primary search term to use in beginning such an audit process is *tartamudez* (stuttering). Currently, such a search of Spanish sites reveals a majority of web sites that emphasize psychological theories of stuttering etiology and persistence. As noted, such views of stuttering are no longer held valid by most American speech-language pathologists or supported by the current research literature. Thus, these sites may convey information that is quite inconsistent with a clinician's approach to therapy and are deserving of discussion with clients and families. Although this trend is subject to change, it appears wise to understand what clients and families might be reading about stuttering outside of clinical contact time.

In considering the use of the Internet to assist in therapy or provision of information, one should keep in mind that a "digital divide" has been documented between middle-income Americans and other segments of American society (Slate, Manuel, & Brinson, 2002). Specifically, in the study just referenced, students from Spanish-speaking families were more anxious about Internet usage than students from English-speaking homes and were more reluctant to use it as a form of information or sharing. Older clients and parents are likely to feel even less comfortable locating and using web resources. Because so much valuable information can be made available through Internet-based sources, it may be wise to explore whether or not the client or family is comfortable with, or has access to, the Internet.

Finally, Listservs have become a very popular outlet for exchanging information and personal experiences about stuttering. A number of the sites linked for Spanish speakers on the Stuttering Home Page either link directly to Listservs directed at the Spanish-speaking community or provide indirect access to them.

SUMMARY

Bilingualism can pose interesting challenges for fluency assessment, therapeutic goal setting, implementation, and evaluation of progress. In assessment, a primary concern is differentiating clinical stuttering from language-formulation disfluency stemming from unbalanced or diminished language ability. Comparison of baseline profiles of behaviors, affective and cognitive features of the fluency disorder across the speaker's languages, and the social contexts in which they are used is very important to therapy planning. The role of code-switching in precipitating fluency failure may also be a therapeutic concern needing attention.

Bilingualism brings with it aspects of biculturalism, and cultural belief systems about the nature of stuttering and its most appropriate treatment may vary quite substantially from that seen in American monolingual English speakers. These variations may be at odds with typical fluency knowledge and practice employed by the clinician, and thus merit exploration and response. The clinician who conceptualizes the ABCs of stuttering will have the conceptual basis and tools to explore the linguistic and sociocultural ramifications of bilingualism and fluency disorder.

REFERENCES

Andrews, G., & Cutler, J. (1974). Stuttering therapy: The relation between changes in symptom level and attitudes. *Journal of Speech and Hearing Disorders, 39,* 312–319.

Bebout, L., & Arthur, B. (1992). Cross-cultural attitudes toward speech disorders. *Journal of Speech and Hearing Research, 35,* 45–52.

Bernstein Ratner, N. (1997a). Leaving Las Vegas: Clinical odds and individual outcomes. *American Journal of Speech-Language Pathology, 6,* 29–33.

Bernstein Ratner, N. (1997b). Stuttering: A psycholinguistic perspective. In R. Curlee & G. Siegel (Eds.), *Nature and treatment of stuttering: New directions.* Boston: Allyn & Bacon.

Bernstein Ratner, N., & Benitez, M. (1985). Linguistic analysis of a bilingual stutterer. *Journal of Fluency Disorders, 10,* 211–219.

Bernstein Ratner, N., & Sisskin, V. (2002). *Intervention strategies for children who stutter.* Rockville, MD: American Speech-Language-Hearing Association.

Boscolo, B., Bernstein Ratner, N., & Rescorla, L. (2002). Fluency characteristics of children with a history of specific expressive language impairment (SLI-E). *American Journal of Speech-Language Pathology, 11,* 41–49.

Brown, C., & Cullinan, W. (1981). Word retrieval difficulty and disfluent speech in adult anomic speakers. *Journal of Speech and Hearing Research, 24,* 358–365.

Brutten, G., & Dunham, S. (1989). The Communication Attitude Test: A normative study of grade school children. *Journal of Fluency Disorders, 14,* 371–377.

Cabrera, V., & Bernstein Ratner, N. (2000, November). *Stuttering patterns in the two languages of a bilingual child.* Paper presented at the American Speech-Language-Hearing Association annual convention, Washington, DC.

Conture, E.G. (2001). *Stuttering: Its nature, diagnosis, and treatment.* Boston: Allyn & Bacon.

Cooper, E., & Cooper, C. (1985). *Cooper personalized fluency control therapy.* Allen, TX: DLM.

Curlee, R., & Yairi, E. (1997). Second opinion. Early intervention with early child-hood stuttering: A critical examination of the data. *American Journal of Speech-Language Pathology, 6*, 8–18.

Gonzales Barbosa, L.M. (1998). Stuttering: Perceptions of Brazilian speech pathol-ogists and undergraduate speech pathology students. *The Multicultural Electronic Journal of Communication Disorders, 1*(1). Retrieved May 14, 2004, from http://www.asha.ucf.edu/gonzales.html

Guitar, B. (1998). *Stuttering: An integrated approach to its nature and treatment.* Bal-timore: Williams & Wilkins.

Gutiérrez-Clellen, V.F., Restrepo, M.A., Bedore, L., Peña, L., & Anderson, R. (2000). Language sample analysis: Methodological considerations. *Language, Speech, and Hearing Services in Schools, 31*, 88–98.

Hall, F. (2000). *Multicultural considerations in the treatment of stuttering.* Paper pre-sented at the Third Annual International Stuttering Awareness Day Online con-ference. Retrieved May 14, 2004, from http://www.mankato.msus.edu/dept/comdis/ISAD3/papers/hall.html

Hernandez, A., Martinez, A., & Kohnert, K. (2000). In search of the language switch: An fMRI study of picture-naming in Spanish-English bilinguals. *Brain & Language, 73*, 421–431.

Humphrey, B. (1999, November). *Bilingual stuttering: Can treating one language improve fluency in both?* Paper presented at the American Speech-Language-Hearing Association Annual Convention, San Francisco, CA.

Jankelowitz, D., & Bortz, M. (1996). The interaction of bilingualism and stutter-ing in an adult. *Journal of Communication Disorders, 29*, 223–234.

Jayaram, M. (1983). Phonetic influences on stuttering in monolingual and bilin-gual stutterers. *Journal of Communication Disorders, 16*, 287–297.

Karniol, R. (1992). Stuttering out of bilingualism. *First Language, 12*, 255–283.

Kathard, H. (1998). *Issues of culture and stuttering: A South African perspective.* Paper published for the First International Stuttering Awareness Day online confer-ence. Archived at http://www.mnsu.edu/dept/comdis/isad/papers/kathard.html

Kempler, D., Teng, E., Dick, M., Taussig, I., & Davis, D. (1998). The effects of age, education, and ethnicity on verbal fluency. *Journal of the International Neu-ropsychological Society, 4*, 531–38.

Kohnert, K., Bates, E., & Hernandez, A. (1999). Balancing bilinguals: Lexical-semantic production and cognitive processing in children learning Spanish and English. *Journal of Speech-Language-Hearing Research, 42*, 1400–1413.

Madding, C. (1999). Mamá e hijo: The Latino mother-infant dyad. *The Multicul-tural Electronic Journal of Communication Disorders, 2*(1). Retrieved May 14, 2004 at http://www.asha.ucf.edu/madding3.html

Maestas, A., & Erickson, J. (1992). Mexican immigrant mothers' beliefs about disabilities. *American Journal of Speech-Language Pathology: A Journal of Clinical Practice, 1*(1), 5–10.

Manning, W. (2001). *Clinical decision-making in fluency disorders* (2nd ed.). Vancou-ver, British Columbia, Canada: Thomson/Singular.

Mattes, L., & Omark, D. (1984). *Speech and language assessment for the bilingual handicapped.* San Diego: College-Hill Press.

Montes, R. (1999). The development of discourse markers in Spanish: Interjections. *Journal of Pragmatics, 3*, 1289–1319.

Muñoz-Duston, E. (1992). *Self-repetitions: Analyzing the speech of Spanish and English bilingual children.* Unpublished doctoral dissertation, Georgetown University.

Murphy, B. (1997). A preliminary look at shame, guilt and stuttering. In N. Bernstein Ratner & E.C. Healey (Eds.), *Stuttering research and practice: Bridging the gap* (pp. 131–144). Mahwah, NJ: Lawrence Erlbaum Associates.

Negy, C., Lachar, D., & Gruber, C. (1998). The Personality Inventory for Youth (PIY): Spanish version. Reliability and equivalence in the English version. *Latino Journal of Behavioral Sciences, 20*, 391–404.

Nwokah, E. (1988). The imbalance of stuttering behavior in bilingual speakers. *Journal of Fluency Disorders, 13*, 357–373.

Ornstein, A., & Manning, W. (1985). Self-efficacy scaling by adult stutterers. *Journal of Communication Disorders, 18*, 313–320.

Oyler, E. (1996, March). Vulnerability in stuttering children. *Dissertation Abstracts International Section A: Humanities & Social Sciences, 56*(9-A), 33–74. Eugene, OR: University Microfilms International.

Pachter, L., Weller, S., Baer, R., de Alba Garcia, J., Trotter, R., Glazer, M., & Klein, R. (2002). Variation in asthma beliefs and practices among mainland Puerto Ricans, Mexican-Americans, Mexicans and Guatemalans. *Journal of Asthma, 39*, 119–134.

Riley, G. (1994). *Stuttering Severity Instrument for Children and Adults* (3rd ed.). Austin, TX: PRO-ED.

Rodriguez Mosequera, P., Manstead, A., & Fischer, A. (2000). The role of honor-related values in the elicitation, experience and communication of pride, shame and anger: Spain and the Netherlands compared. *Personality and Social Psychology Bulletin, 26*, 833–844.

Schrauf, R., & Rubin, D. (2000). Internal languages of retrieval: The bilingual encoding of memories for the personal past. *Memory & Cognition, 28*, 616–623.

Shapiro, D. (1999). *Stuttering intervention.* Austin, TX: PRO-ED.

Sheehan, J. (1975). Conflict theory and avoidance-reduction therapy. In J. Eisenson (Ed.), *Stuttering: A second symposium* (pp. 97–198). New York: Harper & Row.

Shenker, R., Conte, A., Gingras, A., Courcey, A., & Polomeno, L. (1998). The impact of bilingualism on developing fluency in a preschool child. In E. Healey & H.F.M. Peters (Eds.), *Second World Congress on Fluency Disorders: Proceedings* (pp. 200–204). The Netherlands: Nijmegen University Press.

Slate, J., Manuel, M., & Brinson, K. (2002). The "digital divide": Hispanic college students' views of educational uses of the Internet. *Assessment and Evaluation in Higher Education, 27*(1), 75–93.

Stahl, V., & Totten, G. (1995). Bilingualism in young dysfluent children. In C.W. Starkweather & H.F.M. Peters (Eds.), *Stuttering: Proceedings of the First World Congress on Fluency Disorders.* Nijmegen: Nijmegen University Press, 213.

Tellis, G. (2000). Hispanic-American college students' perceptions about stuttering. *Dissertation Abstracts International: Section B, 60*, 38–98.

Von Borsel, J., Maes, E., & Foulon, S. (2001). Stuttering and bilingualism: A review. *Journal of Fluency Disorders, 26*, 179–206.

Van Riper, C. (1982). *The nature of stuttering* (2nd ed.). Englewood Cliffs, NJ: Prentice-Hall.

Watson, J., & Kayser, H. (1994). Assessment of bilingual/bicultural children and adults who stutter. *Seminars in Speech and Language, 15,* 149–163.

Watson, J.B. (1988). A comparison of stutterers' and nonstutterers' affective, cognitive and behavioral self-reports. *Journal of Speech and Hearing Research, 31,* 377–385.

Yairi E., & Ambrose, N. (1992). Onset of stuttering in preschool children: Selected factors. *Journal of Speech and Hearing Research, 35*(4), 782–788.

Yairi, E., Ambrose, N., Paden, E., & Throneberg, R. (1996). Predictive factors of persistence and recovery: Pathways of childhood stuttering. *Journal of Communication Disorders, 29,* 51–77.

Zambrana, R., & Dorrington, C. (1998). Economic and social vulnerability of Latino children and families by subgroup: Implications for child welfare. *Child Welfare, 77*(1), 5–28.

Intervention

CHAPTER 13

Language Intervention with Bilingual Children

KATHRYN KOHNERT AND ANN DERR

T he vast majority of children who learn two (or more) languages during childhood are "typical" learners; with appropriate time and experience they will be skilled in the languages used consistently in their environments. These typically developing children have "intact" language mechanisms, and it is incumbent on their families and communities (including the educational system) to ensure that they have sufficient opportunities to hone their language skills. Our concern in this chapter is not these typically developing children with diverse language experiences, however. Rather, our concern is with those bilingual children whose underlying language or cognitive-linguistic system is somehow compromised.

Primary developmental language impairments due to inefficiencies in children's internal language systems are chronic. Children with language impairments are at significant risk for negative social and academic outcomes. Timely, effective intervention is needed to ameliorate the potential negative long-term effects of language impairments. A critical first (and ongoing) step in successful intervention is appropriate language assessment. Each of the previous chapters in this volume has provided important information related to different aspects of the bilingual assessment process. (The reader is also referred to the following sources for additional information on assessment with bilingual children: Goldstein, 2001; Gutierrez-Clellen, 1996; Kayser, 1998; Langdon & Saenz, 1996; and Roseberry-McKibbin, 1995.) Using these sources as a springboard, we jump into intervention is-

The writing of this chapter was supported by research grants from the National Institute on Deafness and Other Communication Disorders (R03 DC05542-01, titled *Cognitive-Linguistic Processing in L1 and L2 Learners*) and the University of Minnesota (Grant-in-Aid of Research, Artistry and Scholarship).

311

sues with bilingual children who have already participated in valid assessments of their communication skills in both languages, in a variety of contexts, using culturally appropriate formal and informal methods. We use these fair and substantial assessments as our point of departure, turning our attention directly to intervention with Spanish-English bilingual children with diagnosed language impairment.

This chapter includes four sections. The first section provides an overview of the major purposes and processes of clinical intervention for children with language disorders. The second section focuses on the issue that dominates all discussions of intervention with Spanish-English bilingual language-impaired children—language choice. That is, should interventions be conducted in Spanish, in English, or in both? The third section discusses potential ways to structure the language of intervention, with respect to areas of overlap and divergence between Spanish, English, the developing child, and the many contexts in which he or she uses languages. The final section discusses the role of clinical professionals, including those who speak both languages of the child as well as those who speak only one of the child's languages.

PURPOSE AND PROCESS OF BILINGUAL INTERVENTION

Clearly, most bilingual children become extraordinarily skilled in speaking their languages, just as most monolingual children do. It is also clear, however, that a small yet significant subset of bilingual children will have chronic deficits in language. Such deficits in language may negatively affect these children's social interactions and cognitive development in the early years and compromise learning and literacy during the school years. These impairments in language are most likely not due to environmental differences but, rather, to some breach in the integrity of the child's internal language acquisition or processing system as it interacts with the available input. Prevalence rates for primary language disorders and language-based learning disabilities range from 5% to 10% for English-only–speaking children (Leonard, 1998; Paul, 2001). The percentage of children with language impairments increases if those children with associated sensory, neurological, or cognitive impairments (e.g., hearing loss, autism, mental retardation) are included. Although at the time this book was published, no studies had been conducted on the extent to which primary language disorders exist among Spanish-English bilingual children, we anticipate that the rates are similar for this population as they are across other populations.

Intervention is needed to reduce the potential negative long-term effects of language impairments. Roth and Paul stressed that the overall purpose of clinical intervention "is to affect change in communicative behavior to maximize an individual's potential to communicate effectively" (2002, p. 159). This chapter focuses on developing bilinguals, with an emphasis on children who live in homes and communities in which they are exposed to both Spanish and English. In many cases, these children are from families in which Spanish is the primary language at home and English is the primary language of the school and larger community. In other cases, children live in bilingual homes and communities, with Spanish used alongside of English. The point here is that these children regularly function in environments in which two different languages are used. In order to be successful in these environments, both languages are needed. Thus, the overall purpose of intervention with bilingual children with language impairments must be to effect positive change in children's ability to communicate in both Spanish and English—a point we take up more substantially in the following section.

The specific goals, procedures, and activities used in a bilingual language intervention program depend on a number of factors, including a child's age, developmental stage (in terms of cognitive, social, emotional, and motor achievements), and his or her communicative strengths, weaknesses, and preferred learning style. Language intervention implemented by a culturally competent clinical professional is a systematic process aimed at helping the child reach his or her potential as a communicator (Goldstein & Iglesias, 2002). The approach for structuring the language of intervention can be bilingual (with skills common to both languages receiving attention) or cross-linguistic (with attention directed at specific aspects of either Spanish or English). (These approaches are further described in the section called Intervention Designed to Promote Gains in Two Languages.) The specific methods may be direct, indirect, or somewhere in between. A list of resources for intervention is included in an appendix at the end of this chapter.

Regardless of the general approach taken or the specific methods employed in language intervention, the long-term goal is to teach strategies to improve the child's overall communication (e.g., Roth & Paul, 2002). Clearly, specific behaviors are taught along the way (e.g., new words, sound sequences), but the end goal is much broader. For example, not only do clinicians teach the late-talking 2-year-old child to say "ball" and "more" but also they help him or her use these words to request objects or actions from communicative partners. More important, they teach the child to pair increasingly complex linguistic forms with a wider range of meanings and social functions so that he or she can continue to use and develop his or her language skills with diverse partners, in a wide range of environments. Similarly, in working on inflectional morphology with a 6-year-old child with obvious deficits in noun–verb agreement, the clinician goes beyond teaching only these target grammatical forms. He or she helps the child attend to word endings and related subtle differences in form that signal changes in meaning, in both aural and written language. This increased attention to the details of linguistic form and their corresponding semantic values is fundamental to advanced discourse skills and reading fluency.

Thus, the purpose or product of language intervention is to assist the child in achieving his or her full potential as a communicator, considering both capacity (e.g., current weaknesses relative to strengths) and the environmental demands that determine success (e.g., literacy or communicative competency in more than one language). Specific intervention goals are often determined with respect to what is known about "normal" or typical development. Careful descriptions of typical development in bilingual preschool and school-age children at the phonological, grammatical, and lexical-semantic levels are included in previous chapters in this volume. From this information, the reader can begin to identify specific intervention goals. This chapter concentrates on those aspects of the clinical process that are common to all levels of language intervention with bilingual children. These common aspects include choosing the language(s) of intervention, determining how these languages will be used in the intervention process, and the undertaking the roles of the clinical experts charged with helping children with language impairments become successful communicators. The following section examines the issue of language choice.

CHOOSING THE LANGUAGE(S) TO BE USED IN INTERVENTION

Once language impairment has been identified in a bilingual child and it is clear that treatment to promote language gains is warranted, professionals are faced with the issue of language choice; that is, which language should be the focus of intervention? Clinicians working with bilingual children with language impairment have struggled with this question for decades, armed with few studies and no comprehensive theoretical framework to guide their thinking. Because the stakes of selecting only one of a child's two languages for special training are so high, the decision can be overwhelming, making many clinicians reluctant to work with bilingual children for fear of making the critical "wrong" decision from the beginning. Other clinicians have plunged ahead, emphatically stating that the community language was more important because that is the language that will allow the child to be successful in school and beyond. In the absence of a coherent, convergent literature addressing the issue of language choice, some well-intended professionals have been forced to make their decisions on the basis of anecdotal evidence or bias.

As noted previously, primary language impairments in monolingual and bilingual children are not caused by observable deficits in the environment (although clearly, environmental deprivation can cause severe delays in all areas of development, including language). When inefficiencies in language exist due to some breach in the integrity of the child's internal language system as it interacts with the available input, however, most believe the environment can play an important role. Some environments exacerbate difficulties; other environments facilitate language learning and performance. Indeed, this fundamental belief in the role of the language-learning environment (i.e., input) lies at the heart of all clinical intervention for children with language impairments. Clinical experts improve children's skill in communication by manipulating input (e.g., reducing rate; highlighting certain sounds, words, grammatical structures, or social functions) within carefully constructed environments intended to either strip away or replicate influential factors found in natural contexts (see Fey, Windsor, & Warren, 1995; Paul, 2001, 2002). We ask parents to similarly manipulate the environment to enhance their children's opportunities to successfully interact with language. Depending on the level of the child, we teach parents to recast their children's utterances, share books and pictures with their children in ways that increase the availability of meaningful language, and supplement their verbal instructions with visual cues such as gestures or charts to improve comprehension.

Although all informed individuals recognize that systematic exposure to two languages in no way causes language impairments, many believe that dual-language input exacerbates an already existing problem. The reasoning is that if one language is difficult for the child (as is clearly the case for a child with language impairments), two languages must be exponentially harder (e.g., Toppelberg, Snow, & Tager-Flusberg, 1999). The logical recommendation that follows is to scale back to a single language to improve the child's chances for success, in light of the disproportionate disadvantage presented by the internal language impairment coupled with the dual-language environment. Not all experts agree that continuous bilingual input will retard development in the child with language impairment, however, beyond those delays observed in the monolingual child with a similar type of deficit. For example, Gutiérrez-Clellen (1999) argued that children with language impairment require comprehensible input above and beyond what is needed by the child who is typically developing. She explained that for the child who functions in environments in which both Spanish and English are used, comprehensible input, by definition, involves input and experience in two languages. Based on her review of the bilingual education literature and the few available treatment studies with second language (L2) learners, Gutiérrez-Clellen asserted that

> Interventions conducted with incomprehensible input may not facilitate language development in L1 [the first language] or L2. Limiting input by forcing a family to "choose" the language of intervention (typically the majority language) does not appear to be an optimal choice for children who are exposed to a bilingual learning environment outside monolingual clinical or school settings. (1999, p. 300)

So, does bilingual input help or hurt the development of communication skills in children with language impairments? To answer this question, one would need to compare the severity and long-term outcomes of communication skills in monolingual children with language impairments with those of bilingual children with language impairments. The two groups of language-impaired children (monolingual and bilingual) would need to be matched on a number of potentially influential factors, including nonverbal intelligence, family income and literacy levels, adequacy of treatment, and educational opportunities. These two groups would differ only in terms of the number of input languages. Note that it would be important to look at long-term outcomes, say, a decade after diagnosis and the beginning of intervention, in order to fully account for the protracted timeframes of skill acquisition characteristic of both language impairment and second language learning (e.g., Bialystok, 2001; Kohnert, Bates, & Hernandez, 1999; Leonard, 1998). On the one hand, if, in the long term, researchers found that children who received bilingual input had more severe communication deficits than their monolingual peers, all else being equal, they would have direct evidence that bilingual input is a significant risk factor for children with language impairments. On the other hand, if no differences in long-term outcomes between bilingual children with language impairments and their monolingual peers were found, this would provide strong support for continuous bilingual input.

It would also be important to compare the long-term outcomes for an additional group of bilingual children with language impairments. This third group would include children who had received consistent input in Spanish and English for several years. This consistent bilingual input would then be interrupted when the children had reached age 4 or 5, to be replaced by a dramatic and conscious shift to input in English only. This shift to English only would be based on a professional recommendation to limit input to only one language to improve the child's chances to succeed. If this third group of children outperformed the bilingual group that had received continuous input in two languages, this would further support the hypothesis that dual-language input places children with language impairment at an additional disadvantage. We strongly suspect, however, that the long-term outcome for this third group of children would be much worse.

Unfortunately, longitudinal studies of this nature are not available to inform clinical decisions regarding language choice for bilingual children with diagnosed language impairments. In the absence of such direct evidence, we must take a critical look at the series of questions commonly used to determine the language of intervention. Recommendations related to language choice typically depend on the specific way the question is formulated and applied to different children. For example, if a child speaks Spanish at home but needs English to be successful in school, the clinical question is generally, "Should intervention be provided in the language of the home or school?" If assessment results indicate that one language is relatively dominant, clinicians ask, "Should this stronger language be the exclusive focus of intervention to maximize gains?" When both Spanish and English are used in the home of a preschooler with language impairment, the question becomes "Should we consolidate resources and minimize the cognitive demands presumed present in mixed-language input by restricting parent-talk and intervention to a single language?" Responses to these questions must be based on several interwoven layers of theory and practice from diverse literatures. The following sections briefly summarize the literature related to each of these questions, drawing heavily on discussions presented in previous chapters of this volume.

Should Intervention Be Provided in the Language of the Home or the School?

This question is most relevant for school-age children of immigrant families. These children's primary caregivers, including parents or grandparents, generally speak the home language (in this case, Spanish) but not English, and the children attend educational programs in which English, not Spanish, is the primary or sole language. In this situation, providing intervention in the home language (Spanish) is important for at least three reasons. First, for immigrant children with family members who do not speak the community language, preservation of the home language is paramount for maintaining the inter-generational family connections and cultural links required for adequate social-emotional development. Arguments that emphasize the need to support the home language of immigrant children from a social-emotional standpoint have been formulated for "intact" language learners (e.g., Wong-Fillmore, 1991). It is unfortunate that these same fundamental arguments are often dismissed if a child is identified as having a language impairment or language-based learning deficit. The relationship between the communication environment and social-emotional development is heightened, not diminished, in the case of language impairment. (See also Chapters 2, 8, and 9 for more on this relationship.)

A second reason to support the home language (L1) is to more efficiently pave the way for L2 learning. For both intact and impaired language learners, preliminary evidence supports greater and faster gains in L2 when there is a stronger L1 base (see Gutiérrez-Clellen, 1999, and Krashen, 1999, for reviews). This is because language acquisition is a process built up over time and experience. For example, in their seminal work with English-only speakers of various income levels, Hart and Risley (1995) estimated that children from working-class families hear an average of 6,500,000 words per year, embedded in sentences and used within an interactive context. By the time these English-only–speaking children enter kindergarten at age 5, they have had an enormous amount of experience with their ambient language—approximately 32,500,000 words! This rich and continuous experience with spoken language during early childhood provides typical learners with the necessary foundation for a leap from early language into literacy (Bialystok, 2001; Snow, Burns, & Griffin, 1999). English-only–speaking children who are not able to take full advantage of this rich input because of internal deficits in their language-processing mechanisms will struggle with reading and learning during the school years (Bashir & Scavuzzo, 1992; Catts, Fey, Tomblin, & Zhang, 2002). Children from Spanish-speaking families attending English-speaking educational programs are required to make a much greater leap. These children must take their early experiences with spoken language in Spanish and apply it to reading in English. Only those children who are truly precocious in language are expected to independently make this leap from input and experience in one language during the preschool years to literacy in a different language beginning in elementary school, with no stops in between. This is clearly not the case for children with language impairments. These children will require direct intervention, first to shore up skills in L1 to lay the foundation for literacy, then to facilitate the cross-linguistic transfer of information.

A third reason for supporting the L1 in intervention is to provide a foundation for the generalization of communicative gains across settings. Paul defined generalization as "the carryover of trained behavior into settings other than the training context" (2002, p. 342). Generalization of skills from trained to untrained settings is the single most important marker of successful intervention. For instance, many teenagers first experience challenging aspects of driving through computer simulations of inclement weather or oncoming traffic. These structured situations are designed to provide the novice driver with multiple opportunities to learn and practice specific skills in a safe, supportive environment. Of course, ultimately it is unimportant how well these teens perform on the computer-generated driving programs. The real test is if they can generalize their new driving skills to real traffic, in real time. In language intervention, expert professionals train communicative behaviors and strategies through skilled manipulation of cueing hierarchies, structure, and task complexities to provide a springboard for children to transfer skills demonstrated in the clinical setting to communication in the real world. Clinical experts specifically plan for the transfer of skills across settings. If newly acquired communication skills are not transferred from the treatment setting to the child's daily life, then treatment has failed. It is not reasonable to believe that, independent of clinical planning and appropriate scaffolding, children with language impairments will independently be able to transfer skills trained in English only to the Spanish needed to communicate with family members.

Clearly, for the child with language impairment who speaks Spanish at home, Spanish must somehow be incorporated into clinical intervention services. Does this mean that English can be ignored and gains in Spanish planned for only? Absolutely not! All children, including those with language or learning disabilities, need to have access to the primary languages of the school and larger community. When the home and school languages differ, intervention must be designed to ultimately improve communication in both these languages.

Should Intervention Be Provided Only in the Child's "Dominant" Language?

For many professionals, the question of "which language for intervention?" is answered with "whatever language is dominant!" That is, if a student, Gabriel, demonstrates a relative strength in Spanish during the assessment process, intervention should be in Spanish. If his cousin, Teresita, demonstrates a relative strength in English during the assessment process, then she should receive intervention in English. Again, the underlying belief motivating this cross-linguistic triage for the bilingual child with language impairment is that one language is inherently better than two. Motivated by this core belief, professionals look for reasons to discount one language in favor of the other. Discounting the weaker language and recommending intervention in only the stronger language seems an easier position to defend than the reverse. Intervention in the dominant or stronger language is based on the idea that training will be more effective if the child's existing strengths are built on. At first blush, this makes good sense. However, as our understanding of the interactions between L1 and L2 within the developing child increases, it becomes clear that attention to only the dominant language may not be the best approach.

At least three empirical findings undermine the recommendation to provide intervention exclusively in the dominant language. The first finding is that "language dominance" is not constant across all measures. Rather, it seems that what is dominant may vary as a function of tasks, topics, or cognitive demands (Bialystok, 2001; Kohnert & Bates, 2002; Snow, 1990, 1991). For example, children may be stronger on comprehension tasks in one language but relatively better on production tasks in the other language. Children may also be better at talking about some topics in English and other topics in Spanish. Given that what is strongest may vary as a function of what is measured, it seems unreasonable to discount one language as unimportant, particularly given the current limitations in valid assessment procedures with bilingual children.

The second empirical finding that argues against intervention in only the single dominant language is that the relationship between two languages within developing bilinguals is not stable over time. Immigrant children commonly experience a shift in skill level from L1 to L2 (e.g., see Chapters 3 and 8). Thus, a static snapshot of language dominance developed during assessment does not predict the future relationship between the child's two languages. Professionals should not designate a single language as the target of their intervention based on relative cross-linguistic skill levels that are likely to change across tasks and time. By so doing, they might prematurely push children to shift their overall preference from one language to another. If and when a language shift occurs over time and circumstance, this is natural. Indeed, this is to be expected when one language is the more valuable currency in the larger community. It does not seem appropriate that clinical professionals be the instruments of that shift, however, particularly when the other language is needed to maintain family ties and cultural identity.

A third finding that undermines the recommendation to provide intervention exclusively in the perceived dominant language is that skills may be distributed *across* the child's two languages. Distributed (as opposed to duplicated) skills mean that the weaker language does not simply form a subset of information encoded in the stronger language. Rather, some linguistic representations are present only in the relatively weaker language and others (presumably more) are present only in the relatively dominant language. At the lexical-semantic level, distributed skills have been a consistent finding among typical Spanish-English–speaking children and adults (Kohnert, Hernandez, & Bates, 1998; Pearson & Fernández, 1994; Peña, Bedore, & Zlatic, 2002). As Peña and Kester noted in Chapter 5, children who are bilingual learn vocabulary in both the dominant and nondominant languages, with the words learned in each varying with topic and context. These recent findings documenting the interrelatedness of the two languages within the developing child, along with the very dynamic nature of relative language skill across tasks and experience, caution against choosing a language for intervention based on static notions of "language dominance."

Even when one language is found to be clearly stronger, it does not mean that the other language is unimportant. Consider the relationship between your two hands. For most individuals, one hand is clearly dominant. Working independently, this dominant hand can write, grasp a spoon to eat soup, or screw in light bulbs. For other tasks, the nondominant hand plays an important supporting role, holding the telephone receiver as you jot down a note, steadying the needle as the other hand threads it, or securing the mixing bowl as the dominant hand spoons out the batter. In other tasks, the functional neural circuitry established over time and experience allows the two hands to coordinate their equal efforts to tie a shoe, braid strands of hair, or type on the keyboard. Few would argue that the nondominant hand is unimportant. The relationship between the two hands is analogous to the relationship between the two languages in bilingual children. The two languages are interrelated in complex ways, at both the neurological and functional levels (e.g., Chee, Tan, & Thiel, 1999; Conboy, 2002; Paradis, 1997; Perani et al., 1998). Therefore, it seems unreasonable to restrict our efforts to only a single language, even if it that language is relatively stronger.

Should Input Be Restricted to Just One Language When Parents Are Bilingual?

Many proficient bilingual adults use Spanish as their primary language at home, and English in their professional interactions. Other adults use both

Spanish and English in interactions at home and in the community. When a child from a bilingual family is diagnosed with a language impairment, the family is frequently counseled to use only a single language with their child if at all possible. One reason for recommending single language input for the child with language impairment relates to the belief that there will be more opportunities to develop communicative competency if resources are consolidated. Conversely, if two languages are used with the child, it is believed that there will be insufficient opportunities to develop either system fully—thus a return to the "one language is better than none" argument. The relevant issue here is whether restricting input to a single linguistic code (Spanish or English) increases language-learning opportunities for the child who lives in a bilingual environment. Does a *monolingual* child, with or without language impairment, have more opportunities to interact in a *bilingual* community than a bilingual child? This does not seem likely, as there would be far more instances of "incomprehensible input" for the child who knows only English yet is often present as his or her parents use Spanish to communicate with each other or to interact with neighbors and extended family members. It is inappropriate to use a monolingual lens to determine comprehensible input or facilitative language experience for the bilingual child (Gutiérrez-Clellen, 1999). Rather, the validity of language experience is context dependent, and must be determined relative to functional needs.

The potential negative consequences of discontinuous language input (an abrupt switch from two languages to one) on the child with language impairment are also important to note. Even if such a switch increased the quantity of input available in a single language, it would likely decrease the quality of input in terms of linguistic complexity and semantic variability. This is indeed an important trade-off to consider because abundant evidence indicates that both quality and quantity of language experience play fundamental roles in the development of language and literacy (e.g., Hart & Risley, 1995; Weizman & Snow, 2001). Furthermore, a switch from two languages to one may reduce the child's ability to rely on context-embedded cues and cross-linguistic associations built up over time and experience.

A second reason for the recommendation to scale back to a single language for the child from a bilingual home is the belief that two languages are very confusing or cognitively demanding for the child with a language impairment. This presumes that it is harder, even for typically developing bilinguals, to learn and control two languages. Yet we know that for typical learners, acquiring two languages from birth is no harder than acquiring a single language. Children learning two languages from birth—even when these languages involve different modalities—achieve early language milestones at the rate expected for monolingual children (Pettito et al., 2001; Pearson, Fernandez, & Oller, 1993; see also Chapter 7).

Evidence indicates, then, that it is not more difficult for children who are typically developing to learn two different linguistic codes given sufficient opportunity; however, is it cognitively harder for children to keep these two languages separate during real-time? Do children have to use their developing cognitive resources to inhibit one language so that they can activate the other? Does this slow them down or cause them to make more errors during mixed language processing tasks? Answers to these questions seem to be dependent on the circumstances. For example, Kohnert and Bates (2002) tested the speed and accuracy with which bilingual children and adults (ages 5–25 years) were able to access lexical items in two different conditions: single language input (blocks of Spanish or English only) and mixed bilingual-language input (with stimulus words alternating between Spanish and English). On this lexical access task there was no increased processing cost (indexed by slower responses or increased errors), at any age, for the mixed bilingual language condition relative to the single-language-only condition. In contrast, in a task that required children and adults (again, ages 5–25 years) to both access and generate lexical terms in either a single language (Spanish or English) or in a bilingual mixed-language condition (alternating between Spanish and English), Kohnert and colleagues (1999) documented a clear processing cost for all participants in the mixed-bilingual condition relative to the single-language-only condition. Tasks that require both inhibition and activation (e.g., generating the names of pictures out of context as one is cued to switch between two languages) appear to be more cognitively demanding than tasks that involve activation only (as when listening to words presented in two different languages).

Of note, context-embedded communicative interactions that involve a code-switch (a change from Spanish to English and back again) rely primarily on cognitive activation, so there should be no additional cognitive load imposed on bilinguals who have experience with such input (cf., Grosjean, 1997). Indeed, because of the communicative relevancy and increased semantic value of bilingual discourse, it is likely that interactions that involve a switch between Spanish and English facilitate language processing in some instances. It is also true that different languages in the bilingual home become associated with different topics. This context-embedded language provides additional sources of meaningful language input for the bilingual child without incurring an additional processing cost.

In summary, although it is true that additional cognitive resources are needed by bilingual children to perform some tasks that involve mixed language input, it does not seem to be the case that processing two languages always involves an increased processing load or disproportionately slows down the language acquisition process. Indeed, the cost of switching to one language relative to the benefit of continuing with two seems to clearly favor continued input in two languages for those children who have been consistently exposed to two languages from birth.

A New Question

The common thread between the clinical questions reviewed in this section, then, is the persistent notion that a single language is always best for the bilingual child with language impairment. Most of us would agree with the common clinical adage that "one language is better than none," but is that really the only option? As noted previously, there is no direct evidence to support the assumption that a child with language impairment who receives continuous input in two languages would fare worse than the monolingual child with a similar impairment. On the flip side, based on what is known about the positive effects of cumulative, emotionally responsive, and increasingly complex input for language development, along with our understanding of the common cognitive underpinnings, the inter-relatedness of the two languages within the developing bilingual child, and the basic necessity for communicative skill in the primary languages used in the home and community, we must consider the potential negative consequences of input in only a single language for the child who needs two. So perhaps the more relevant clinical adage for the bilingual children who are the subject of this volume is "two languages are better than none." When asked which language long-term intervention goals are designed to support and increase, speech-language professionals must answer, "Both!" We can now move on to a new question: How can the language of intervention be structured to promote gains in both languages of the bilingual child with language impairment?

INTERVENTION DESIGNED TO PROMOTE GAINS IN TWO LANGUAGES

These arguments strongly indicate that the overall goal in language intervention is to affect positive change in both languages used by a bilingual child with language impairment in an effort to maximize his or her potential to communicate effectively. Readers may now turn their attention to a more tangible aspect of implementing a clinical intervention program designed to increase skills in Spanish and English—structuring language within and across sessions. Supporting development in both languages does not necessarily mean always using both languages in a single intervention session or even treating directly in both languages during the same time period, although this may be optimal in some cases. Rather, a holistic, interactive view of bilingual development requires planning for generalization of treated gains across languages, and that both languages are considered in treatment goals. Precisely how this plan is implemented will vary with each child.

Two general approaches to structuring language during the intervention process are recommended. The Bilingual Approach is aimed at those cognitive-linguistic skills that are common to both languages. The Cross-Linguistic Approach is directed at linguistic features or social uses of language that are unique to each language. Each of these primary approaches to structuring language intervention is presented separately, although in most cases it is likely that both will be used at different stages in the intervention process.

Bilingual Approach

A bilingual approach to intervention, as defined here, simultaneously directs attention to improving communicative competency in both Spanish and English. This dual-language focus may be achieved in at least three different ways: 1) by focusing on the cognitive underpinnings common to all languages (e.g., the ability to process information efficiently or to attend to slight changes in signal form); 2) by directly training those aspects of language content, form, or use that are shared by Spanish and English (such as the phonemes or noun-final morphological inflections common to both languages); and 3) by highlighting the interactions between cognition and language or between L1 and L2 (as in contrastive analysis or translation).

Figure 13.1 illustrates one way to conceive of the links and interactions among language and the underlying general cognitive processing mechanisms. This conceptualization can be used as a framework for the bilingual approach to intervention. Both input (language in the child's environment, including intervention), and uptake (the child's comprehension and production of language) include Spanish and English. The middle section in Figure 13.1 shows that language input and uptake are mediated by basic cognitive processing mechanisms internal to the child. Conventionally, these basic cognitive processing mechanisms include working mem-

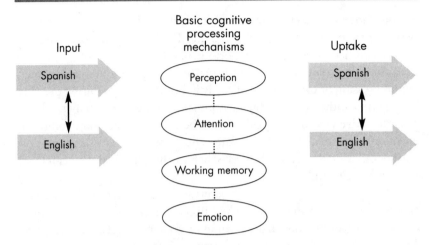

Figure 13.1.   The links and interactions among language and the underlying general cognitive processing mechanisms. Input includes language in a child's environment, including intervention, and uptake includes the child's comprehension and production of language in Spanish and English. Language input and uptake are mediated by basic cognitive processing mechanisms internal to the child. Dotted lines indicate linguistic overlap and potential interactions between the two languages.

ory, perception, attention, and emotion as the basic building blocks for all learning (e.g., Bates & MacWhinney, 1987; Elman et al., 1996). These basic cognitive processing mechanisms allow the efficient language learner to discern patterns in the input, to unpack rapidly presented sequential pieces of information that are loaded with fine-grained details, to discern the semantic and pragmatic value of this information relative to the immediate context, to quickly access known information to formulate responses in a timely manner, and to engage in analogous learning to acquire new information. The efficiency with which individuals are able to act on the incoming language input is critical. Children with language impairments are less efficient then their typically developing peers in this type of processing efficiency, even on tasks that do not involve language (e.g., Kohnert & Windsor, in press; Miller, Kail, Leonard, & Tomblin, 2001; Windsor & Hwang, 1999; see also Leonard, 1998, for review).

A cognitive approach to bilingual intervention leaves open the possibility that, at least in some cases, treatment that strengthens underlying cognitive processing mechanisms will lead to gains in overall language ability. This may be a preliminary step toward more language-specific training or it may form an ongoing sub-component of language intervention. The emphasis here is on increasing a child's ability to process information (nonverbal as well as verbal). Specific activities may include categorization tasks (determining which objects go together); digit searches, or "I spy" games (finding target numbers, letters or shapes "hidden" among distractors of varying complexity); "same or different" auditory tasks (discerning increasingly subtle differences between sounds); imitation-recall tasks (reproducing sequences of actions, sounds, or object manipulation), or speeded identification or naming tasks (over-rehearsing known information to increase automatic access). The selection of appropriate activities will, of course, vary with the child's age and developmental stage. (See Scarry-Larkin, 1999, and Windsor, 2002, for additional tasks and descriptions.)

Referring again to Figure 13.1, the dotted line between Spanish and English in both input and uptake serves two important functions. First, this dotted line represents the linguistic overlap between Spanish and English in terms of meaning, linguistic structure, or communication function. For example, both languages contain words that indicate family relationships (*tío*/uncle; *abuela*/grandmother), inflected forms for nouns and verbs (plural *-es/-s* and gerund *-iendo, -ando/-ing*), conventions for giving instructions and requesting information (i.e., command and question forms), and mechanisms to ensure cohesion in connected discourse (e.g., referencing and complex syntax). The second important function this dotted line serves is to represent the ways Spanish and English may interact. Cross-linguistic interactions occur when different languages are used in the same context or conversational exchange (as in code-switching or language-mixing), or through internal transfer of information from one language to the other language (as when the child needs to transfer a story heard at home in Spanish into English to perform in the English-only classroom).

In intervention, professionals can direct their attention to manipulating the input to directly highlight the similarities between the languages in terms of their content, form, or use. For example, the Spanish and English languages share approximately 15 phonemes. For a child with a very limited repertoire of sounds that he or she is able to use contrastively (a requisite for intelligibility in any language), the initial phases of intervention may be geared toward increasing his or her phonemic repertoire by focusing on those sounds common to both languages (see Chapter 11). For a young child with a restricted vocabulary, interventionists may want to focus initially on lexical referents for concepts that are more likely to be shared across language settings. In Chapter 5, Peña and Kester note that these shared concepts are more likely to include people, part–whole relationships, and functions and are less likely to be about food, household items, shapes, or colors.

Professionals also can structure the language input or stimuli used in intervention to directly highlight the interactions between the two languages. For example, for the school-age child with impaired language, interventionists can highlight the interaction between content and form with respect to phonological awareness, building a child's vocabulary to aid his or her transition to literacy. Toward this end, professionals may select a number of cross-linguistic cognates (translation equivalents in Spanish and English with significant phonological or graphemic overlap, e.g., *elephant* and *elefante*). We may embed these carefully selected words into meaningful contexts, such as short narratives or scripted events. Although the relationships between cross-linguistic cognates are clear for those with good language skills, this may not be the case for children with language impairments or reading difficulties (e.g., Durgunoglu, 1998; Jiménez, García, & Pearson, 1996; Kohnert, Windsor, & Miller, in press). The point is, when providing intervention, one may need to take what is an implicit understanding about the relationship between two languages for the language-intact learner and make it explicit for the bilingual child with language impairment (cf. Kohnert, in press).

In summary, a bilingual approach to intervention is designed to directly target those skills needed for communicative competency in both Spanish and English. This can be achieved by providing training in the basic cognitive processing mechanisms that underlie communicative efficiency, in the linguistic and functional elements that are shared by both Spanish and English, or in the interactions between the cognitive and linguistic elements. A clinical expert who speaks both of the child's languages or a team consisting of a clinical expert that speaks only one of the child's languages and a bilingual paraprofessional may implement bilingual intervention.

Cross-Linguistic Approach

A cross-linguistic approach to intervention, as defined here, is directed at those linguistic features or communicative functions that are unique to each language. These nonoverlapping features of Spanish and English can be at the sound, meaning, structural, discourse, or pragmatic levels. Cross-linguistic intervention alternately focuses attention on Spanish and English in separate sessions during the same period or at different points in time during the intervention process.

Cross-linguistic variation stems from many potential sources. In Table 13.1, Spanish and English are compared on 10 representative linguistic features. At the structural level are a number of important differences between the two languages. For example, the permissibility of word order variation in English sentences is very low. The canonical—and by far

Table 13.1.   Non-overlapping features of Spanish and English languages

Linguistic feature	Spanish	English	Comment
1. Word order variation	High	Low	Refers to the number of different orders of subject, verb, and object possible in the spoken language
2. Inflectional morphology	Rich	Sparse	Refers to bound morphemes added to freestanding words to indicate changes in tense, person, number, and gender
3. Morphologic regularity	Multiple regular and irregular forms	One regular; multiple irregulars (for plural and past)	Refers to the consistency of inflectional morphology in the language. The single regular past form in English is -ed, but there are many irregulars such as eat/ate, do/did, drink/drank, and drive/drove
4. Omission of constituents in sentences	Subject can be omitted	Not permitted	Subject omission is grammatical and frequent in Spanish. For example, to translate the sentence I already read it, Spanish speakers would drop the I and say "Ya lo leí."
5. Lexical ambiguity	Low (due to inflectional markings)	High (especially for nouns and verbs)	English has many words that need to be interpreted with respect to context. For example, chair can be either an object (the chair) or action (to chair the meeting); the word scale used with fish or pounds conjures up two different referents.
6. Use of compounding	Low	High	Refers to words that are composed of other freestanding words (e.g., bluebird; laptop)
7. Grammatical cues to word identity	Gender and form class (masculine and feminine singular and plurals)	Form class only	Both languages use form class cues that reliably distinguish between nouns, verbs, and other grammatical classes

(continued)

Table 13.1.   *(continued)*

Linguistic feature	Spanish	English	Comment
			(e.g., *I went to the store* versus *I want to store the items*). However, only Spanish uses gender *(el, la, los, las)* as an additional cue within the nominal category.
8. Word length in syllables	Long	Short	An analysis of 520 non-inflected nouns showed Spanish words contained an average of 2.76 syllables (with 54% of words having 3 syllables or greater); average syllable length in English was 1.74 (and 84% of words were 2 syllables or less).
9. Canonical syllable shape	CV	CVC	The default syllable shape and most common sound combinations vary across languages. For example, post-vocalic consonant singletons and clusters are frequent in English. Spanish has only five consonant singletons that can be used in word-final position /d,l,n,r,s/ and no consonant clusters.
10. Orthographic regularity	Highly regular	Highly opaque	Both languages are alphabetic in that writing is based on sound–symbol correspondence. However, this sound-symbol relationship is much less transparent in English (e.g., *sh* sound written with *s* in *sugar*, *-tion* in *nation*, or *sh* in *cushion*).

Parts of this table are adapted from Bates et al. (in press) and Kohnert, Scarry-Larkin and Price (2000).   (Key: C = consonant; V = vowel.)

most predominant—word order for English sentences is subject–verb–object (S–V–O), thereby providing a very robust cue to meaning in English. In contrast, Spanish is much more flexible in the ways in which words can be combined in sentences. Because many more syntactic variations are used in Spanish sentences, word order is not a reliable cue to meaning, and bilingual children with language impairment may make more errors. As an example, the sentence *The girl ate the apple* has the canonical shape of S–V–O. Pronominal referents could also be used, as in *She ate it*—again, S–V–O. In Spanish, the first sentence also has the S–V–O shape (*La niña comió la manzana*); however, *She ate it* becomes *La comió* in Spanish and the structure changes to O–V (with the subject indicated by verb morphology). This cross-linguistic difference may require specific attention in Spanish. The opposite is true for inflectional morphology. That is, English has relatively few bound morphemes, particularly for verb endings. Consider the present tense conjugation of the verb *to drink* in English relative to Spanish (*tomar*): *(I) drink/tomo; (you) drink/tomas; (he, she, it) drinks/toma; (we) drink/tomamos; (they) drink/toman*. Verb inflections for English are both few (*-s, -ing, -ed*) and inconsistent (*-s* is used only for third person singular; many irregular past-tense forms exist). These relatively infrequent morphological inflections present particular difficulty for language-impaired children learning English but much less difficulty for children learning more highly inflected languages such as Spanish (Leonard, 1998). (See also Chapter 6 and Chapter 7.)

Important cross-linguistic differences also occur at the lexical-semantic level. For example, English has many words that are ambiguous out of context (see Table 13.1). The word *ring* can be a circular object or the sound associated with the telephone; *bank* can be the land alongside a river, a place to deposit money, or even the action of stockpiling money. English is rich with these types of polysemous words, and context plays an important role in determining the correct meaning. This is not the case for Spanish, so this unique feature of English needs to be highlighted.

Another important cross-linguistic difference at the lexical-semantic level as it interacts with the linguistic context is the availability of grammatical cues to word identity. Spanish provides gender cues to word identity (e.g., masculine *el* and feminine *la* for the neutral English *the*). These gender cues facilitate lexical access—an important consideration when designing intervention programs for bilingual children to facilitate word recall. Lexical knowledge in each language is also closely associated with different topics. Striking differences will likely occur in the vocabulary a child uses at home to discuss food preparation and negotiate household duties and the language the child uses at school to discuss basic math concepts such as numbers and shapes (see Chapter 5).

In using sounds to construct words, we noted that there were approximately 15 sounds that were used contrastively by both Spanish and English. A number of sounds are unique to each language, however. For example, Spanish, not English, has both tapped and trilled /r/ sounds, and English, not Spanish, has the voiced fricatives /z/ and /v/. For the bilingual child with delayed phonology or reduced phonological awareness, cross-linguistic intervention is needed to separately target those unique features of Spanish and English that are in error (see Chapter 11). Moreover, as shown in Table 13.1, important cross-linguistic differences are found in word length in syllables and in the frequency of occurrence of different syllable shapes. For example, Spanish words generally include more syllables than English words. Consider these common object names that are part of a toddler's early vocabulary: *pelota/ball*, *zapato/shoe*, and *manzana/apple*. In each case, the Spanish word is three syllables in length. In comparing word length in syllables, 84% of common object names in English are two syllables or less, in contrast with the 54% of Spanish object names that are three syllables or more (Bates et al., in press; Kohnert, Scarry-Larkin, & Price, 2000). This means that the phonological process of syllable deletion will have a much greater negative impact on overall speech intelligibility in Spanish and must receive additional attention. Within each syllable, however, English is generally more complex. The most common syllable shape in English is consonant–vowel–consonant (as in *hat*, *boat*, and *pig*). Children who omit the post-vocalic consonant in English (so that *boat* becomes "bo") can be extremely difficult to understand. In contrast, the most common syllable shape in Spanish is consonant-vowel, so the consistent reduction of syllable final consonants will have much less of an impact on the child's speech in Spanish. It is likely that bilingual children with phonological deficits will need additional attention in Spanish to target longer words, and in English to facilitate the consistent inclusion of final consonants (see Kohnert, Scarry-Larkin, & Price, 2000).

In summary, a cross-linguistic approach provides separate special training in English and Spanish. Although many intervention goals may apply to both languages, each language will have unique intervention goals as well. In the cross-linguistic approach, individuals are trained in these nonoverlapping goals. Of course, at some point this cross-linguistic approach may be merged with the bilingual approach to further promote skills at the metalinguistic level. For example, with some children, professionals may want to use contrastive analyses activities, directly comparing selected features of Spanish and English to facilitate understanding. Intervention in Spanish and English may be concurrent (sessions in Spanish or English during the same period) or sequential (Spanish only for several months followed by a gradual addition of English sessions). These sessions may be conducted by a single bilingual professional or by a team of professionals, both monolingual and bilingual. These clinical professionals and their roles in treatment with the bilingual child are discussed next.

IMPLICATIONS FOR INTERVENTION

In this final section, we turn our attention to those individuals who have primary responsibility for developing, implementing, and determining the effectiveness of language treatment—speech-language pathologists (SLPs). Although SLPs are the primary professionals responsible for affecting positive change in the communication skills of bilingual children with language impairment, they do not work in isolation. Parents and other family members are essential partners in the intervention process. Additional partners may include child care providers, classroom and English as a Second Language (ESL) instructors, special educators, and older children or same-age peers with strong communication skills. Increasingly, SLP assistants and professional interpreters/translators are becoming integral team members (Langdon & Cheng, 2002; Paul-Brown & Goldberg, 2001).

Ideally, every SLP would speak all the languages of his or her clients. Indeed, the number of proficient Spanish-English bilingual SLPs is growing; however, the demand continues to far exceed the supply. And, although our attention here is focused on Spanish-English bilingual children, we recognize that there will be many times when SLPs are called to serve children who speak languages other than Spanish or English (e.g., Tagalog, Urdu, Vietnamese, Turkish, Somali) (Kohnert, Kennedy, Glaze, Kan, & Carney, 2003). Both bilingual language-matched SLPs and SLPs who do not share one of the child's primary languages have important professional roles in the provision of effective intervention to the bilingual child with language impairment.

The SLP who speaks both Spanish and English may choose to be the primary provider of intervention in both languages. These languages may be combined in a single session when the focus is on skills common to both languages. For example, if the goal is to increase the frequency with which a child initiates verbal interactions, the bilingual SLP may follow the child's lead, alternating his or her response language to match the language produced by the child. The bilingual SLP may also engage in pre-teaching activities in Spanish, priming specific concepts prior to classroom lessons in English. Or the bilingual SLP may use more of a cross-linguistic approach, working on nonoverlapping phonological error patterns in Spanish in one of two weekly sessions, and in English the other session. Parallel home or extension programs can also be established and monitored by the bilingual SLP. The family may be specifically trained to reinforce intervention targets in Spanish and the classroom teaching assistant or SLP assistant may be taught to help with generalization in English.

The SLP who speaks both of the child's languages may implement a team approach to direct intervention. In this case, the bilingual SLP provides direct services in Spanish, with a parallel program developed and implemented in English by a different SLP. These parallel direct service programs, administered by different professionals in different languages, can be very effective in meeting a child's overall communication goals. Bilingual SLPs also may serve as consultants. This may be the preferred model when there are few Spanish-English SLPs and many bilingual children to be served. As the consultant, the bilingual SLP provides the family with direct training in intervention objectives and strategies, then coordinates the efforts of an English-speaking SLP and Spanish-speaking SLP assistant to work directly with the child in each language. In this case, the bilingual SLP maintains primary responsibility for ensuring the intervention goals are met. The bilingual SLP consultant monitors the child's progress, provides ongoing training and supervision to the SLP, implements strategic changes in treatment goals and procedures as needed, consults with the English-speaking SLP on a regular basis, and coordinates efforts between all team members to facilitate the cross-linguistic and cross-setting transfer of skills. In all cases, it is incumbent on the bilingual SLP to maintain close, respectful, and productive partnerships with the family, attending carefully to their preferences for the language of intervention and their impressions of progress.

The SLP who does not speak both of the child's languages maintains an important professional role in providing intervention services to bilingual children, in both of their languages. In the absence of a bilingual professional, this SLP will need to be skilled in working with interpreters/translators, in training and supervising SLP assistants, and in implementing alternative treatment procedures such as mediated peer-tutoring (McGregor, 2000). In developing appropriate goals, the SLP may consult with other language and community professionals such as English or foreign language instructors, bilingual SLPs in other settings, interpreters, and culturally matched paraprofessionals to identify the salient cross-linguistic features that are shared or different across languages and cultural communication settings. In this model, the SLP serves as team coordinator as well as the direct provider of some services, maintaining primary responsibility for ensuring that the child's communication goals are met.

It is clear that additional knowledge and skills are needed by professionals to provide services to bilingual children with language impairment. At a minimum, specific knowledge related to typical and atypical language development in the bilingual child is needed, as well as a heightened ability to collaborate effectively with a wider range of individuals with a broad set of cultural, linguistic, and professional skills (see Kohnert et al., 2003, for additional discussion).

SUMMARY

In this chapter we have provided an overview of the major purposes and procedures of language intervention, specifically focused on Spanish-English bilingual children with language impairment. We have directly addressed the question of language choice. Based on a review of the literature and the common arguments used in discussions of "which language?," we step back from the common wisdom that two languages are always worse for the child with language impairment. Consistent with discussions by authors of previous chapters in this book, we advocate an approach that systematically considers both languages in the planning and implementation of intervention for the bilingual child. We have presented two complementary approaches (bilingual and cross-linguistic) for organizing language within and across sessions. In the next section, we introduced SLPs—the professionals with primary responsibility for ensuring that children with language impairment receive appropriate intervention services so that they will achieve their potential as communicators. Here we emphasized the importance of collaboration within and across professions to meet the needs of bilingual children with language impairment.

REFERENCES

Bashir, A.S., & Scavuzzo, A. (1992). Children with language disorders: Natural history and academic success. *Journal of Learning Disabilities, 25*, 53–65.

Bates, E., D'Amico, S., Jacobsen, T., Szekely, A., Andonova, E., Herron, D., Lu, C.C., et al. (in press). Timed picture naming in seven languages. *Psychonomic Bulletin & Review.*

Bates, E., & MacWhinney, B. (1987). Competition, variation, and language learning. In B. MacWhinney (Ed.), *Mechanisms of language and acquisition* (pp. 157–193). Mahwah, NJ: Lawrence Erlbaum Associates.

Bialystok, E. (2001). *Bilingualism in development: Language, literacy, & cognition.* New York: Cambridge University Press.

Catts, H., Fey, M., Tomblin, B., & Zhang, X. (2002). A longitudinal investigation of reading outcomes in children with language impairments. *Journal of Speech, Language, and Hearing Research, 45,* 1142–1157.

Chee, M., Tan, E., & Thiel, T. (1999). Mandarin and English single word processing studied with functional magnetic resonance imaging. *The Journal of Neuroscience, 19*(8), 3050–3056.

Conboy, B. (2002). *Patterns of language processing and growth in early English-Spanish bilinguals.* Unpublished doctoral dissertation, University of California, San Diego, and San Diego State University.

Durgunoglu, A.Y. (1998). Acquiring literacy in English and Spanish in the United States. In A.Y. Durgunoglu & L. Verhoeven (Eds.), *Literacy development in a multilingual context: Cross-cultural perspectives* (pp. 135–145). Mahwah, NJ: Lawrence Erlbaum Associates.

Elman, J., Bates, E., Johnson, M., Karmiloff-Smith, A., Parisi, D., & Plunkett, K. (1996). *Rethinking innateness: A connectionist perspective on development.* Cambridge: MIT Press.

Fey, M.E., Windsor, J., & Warren, S.F. (Eds.) (1995). *Language intervention: Preschool through the elementary years.* Baltimore: Paul H. Brookes Publishing Co.

Goldstein, B. (2001). *Cultural and linguistic diversity resource guide for speech-language pathologists.* San Diego, CA: Singular/Thomson Learning.

Goldstein, B., & Iglesias, A. (2002). Issues of cultural and linguistic diversity. In R. Paul (Ed.), *Introduction to clinical methods in communication disorders* (pp. 261–279). Baltimore: Paul H. Brookes Publishing Co.

Grosjean, F. (1997). Processing mixed languages: Issues, findings, and models. In A.M.B. de Groot & J.F. Kroll (Eds.), *Tutorials in bilingualism: Psycholinguistic perspectives* (pp. 225–254). Mahwah, NJ: Lawrence Erlbaum Associates.

Gutiérrez-Clellen, V. (1996). Language diversity: Implications for assessment. In S.F. Warren & J. Reichle (Series Eds.) & K.N. Cole, P.S. Dale, & D.J. Thal (Vol. Eds.), *Communication and language intervention series: Vol. 6. Advances in Assessment of communication and language* (pp. 29–56). Baltimore: Paul H. Brookes Publishing Co.

Gutiérrez-Clellen, V. (1999). Language choice in intervention with bilingual children. *American Journal of Speech-Language Pathology, 8,* 291–302.

Hart, B., & Risley, T.R. (1995). *Meaningful differences in the everyday experience of young American children.* Baltimore: Paul H. Brookes Publishing Co.

Jiménez, R., García, G., & Pearson, D. (1996). The reading strategies of bilingual Latina/o students who are successful English readers: Opportunities and obstacles. *Reading Research Quarterly, 31,* 90–112.

Kayser, H. (1998). *Assessment and intervention resource for Hispanic children.* San Diego: Singular Publishing Group.

Kohnert, K. (in press). Cognitive and cognate treatments for bilingual aphasia: A case study. *Brain and Language.*

Kohnert, K., & Bates, E. (2002). Balancing bilinguals, II: Lexical comprehension and cognitive processing in children learning Spanish and English. *Journal of Speech, Language, and Hearing Research, 45,* 347–359.

Kohnert, K., Bates, E., & Hernandez, A.E. (1999). Balancing bilinguals: Lexical-semantic production and cognitive processing in children learning Spanish and English. *Journal of Speech, Language, and Hearing Research, 42,* 1400–1413.

Kohnert, K.J., Hernandez, A.E., & Bates, E. (1998). Bilingual performance on the Boston Naming Test: Preliminary norms in Spanish and English. *Brain and Language, 65,* 422–440.

Kohnert, K., Kennedy, M., Glaze, L., Kan, P., & Carney, E. (2003). Breadth and depth of diversity in Minnesota: Challenges to clinical competency. *American Journal of Speech-Language Pathology, 12,* 259–272.

Kohnert, K.J., Scarry-Larkin, M., & Price, E. (2000). *Spanish phonology: Intervention.* San Luis Obispo, CA: LocuTour Multimedia Cognitive Rehabilitation/ Learning Fundamentals.

Kohnert, K., & Windsor, J. (in press). In search of common ground, Part II: Non-linguistic performance by linguistically diverse learners. *Journal of Speech, Language, and Hearing Research.*

Kohnert, K., Windsor, J., & Miller, R. (in press). Crossing borders: Recognition of Spanish words by English speaking children with and without language impairment. *Applied Psycholinguistics.*

Krashen, S. (1999). *Condemned without a trial: Bogus arguments against bilingual education.* Portsmouth, NH: Heinemann.

Langdon, H., & Cheng, L. (2002). *Interpreting and translating in speech-language pathology and audiology.* Eau Claire, WI: Thinking Publications.

Langdon, H., & Saenz, T.I. (Eds.). (1996). *Language assessment and intervention with multicultural students.* Oceanside, CA: Academic Communication Associates.

Leonard, L. (1998). *Children with specific language impairment.* Cambridge, MA: MIT Press.

McGregor, K. (2000). The development and enhancement of narrative skills in a preschool classroom: Towards a solution to clinician-client mismatch. *American Journal of Speech-Language Pathology, 9,* 55–71.

Miller, C., Kail, R., Leonard, L., & Tomblin, B. (2001). Speed of processing in children with specific language impairment. *Journal of Speech, Language, and Hearing Research, 44,* 416–433.

Paradis, M. (1997). The cognitive neuropsychology of bilingualism. In A.M.B. de Groot & J. Kroll (Eds.), *Tutorials in bilingualism: Psycholinguistic perspectives* (pp. 331–354). New York: Routledge.

Paul, R. (2001). *Language disorders from infancy through adolescence: Assessment and intervention* (2nd ed). St. Louis, MO: Mosby.

Paul, R. (Ed.). (2002). *Introduction to clinical methods in communication disorders.* Baltimore: Paul H. Brookes Publishing Co.

Paul-Brown, D., & Goldberg, L. (2001). Current policies and new directions for speech-language pathology assistants. *Language, Speech, and Hearing Services in Schools, 32,* 4–17.

Pearson, B., & Fernández, S. (1994). Patterns of interaction in the lexical development in two languages of bilingual infants. *Language Learning, 44,* 617–653.

Pearson, B., Fernández, S., & Oller, D. (1993). Lexical development in bilingual infants and toddlers: Comparison to monolingual norms. *Language Learning, 43,* 93–120.

Peña, E., Bedore, L., & Zlatic, R. (2002). Category generation in performance of young bilingual children: The influence of condition, category, and language. *Speech, Language, and Hearing Research, 45,* 938–947.

Perani, D., Paulesu, E., Sebastian Galles, N., Dupoux, E., Dehaene, S., Bettinardi, V., et al. (1998). The bilingual brain: Proficiency and age of acquisition of the second language. *Brain, 121,* 1841–1852.

Pettito, L., Katerelos, M., Levy, B., Gauna, K., Tétreault, K., & Ferraro, V. (2001). Bilingual signed and spoken language acquisition from birth: Implications for the mechanisms underlying early bilingual language acquisition. *Journal of Child Language, 28,* 453–496.

Roseberry-McKibbin, C. (1995). Distinguishing language difference from language disorder in linguistically and culturally diverse students. *Multicultural Education, 4,* 12–16.

Roth, F.P., & Paul, R. (2002). Principles of intervention. In R. Paul (Ed.) *Introduction to clinical methods in communication disorders* (pp. 159–181). Baltimore: Paul H. Brookes Publishing Co.

Scarry-Larkin, M. (1999). *Attention and memory* (Vol. 1.). San Luis Obispo, CA: LocuTour Multimedia Cognitive Rehabilitation/Learning Fundamentals.

Snow, C.E. (1990). The development of definitional skill. *Journal of Child Language, 17,* 697–710.

Snow, C.E. (1991). Language proficiency: Towards a definition. In H. Dechert & G. Appel (Eds.), *A case for psycholinguistic cases* (pp. 63–89). Amsterdam: John Benjamins.

Snow, C.E., Burns, M.S., & Griffin, P. (Eds.). (1998). *Preventing reading difficulties in young children.* Washington, DC: National Academy Press.

Toppelberg, C., Snow, C.E., & Tager-Flusberg, H. (1999). Severe developmental disorders and bilingualism. *Journal of the American Academy of Child & Adolescent Psychiatry, 38,* 1197–1199.

Weizman, Z.O., & Snow, C.E. (2001). Lexical input as related to children's vocabulary acquisition: Effects of sophisticated exposure and support for meaning. *Developmental Psychology, 37,* 265–279.

Windsor, J. (2002). Contrasting general and process-specific slowing in language impairment. *Topics in Language Disorders, 22*(3), 49–61.

Windsor, J., & Hwang, M. (1999). Testing the generalized slowing hypothesis in specific language impairment. *Journal of Speech, Language, and Hearing Research, 42,* 1205–1218.

Wong-Fillmore, L. (1991). Second language learning in children: A model of language learning in social context. In E. Bialystok (Ed.), *Language processing in bilingual children* (pp. 49–69). Cambridge, UK: Cambridge University Press.

RESOURCES FOR SPANISH-ENGLISH SPEECH-LANGUAGE THERAPY

VIDEOS

Developing the Young Bilingual Learner   http://www.naeyc.org
First Steps: Supporting Early Language Development (Spanish)
   http://www.edpro.com
Starting Points—Getting Your Message Across   http://www.edpro.com
Language is the Key—El Hablar y el Jugar & El Hablar y los Libros
   http://www.wri-edu.org

PROFESSIONAL/PARENT INFORMATIONAL BOOKS

Assessment and Intervention Resource for Hispanic Children
Hortencia Kayser (Singular Spiralbound, 1998)
http://www.delmarhealthcare.com/comsci/

Bebes con Sindrome de Down: Guia para Padres
Karen Stray-Gundersen (Woodbine House, 1998)
http://www.woodbinehouse.com

Bilingual Speech-Language Pathology—An Hispanic Focus
Hortencia Kayser (Academic Communication Associates, 1995)
http://www.acadcom.com

Celebrating Families Strengths: A Handbook for Families (Spanish)
(Pacer Center, 1993) http://www.pacer.org

Cleft Palate Foundation Publications
http://www.cleftline.org/

Cultural and Linguistic Diversity Resource Guide for Speech-Language Pathologists
Brian A. Goldstein (Academic Communication Associates, 2000)
http://www.acadcom.com

The Hispanic Child
Alejandro E. Brice (Allyn & Bacon, 2002)
http://www.ablongman.com

Hispanic Children and Adults with Communication Disorders: Assessment and Intervention
Henriette Langdon, with Li-Rong Lilly Cheng (PRO-ED, 2005)
http://www.amazon.com

Multicultural Students with Special Language Needs
Celeste Roseberry-McKibbin (Academic Communication Associates, 2002)
http://www.acadcom.com

Ninos Autistas
Michael D. Powers (Woodbine House, 1999)
http://www.woodbinehouse.com

Padres de Sesame Street (Sesame Workshop)
http://www.sesamestreet.com

Partners in Speech, Language, and Hearing: A Guide for Parents and Caregivers of Babies,
   Toddlers, and Young Children (Spanish version)
(American Speech-Language Hearing Association)
http://www.asha.org

Speech and Language Handouts (Spanish)
Mary Brooks and Deedra Hartung (PRO-ED, 2002)
http://www.proedinc.com

Stuttering and the Bilingual Child
Rosalee G. Shenker, Ph.D. (Stuttering Foundation of America, 2003)
http://www.stutteringhelp.org

Talk with Me: A resource guide for speech-language pathologists and early childhood special
   education teams working with linguistically diverse young children and their families
Minnesota Speech-Language Hearing Association, Multicultural Affairs Committee,
   and the DCFL (Minnesota Metro Educational Cooperative Service Unit, 2002)
http://www.ecsu.k12.mn.us/pub.htm

CD ROMS IN SPANISH OR SPANISH/ENGLISH BILINGUAL

Davidson and Associates, Inc.   http://www.education.com
   Baba Yaga y Los Gansos Magicos
   El Pequeno Samurai
   Las Grandes Aventuras de Fisher Price: El Barco de los Piratas
   Imo y el Rey
   Jump Start for Kids: Spanish

Edmark   http://www.edmark.com
   Travel the World with Timmy!
   Words Around Me: Vocabulary Development for Students with Unique Learn-
      ing Needs
   Berenstain Bears get in a Fight
   Harry and the Haunted House
   The Tortoise and the Hare

Icono Multimedia   http://www.iconokids.com
   El Mundo de Chabelo

Laureate Learning Systems   http://www.LaureateLearning.com
   First Words II (Spanish/English)
   First Verbs
   Words and Concepts

The Learning Company, Inc.   http://www.broderbund.com
   Just Grandma and Me
   Rugrats: Aventuras en Panales. Al Rescate de Reptar
   Rugrats: Aventuras en Panales. Juegos y Desafios

Locutour Multimedia   http://www.LocuTour.com
   "Es . . ." Todo
   Fonologia en espanol: Tratamiento/Spanish Phonology: Intervention
   Fonologia en Espanol: Dibujos y Actividades/Spanish Phonology: Picture Cards
      and Carryover Activities
   Palabras Básicas para Los Niños

Mind Play   http://www.mindplay.com/
   Race the Clock: Language Arts Edition

Scholastic   http://www.ScholasticNetwork.com
   Dora the Explorer Backpack Adventure

Transparent Language   http://www.transparent.com
   KidSpeak: 6-in-1 Language Learning

MUSIC

Alerta Sings and Songs for the Playground
http://www.redleafpress.org

CantoAlegre Volume 1, Volume 2, Rockerito
http://www.mtm-music.com/

Cien por ciento Para Ninos
http://www.bmgentertainment.com/

Colibri in the Faraway Forest
http://www.redleafpress.org

Fiesta Musical
http://www.mflp.com/

Jose Luis Orozco
http://www.joseluisorozco.com

Las Canciones de Barney
http://www.expressmusic.com.mx/catalogo_Detail.cfm?ID=7509662710096

Los 60 mejores canticuentos
http://www.festival.valledupar.com/discotienda/infantil.html

Mama Lisa's World
http://www.mamalisa.com/world/

Nelson Gill
http://www.NelsonGill.com

Spanish Piggyback Songs
http://www.teachersparadise.com/

CATALOG COMPANIES FOR
BILINGUAL BOOKS AND THERAPY MATERIALS

Academic Communication Associates Inc.   http://www.acadcom.com
Bilingual Speech Source   (800) 825-7133
Children's Book Press   (510) 655-3395
Claudia's Caravan   (510) 521-7871
Disney Catalogue   http://www.disneystore.com
Ejercitacion Fonetica del Lenguaje (Panama) 617185-617697
Hampton-Brown Books   http://www.hampton-brown.com/
Kaplan Early Learning Company   http://www.kaplanco.com/
Lakeshore Learning Store   http://www.lakeshorelearning.com
Lectorum Publications   http://www.lectorum.com/
LinguiSystems   http://www.linguisystems.com
Pasitos—D.F. Schott Educational materials   http://www.pasitos.net/
Redleaf Press   http://www.redleafpress.org
Rigby   http://www.rigby.com/
Rourke Publishing Group   http://www.rourkepublishing.com/
Sentient Systems Technology   http://www.Sentient-sys.com
Scholastic Inc.   http://www.scholastic.com
SRA MacMillen/McGraw-Hill   http://www.mhln.com/
SuperDuper   http://www.superduperinc.com/

WEB SITES

American Speech-Language-Hearing Association (ASHA)   http://www.asha.org
Autism Society of America   http://www.autism-society.org
Bilingual Therapies   http://www.bilingualtherapies.com
Center for the Study of Autism   http://www.autism.org/
Center for the Study of Books in Spanish for Children and Adolescents
    http://www.csusm.edu/csb/english/
Council for Exceptional Children (CEC)   http://www.cec.sped.org/index.html
Culturally and Linguistically Appropriate Services (CLAS)   http://clas.uiuc.edu
Cultural and Ethnic Differences in Stuttering   http://casafuturatech.com
ERIC   http://www.eric.ed.gov/
The Hanen Centre   http://www.hanen.org/
National Association for the Education of Young People (NAEYC)
    http://www.naeyc.org
National Information Center for Children and Youth with Disabilities (NICHCY)/
    National Dissemination Center for Children with Disabilities
    http://www.nichcy.org
Schwab Foundation for Learning   http://www.schwablearning.org/
Shen's.com (Children's books in Spanish)   http://www.shens.com
Sobresalud   http://sobresalud.com
World Language Resources   http://www.worldlanguage.com

Index

Page numbers followed by *t* and *f* indicate tables and figures, respectively.